LAURELL K. HAMILTON

ANITA BLAKE™
VAMPIRE HUNTER
Guilty Pleasures

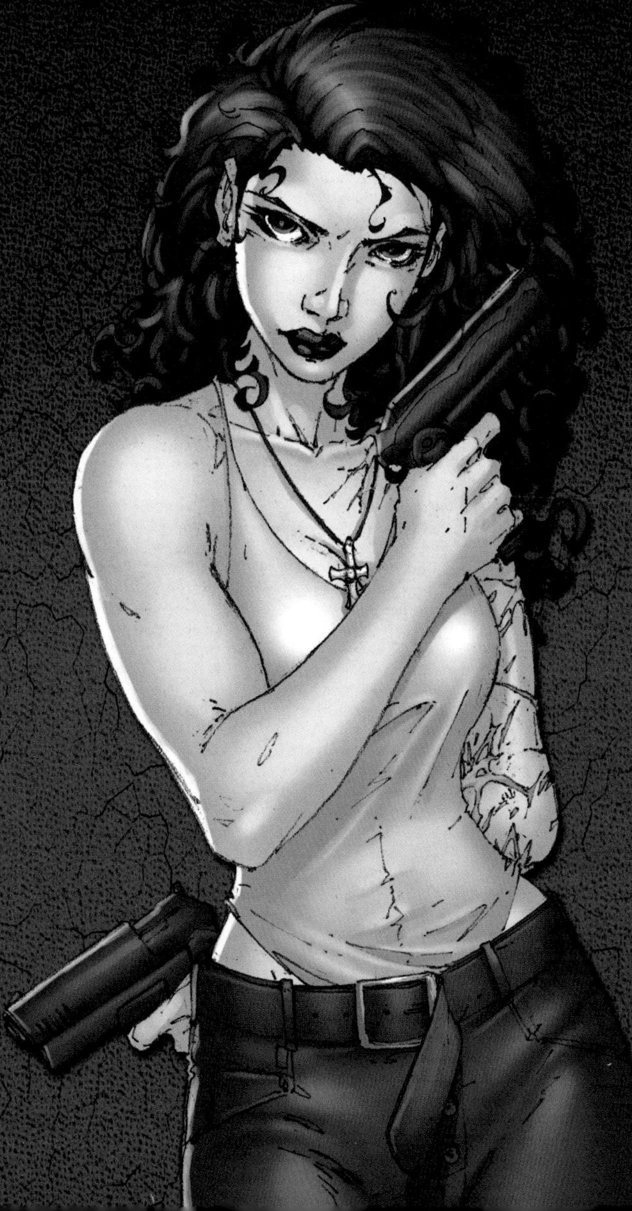

ANITA BLAKE™
VAMPIRE HUNTER
Guilty Pleasures

Anita Blake is the Executioner.
She raises the dead and kills vampires.
So you would think that vampires would avoid her like the proverbial plague. But there's something out there they fear even more, a killer targeting the most powerful vampires in the city. The Master Vampire of St. Louis makes her an offer she can't refuse: if she wants to save the life of her best friend, the Executioner will join forces with the very creatures she would rather kill.

WRITER **LAURELL K. HAMILTON**
ADAPTATION **STACIE RITCHIE** (ISSUES 1-5) & **JESS RUFFNER-BOOTH** (ISSUE 6)
ARTWORK **BRETT BOOTH** COLORS **IMAGINARY FRIENDS STUDIOS** (WITH MATT MOYLAN)
LETTERS & DESIGN **BILL TORTOLINI** (WITH SIMON BOWLAND) EDITORS **MIKE RAICHT & SEAN JORDAN**
SPECIAL THANKS TO **MELISSA MCALISTER, ANN TREDWAY, JONATHON GREEN, JASON & DARLA COOK**

DABEL BROTHERS PRODUCTIONS

MARVEL

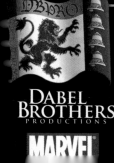

For Dabel Brothers: Matt Hansen *Editor in Chief,* Mike Raicht *Managing Editor,* Bill Tortolini *Art Director,* Les Dabel *Vice President* , Ernst Dabel *President*

For Marvel: Jeff Youngquist *Senior Editor, Special Projects* , David Gabriel *Senior Vice President of Sales,* Tom Marvelli *Vice President of Creative,* Joe Quesada *Editor in Chief* , Dan Buckley *Publisher*

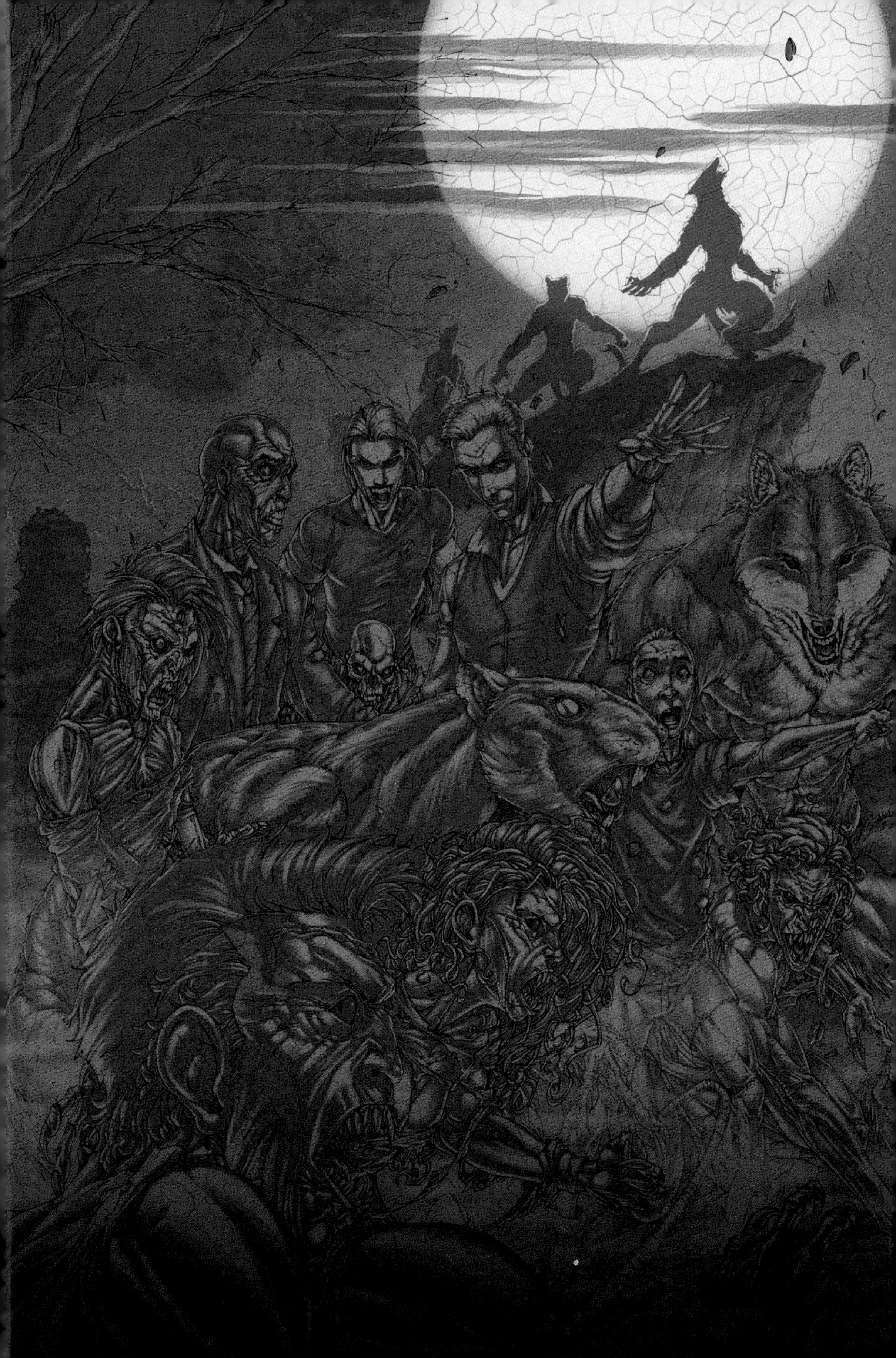

CHAPTER ONE

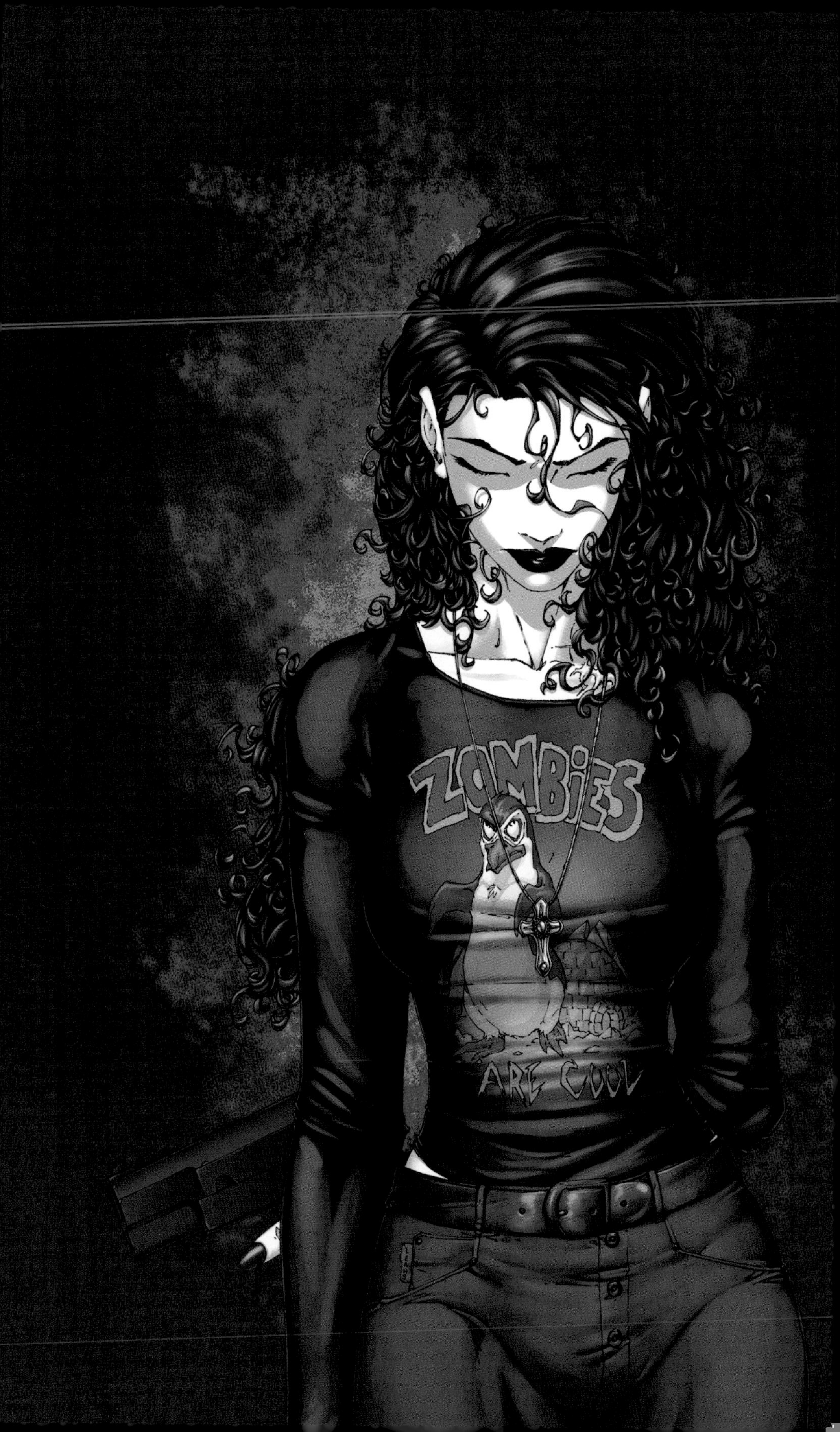
ZOMBIES
ARE COOL

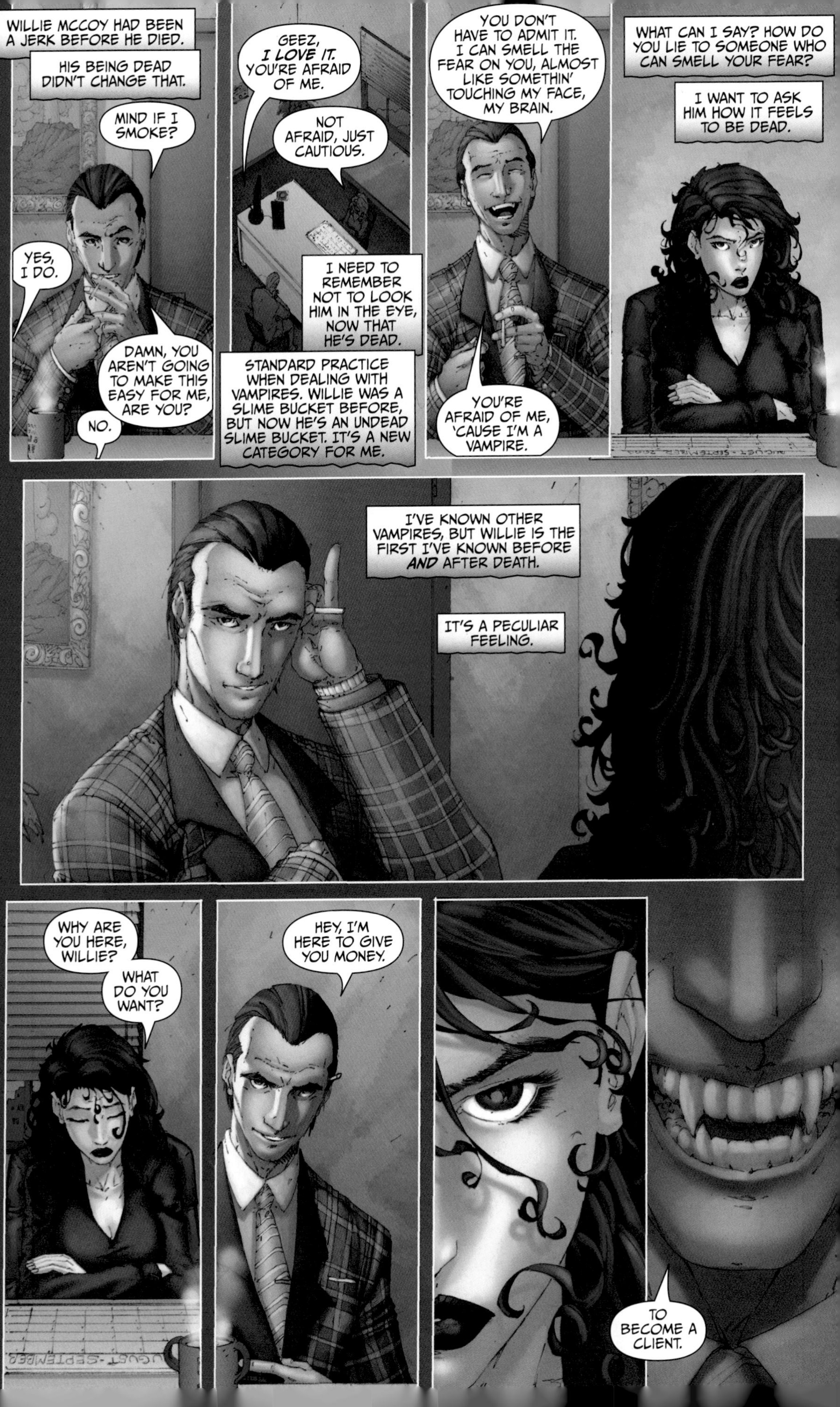
WILLIE MCCOY HAD BEEN A JERK BEFORE HE DIED.
HIS BEING DEAD DIDN'T CHANGE THAT.
MIND IF I SMOKE?
YES, I DO.
DAMN, YOU AREN'T GOING TO MAKE THIS EASY FOR ME, ARE YOU?
NO.
GEEZ, I LOVE IT. YOU'RE AFRAID OF ME.
NOT AFRAID, JUST CAUTIOUS.
I NEED TO REMEMBER NOT TO LOOK HIM IN THE EYE, NOW THAT HE'S DEAD.
STANDARD PRACTICE WHEN DEALING WITH VAMPIRES. WILLIE WAS A SLIME BUCKET BEFORE, BUT NOW HE'S AN UNDEAD SLIME BUCKET. IT'S A NEW CATEGORY FOR ME.
YOU DON'T HAVE TO ADMIT IT. I CAN SMELL THE FEAR ON YOU, ALMOST LIKE SOMETHIN' TOUCHING MY FACE, MY BRAIN.
YOU'RE AFRAID OF ME, 'CAUSE I'M A VAMPIRE.
WHAT CAN I SAY? HOW DO YOU LIE TO SOMEONE WHO CAN SMELL YOUR FEAR?
I WANT TO ASK HIM HOW IT FEELS TO BE DEAD.
I'VE KNOWN OTHER VAMPIRES, BUT WILLIE IS THE FIRST I'VE KNOWN BEFORE AND AFTER DEATH.
IT'S A PECULIAR FEELING.
WHY ARE YOU HERE, WILLIE?
WHAT DO YOU WANT?
HEY, I'M HERE TO GIVE YOU MONEY.
TO BECOME A CLIENT.

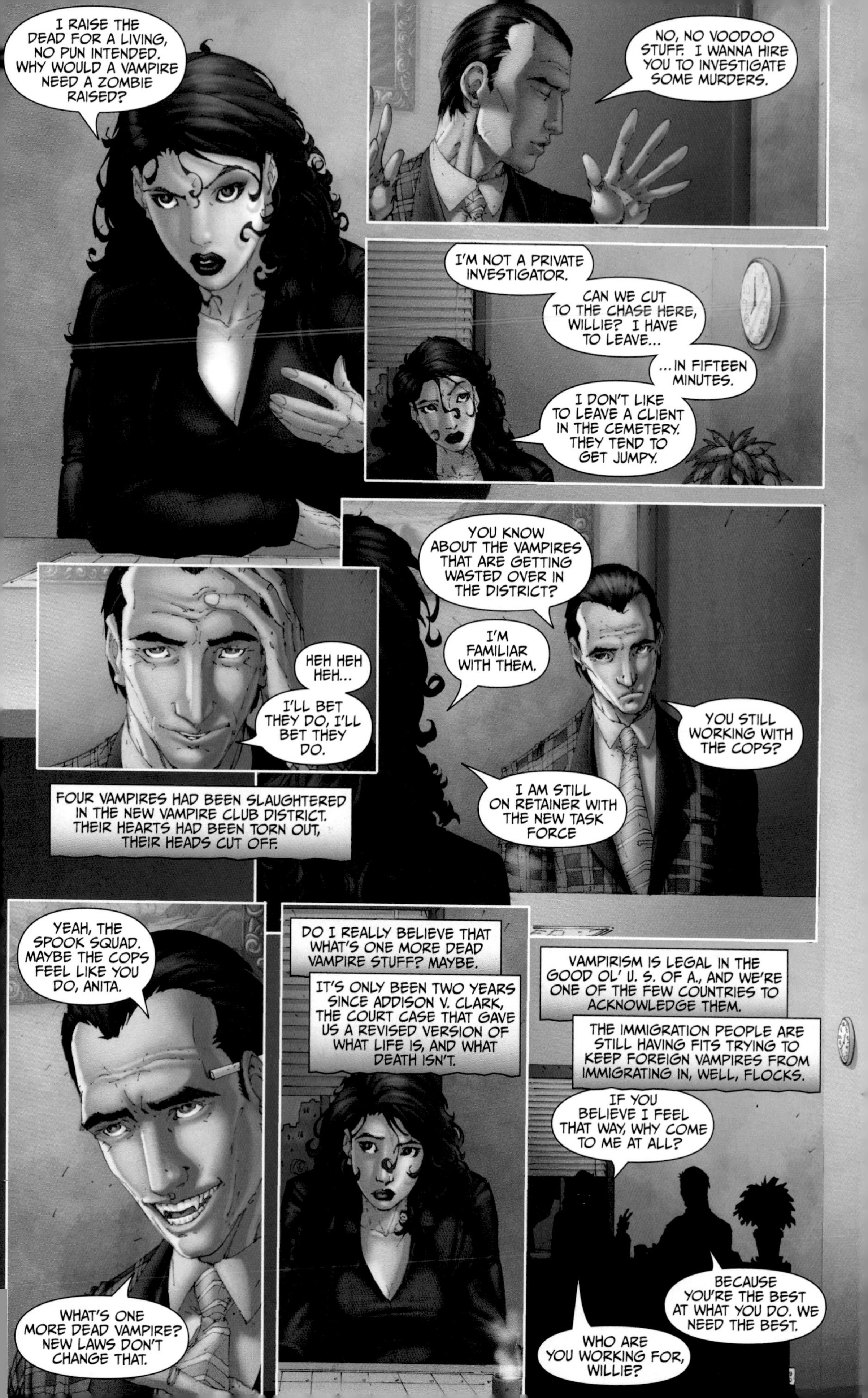
I RAISE THE DEAD FOR A LIVING, NO PUN INTENDED. WHY WOULD A VAMPIRE NEED A ZOMBIE RAISED?
NO, NO VOODOO STUFF. I WANNA HIRE YOU TO INVESTIGATE SOME MURDERS.
I'M NOT A PRIVATE INVESTIGATOR.
CAN WE CUT TO THE CHASE HERE, WILLIE? I HAVE TO LEAVE...
...IN FIFTEEN MINUTES.
I DON'T LIKE TO LEAVE A CLIENT IN THE CEMETERY. THEY TEND TO GET JUMPY.
YOU KNOW ABOUT THE VAMPIRES THAT ARE GETTING WASTED OVER IN THE DISTRICT?
I'M FAMILIAR WITH THEM.
HEH HEH HEH...
I'LL BET THEY DO, I'LL BET THEY DO.
YOU STILL WORKING WITH THE COPS?
I AM STILL ON RETAINER WITH THE NEW TASK FORCE
FOUR VAMPIRES HAD BEEN SLAUGHTERED IN THE NEW VAMPIRE CLUB DISTRICT. THEIR HEARTS HAD BEEN TORN OUT, THEIR HEADS CUT OFF.
YEAH, THE SPOOK SQUAD. MAYBE THE COPS FEEL LIKE YOU DO, ANITA.
WHAT'S ONE MORE DEAD VAMPIRE? NEW LAWS DON'T CHANGE THAT.
DO I REALLY BELIEVE THAT WHAT'S ONE MORE DEAD VAMPIRE STUFF? MAYBE.
IT'S ONLY BEEN TWO YEARS SINCE ADDISON V. CLARK, THE COURT CASE THAT GAVE US A REVISED VERSION OF WHAT LIFE IS, AND WHAT DEATH ISN'T.
VAMPIRISM IS LEGAL IN THE GOOD OL' U. S. OF A., AND WE'RE ONE OF THE FEW COUNTRIES TO ACKNOWLEDGE THEM.
THE IMMIGRATION PEOPLE ARE STILL HAVING FITS TRYING TO KEEP FOREIGN VAMPIRES FROM IMMIGRATING IN, WELL, FLOCKS.
IF YOU BELIEVE I FEEL THAT WAY, WHY COME TO ME AT ALL?
BECAUSE YOU'RE THE BEST AT WHAT YOU DO. WE NEED THE BEST.
WHO ARE YOU WORKING FOR, WILLIE?

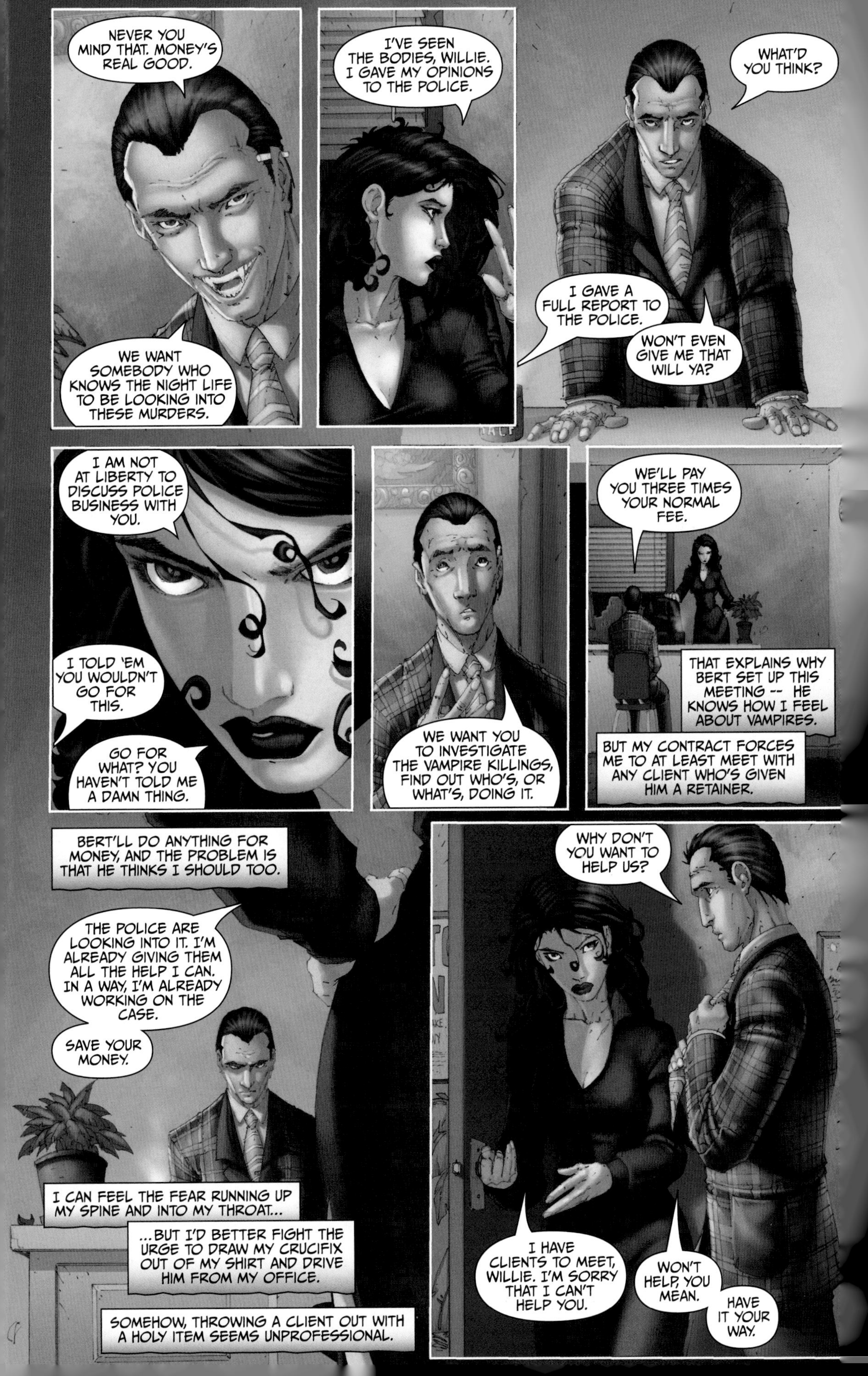
NEVER YOU MIND THAT. MONEY'S REAL GOOD.
WE WANT SOMEBODY WHO KNOWS THE NIGHT LIFE TO BE LOOKING INTO THESE MURDERS.
I'VE SEEN THE BODIES, WILLIE. I GAVE MY OPINIONS TO THE POLICE.
WHAT'D YOU THINK?
I GAVE A FULL REPORT TO THE POLICE.
WON'T EVEN GIVE ME THAT WILL YA?
I AM NOT AT LIBERTY TO DISCUSS POLICE BUSINESS WITH YOU.
I TOLD 'EM YOU WOULDN'T GO FOR THIS.
GO FOR WHAT? YOU HAVEN'T TOLD ME A DAMN THING.
WE WANT YOU TO INVESTIGATE THE VAMPIRE KILLINGS, FIND OUT WHO'S, OR WHAT'S, DOING IT.
WE'LL PAY YOU THREE TIMES YOUR NORMAL FEE.
THAT EXPLAINS WHY BERT SET UP THIS MEETING -- HE KNOWS HOW I FEEL ABOUT VAMPIRES.
BUT MY CONTRACT FORCES ME TO AT LEAST MEET WITH ANY CLIENT WHO'S GIVEN HIM A RETAINER.
BERT'LL DO ANYTHING FOR MONEY, AND THE PROBLEM IS THAT HE THINKS I SHOULD TOO.
THE POLICE ARE LOOKING INTO IT. I'M ALREADY GIVING THEM ALL THE HELP I CAN. IN A WAY, I'M ALREADY WORKING ON THE CASE.
SAVE YOUR MONEY.
I CAN FEEL THE FEAR RUNNING UP MY SPINE AND INTO MY THROAT...
...BUT I'D BETTER FIGHT THE URGE TO DRAW MY CRUCIFIX OUT OF MY SHIRT AND DRIVE HIM FROM MY OFFICE.
SOMEHOW, THROWING A CLIENT OUT WITH A HOLY ITEM SEEMS UNPROFESSIONAL.
WHY DON'T YOU WANT TO HELP US?
I HAVE CLIENTS TO MEET, WILLIE. I'M SORRY THAT I CAN'T HELP YOU.
WON'T HELP, YOU MEAN.
HAVE IT YOUR WAY.

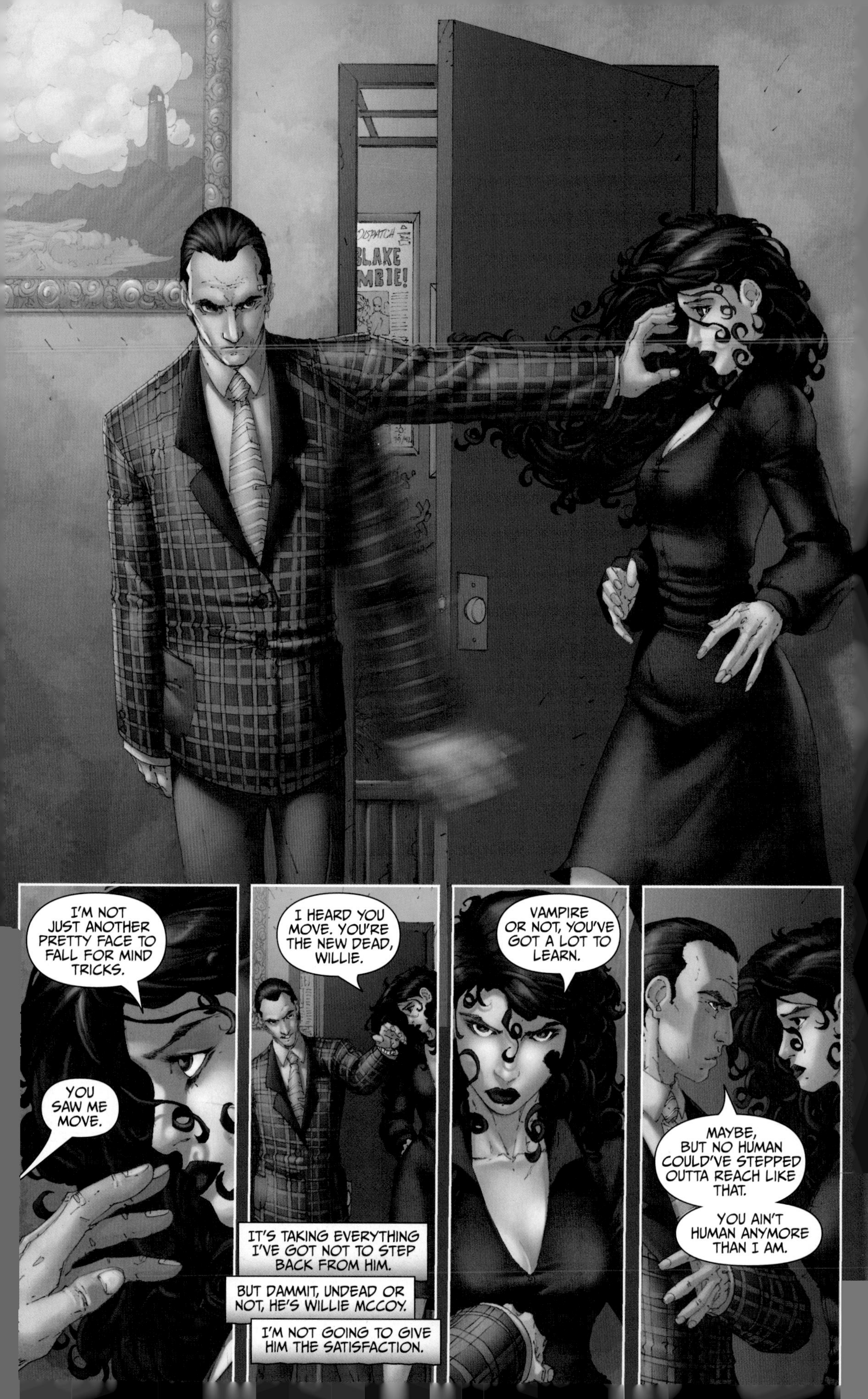
DISPATCH
BLAKE
MBIE!
I'M NOT JUST ANOTHER PRETTY FACE TO FALL FOR MIND TRICKS.
YOU SAW ME MOVE.
I HEARD YOU MOVE. YOU'RE THE NEW DEAD, WILLIE.
IT'S TAKING EVERYTHING I'VE GOT NOT TO STEP BACK FROM HIM.
BUT DAMMIT, UNDEAD OR NOT, HE'S WILLIE MCCOY.
I'M NOT GOING TO GIVE HIM THE SATISFACTION.
VAMPIRE OR NOT, YOU'VE GOT A LOT TO LEARN.
MAYBE, BUT NO HUMAN COULD'VE STEPPED OUTTA REACH LIKE THAT.
YOU AIN'T HUMAN ANYMORE THAN I AM.

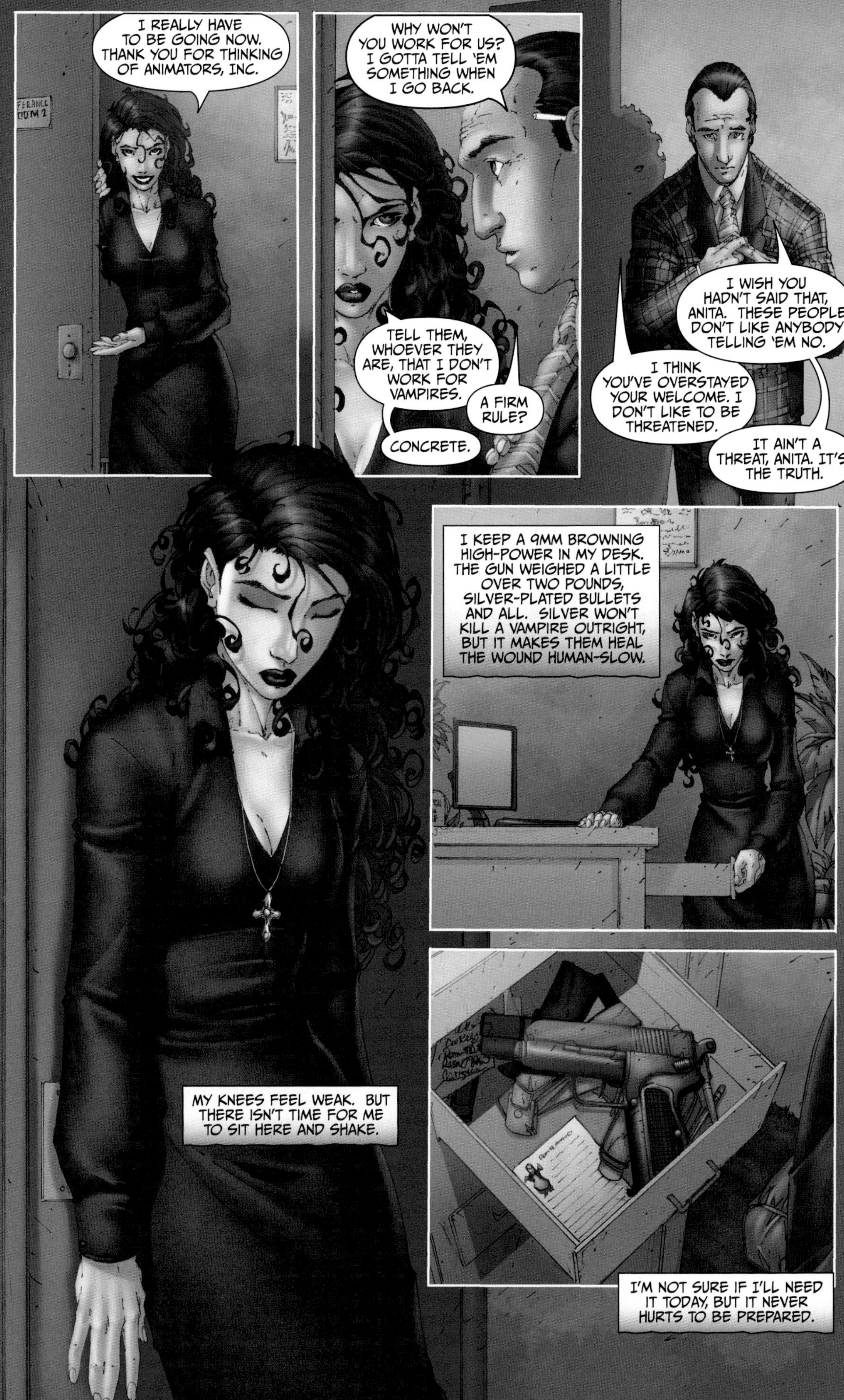
I REALLY HAVE TO BE GOING NOW. THANK YOU FOR THINKING OF ANIMATORS, INC.
WHY WON'T YOU WORK FOR US? I GOTTA TELL 'EM SOMETHING WHEN I GO BACK.
TELL THEM, WHOEVER THEY ARE, THAT I DON'T WORK FOR VAMPIRES.
A FIRM RULE?
CONCRETE.
I WISH YOU HADN'T SAID THAT, ANITA. THESE PEOPLE DON'T LIKE ANYBODY TELLING 'EM NO.
I THINK YOU'VE OVERSTAYED YOUR WELCOME. I DON'T LIKE TO BE THREATENED.
IT AIN'T A THREAT, ANITA. IT'S THE TRUTH.
MY KNEES FEEL WEAK. BUT THERE ISN'T TIME FOR ME TO SIT HERE AND SHAKE.
I KEEP A 9MM BROWNING HIGH-POWER IN MY DESK. THE GUN WEIGHED A LITTLE OVER TWO POUNDS, SILVER-PLATED BULLETS AND ALL. SILVER WON'T KILL A VAMPIRE OUTRIGHT, BUT IT MAKES THEM HEAL THE WOUND HUMAN-SLOW.
I'M NOT SURE IF I'LL NEED IT TODAY, BUT IT NEVER HURTS TO BE PREPARED.

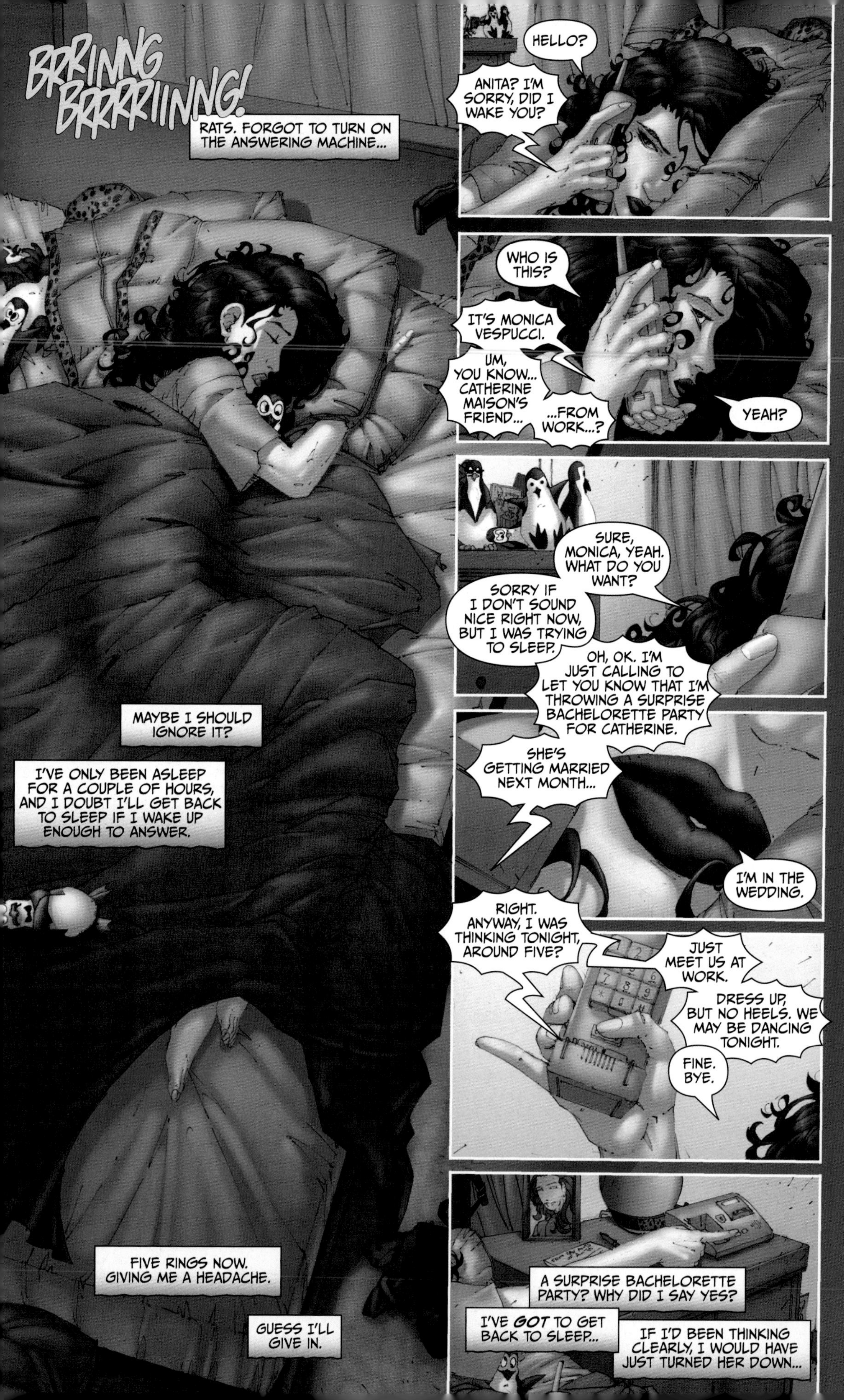
BRRINNG BRRRRIINNG!
RATS. FORGOT TO TURN ON THE ANSWERING MACHINE...
MAYBE I SHOULD IGNORE IT?
I'VE ONLY BEEN ASLEEP FOR A COUPLE OF HOURS, AND I DOUBT I'LL GET BACK TO SLEEP IF I WAKE UP ENOUGH TO ANSWER.
FIVE RINGS NOW. GIVING ME A HEADACHE.
GUESS I'LL GIVE IN.
HELLO?
ANITA? I'M SORRY, DID I WAKE YOU?
WHO IS THIS?
IT'S MONICA VESPUCCI.
UM, YOU KNOW... CATHERINE MAISON'S FRIEND...
...FROM WORK...?
YEAH?
SURE, MONICA, YEAH. WHAT DO YOU WANT?
SORRY IF I DON'T SOUND NICE RIGHT NOW, BUT I WAS TRYING TO SLEEP.
OH, OK. I'M JUST CALLING TO LET YOU KNOW THAT I'M THROWING A SURPRISE BACHELORETTE PARTY FOR CATHERINE.
SHE'S GETTING MARRIED NEXT MONTH...
I'M IN THE WEDDING.
RIGHT. ANYWAY, I WAS THINKING TONIGHT, AROUND FIVE?
JUST MEET US AT WORK.
DRESS UP, BUT NO HEELS. WE MAY BE DANCING TONIGHT.
FINE. BYE.
A SURPRISE BACHELORETTE PARTY? WHY DID I SAY YES?
I'VE GOT TO GET BACK TO SLEEP...
IF I'D BEEN THINKING CLEARLY, I WOULD HAVE JUST TURNED HER DOWN...

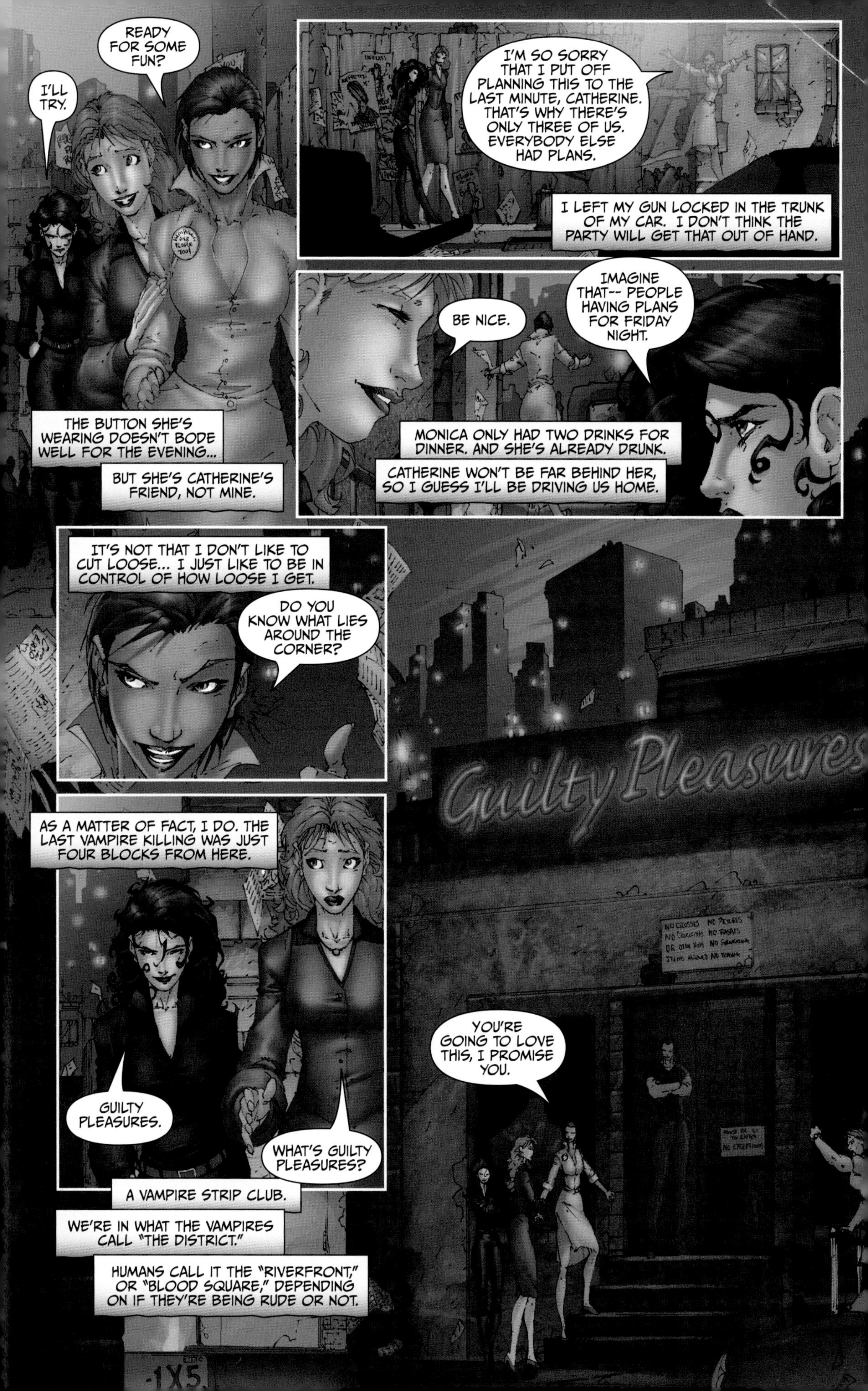
READY FOR SOME FUN?
I'LL TRY.
THE BUTTON SHE'S WEARING DOESN'T BODE WELL FOR THE EVENING...
BUT SHE'S CATHERINE'S FRIEND, NOT MINE.
I'M SO SORRY THAT I PUT OFF PLANNING THIS TO THE LAST MINUTE, CATHERINE. THAT'S WHY THERE'S ONLY THREE OF US. EVERYBODY ELSE HAD PLANS.
I LEFT MY GUN LOCKED IN THE TRUNK OF MY CAR. I DON'T THINK THE PARTY WILL GET THAT OUT OF HAND.
IMAGINE THAT-- PEOPLE HAVING PLANS FOR FRIDAY NIGHT.
BE NICE.
MONICA ONLY HAD TWO DRINKS FOR DINNER. AND SHE'S ALREADY DRUNK.
CATHERINE WON'T BE FAR BEHIND HER, SO I GUESS I'LL BE DRIVING US HOME.
IT'S NOT THAT I DON'T LIKE TO CUT LOOSE... I JUST LIKE TO BE IN CONTROL OF HOW LOOSE I GET.
DO YOU KNOW WHAT LIES AROUND THE CORNER?
AS A MATTER OF FACT, I DO. THE LAST VAMPIRE KILLING WAS JUST FOUR BLOCKS FROM HERE.
GUILTY PLEASURES.
WHAT'S GUILTY PLEASURES?
A VAMPIRE STRIP CLUB.
WE'RE IN WHAT THE VAMPIRES CALL "THE DISTRICT."
HUMANS CALL IT THE "RIVERFRONT," OR "BLOOD SQUARE," DEPENDING ON IF THEY'RE BEING RUDE OR NOT.
Guilty Pleasures
YOU'RE GOING TO LOVE THIS, I PROMISE YOU.

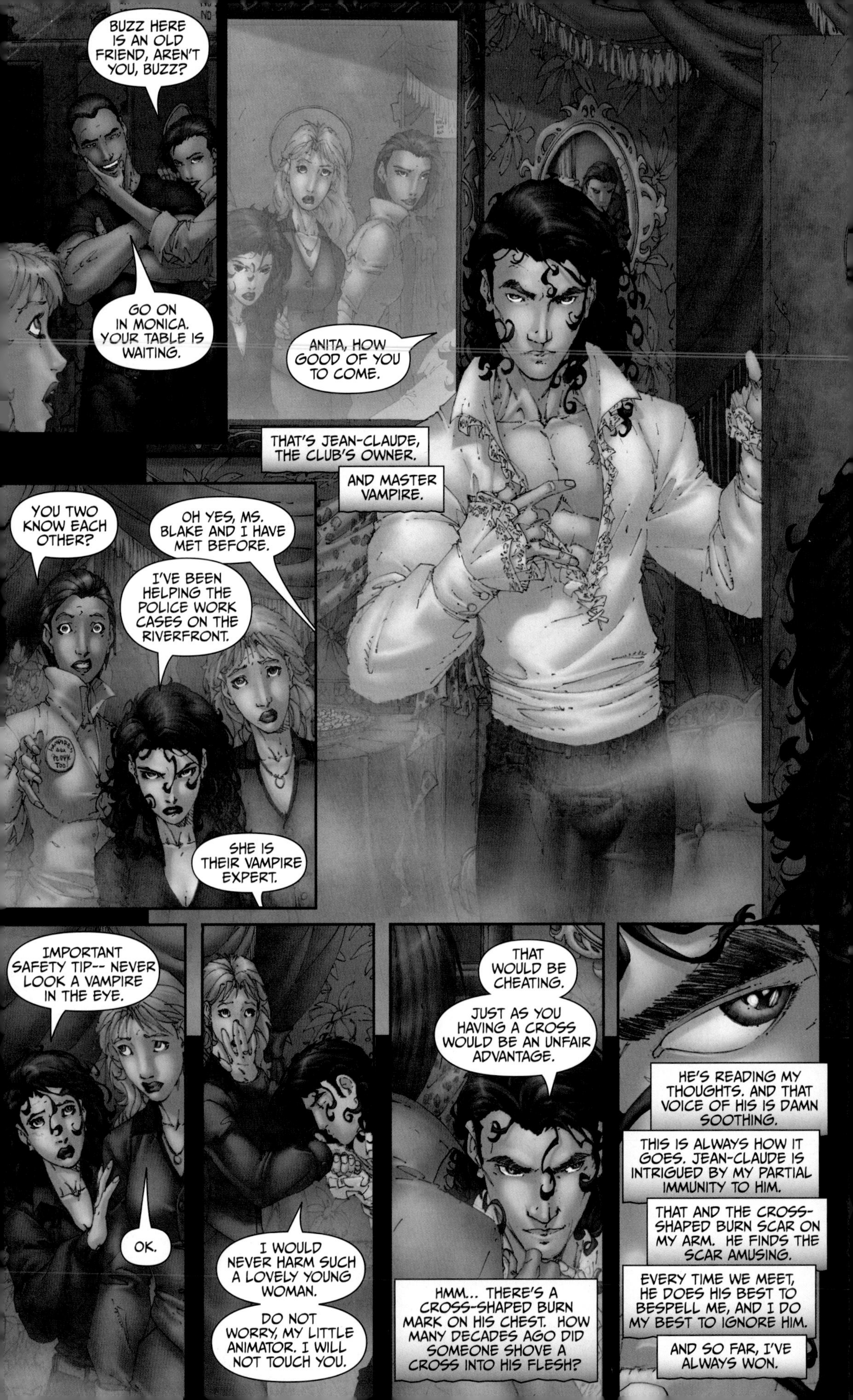
BUZZ HERE IS AN OLD FRIEND, AREN'T YOU, BUZZ?
GO ON IN MONICA. YOUR TABLE IS WAITING.
ANITA, HOW GOOD OF YOU TO COME.
THAT'S JEAN-CLAUDE, THE CLUB'S OWNER.
AND MASTER VAMPIRE.
YOU TWO KNOW EACH OTHER?
OH YES, MS. BLAKE AND I HAVE MET BEFORE.
I'VE BEEN HELPING THE POLICE WORK CASES ON THE RIVERFRONT.
SHE IS THEIR VAMPIRE EXPERT.
IMPORTANT SAFETY TIP-- NEVER LOOK A VAMPIRE IN THE EYE.
OK.
I WOULD NEVER HARM SUCH A LOVELY YOUNG WOMAN.
DO NOT WORRY, MY LITTLE ANIMATOR. I WILL NOT TOUCH YOU.
THAT WOULD BE CHEATING.
JUST AS YOU HAVING A CROSS WOULD BE AN UNFAIR ADVANTAGE.
HMM... THERE'S A CROSS-SHAPED BURN MARK ON HIS CHEST. HOW MANY DECADES AGO DID SOMEONE SHOVE A CROSS INTO HIS FLESH?
HE'S READING MY THOUGHTS. AND THAT VOICE OF HIS IS DAMN SOOTHING.
THIS IS ALWAYS HOW IT GOES. JEAN-CLAUDE IS INTRIGUED BY MY PARTIAL IMMUNITY TO HIM.
THAT AND THE CROSS-SHAPED BURN SCAR ON MY ARM. HE FINDS THE SCAR AMUSING.
EVERY TIME WE MEET, HE DOES HIS BEST TO BESPELL ME, AND I DO MY BEST TO IGNORE HIM.
AND SO FAR, I'VE ALWAYS WON.

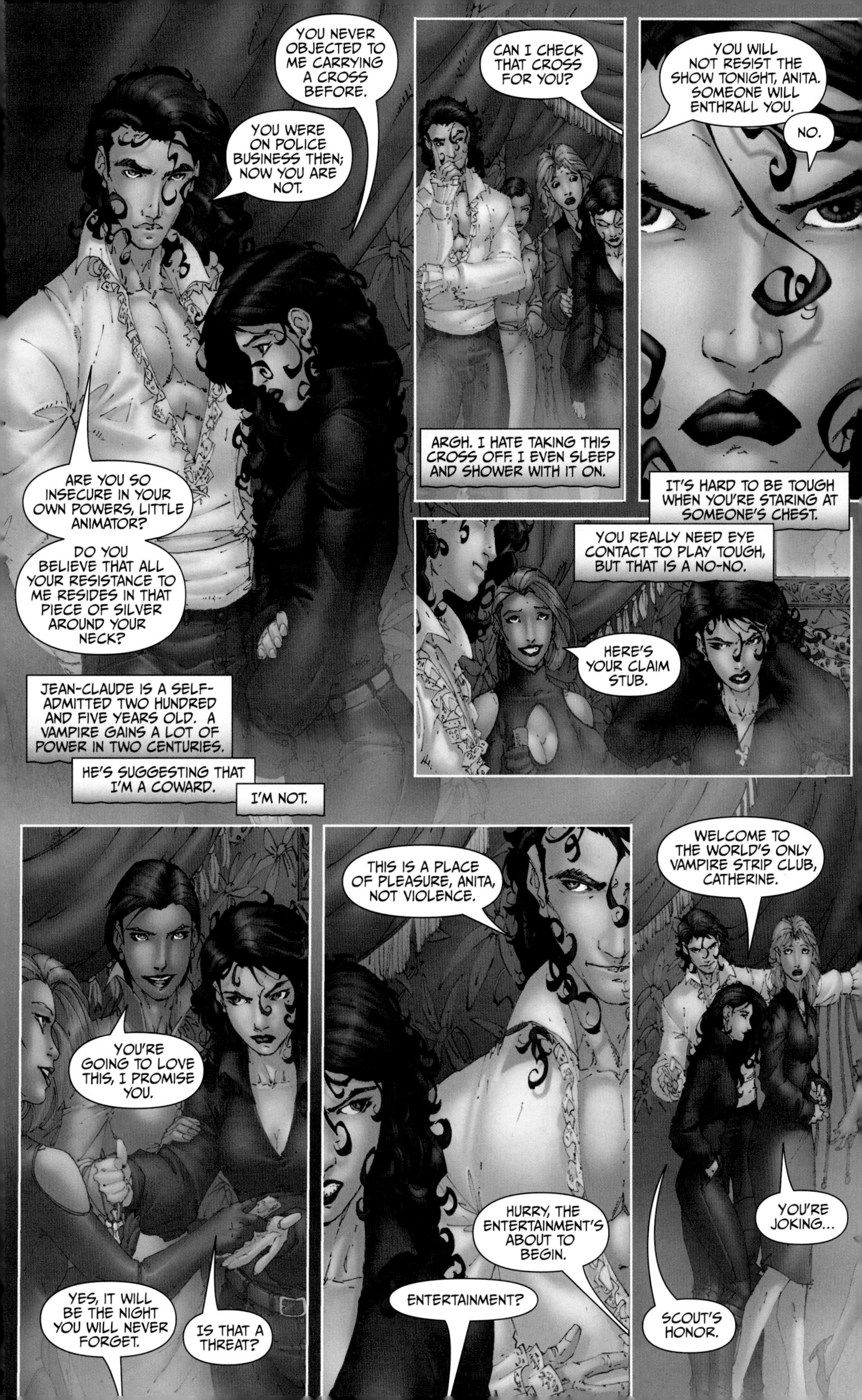
YOU NEVER OBJECTED TO ME CARRYING A CROSS BEFORE.
YOU WERE ON POLICE BUSINESS THEN; NOW YOU ARE NOT.
ARE YOU SO INSECURE IN YOUR OWN POWERS, LITTLE ANIMATOR?
DO YOU BELIEVE THAT ALL YOUR RESISTANCE TO ME RESIDES IN THAT PIECE OF SILVER AROUND YOUR NECK?
JEAN-CLAUDE IS A SELF-ADMITTED TWO HUNDRED AND FIVE YEARS OLD. A VAMPIRE GAINS A LOT OF POWER IN TWO CENTURIES.
HE'S SUGGESTING THAT I'M A COWARD.
I'M NOT.
CAN I CHECK THAT CROSS FOR YOU?
ARGH. I HATE TAKING THIS CROSS OFF. I EVEN SLEEP AND SHOWER WITH IT ON.
YOU WILL NOT RESIST THE SHOW TONIGHT, ANITA. SOMEONE WILL ENTHRALL YOU.
NO.
IT'S HARD TO BE TOUGH WHEN YOU'RE STARING AT SOMEONE'S CHEST.
YOU REALLY NEED EYE CONTACT TO PLAY TOUGH, BUT THAT IS A NO-NO.
HERE'S YOUR CLAIM STUB.
YOU'RE GOING TO LOVE THIS, I PROMISE YOU.
YES, IT WILL BE THE NIGHT YOU WILL NEVER FORGET.
IS THAT A THREAT?
THIS IS A PLACE OF PLEASURE, ANITA, NOT VIOLENCE.
HURRY, THE ENTERTAINMENT'S ABOUT TO BEGIN.
ENTERTAINMENT?
WELCOME TO THE WORLD'S ONLY VAMPIRE STRIP CLUB, CATHERINE.
YOU'RE JOKING...
SCOUT'S HONOR.

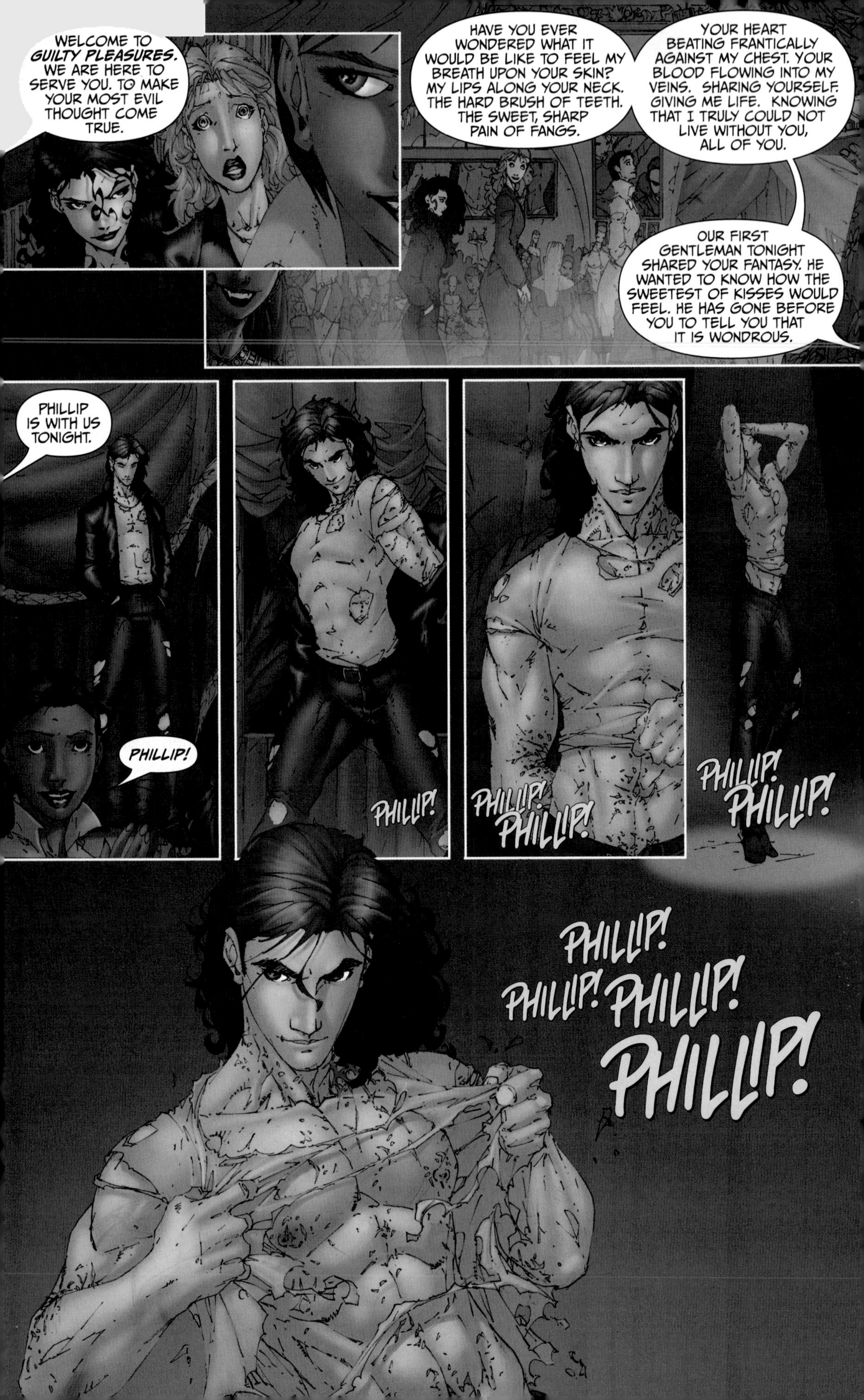

WELCOME TO *GUILTY PLEASURES.* WE ARE HERE TO SERVE YOU. TO MAKE YOUR MOST EVIL THOUGHT COME TRUE.
HAVE YOU EVER WONDERED WHAT IT WOULD BE LIKE TO FEEL MY BREATH UPON YOUR SKIN? MY LIPS ALONG YOUR NECK. THE HARD BRUSH OF TEETH. THE SWEET, SHARP PAIN OF FANGS.
YOUR HEART BEATING FRANTICALLY AGAINST MY CHEST. YOUR BLOOD FLOWING INTO MY VEINS. SHARING YOURSELF. GIVING ME LIFE. KNOWING THAT I TRULY COULD NOT LIVE WITHOUT YOU, ALL OF YOU.
OUR FIRST GENTLEMAN TONIGHT SHARED YOUR FANTASY. HE WANTED TO KNOW HOW THE SWEETEST OF KISSES WOULD FEEL. HE HAS GONE BEFORE YOU TO TELL YOU THAT IT IS WONDROUS.
PHILLIP IS WITH US TONIGHT.
PHILLIP!
PHILLIP!
PHILLIP! PHILLIP!
PHILLIP! PHILLIP!
PHILLIP! PHILLIP! PHILLIP! PHILLIP!

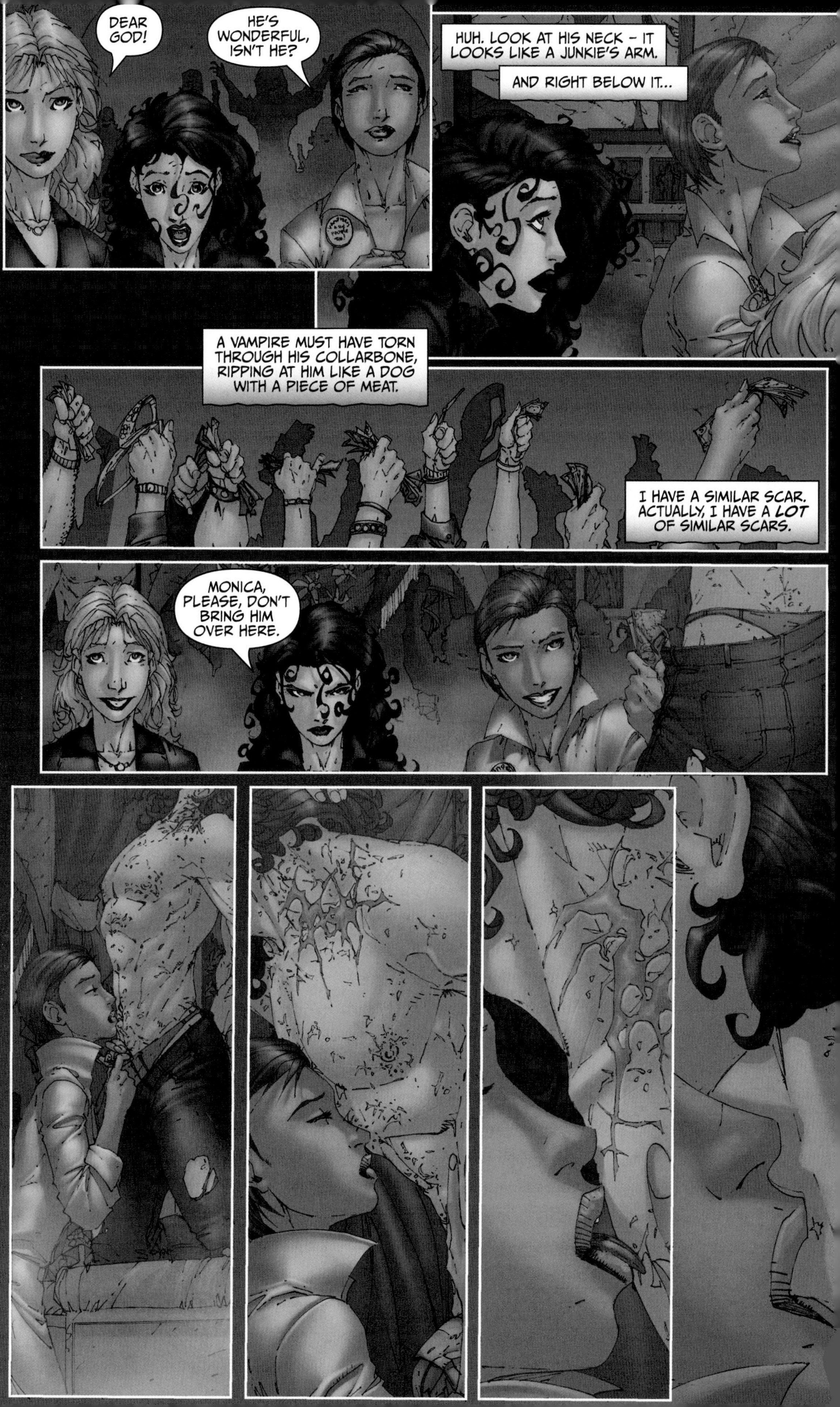
DEAR GOD!
HE'S WONDERFUL, ISN'T HE?
HUH. LOOK AT HIS NECK – IT LOOKS LIKE A JUNKIE'S ARM.
AND RIGHT BELOW IT...
A VAMPIRE MUST HAVE TORN THROUGH HIS COLLARBONE, RIPPING AT HIM LIKE A DOG WITH A PIECE OF MEAT.
I HAVE A SIMILAR SCAR. ACTUALLY, I HAVE A LOT OF SIMILAR SCARS.
MONICA, PLEASE, DON'T BRING HIM OVER HERE.

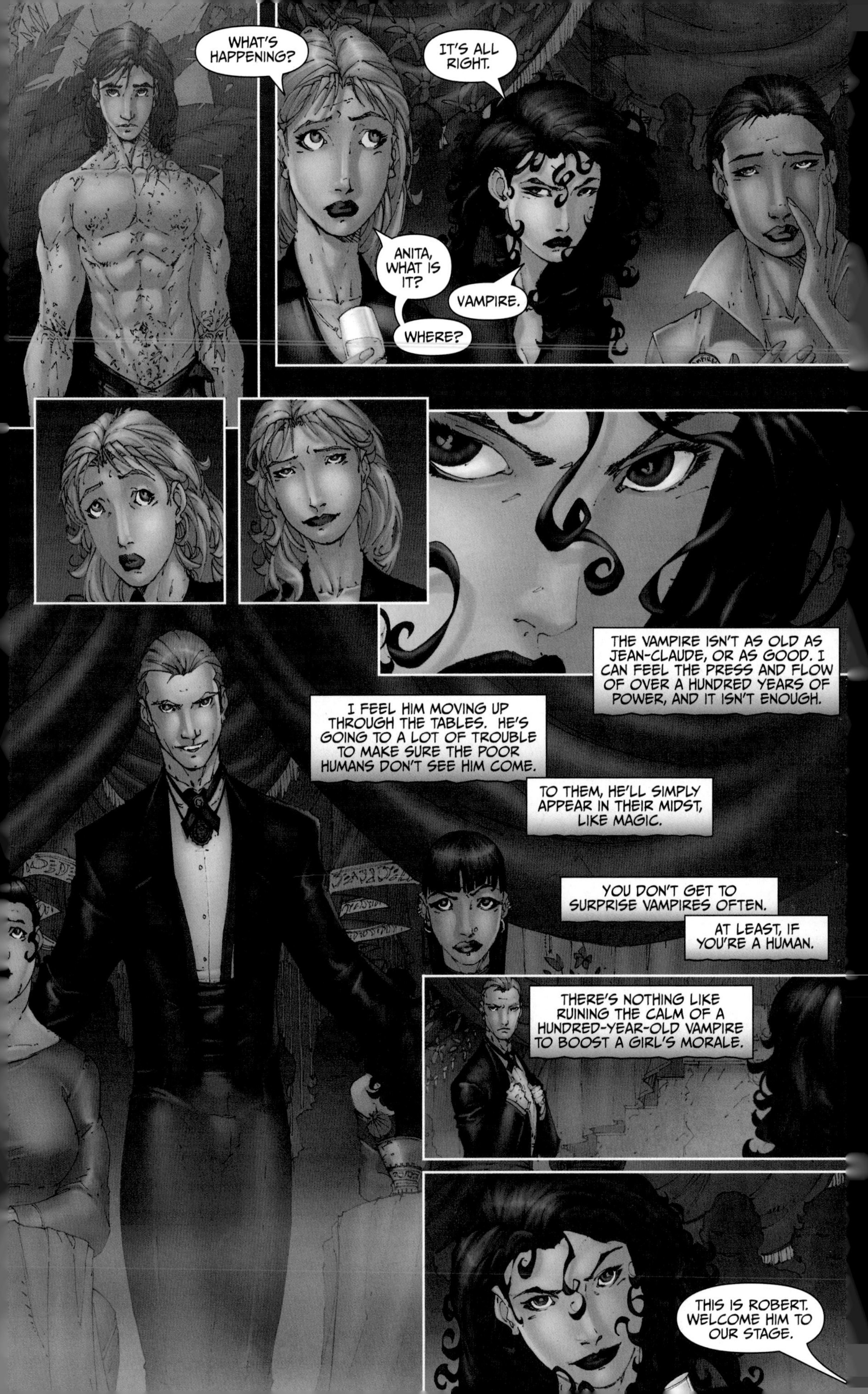
WHAT'S HAPPENING?
IT'S ALL RIGHT.
ANITA, WHAT IS IT?
VAMPIRE.
WHERE?
THE VAMPIRE ISN'T AS OLD AS JEAN-CLAUDE, OR AS GOOD. I CAN FEEL THE PRESS AND FLOW OF OVER A HUNDRED YEARS OF POWER, AND IT ISN'T ENOUGH.
I FEEL HIM MOVING UP THROUGH THE TABLES. HE'S GOING TO A LOT OF TROUBLE TO MAKE SURE THE POOR HUMANS DON'T SEE HIM COME.
TO THEM, HE'LL SIMPLY APPEAR IN THEIR MIDST, LIKE MAGIC.
YOU DON'T GET TO SURPRISE VAMPIRES OFTEN.
AT LEAST, IF YOU'RE A HUMAN.
THERE'S NOTHING LIKE RUINING THE CALM OF A HUNDRED-YEAR-OLD VAMPIRE TO BOOST A GIRL'S MORALE.
THIS IS ROBERT. WELCOME HIM TO OUR STAGE.

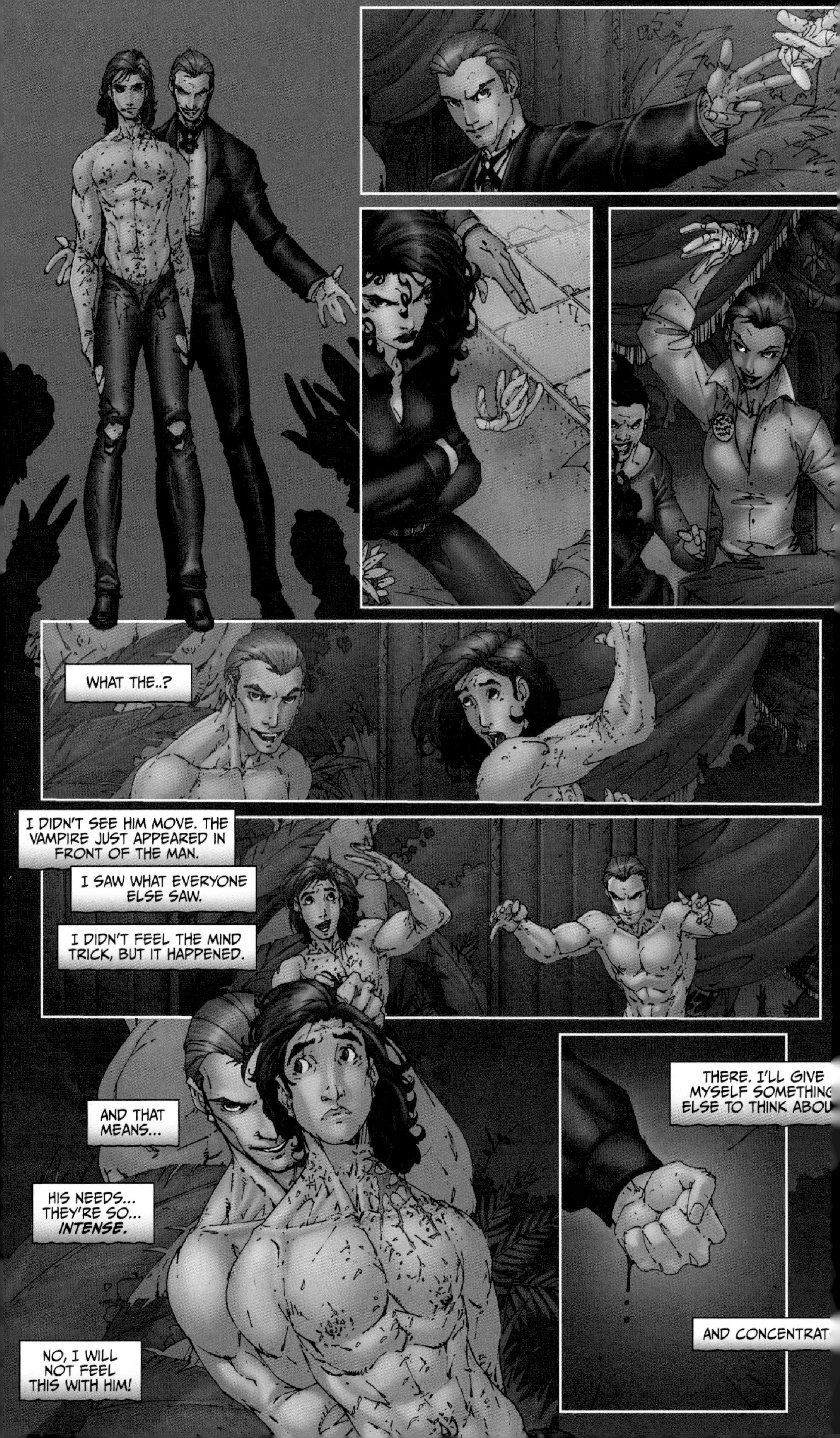

WHAT THE..?
I DIDN'T SEE HIM MOVE. THE VAMPIRE JUST APPEARED IN FRONT OF THE MAN.
I SAW WHAT EVERYONE ELSE SAW.
I DIDN'T FEEL THE MIND TRICK, BUT IT HAPPENED.
AND THAT MEANS...
HIS NEEDS... THEY'RE SO... *INTENSE.*
NO, I WILL NOT FEEL THIS WITH HIM!
THERE. I'LL GIVE MYSELF SOMETHING ELSE TO THINK ABOU
AND CONCENTRAT

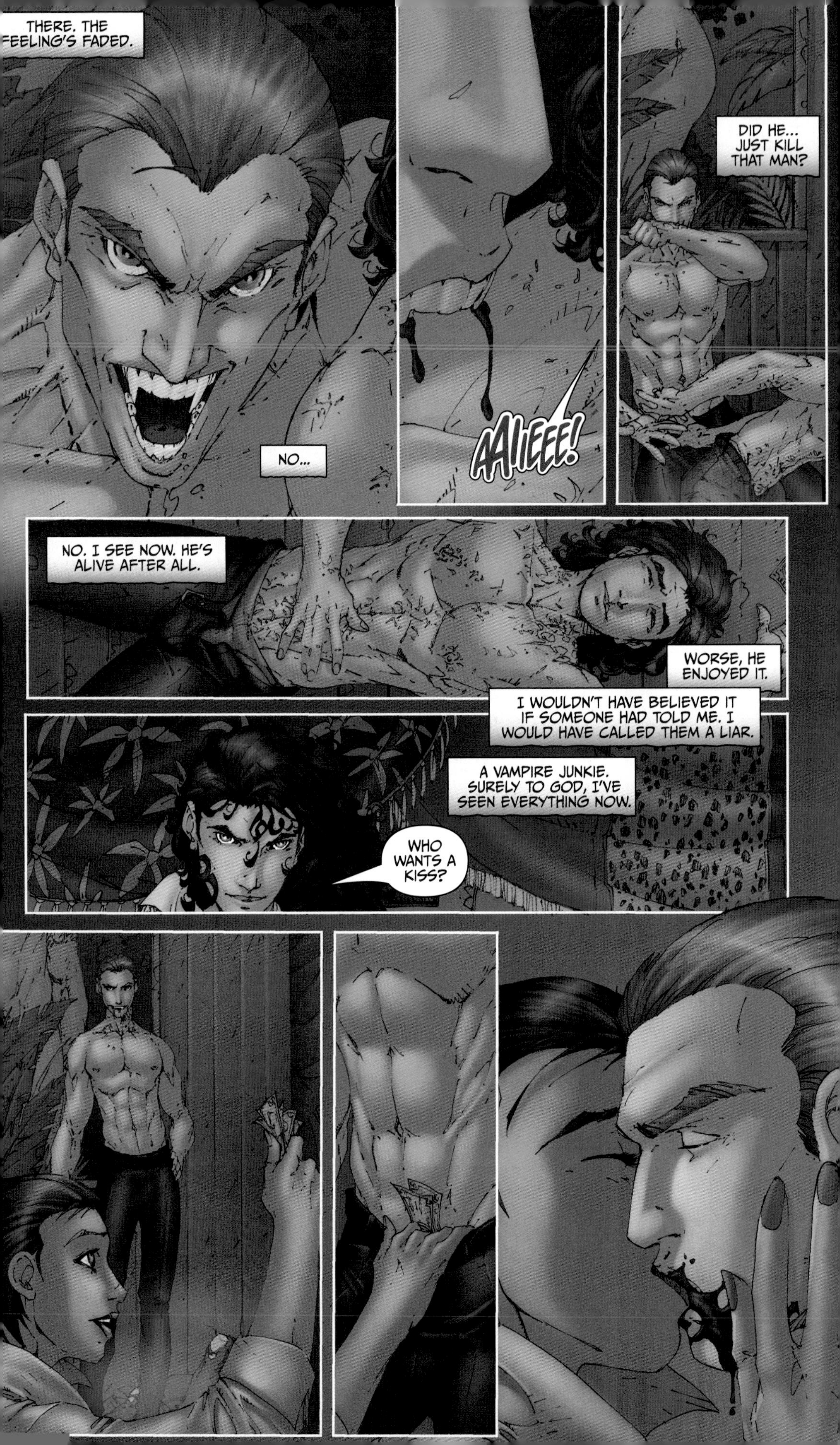
THERE. THE FEELING'S FADED.
NO...
AAIIEEE!
DID HE... JUST KILL THAT MAN?
NO. I SEE NOW. HE'S ALIVE AFTER ALL.
WORSE, HE ENJOYED IT.
I WOULDN'T HAVE BELIEVED IT IF SOMEONE HAD TOLD ME. I WOULD HAVE CALLED THEM A LIAR.
A VAMPIRE JUNKIE. SURELY TO GOD, I'VE SEEN EVERYTHING NOW.
WHO WANTS A KISS?

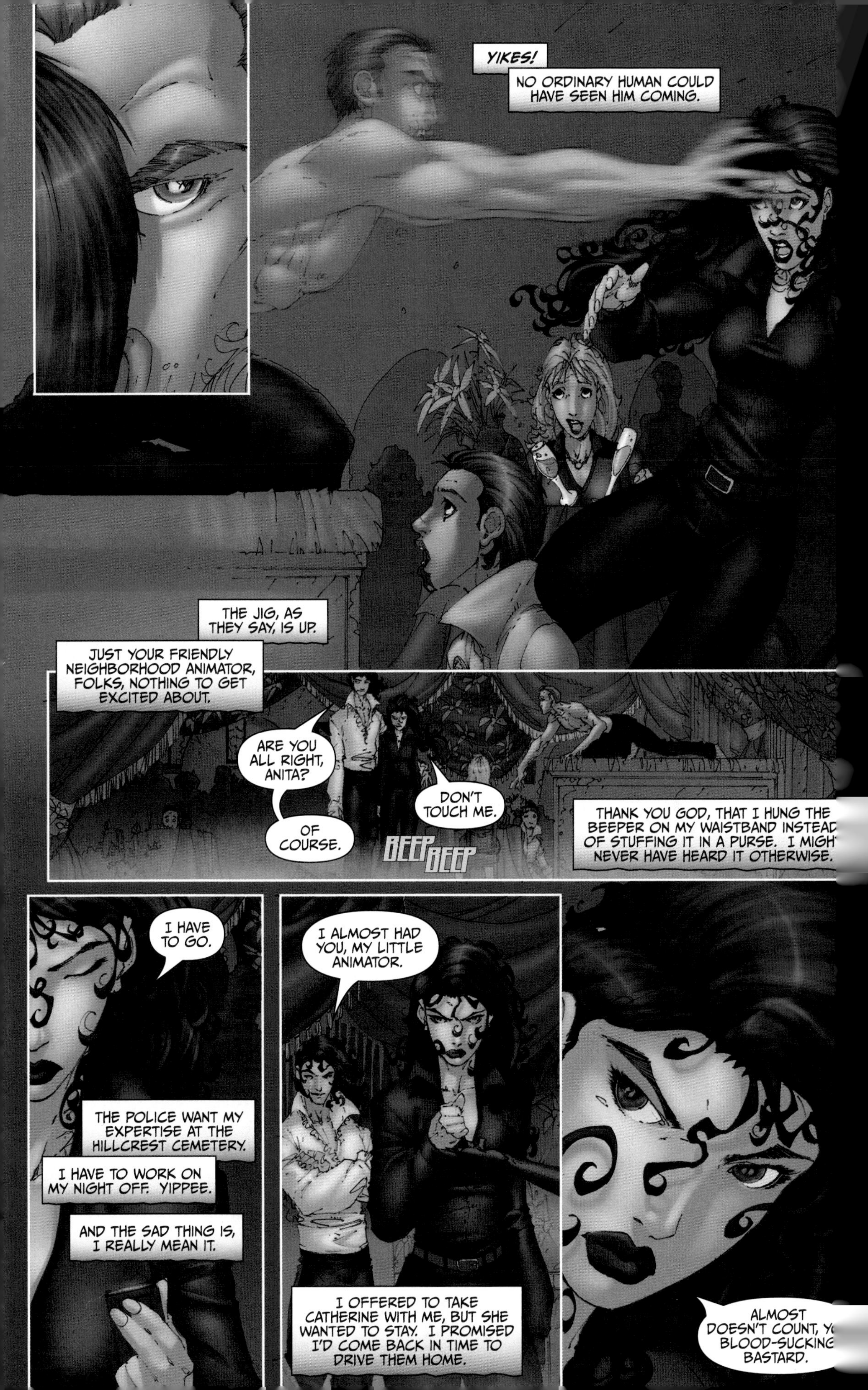
YIKES!
NO ORDINARY HUMAN COULD HAVE SEEN HIM COMING.
THE JIG, AS THEY SAY, IS UP.
JUST YOUR FRIENDLY NEIGHBORHOOD ANIMATOR, FOLKS, NOTHING TO GET EXCITED ABOUT.
ARE YOU ALL RIGHT, ANITA?
OF COURSE.
DON'T TOUCH ME.
BEEP BEEP
THANK YOU GOD, THAT I HUNG THE BEEPER ON MY WAISTBAND INSTEAD OF STUFFING IT IN A PURSE. I MIGHT NEVER HAVE HEARD IT OTHERWISE.
I HAVE TO GO.
THE POLICE WANT MY EXPERTISE AT THE HILLCREST CEMETERY.
I HAVE TO WORK ON MY NIGHT OFF. YIPPEE.
AND THE SAD THING IS, I REALLY MEAN IT.
I ALMOST HAD YOU, MY LITTLE ANIMATOR.
I OFFERED TO TAKE CATHERINE WITH ME, BUT SHE WANTED TO STAY. I PROMISED I'D COME BACK IN TIME TO DRIVE THEM HOME.
ALMOST DOESN'T COUNT, YO BLOOD-SUCKING BASTARD.

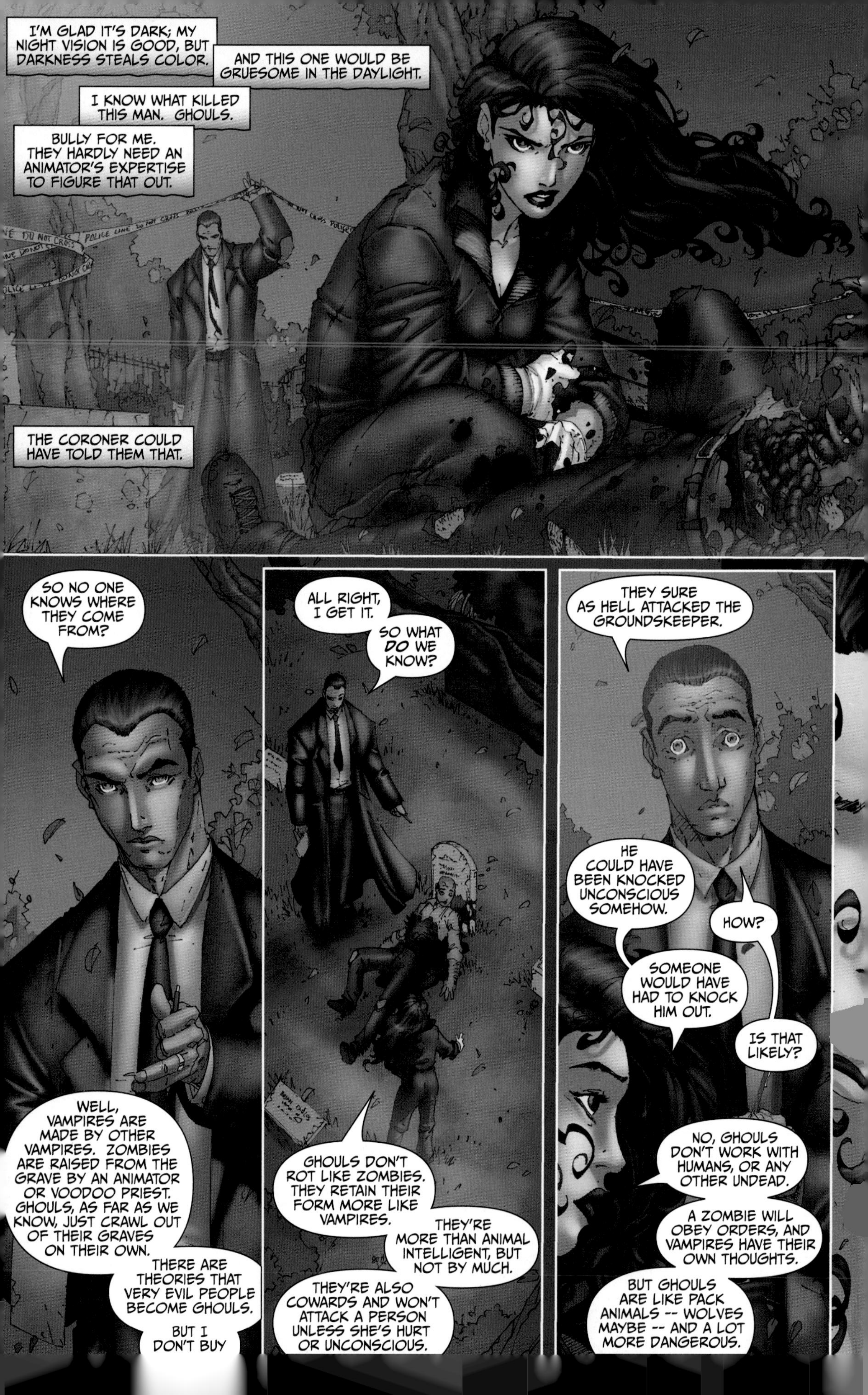
I'M GLAD IT'S DARK; MY NIGHT VISION IS GOOD, BUT DARKNESS STEALS COLOR.
AND THIS ONE WOULD BE GRUESOME IN THE DAYLIGHT.
I KNOW WHAT KILLED THIS MAN. GHOULS.
BULLY FOR ME. THEY HARDLY NEED AN ANIMATOR'S EXPERTISE TO FIGURE THAT OUT.
THE CORONER COULD HAVE TOLD THEM THAT.
SO NO ONE KNOWS WHERE THEY COME FROM?
WELL, VAMPIRES ARE MADE BY OTHER VAMPIRES. ZOMBIES ARE RAISED FROM THE GRAVE BY AN ANIMATOR OR VOODOO PRIEST. GHOULS, AS FAR AS WE KNOW, JUST CRAWL OUT OF THEIR GRAVES ON THEIR OWN.
THERE ARE THEORIES THAT VERY EVIL PEOPLE BECOME GHOULS.
BUT I DON'T BUY
ALL RIGHT, I GET IT.
SO WHAT DO WE KNOW?
GHOULS DON'T ROT LIKE ZOMBIES. THEY RETAIN THEIR FORM MORE LIKE VAMPIRES.
THEY'RE MORE THAN ANIMAL INTELLIGENT, BUT NOT BY MUCH.
THEY'RE ALSO COWARDS AND WON'T ATTACK A PERSON UNLESS SHE'S HURT OR UNCONSCIOUS.
THEY SURE AS HELL ATTACKED THE GROUNDSKEEPER.
HE COULD HAVE BEEN KNOCKED UNCONSCIOUS SOMEHOW.
HOW?
SOMEONE WOULD HAVE HAD TO KNOCK HIM OUT.
IS THAT LIKELY?
NO, GHOULS DON'T WORK WITH HUMANS, OR ANY OTHER UNDEAD.
A ZOMBIE WILL OBEY ORDERS, AND VAMPIRES HAVE THEIR OWN THOUGHTS.
BUT GHOULS ARE LIKE PACK ANIMALS -- WOLVES MAYBE -- AND A LOT MORE DANGEROUS.

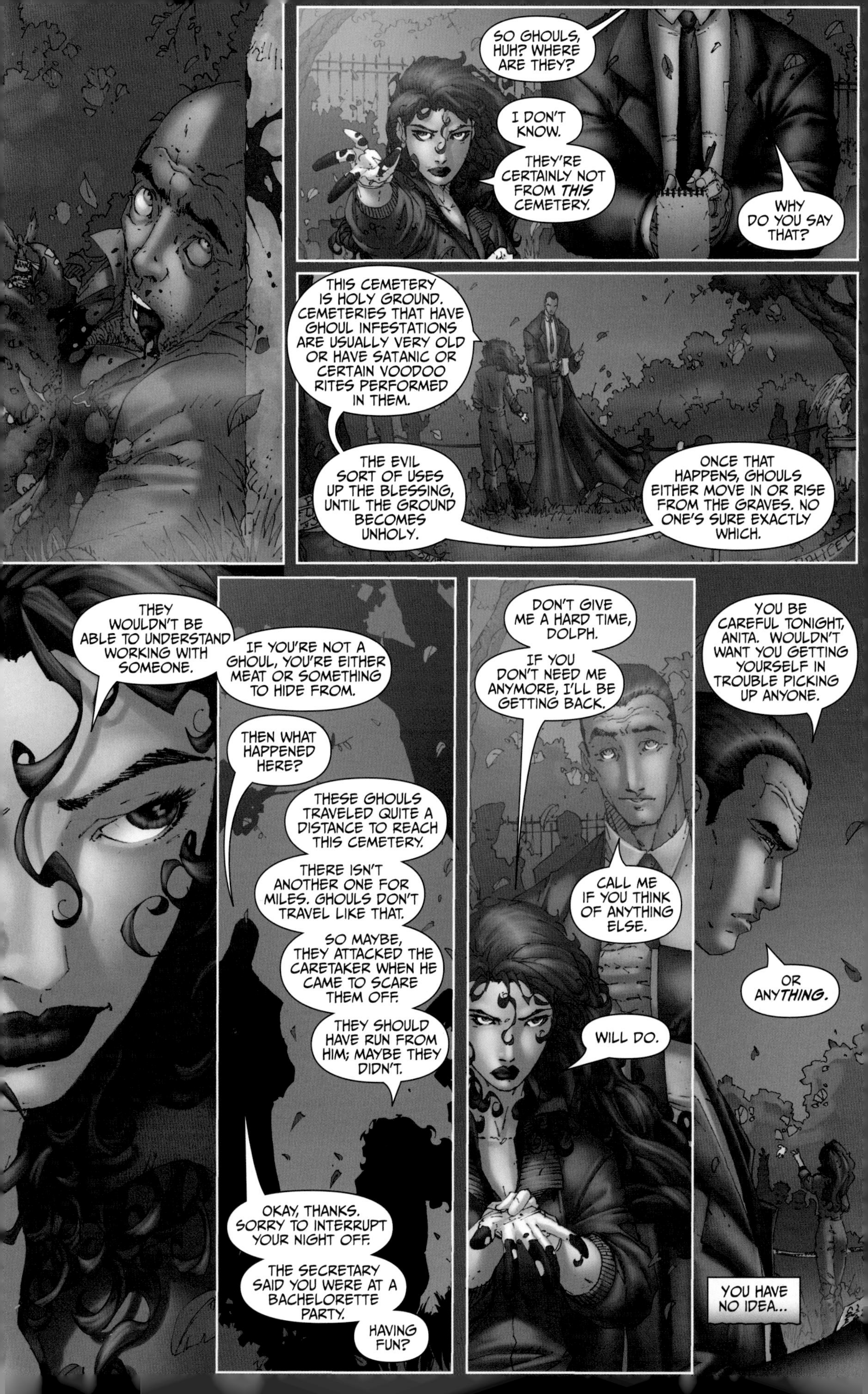

SO GHOULS, HUH? WHERE ARE THEY?
I DON'T KNOW.
THEY'RE CERTAINLY NOT FROM *THIS* CEMETERY.
WHY DO YOU SAY THAT?
THIS CEMETERY IS HOLY GROUND. CEMETERIES THAT HAVE GHOUL INFESTATIONS ARE USUALLY VERY OLD OR HAVE SATANIC OR CERTAIN VOODOO RITES PERFORMED IN THEM.
THE EVIL SORT OF USES UP THE BLESSING, UNTIL THE GROUND BECOMES UNHOLY.
ONCE THAT HAPPENS, GHOULS EITHER MOVE IN OR RISE FROM THE GRAVES. NO ONE'S SURE EXACTLY WHICH.
THEY WOULDN'T BE ABLE TO UNDERSTAND WORKING WITH SOMEONE.
IF YOU'RE NOT A GHOUL, YOU'RE EITHER MEAT OR SOMETHING TO HIDE FROM.
THEN WHAT HAPPENED HERE?
THESE GHOULS TRAVELED QUITE A DISTANCE TO REACH THIS CEMETERY.
THERE ISN'T ANOTHER ONE FOR MILES. GHOULS DON'T TRAVEL LIKE THAT.
SO MAYBE, THEY ATTACKED THE CARETAKER WHEN HE CAME TO SCARE THEM OFF.
THEY SHOULD HAVE RUN FROM HIM; MAYBE THEY DIDN'T.
OKAY, THANKS. SORRY TO INTERRUPT YOUR NIGHT OFF.
THE SECRETARY SAID YOU WERE AT A BACHELORETTE PARTY.
HAVING FUN?
DON'T GIVE ME A HARD TIME, DOLPH.
IF YOU DON'T NEED ME ANYMORE, I'LL BE GETTING BACK.
CALL ME IF YOU THINK OF ANYTHING ELSE.
WILL DO.
YOU BE CAREFUL TONIGHT, ANITA. WOULDN'T WANT YOU GETTING YOURSELF IN TROUBLE PICKING UP ANYONE.
OR ANY*THING.*
YOU HAVE NO IDEA...

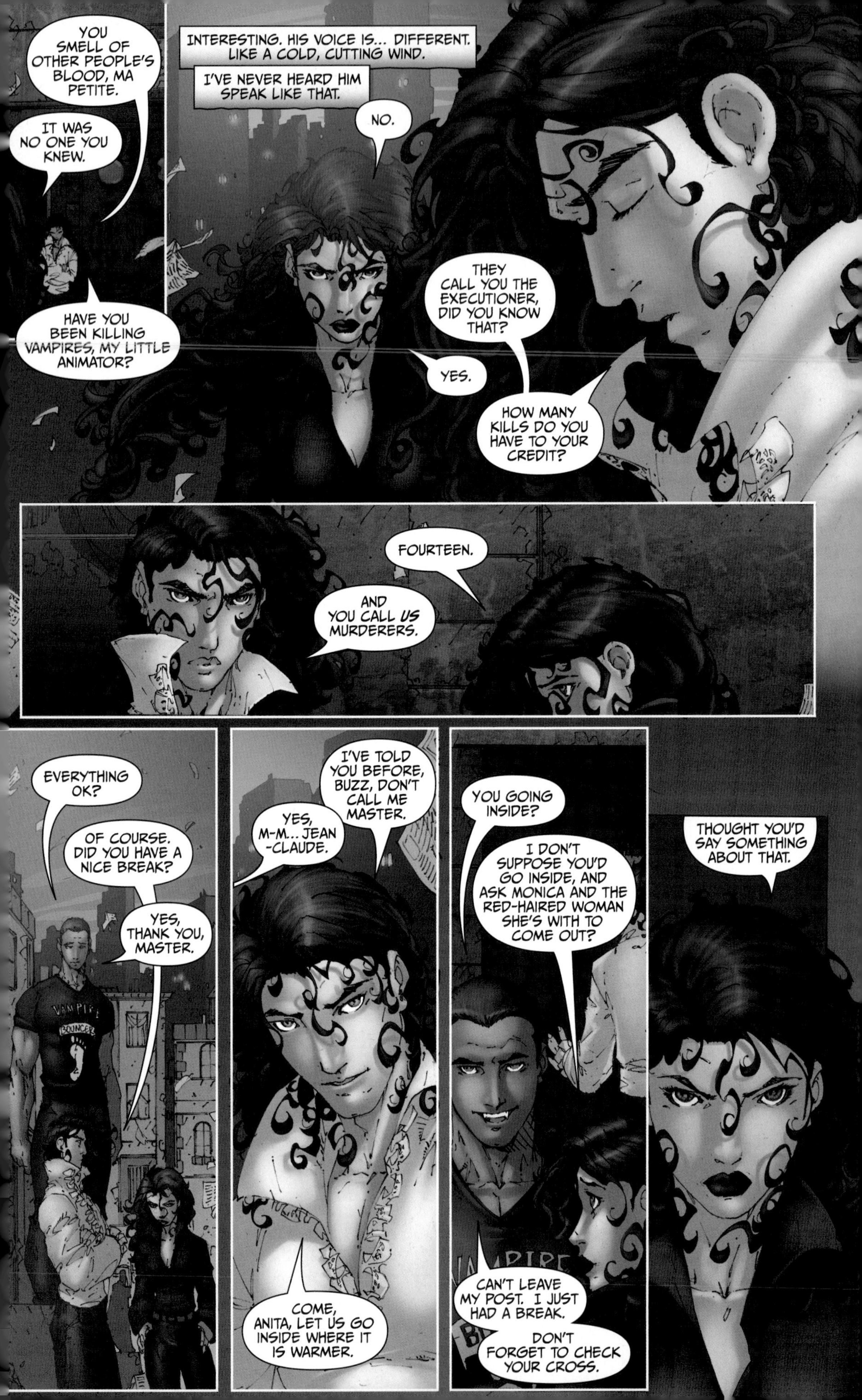
YOU SMELL OF OTHER PEOPLE'S BLOOD, MA PETITE.
IT WAS NO ONE YOU KNEW.
HAVE YOU BEEN KILLING VAMPIRES, MY LITTLE ANIMATOR?
INTERESTING. HIS VOICE IS... DIFFERENT. LIKE A COLD, CUTTING WIND.
I'VE NEVER HEARD HIM SPEAK LIKE THAT.
NO.
THEY CALL YOU THE EXECUTIONER, DID YOU KNOW THAT?
YES.
HOW MANY KILLS DO YOU HAVE TO YOUR CREDIT?
FOURTEEN.
AND YOU CALL *US* MURDERERS.
EVERYTHING OK?
OF COURSE. DID YOU HAVE A NICE BREAK?
YES, THANK YOU, MASTER.
VAMPIRE BOUNCER
I'VE TOLD YOU BEFORE, BUZZ, DON'T CALL ME MASTER.
YES, M-M... JEAN -CLAUDE.
COME, ANITA, LET US GO INSIDE WHERE IT IS WARMER.
YOU GOING INSIDE?
I DON'T SUPPOSE YOU'D GO INSIDE, AND ASK MONICA AND THE RED-HAIRED WOMAN SHE'S WITH TO COME OUT?
CAN'T LEAVE MY POST. I JUST HAD A BREAK.
DON'T FORGET TO CHECK YOUR CROSS.
THOUGHT YOU'D SAY SOMETHING ABOUT THAT.

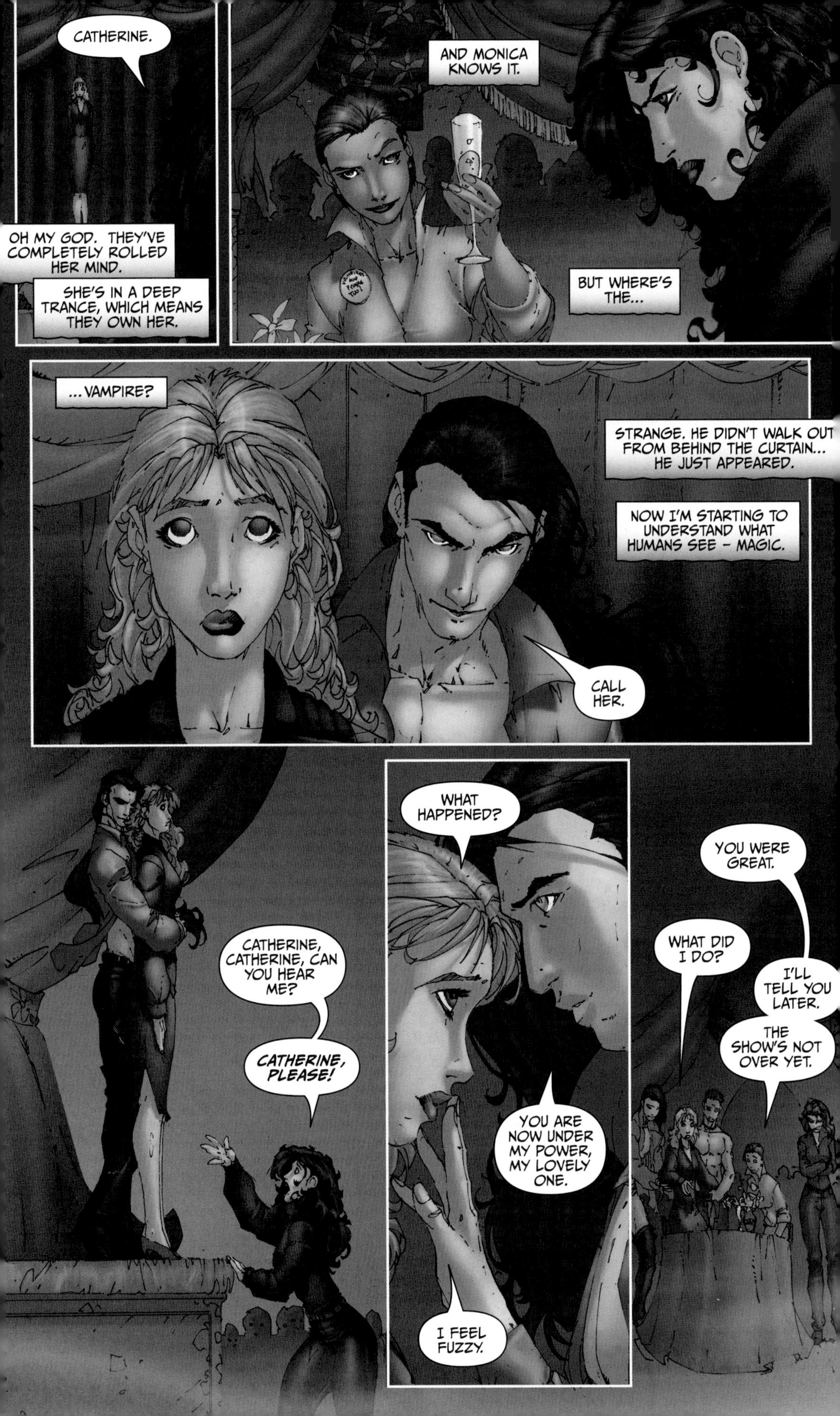

CATHERINE.
OH MY GOD. THEY'VE COMPLETELY ROLLED HER MIND.
SHE'S IN A DEEP TRANCE, WHICH MEANS THEY OWN HER.
AND MONICA KNOWS IT.
BUT WHERE'S THE...
...VAMPIRE?
STRANGE. HE DIDN'T WALK OUT FROM BEHIND THE CURTAIN... HE JUST APPEARED.
NOW I'M STARTING TO UNDERSTAND WHAT HUMANS SEE – MAGIC.
CALL HER.
CATHERINE, CATHERINE, CAN YOU HEAR ME?
CATHERINE, PLEASE!
WHAT HAPPENED?
YOU ARE NOW UNDER MY POWER, MY LOVELY ONE.
I FEEL FUZZY.
YOU WERE GREAT.
WHAT DID I DO?
I'LL TELL YOU LATER.
THE SHOW'S NOT OVER YET.

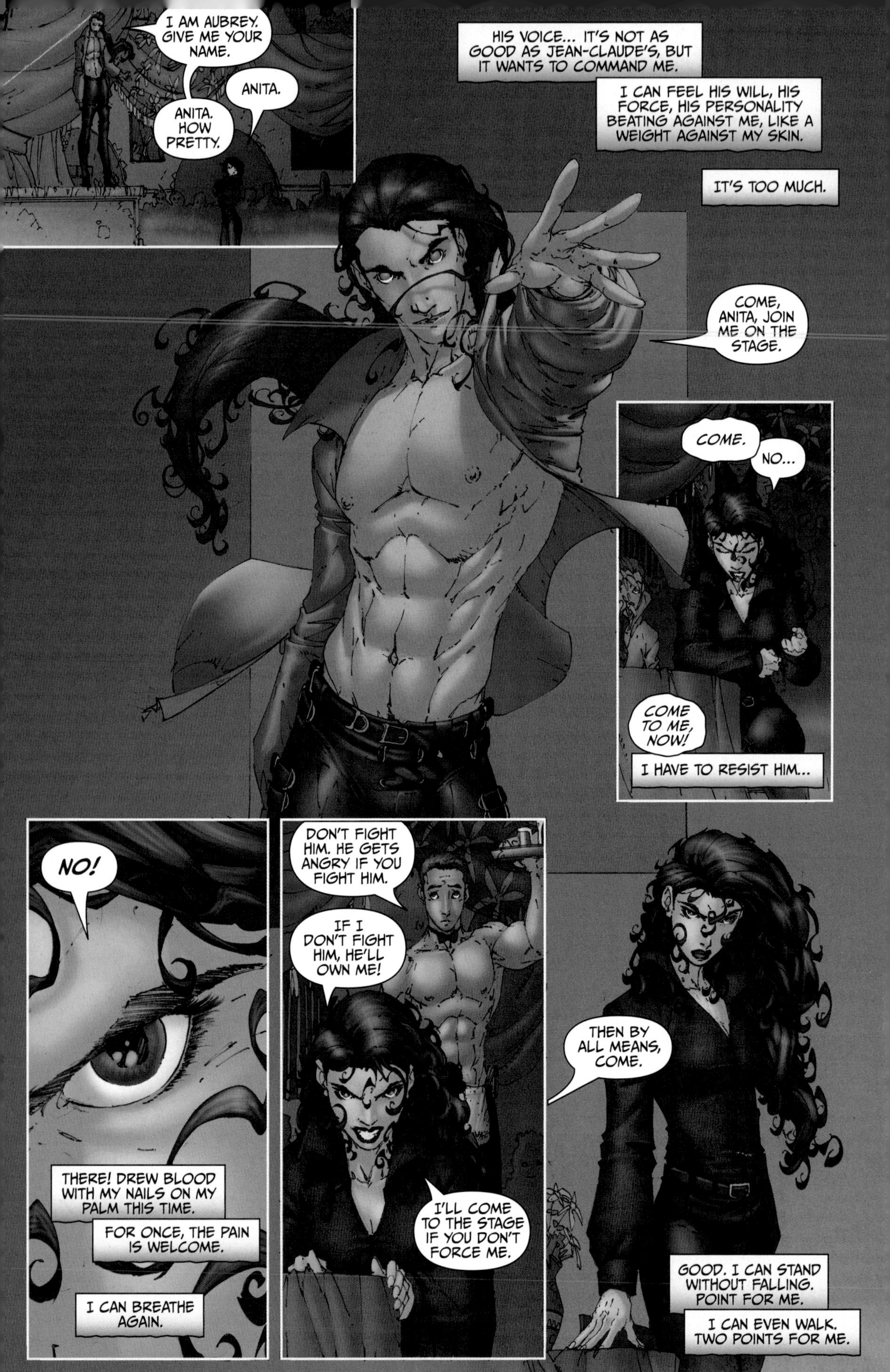
I AM AUBREY. GIVE ME YOUR NAME.
ANITA.
ANITA. HOW PRETTY.
HIS VOICE... IT'S NOT AS GOOD AS JEAN-CLAUDE'S, BUT IT WANTS TO COMMAND ME.
I CAN FEEL HIS WILL, HIS FORCE, HIS PERSONALITY BEATING AGAINST ME, LIKE A WEIGHT AGAINST MY SKIN.
IT'S TOO MUCH.
COME, ANITA, JOIN ME ON THE STAGE.
COME.
NO...
COME TO ME, NOW!
I HAVE TO RESIST HIM...
NO!
THERE! DREW BLOOD WITH MY NAILS ON MY PALM THIS TIME.
FOR ONCE, THE PAIN IS WELCOME.
I CAN BREATHE AGAIN.
DON'T FIGHT HIM. HE GETS ANGRY IF YOU FIGHT HIM.
IF I DON'T FIGHT HIM, HE'LL OWN ME!
I'LL COME TO THE STAGE IF YOU DON'T FORCE ME.
THEN BY ALL MEANS, COME.
GOOD. I CAN STAND WITHOUT FALLING. POINT FOR ME.
I CAN EVEN WALK. TWO POINTS FOR ME.

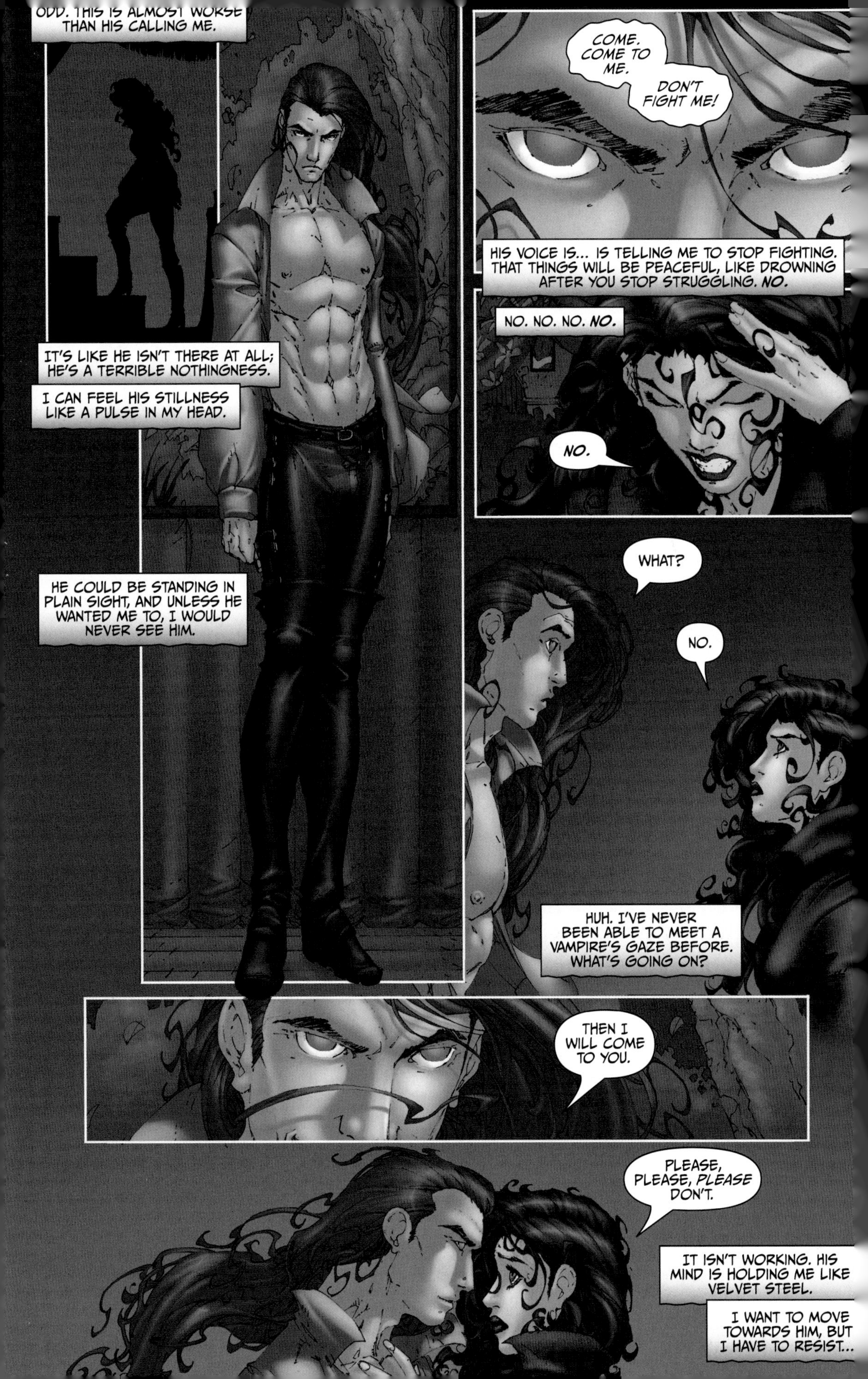
ODD. THIS IS ALMOST WORSE THAN HIS CALLING ME.
IT'S LIKE HE ISN'T THERE AT ALL; HE'S A TERRIBLE NOTHINGNESS.
I CAN FEEL HIS STILLNESS LIKE A PULSE IN MY HEAD.
HE COULD BE STANDING IN PLAIN SIGHT, AND UNLESS HE WANTED ME TO, I WOULD NEVER SEE HIM.
COME. COME TO ME.
DON'T FIGHT ME!
HIS VOICE IS... IS TELLING ME TO STOP FIGHTING. THAT THINGS WILL BE PEACEFUL, LIKE DROWNING AFTER YOU STOP STRUGGLING. NO.
NO. NO. NO. NO.
NO.
WHAT?
NO.
HUH. I'VE NEVER BEEN ABLE TO MEET A VAMPIRE'S GAZE BEFORE. WHAT'S GOING ON?
THEN I WILL COME TO YOU.
PLEASE, PLEASE, PLEASE DON'T.
IT ISN'T WORKING. HIS MIND IS HOLDING ME LIKE VELVET STEEL.
I WANT TO MOVE TOWARDS HIM, BUT I HAVE TO RESIST...

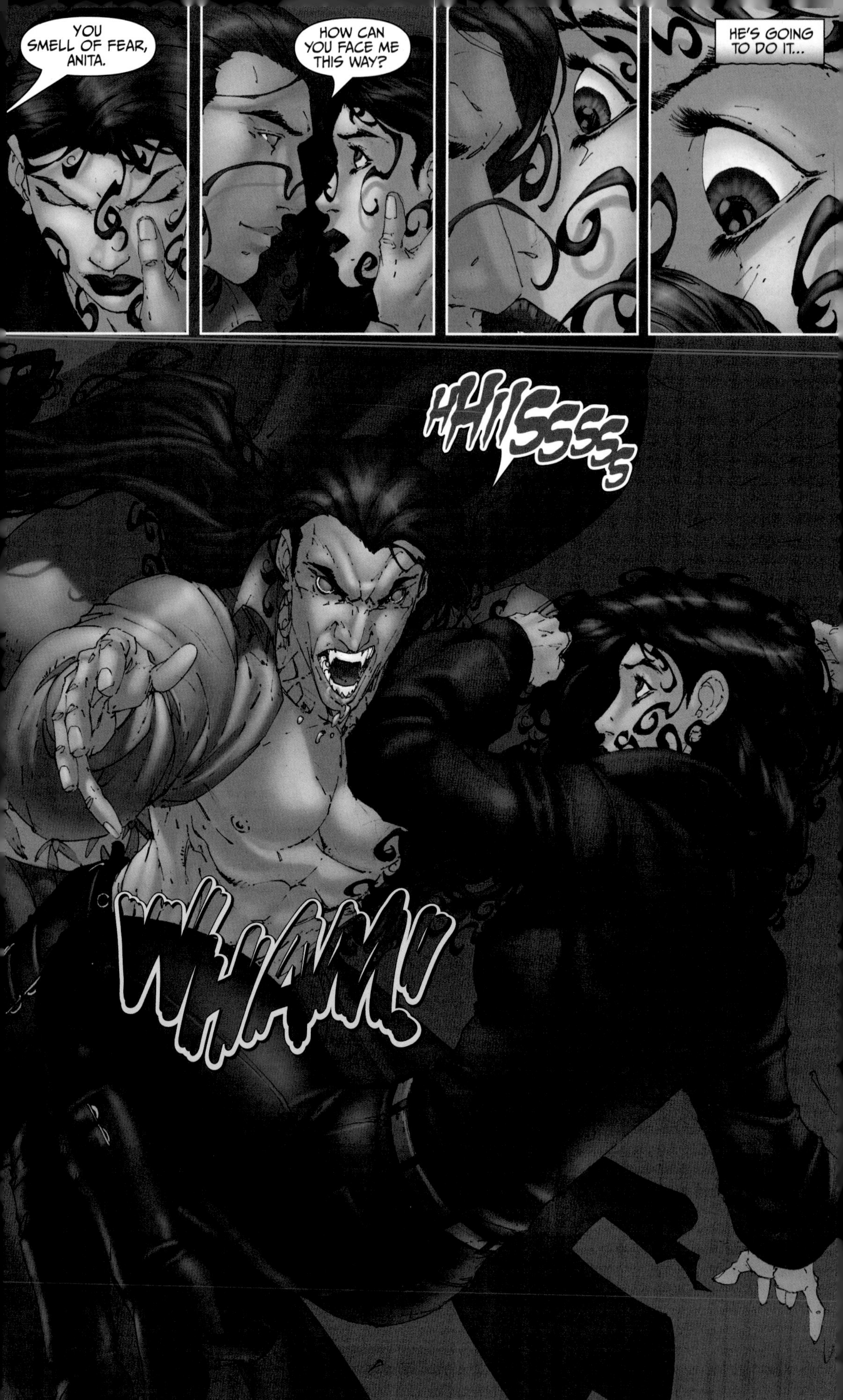
YOU SMELL OF FEAR, ANITA.
HOW CAN YOU FACE ME THIS WAY?
HE'S GOING TO DO IT...
HHHISSSSS
WHAM!

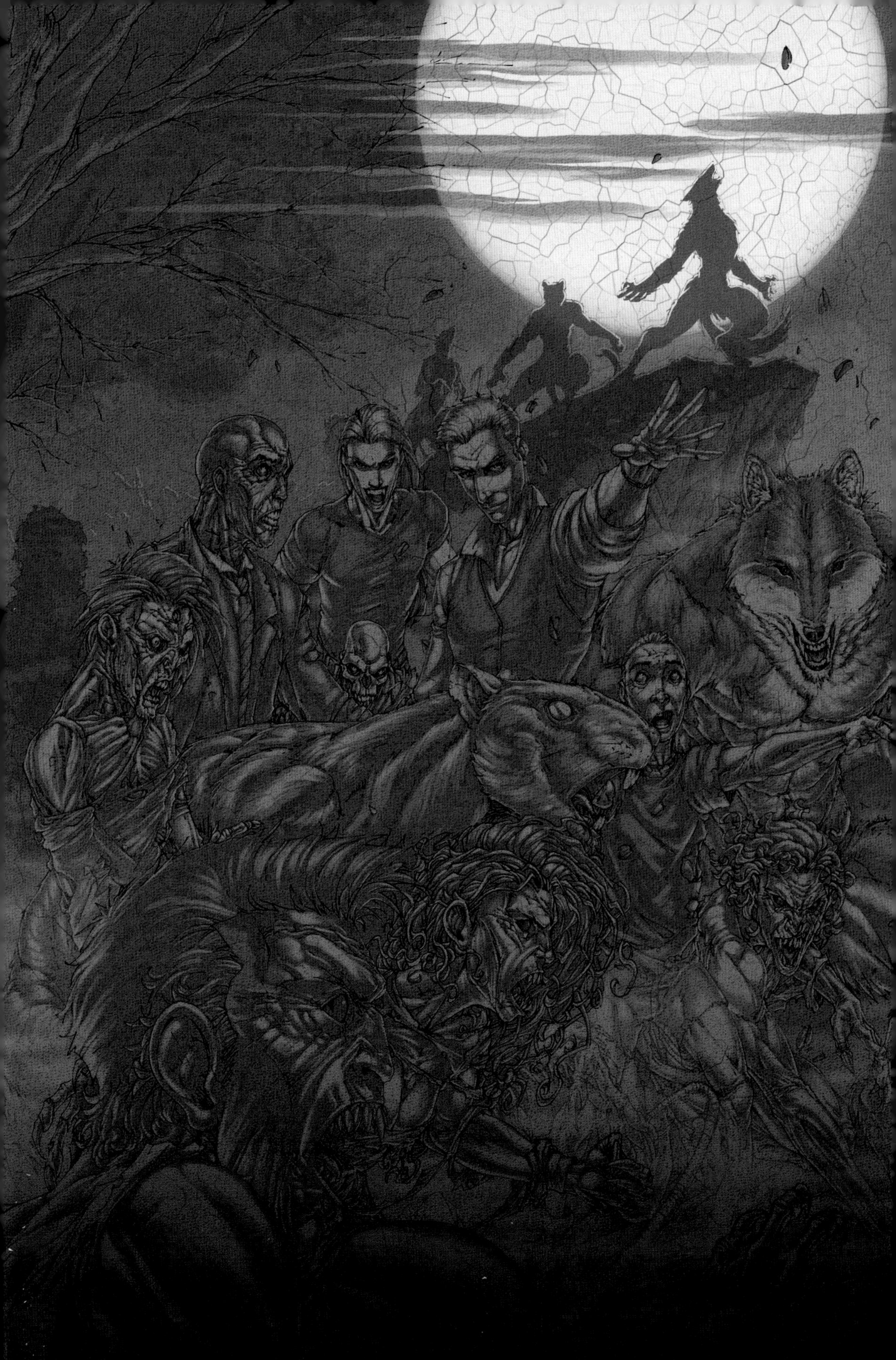

CHAPTER TWO

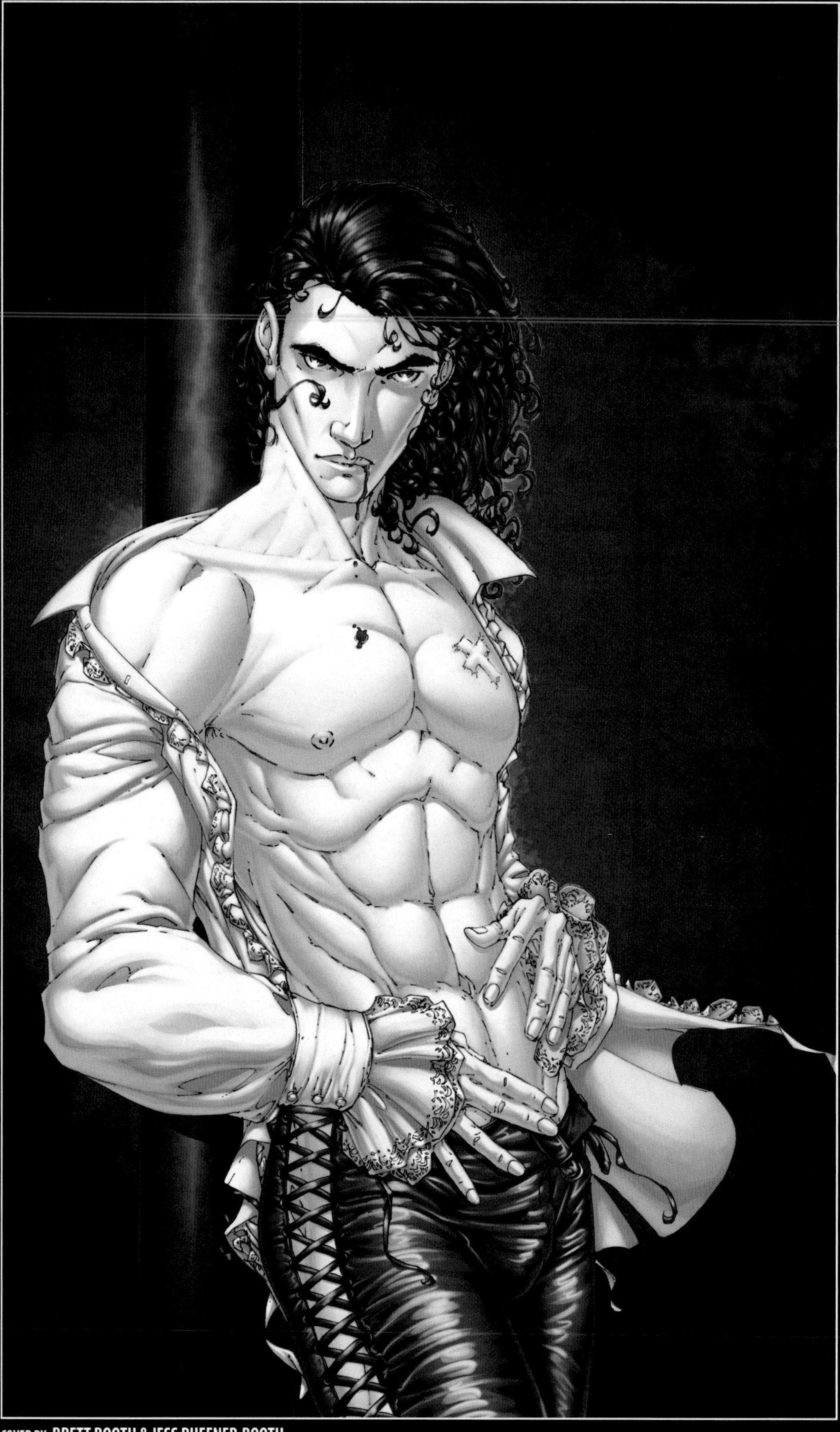

COVER BY: **BRETT BOOTH & JESS RUFFNER-BOOTH**

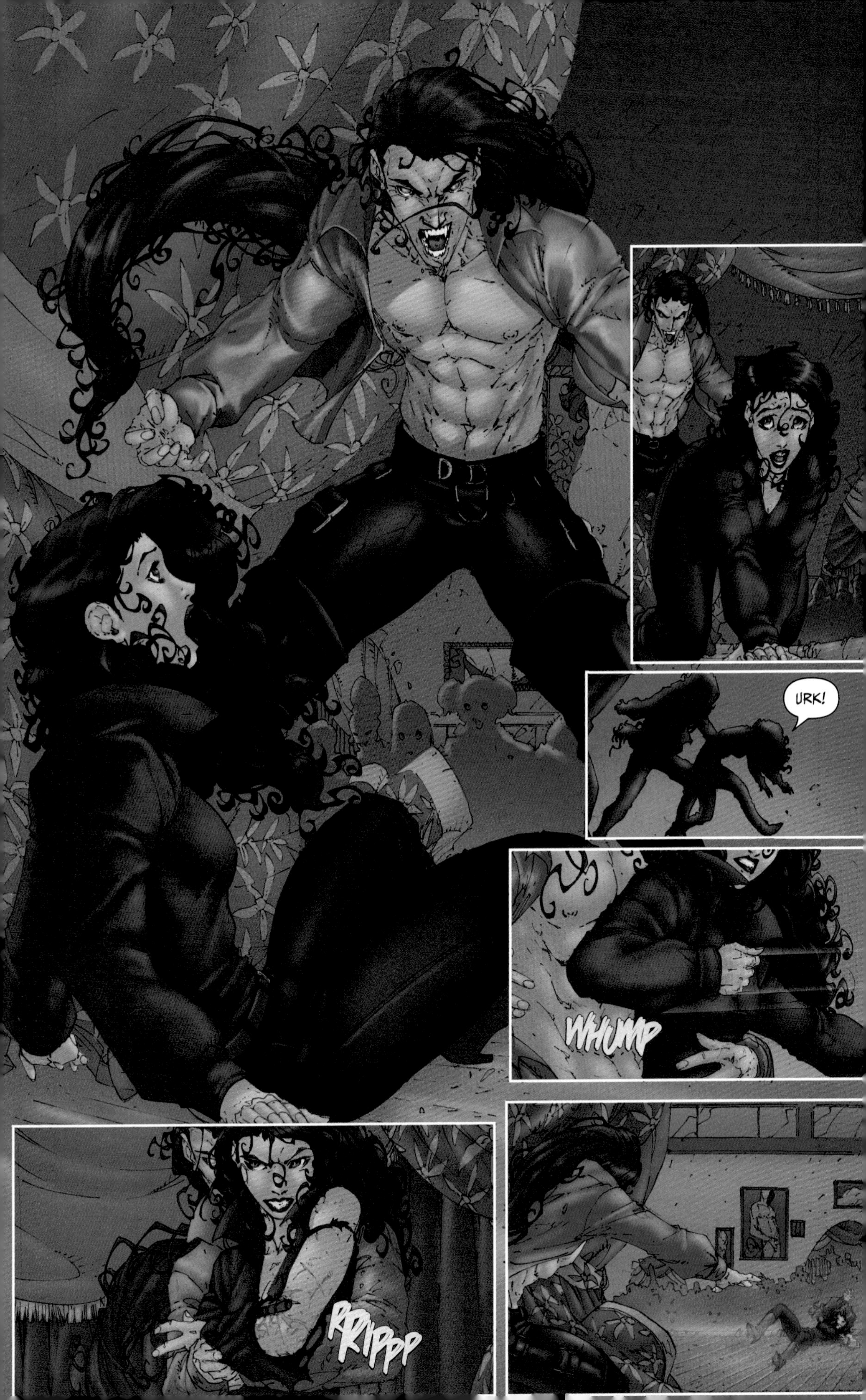
URK!
WHUMP
RRIPPP

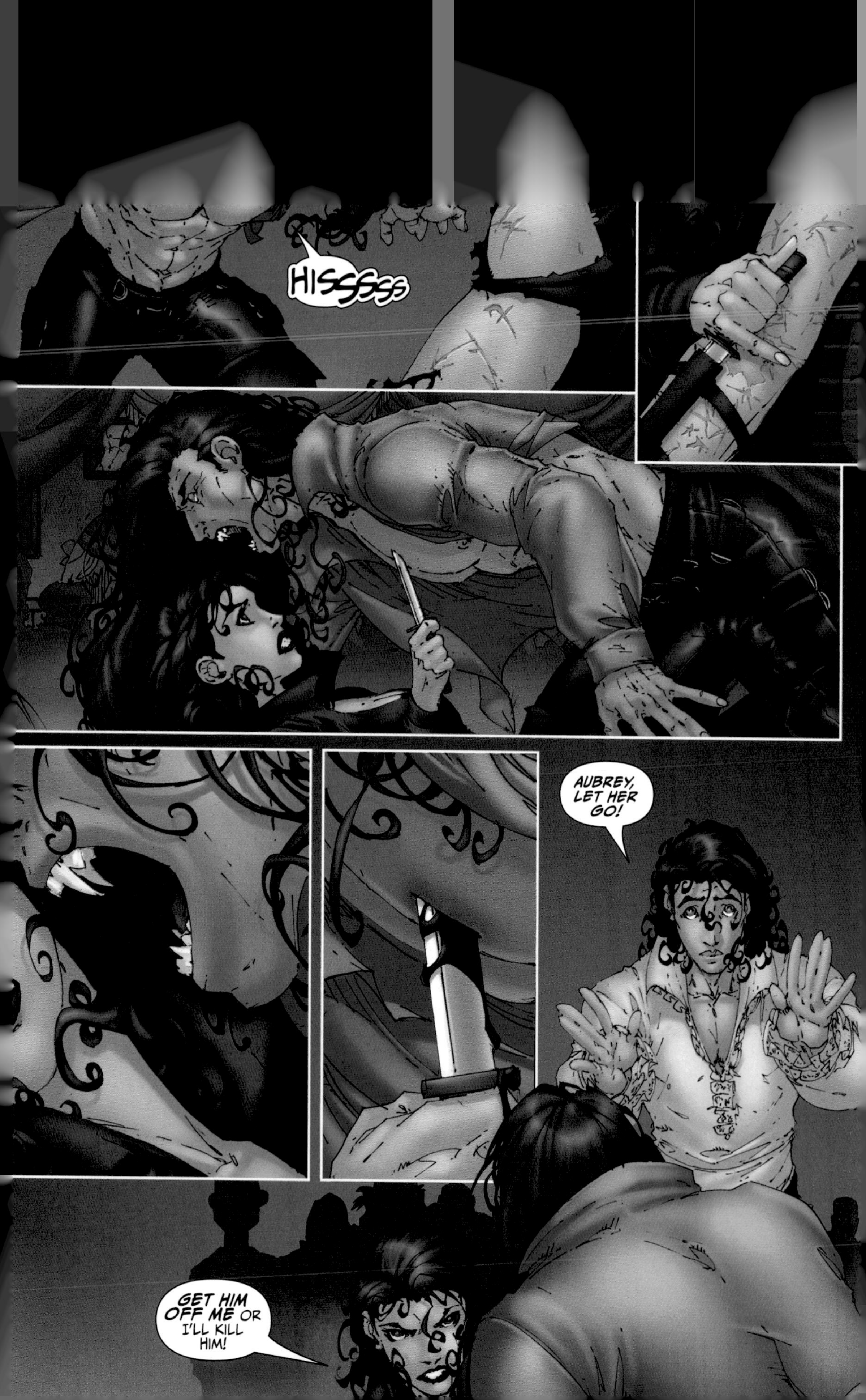
HISSSSSS
AUBREY, LET HER GO!
GET HIM OFF ME OR I'LL KILL HIM!

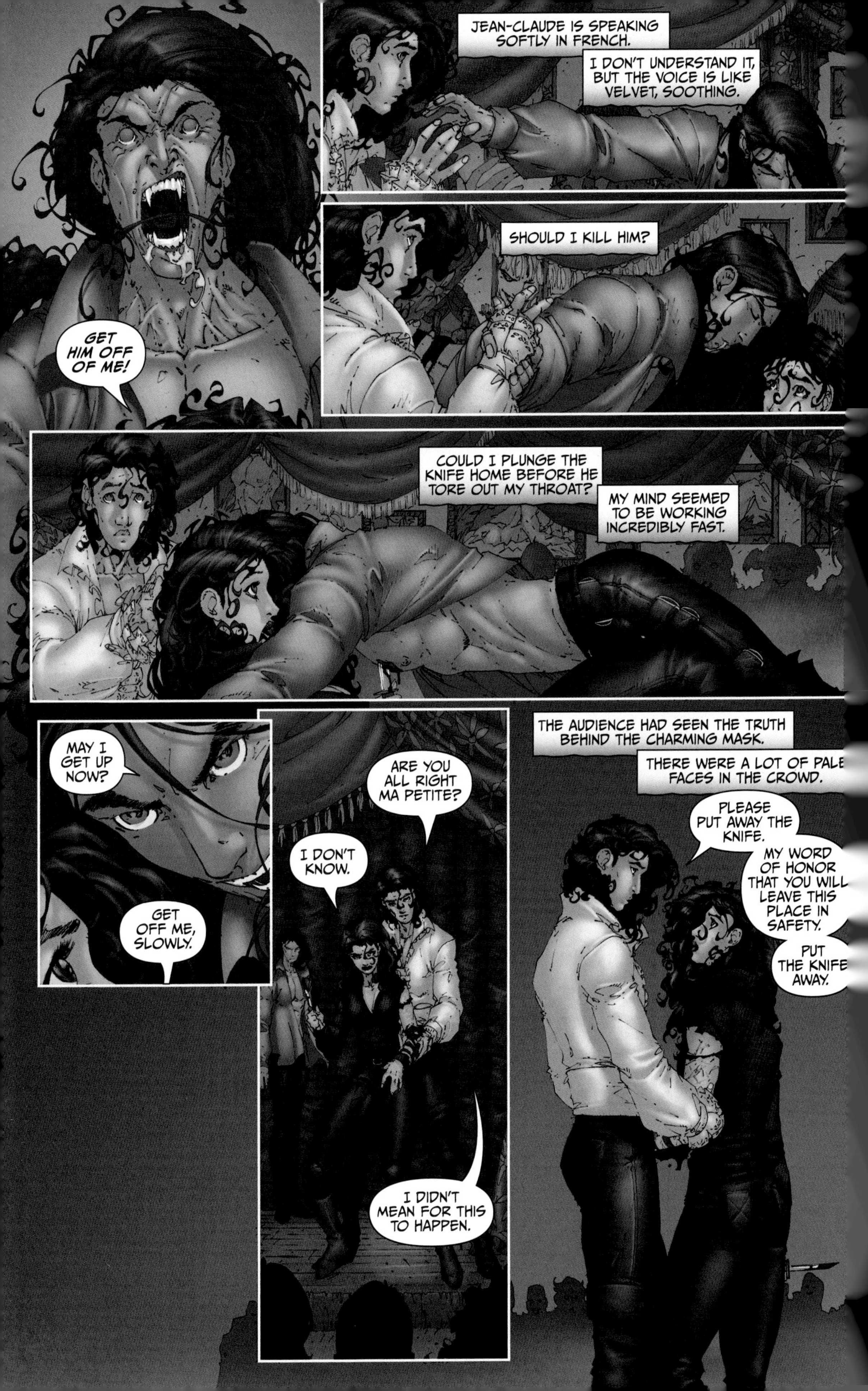
GET HIM OFF OF ME!
JEAN-CLAUDE IS SPEAKING SOFTLY IN FRENCH.
I DON'T UNDERSTAND IT, BUT THE VOICE IS LIKE VELVET, SOOTHING.
SHOULD I KILL HIM?
COULD I PLUNGE THE KNIFE HOME BEFORE HE TORE OUT MY THROAT?
MY MIND SEEMED TO BE WORKING INCREDIBLY FAST.
MAY I GET UP NOW?
GET OFF ME, SLOWLY.
ARE YOU ALL RIGHT MA PETITE?
I DON'T KNOW.
I DIDN'T MEAN FOR THIS TO HAPPEN.
THE AUDIENCE HAD SEEN THE TRUTH BEHIND THE CHARMING MASK.
THERE WERE A LOT OF PALE FACES IN THE CROWD.
PLEASE PUT AWAY THE KNIFE.
MY WORD OF HONOR THAT YOU WILL LEAVE THIS PLACE IN SAFETY.
PUT THE KNIFE AWAY.

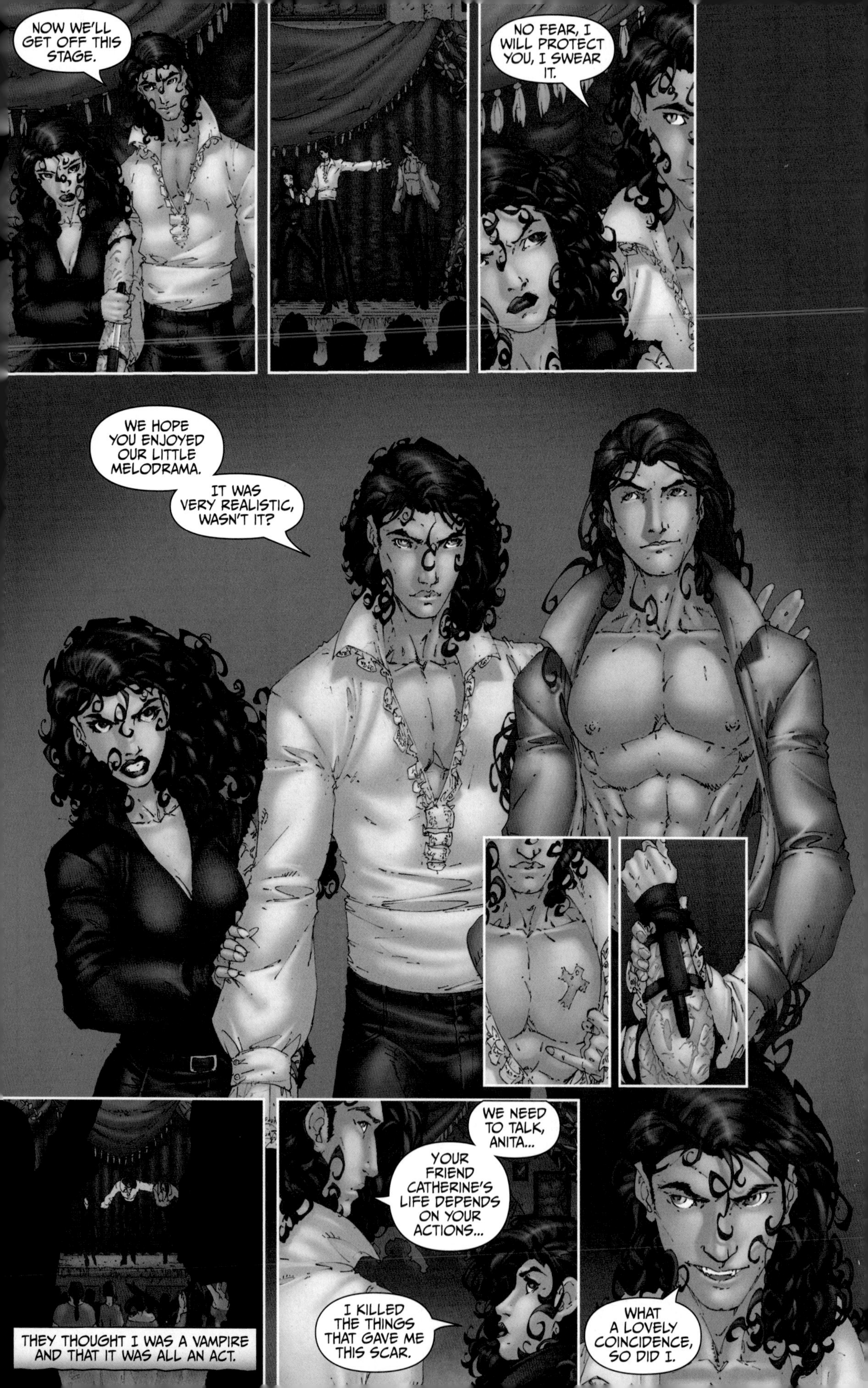
NOW WE'LL GET OFF THIS STAGE.
NO FEAR, I WILL PROTECT YOU, I SWEAR IT.
WE HOPE YOU ENJOYED OUR LITTLE MELODRAMA.
IT WAS VERY REALISTIC, WASN'T IT?
THEY THOUGHT I WAS A VAMPIRE AND THAT IT WAS ALL AN ACT.
WE NEED TO TALK, ANITA...
YOUR FRIEND CATHERINE'S LIFE DEPENDS ON YOUR ACTIONS...
I KILLED THE THINGS THAT GAVE ME THIS SCAR.
WHAT A LOVELY COINCIDENCE, SO DID I.

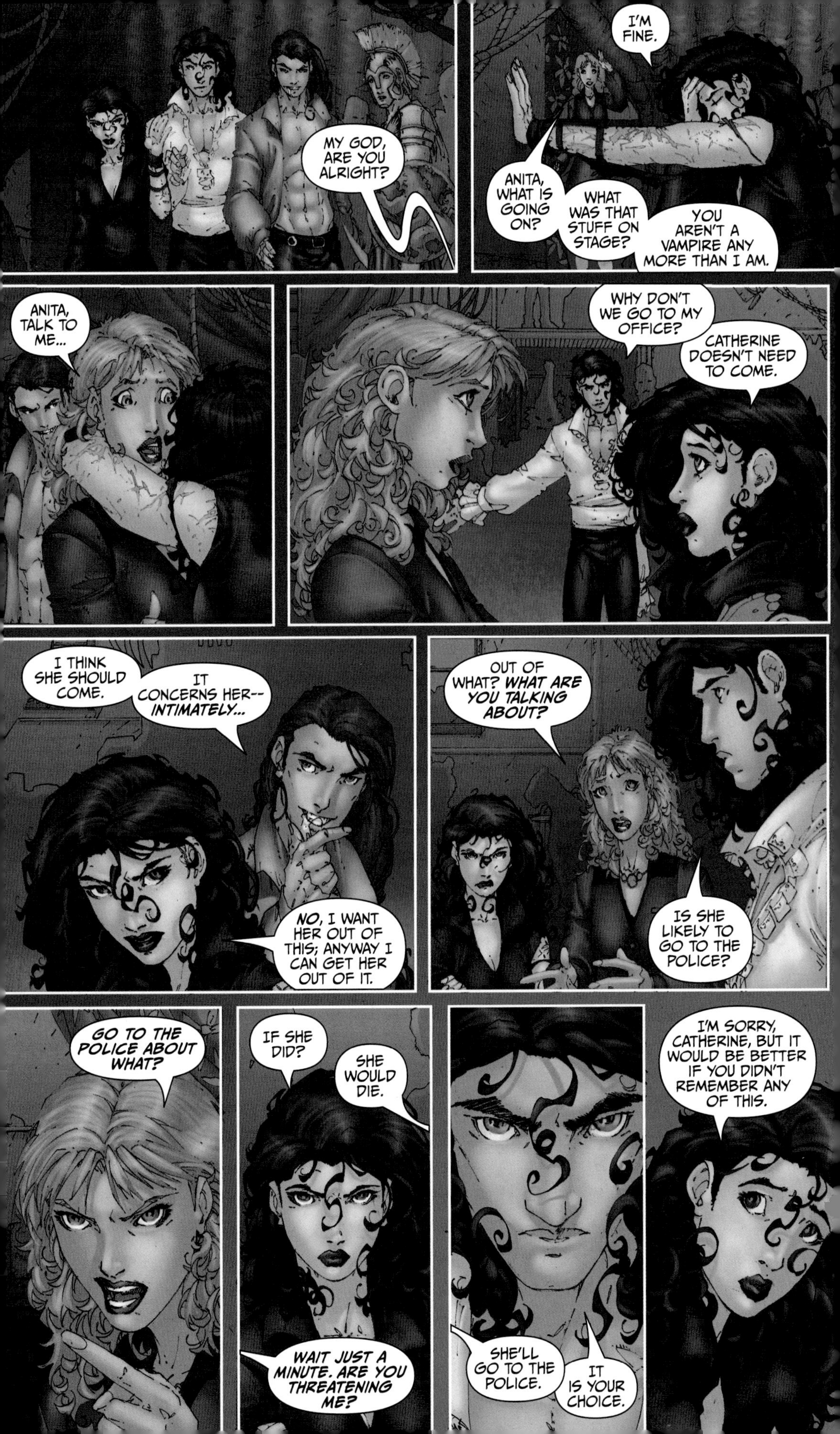
MY GOD, ARE YOU ALRIGHT?
I'M FINE.
ANITA, WHAT IS GOING ON?
WHAT WAS THAT STUFF ON STAGE?
YOU AREN'T A VAMPIRE ANY MORE THAN I AM.
ANITA, TALK TO ME...
WHY DON'T WE GO TO MY OFFICE?
CATHERINE DOESN'T NEED TO COME.
I THINK SHE SHOULD COME.
IT CONCERNS HER-- INTIMATELY...
NO, I WANT HER OUT OF THIS; ANYWAY I CAN GET HER OUT OF IT.
OUT OF WHAT? WHAT ARE YOU TALKING ABOUT?
IS SHE LIKELY TO GO TO THE POLICE?
GO TO THE POLICE ABOUT WHAT?
IF SHE DID?
SHE WOULD DIE.
WAIT JUST A MINUTE. ARE YOU THREATENING ME?
I'M SORRY, CATHERINE, BUT IT WOULD BE BETTER IF YOU DIDN'T REMEMBER ANY OF THIS.
SHE'LL GO TO THE POLICE.
IT IS YOUR CHOICE.

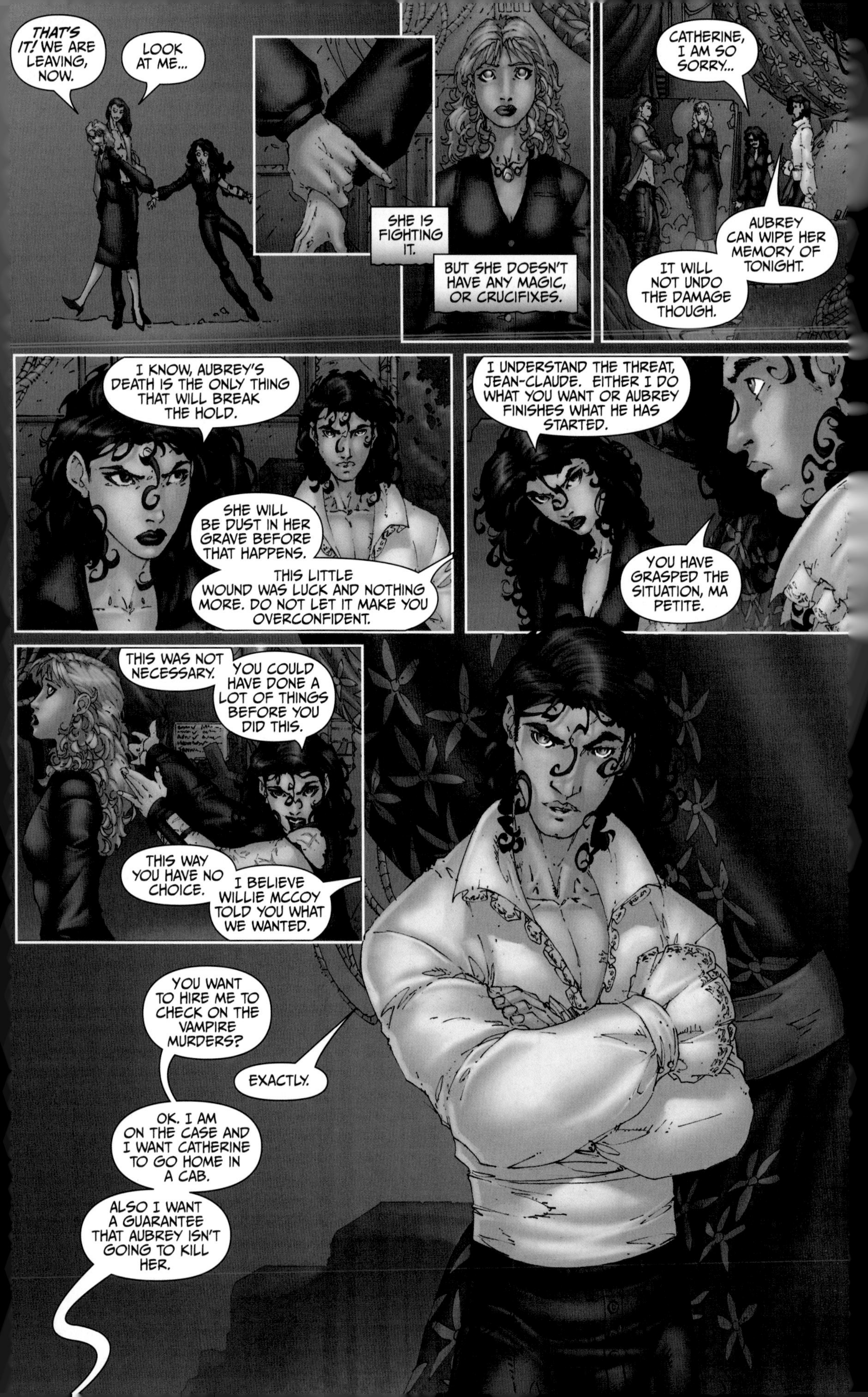
THAT'S IT! WE ARE LEAVING, NOW.
LOOK AT ME...
SHE IS FIGHTING IT.
BUT SHE DOESN'T HAVE ANY MAGIC, OR CRUCIFIXES.
CATHERINE, I AM SO SORRY...
AUBREY CAN WIPE HER MEMORY OF TONIGHT.
IT WILL NOT UNDO THE DAMAGE THOUGH.
I KNOW, AUBREY'S DEATH IS THE ONLY THING THAT WILL BREAK THE HOLD.
SHE WILL BE DUST IN HER GRAVE BEFORE THAT HAPPENS.
THIS LITTLE WOUND WAS LUCK AND NOTHING MORE. DO NOT LET IT MAKE YOU OVERCONFIDENT.
I UNDERSTAND THE THREAT, JEAN-CLAUDE. EITHER I DO WHAT YOU WANT OR AUBREY FINISHES WHAT HE HAS STARTED.
YOU HAVE GRASPED THE SITUATION, MA PETITE.
THIS WAS NOT NECESSARY.
YOU COULD HAVE DONE A LOT OF THINGS BEFORE YOU DID THIS.
THIS WAY YOU HAVE NO CHOICE.
I BELIEVE WILLIE MCCOY TOLD YOU WHAT WE WANTED.
YOU WANT TO HIRE ME TO CHECK ON THE VAMPIRE MURDERS?
EXACTLY.
OK. I AM ON THE CASE AND I WANT CATHERINE TO GO HOME IN A CAB.
ALSO I WANT A GUARANTEE THAT AUBREY ISN'T GOING TO KILL HER.

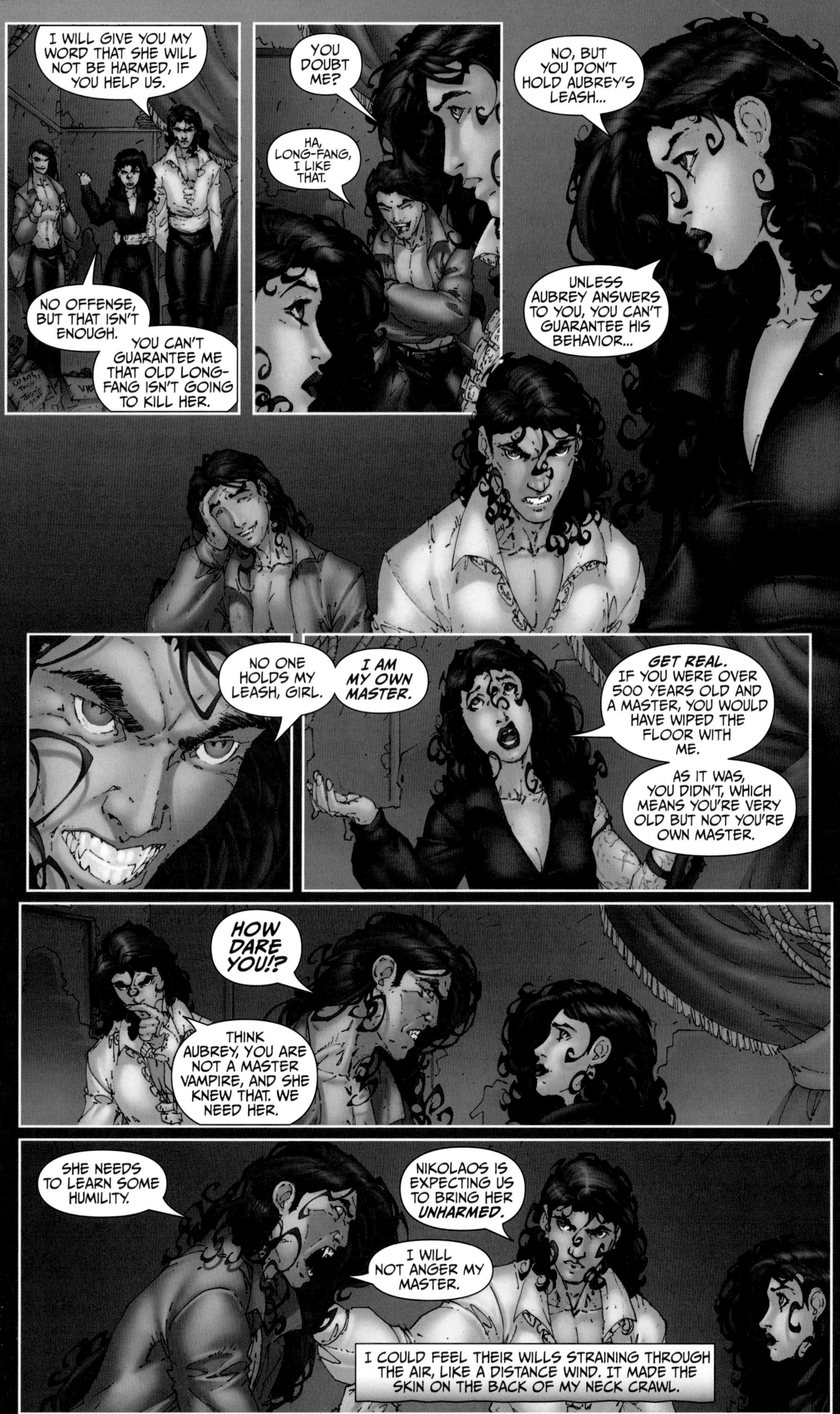
I WILL GIVE YOU MY WORD THAT SHE WILL NOT BE HARMED, IF YOU HELP US.
NO OFFENSE, BUT THAT ISN'T ENOUGH.
YOU CAN'T GUARANTEE ME THAT OLD LONG-FANG ISN'T GOING TO KILL HER.
YOU DOUBT ME?
HA, LONG-FANG, I LIKE THAT.
NO, BUT YOU DON'T HOLD AUBREY'S LEASH...
UNLESS AUBREY ANSWERS TO YOU, YOU CAN'T GUARANTEE HIS BEHAVIOR...
NO ONE HOLDS MY LEASH, GIRL.
I AM MY OWN MASTER.
GET REAL. IF YOU WERE OVER 500 YEARS OLD AND A MASTER, YOU WOULD HAVE WIPED THE FLOOR WITH ME.
AS IT WAS, YOU DIDN'T, WHICH MEANS YOU'RE VERY OLD BUT NOT YOU'RE OWN MASTER.
HOW DARE YOU!?
THINK AUBREY, YOU ARE NOT A MASTER VAMPIRE, AND SHE KNEW THAT. WE NEED HER.
SHE NEEDS TO LEARN SOME HUMILITY.
NIKOLAOS IS EXPECTING US TO BRING HER *UNHARMED.*
I WILL NOT ANGER MY MASTER.
I COULD FEEL THEIR WILLS STRAINING THROUGH THE AIR, LIKE A DISTANCE WIND. IT MADE THE SKIN ON THE BACK OF MY NECK CRAWL.

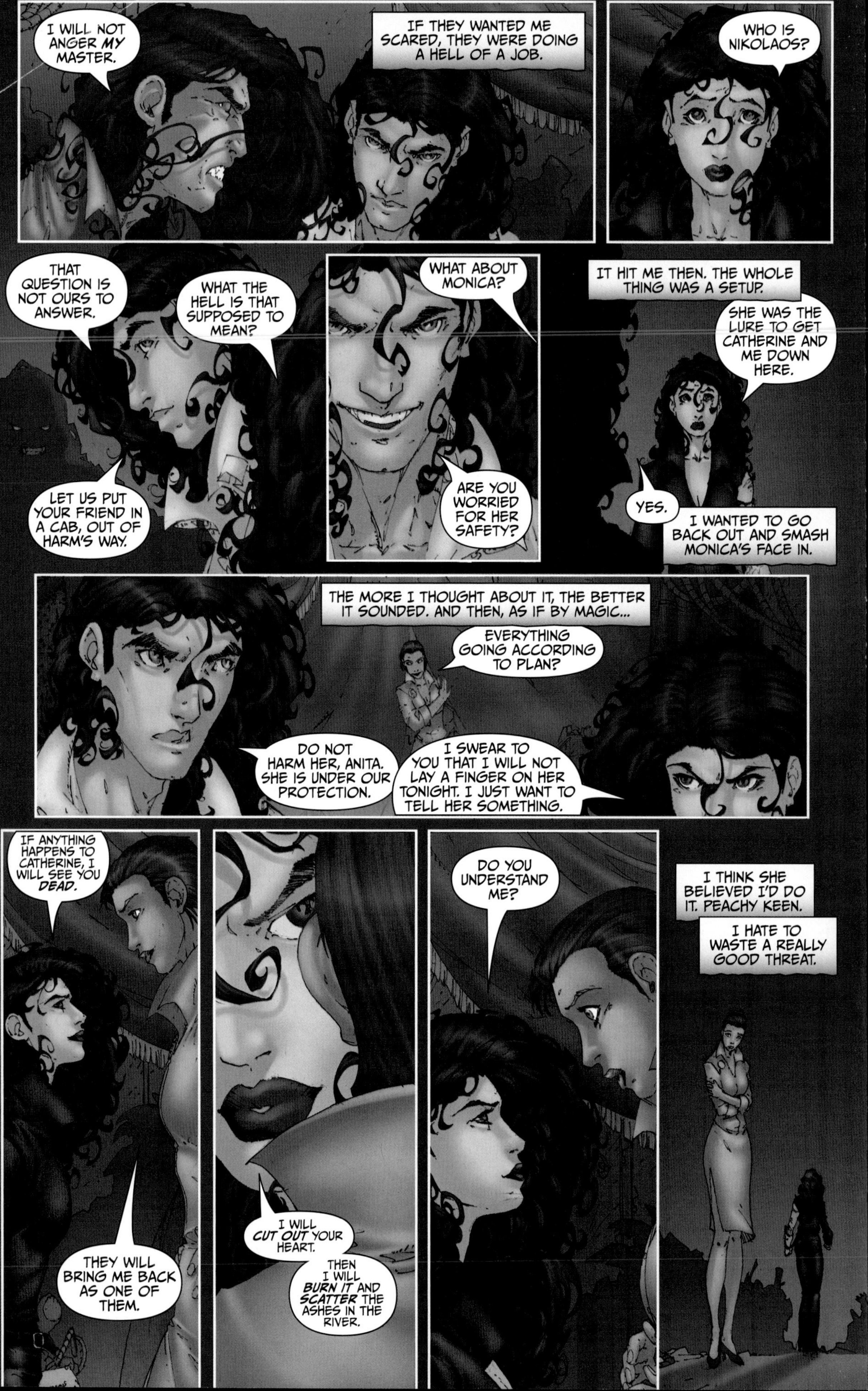
I WILL NOT ANGER *MY* MASTER.
IF THEY WANTED ME SCARED, THEY WERE DOING A HELL OF A JOB.
WHO IS NIKOLAOS?
THAT QUESTION IS NOT OURS TO ANSWER.
WHAT THE HELL IS THAT SUPPOSED TO MEAN?
LET US PUT YOUR FRIEND IN A CAB, OUT OF HARM'S WAY.
WHAT ABOUT MONICA?
ARE YOU WORRIED FOR HER SAFETY?
IT HIT ME THEN. THE WHOLE THING WAS A SETUP.
SHE WAS THE LURE TO GET CATHERINE AND ME DOWN HERE.
YES.
I WANTED TO GO BACK OUT AND SMASH MONICA'S FACE IN.
THE MORE I THOUGHT ABOUT IT, THE BETTER IT SOUNDED. AND THEN, AS IF BY MAGIC...
EVERYTHING GOING ACCORDING TO PLAN?
DO NOT HARM HER, ANITA. SHE IS UNDER OUR PROTECTION.
I SWEAR TO YOU THAT I WILL NOT LAY A FINGER ON HER TONIGHT. I JUST WANT TO TELL HER SOMETHING.
IF ANYTHING HAPPENS TO CATHERINE, I WILL SEE YOU *DEAD*.
THEY WILL BRING ME BACK AS ONE OF THEM.
I WILL *CUT OUT* YOUR HEART.
THEN I WILL *BURN IT* AND *SCATTER* THE ASHES IN THE RIVER.
DO YOU UNDERSTAND ME?
I THINK SHE BELIEVED I'D DO IT. PEACHY KEEN.
I HATE TO WASTE A REALLY GOOD THREAT.

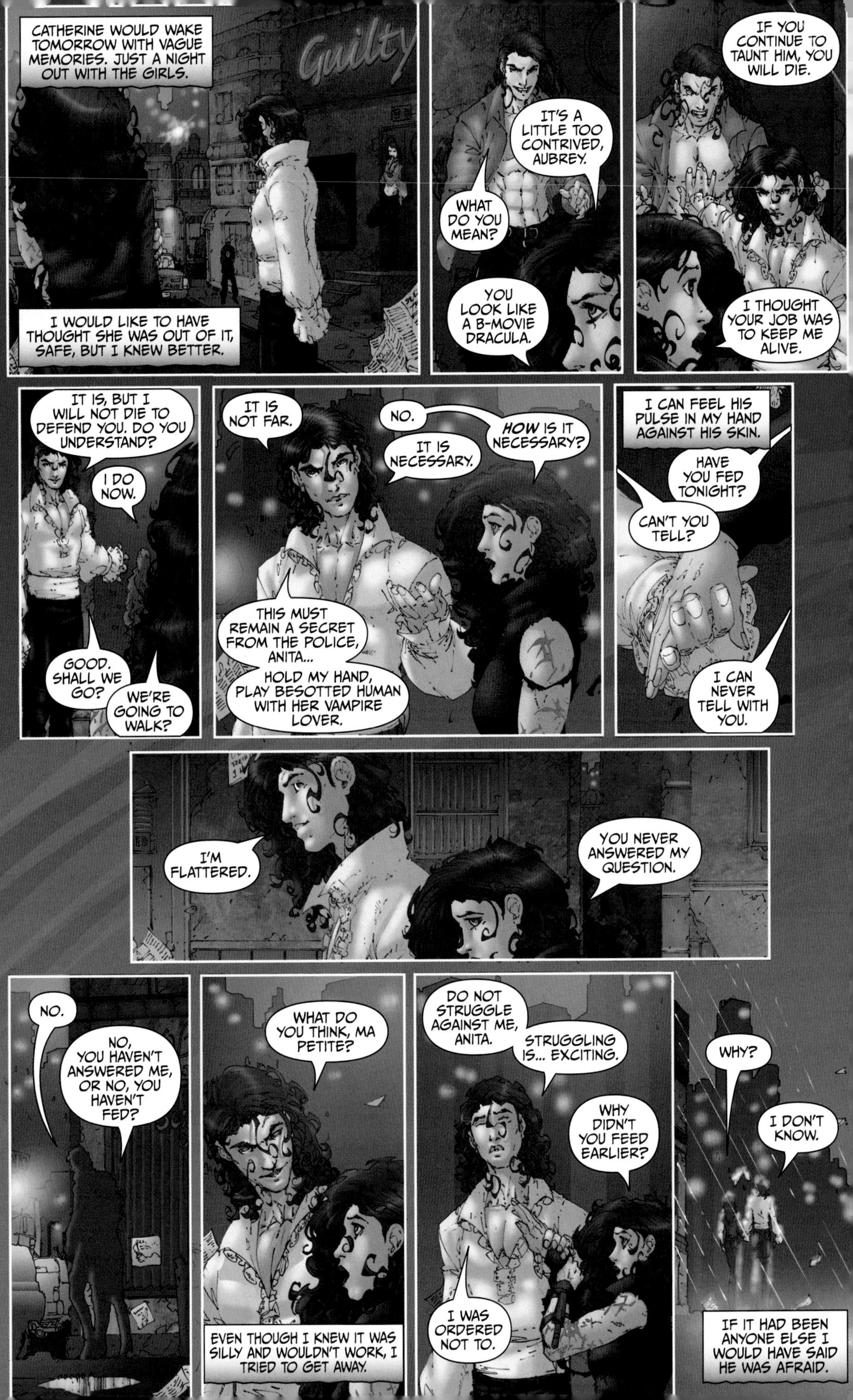

CATHERINE WOULD WAKE TOMORROW WITH VAGUE MEMORIES. JUST A NIGHT OUT WITH THE GIRLS.
Guilty
I WOULD LIKE TO HAVE THOUGHT SHE WAS OUT OF IT, SAFE, BUT I KNEW BETTER.
IT'S A LITTLE TOO CONTRIVED, AUBREY.
WHAT DO YOU MEAN?
YOU LOOK LIKE A B-MOVIE DRACULA.
IF YOU CONTINUE TO TAUNT HIM, YOU WILL DIE.
I THOUGHT YOUR JOB WAS TO KEEP ME ALIVE.
IT IS, BUT I WILL NOT DIE TO DEFEND YOU. DO YOU UNDERSTAND?
I DO NOW.
GOOD. SHALL WE GO?
WE'RE GOING TO WALK?
IT IS NOT FAR.
NO.
HOW IS IT NECESSARY?
IT IS NECESSARY.
THIS MUST REMAIN A SECRET FROM THE POLICE, ANITA...
HOLD MY HAND, PLAY BESOTTED HUMAN WITH HER VAMPIRE LOVER.
I CAN FEEL HIS PULSE IN MY HAND AGAINST HIS SKIN.
HAVE YOU FED TONIGHT?
CAN'T YOU TELL?
I CAN NEVER TELL WITH YOU.
I'M FLATTERED.
YOU NEVER ANSWERED MY QUESTION.
NO.
NO, YOU HAVEN'T ANSWERED ME, OR NO, YOU HAVEN'T FED?
WHAT DO YOU THINK, MA PETITE?
EVEN THOUGH I KNEW IT WAS SILLY AND WOULDN'T WORK, I TRIED TO GET AWAY.
DO NOT STRUGGLE AGAINST ME, ANITA.
STRUGGLING IS... EXCITING.
WHY DIDN'T YOU FEED EARLIER?
I WAS ORDERED NOT TO.
WHY?
I DON'T KNOW.
IF IT HAD BEEN ANYONE ELSE I WOULD HAVE SAID HE WAS AFRAID.

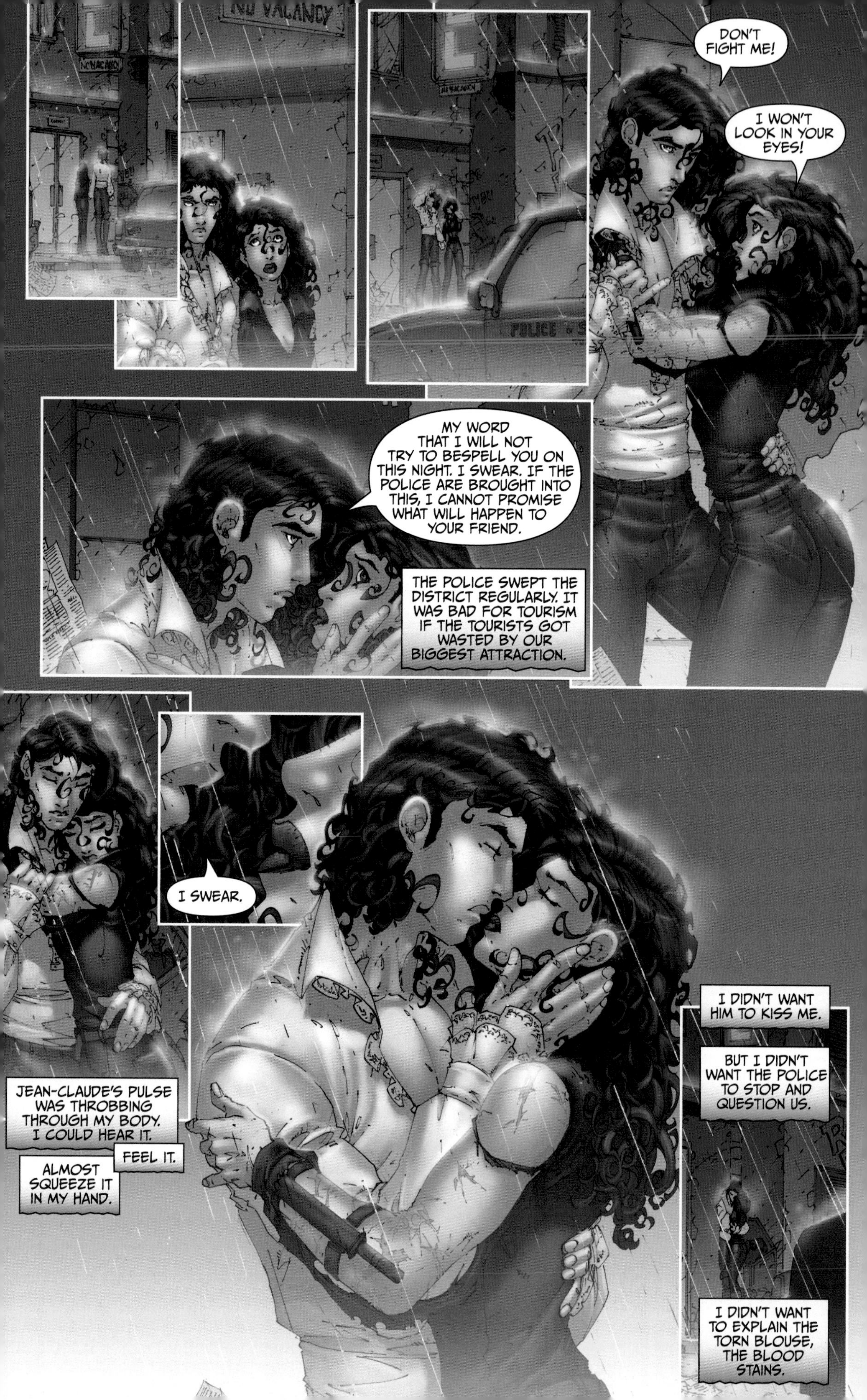
NO VACANCY
DON'T FIGHT ME!
I WON'T LOOK IN YOUR EYES!
MY WORD THAT I WILL NOT TRY TO BESPELL YOU ON THIS NIGHT. I SWEAR. IF THE POLICE ARE BROUGHT INTO THIS, I CANNOT PROMISE WHAT WILL HAPPEN TO YOUR FRIEND.
THE POLICE SWEPT THE DISTRICT REGULARLY. IT WAS BAD FOR TOURISM IF THE TOURISTS GOT WASTED BY OUR BIGGEST ATTRACTION.
JEAN-CLAUDE'S PULSE WAS THROBBING THROUGH MY BODY. I COULD HEAR IT.
FEEL IT.
ALMOST SQUEEZE IT IN MY HAND.
I SWEAR.
I DIDN'T WANT HIM TO KISS ME.
BUT I DIDN'T WANT THE POLICE TO STOP AND QUESTION US.
I DIDN'T WANT TO EXPLAIN THE TORN BLOUSE, THE BLOOD STAINS.

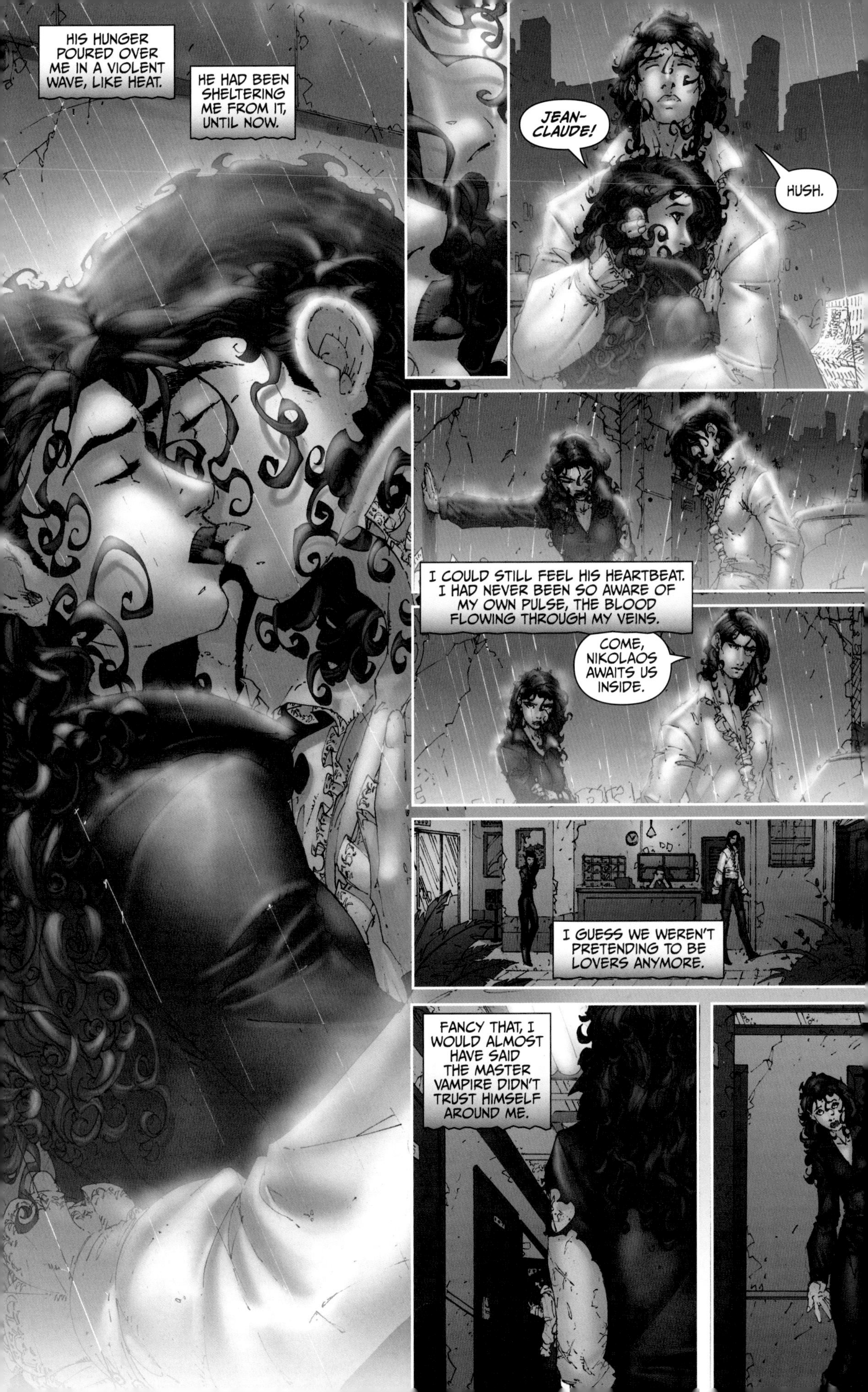
HIS HUNGER POURED OVER ME IN A VIOLENT WAVE, LIKE HEAT.
HE HAD BEEN SHELTERING ME FROM IT, UNTIL NOW.
JEAN-CLAUDE!
HUSH.
I COULD STILL FEEL HIS HEARTBEAT. I HAD NEVER BEEN SO AWARE OF MY OWN PULSE, THE BLOOD FLOWING THROUGH MY VEINS.
COME, NIKOLAOS AWAITS US INSIDE.
I GUESS WE WEREN'T PRETENDING TO BE LOVERS ANYMORE.
FANCY THAT, I WOULD ALMOST HAVE SAID THE MASTER VAMPIRE DIDN'T TRUST HIMSELF AROUND ME.

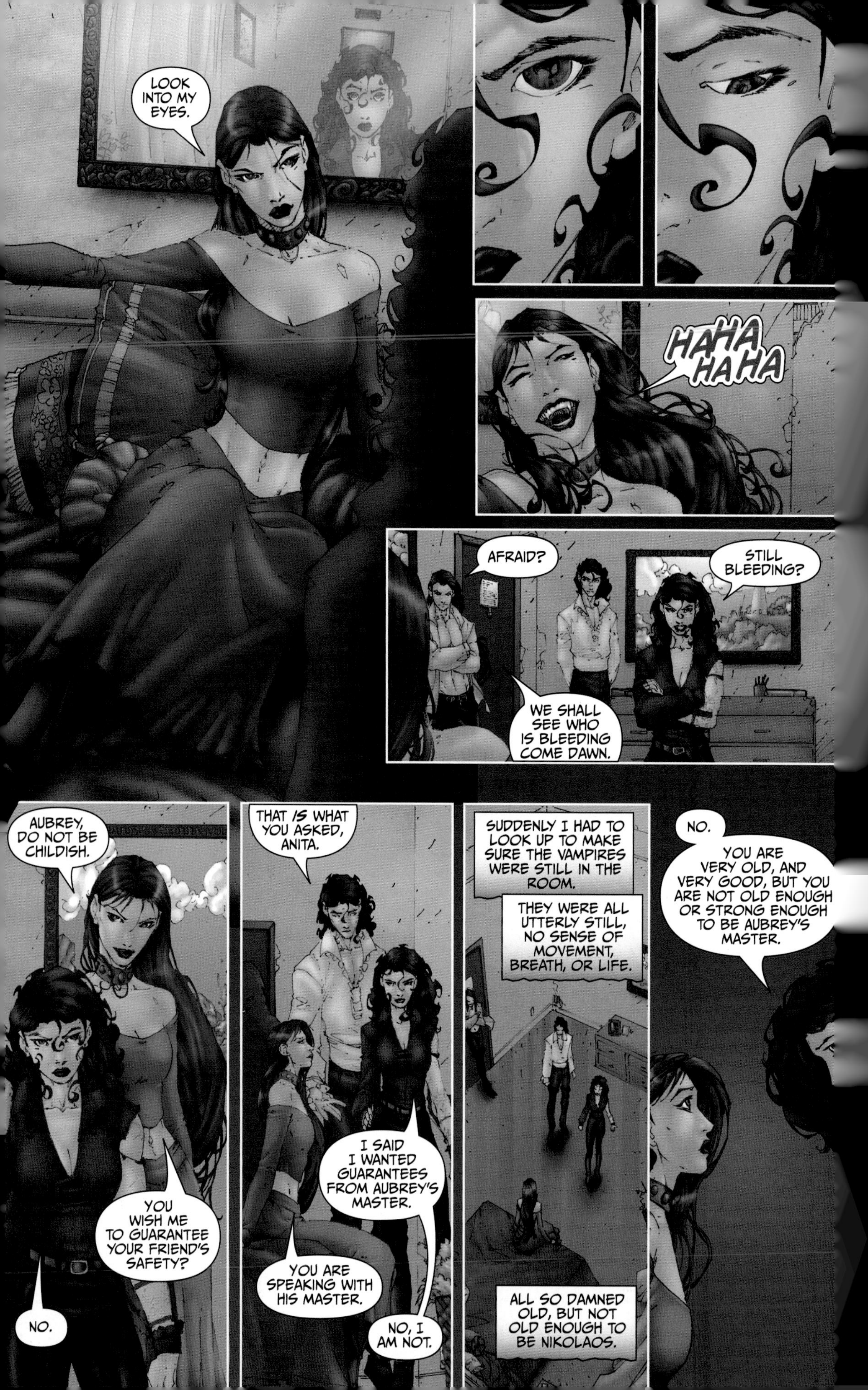
LOOK INTO MY EYES.
HAHA HAHA
AFRAID?
STILL BLEEDING?
WE SHALL SEE WHO IS BLEEDING COME DAWN.
AUBREY, DO NOT BE CHILDISH.
YOU WISH ME TO GUARANTEE YOUR FRIEND'S SAFETY?
NO.
THAT IS WHAT YOU ASKED, ANITA.
I SAID I WANTED GUARANTEES FROM AUBREY'S MASTER.
YOU ARE SPEAKING WITH HIS MASTER.
NO, I AM NOT.
SUDDENLY I HAD TO LOOK UP TO MAKE SURE THE VAMPIRES WERE STILL IN THE ROOM.
THEY WERE ALL UTTERLY STILL, NO SENSE OF MOVEMENT, BREATH, OR LIFE.
ALL SO DAMNED OLD, BUT NOT OLD ENOUGH TO BE NIKOLAOS.
NO.
YOU ARE VERY OLD, AND VERY GOOD, BUT YOU ARE NOT OLD ENOUGH OR STRONG ENOUGH TO BE AUBREY'S MASTER.

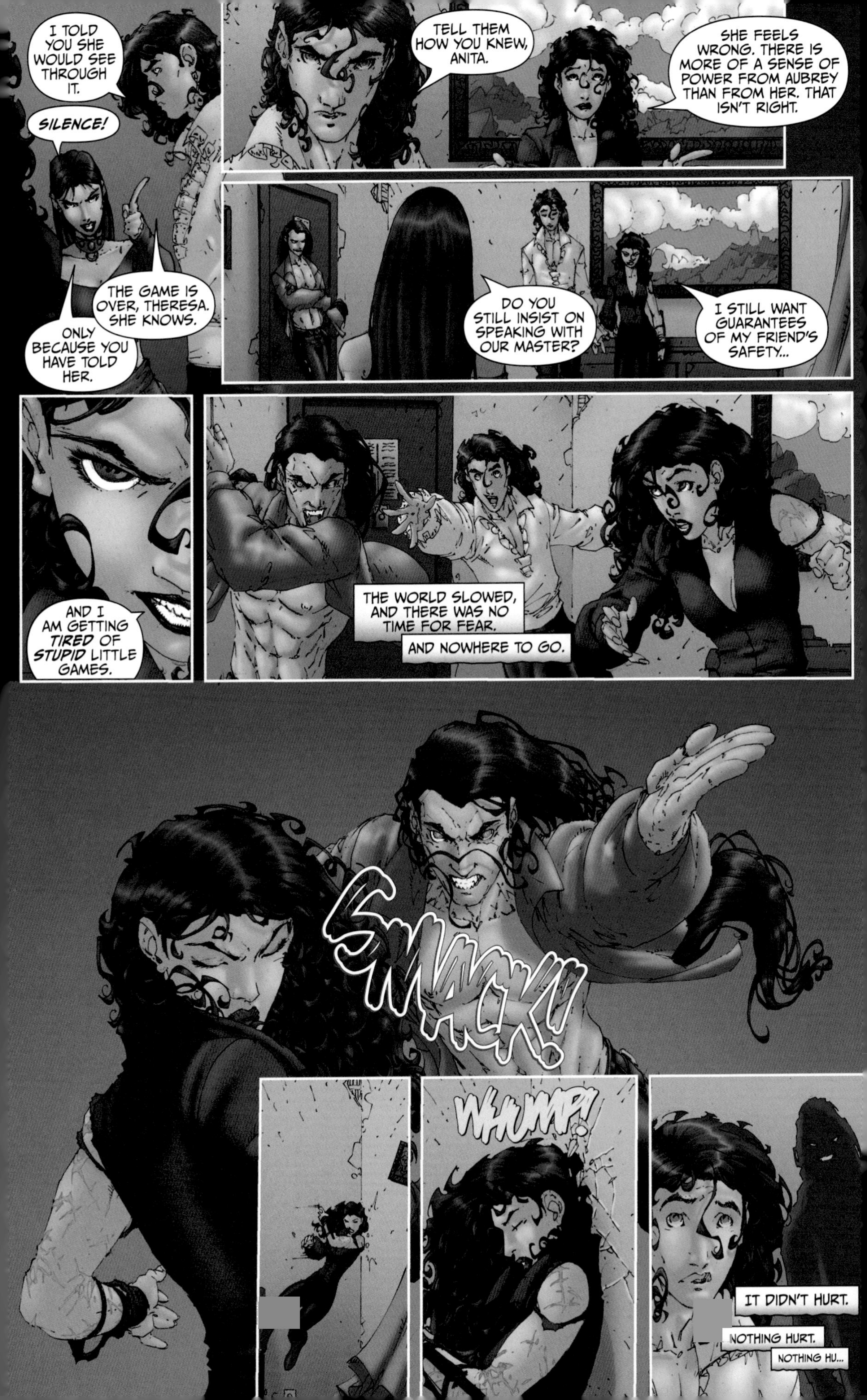
I TOLD YOU SHE WOULD SEE THROUGH IT.
SILENCE!
THE GAME IS OVER, THERESA. SHE KNOWS.
ONLY BECAUSE YOU HAVE TOLD HER.
TELL THEM HOW YOU KNEW, ANITA.
SHE FEELS WRONG. THERE IS MORE OF A SENSE OF POWER FROM AUBREY THAN FROM HER. THAT ISN'T RIGHT.
DO YOU STILL INSIST ON SPEAKING WITH OUR MASTER?
I STILL WANT GUARANTEES OF MY FRIEND'S SAFETY...
AND I AM GETTING TIRED OF STUPID LITTLE GAMES.
THE WORLD SLOWED, AND THERE WAS NO TIME FOR FEAR.
AND NOWHERE TO GO.
SMACK!
WHUMP!
IT DIDN'T HURT.
NOTHING HURT.
NOTHING HU...

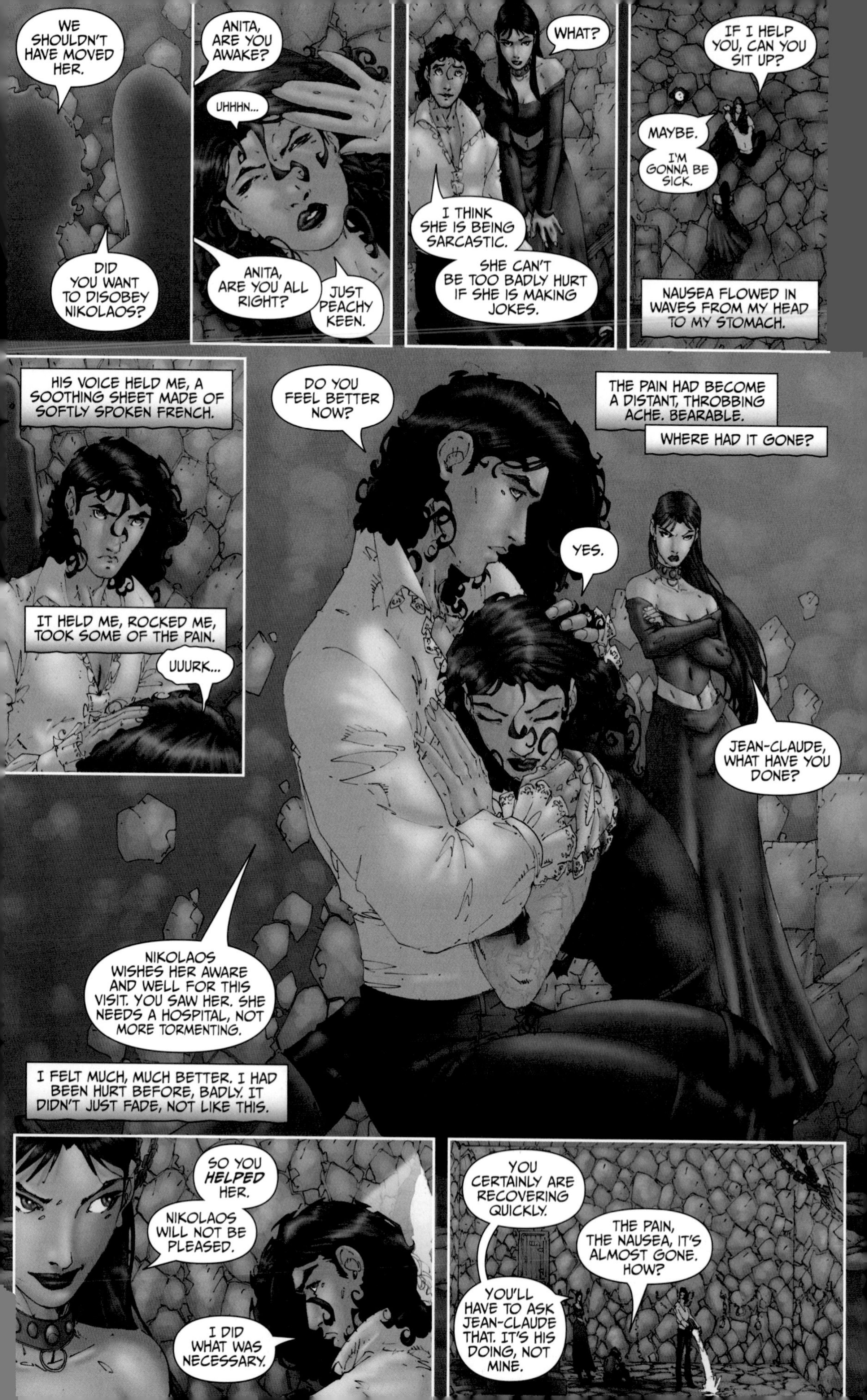

WE SHOULDN'T HAVE MOVED HER.
DID YOU WANT TO DISOBEY NIKOLAOS?
ANITA, ARE YOU AWAKE?
UHHHN...
ANITA, ARE YOU ALL RIGHT?
JUST PEACHY KEEN.
WHAT?
I THINK SHE IS BEING SARCASTIC.
SHE CAN'T BE TOO BADLY HURT IF SHE IS MAKING JOKES.
IF I HELP YOU, CAN YOU SIT UP?
MAYBE.
I'M GONNA BE SICK.
NAUSEA FLOWED IN WAVES FROM MY HEAD TO MY STOMACH.
HIS VOICE HELD ME, A SOOTHING SHEET MADE OF SOFTLY SPOKEN FRENCH.
IT HELD ME, ROCKED ME, TOOK SOME OF THE PAIN.
UUURK...
DO YOU FEEL BETTER NOW?
THE PAIN HAD BECOME A DISTANT, THROBBING ACHE. BEARABLE.
WHERE HAD IT GONE?
YES.
JEAN-CLAUDE, WHAT HAVE YOU DONE?
NIKOLAOS WISHES HER AWARE AND WELL FOR THIS VISIT. YOU SAW HER. SHE NEEDS A HOSPITAL, NOT MORE TORMENTING.
I FELT MUCH, MUCH BETTER. I HAD BEEN HURT BEFORE, BADLY. IT DIDN'T JUST FADE, NOT LIKE THIS.
SO YOU *HELPED* HER.
NIKOLAOS WILL NOT BE PLEASED.
I DID WHAT WAS NECESSARY.
YOU CERTAINLY ARE RECOVERING QUICKLY.
THE PAIN, THE NAUSEA, IT'S ALMOST GONE. HOW?
YOU'LL HAVE TO ASK JEAN-CLAUDE THAT. IT'S HIS DOING, NOT MINE.

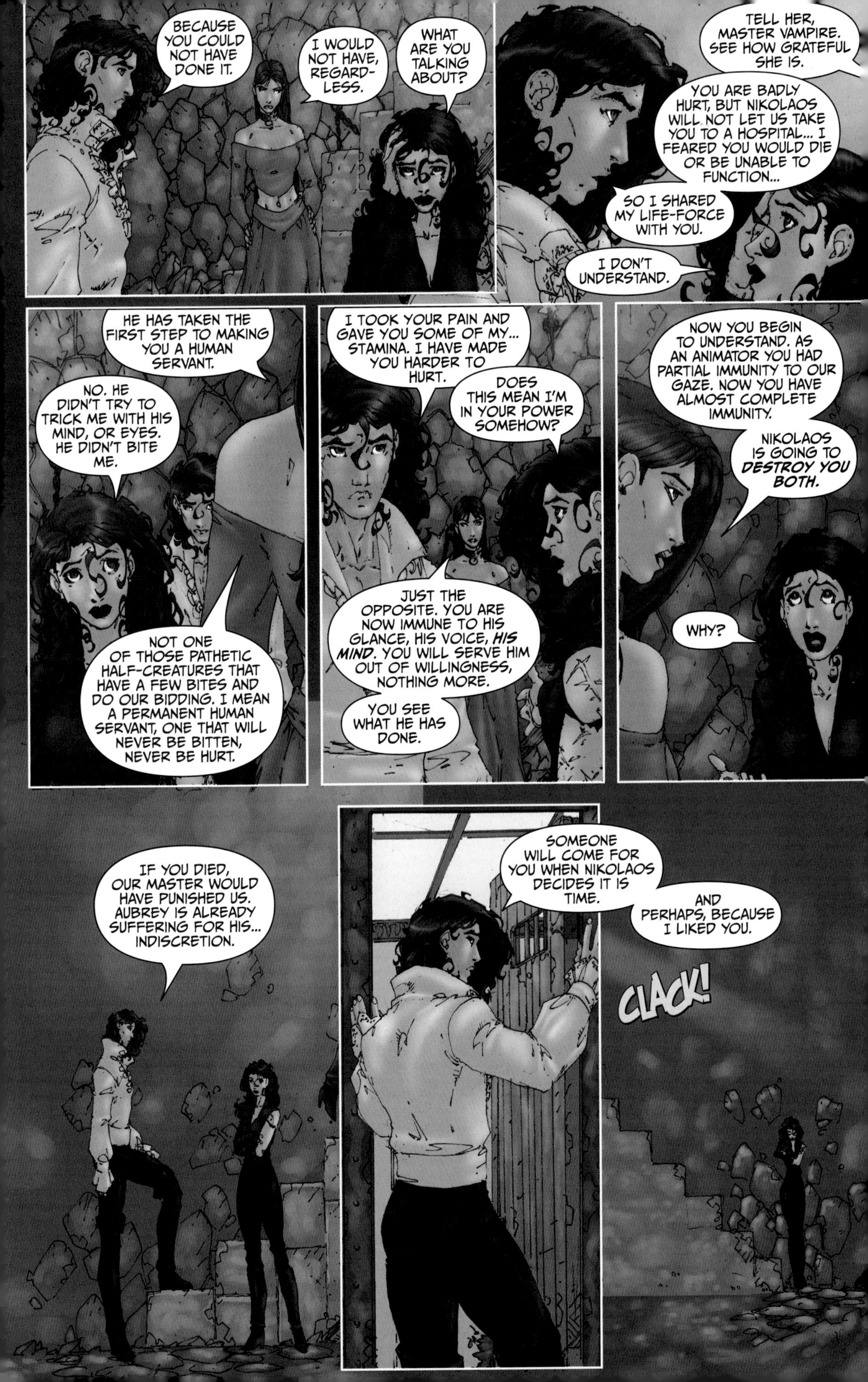
BECAUSE YOU COULD NOT HAVE DONE IT.
I WOULD NOT HAVE, REGARDLESS.
WHAT ARE YOU TALKING ABOUT?
TELL HER, MASTER VAMPIRE. SEE HOW GRATEFUL SHE IS.
YOU ARE BADLY HURT, BUT NIKOLAOS WILL NOT LET US TAKE YOU TO A HOSPITAL... I FEARED YOU WOULD DIE OR BE UNABLE TO FUNCTION...
SO I SHARED MY LIFE-FORCE WITH YOU.
I DON'T UNDERSTAND.
HE HAS TAKEN THE FIRST STEP TO MAKING YOU A HUMAN SERVANT.
NO. HE DIDN'T TRY TO TRICK ME WITH HIS MIND, OR EYES. HE DIDN'T BITE ME.
NOT ONE OF THOSE PATHETIC HALF-CREATURES THAT HAVE A FEW BITES AND DO OUR BIDDING. I MEAN A PERMANENT HUMAN SERVANT, ONE THAT WILL NEVER BE BITTEN, NEVER BE HURT.
I TOOK YOUR PAIN AND GAVE YOU SOME OF MY... STAMINA. I HAVE MADE YOU HARDER TO HURT.
DOES THIS MEAN I'M IN YOUR POWER SOMEHOW?
JUST THE OPPOSITE. YOU ARE NOW IMMUNE TO HIS GLANCE, HIS VOICE, HIS MIND. YOU WILL SERVE HIM OUT OF WILLINGNESS, NOTHING MORE.
YOU SEE WHAT HE HAS DONE.
NOW YOU BEGIN TO UNDERSTAND. AS AN ANIMATOR YOU HAD PARTIAL IMMUNITY TO OUR GAZE. NOW YOU HAVE ALMOST COMPLETE IMMUNITY.
NIKOLAOS IS GOING TO DESTROY YOU BOTH.
WHY?
IF YOU DIED, OUR MASTER WOULD HAVE PUNISHED US. AUBREY IS ALREADY SUFFERING FOR HIS... INDISCRETION.
SOMEONE WILL COME FOR YOU WHEN NIKOLAOS DECIDES IT IS TIME.
AND PERHAPS, BECAUSE I LIKED YOU.
CLACK!

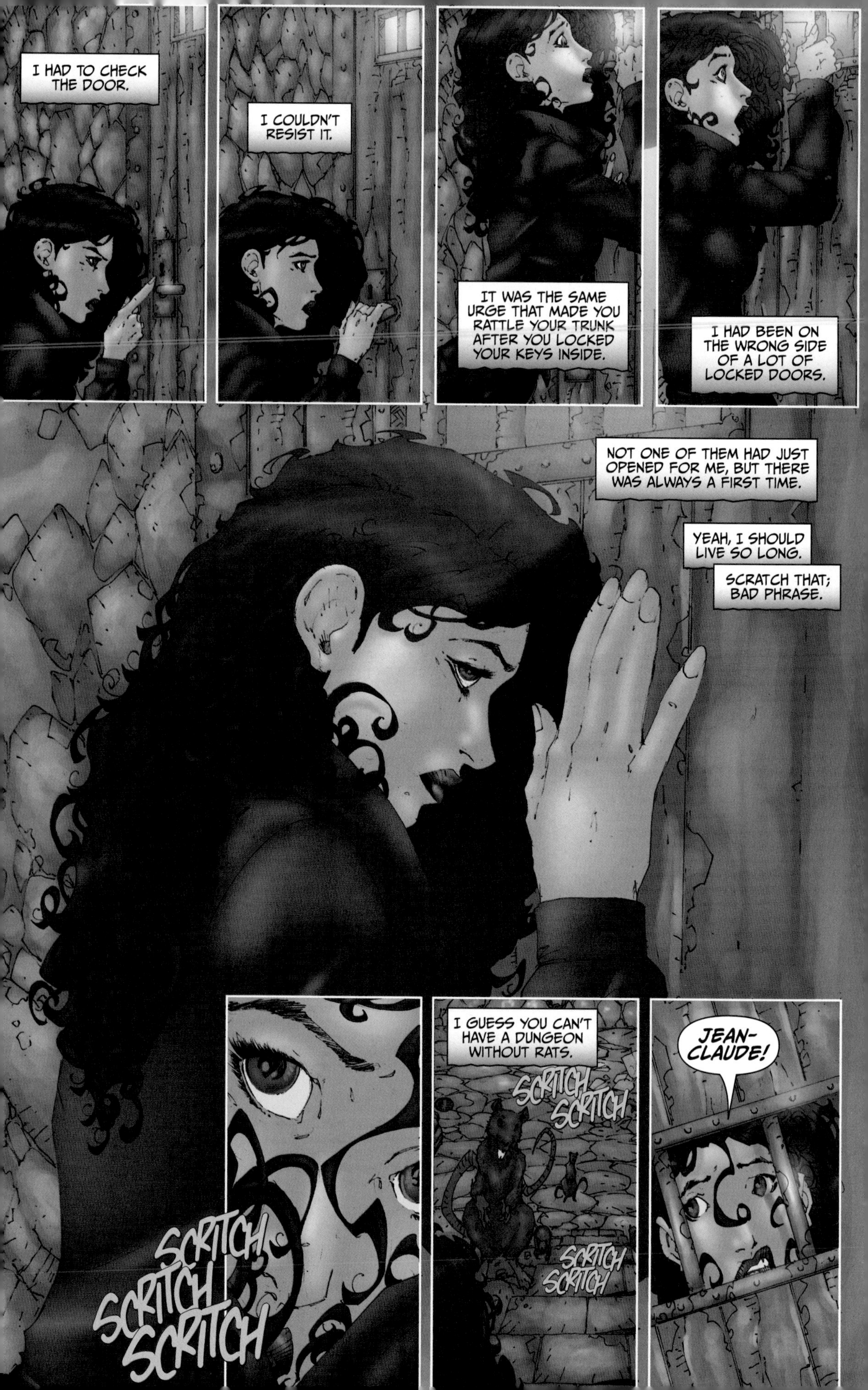

I HAD TO CHECK THE DOOR.
I COULDN'T RESIST IT.
IT WAS THE SAME URGE THAT MADE YOU RATTLE YOUR TRUNK AFTER YOU LOCKED YOUR KEYS INSIDE.
I HAD BEEN ON THE WRONG SIDE OF A LOT OF LOCKED DOORS.
NOT ONE OF THEM HAD JUST OPENED FOR ME, BUT THERE WAS ALWAYS A FIRST TIME.
YEAH, I SHOULD LIVE SO LONG.
SCRATCH THAT; BAD PHRASE.
SCRITCH SCRITCH SCRITCH
I GUESS YOU CAN'T HAVE A DUNGEON WITHOUT RATS.
SCRITCH SCRITCH
SCRITCH SCRITCH
JEAN-CLAUDE!

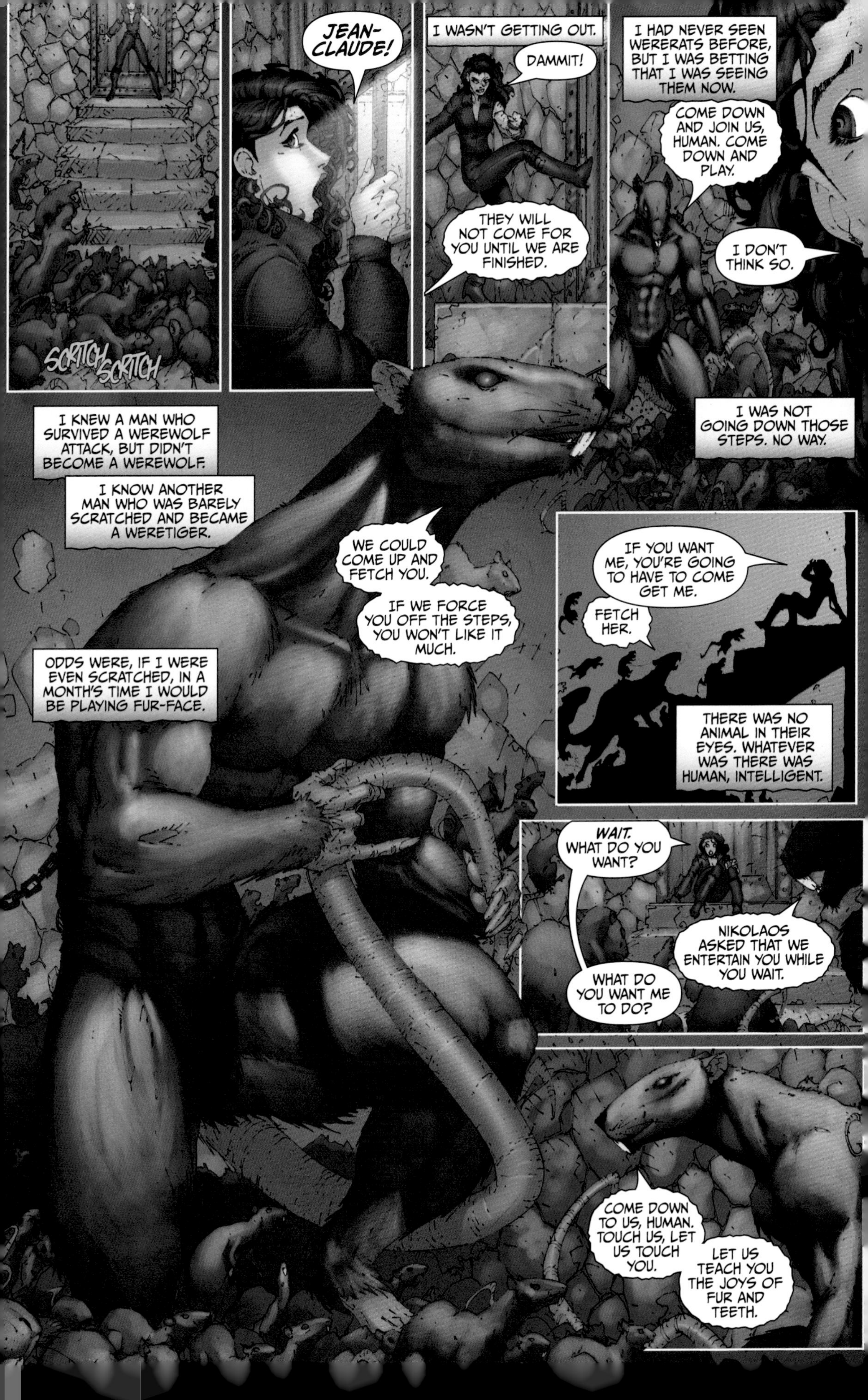
SCRITCH SCRITCH
JEAN-CLAUDE!
I WASN'T GETTING OUT.
DAMMIT!
THEY WILL NOT COME FOR YOU UNTIL WE ARE FINISHED.
I HAD NEVER SEEN WERERATS BEFORE, BUT I WAS BETTING THAT I WAS SEEING THEM NOW.
COME DOWN AND JOIN US, HUMAN. COME DOWN AND PLAY.
I DON'T THINK SO.
I KNEW A MAN WHO SURVIVED A WEREWOLF ATTACK, BUT DIDN'T BECOME A WEREWOLF.
I KNOW ANOTHER MAN WHO WAS BARELY SCRATCHED AND BECAME A WERETIGER.
ODDS WERE, IF I WERE EVEN SCRATCHED, IN A MONTH'S TIME I WOULD BE PLAYING FUR-FACE.
WE COULD COME UP AND FETCH YOU.
IF WE FORCE YOU OFF THE STEPS, YOU WON'T LIKE IT MUCH.
I WAS NOT GOING DOWN THOSE STEPS. NO WAY.
IF YOU WANT ME, YOU'RE GOING TO HAVE TO COME GET ME.
FETCH HER.
THERE WAS NO ANIMAL IN THEIR EYES. WHATEVER WAS THERE WAS HUMAN, INTELLIGENT.
WAIT. WHAT DO YOU WANT?
NIKOLAOS ASKED THAT WE ENTERTAIN YOU WHILE YOU WAIT.
WHAT DO YOU WANT ME TO DO?
COME DOWN TO US, HUMAN. TOUCH US, LET US TOUCH YOU.
LET US TEACH YOU THE JOYS OF FUR AND TEETH.

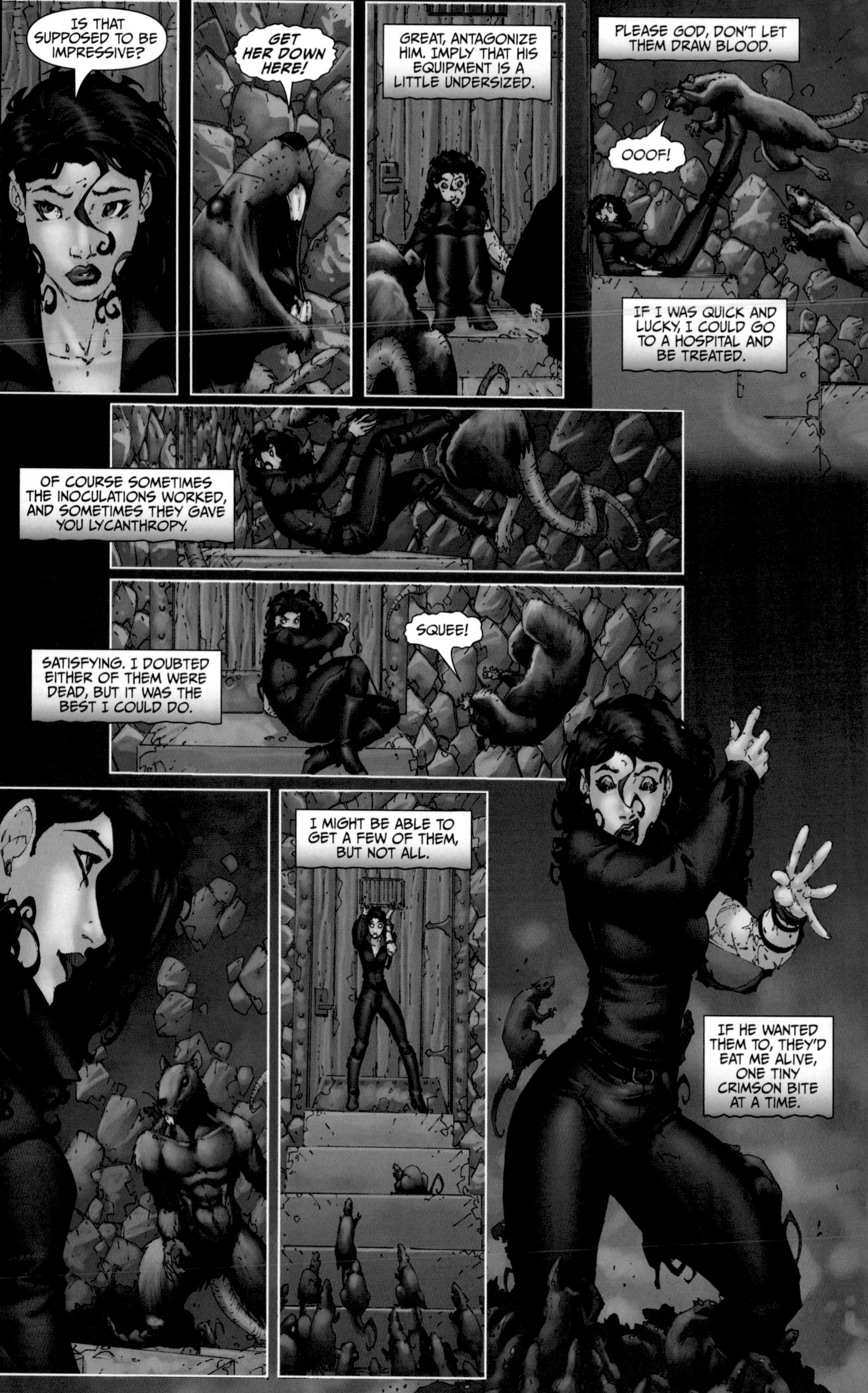
IS THAT SUPPOSED TO BE IMPRESSIVE?
GET HER DOWN HERE!
GREAT, ANTAGONIZE HIM. IMPLY THAT HIS EQUIPMENT IS A LITTLE UNDERSIZED.
PLEASE GOD, DON'T LET THEM DRAW BLOOD.
OOOF!
IF I WAS QUICK AND LUCKY, I COULD GO TO A HOSPITAL AND BE TREATED.
OF COURSE SOMETIMES THE INOCULATIONS WORKED, AND SOMETIMES THEY GAVE YOU LYCANTHROPY.
SATISFYING. I DOUBTED EITHER OF THEM WERE DEAD, BUT IT WAS THE BEST I COULD DO.
SQUEE!
I MIGHT BE ABLE TO GET A FEW OF THEM, BUT NOT ALL.
IF HE WANTED THEM TO, THEY'D EAT ME ALIVE, ONE TINY CRIMSON BITE AT A TIME.

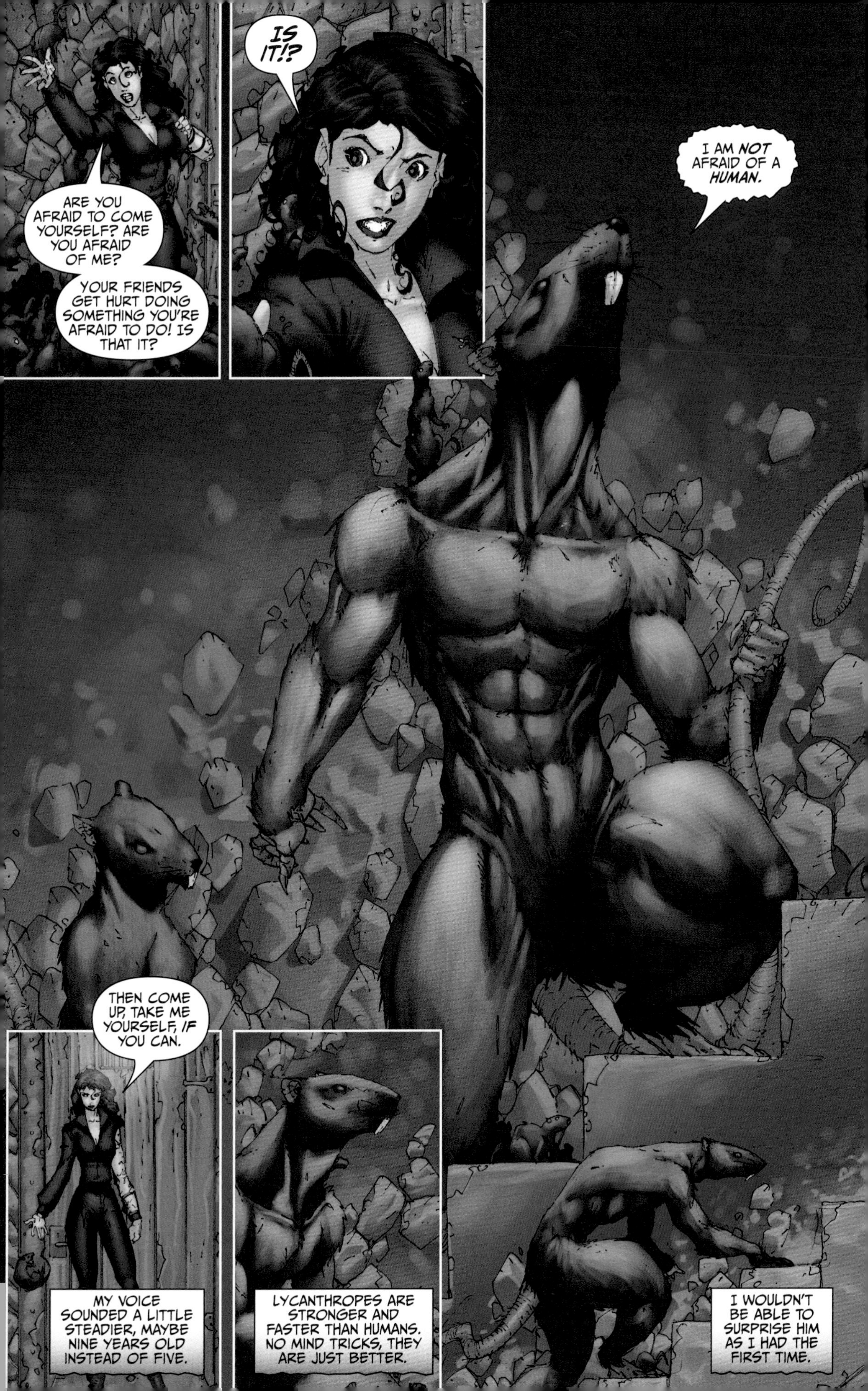
ARE YOU AFRAID TO COME YOURSELF? ARE YOU AFRAID OF ME?
YOUR FRIENDS GET HURT DOING SOMETHING YOU'RE AFRAID TO DO! IS THAT IT?
IS IT!?
I AM NOT AFRAID OF A HUMAN.
THEN COME UP, TAKE ME YOURSELF, IF YOU CAN.
MY VOICE SOUNDED A LITTLE STEADIER, MAYBE NINE YEARS OLD INSTEAD OF FIVE.
LYCANTHROPES ARE STRONGER AND FASTER THAN HUMANS. NO MIND TRICKS, THEY ARE JUST BETTER.
I WOULDN'T BE ABLE TO SURPRISE HIM AS I HAD THE FIRST TIME.

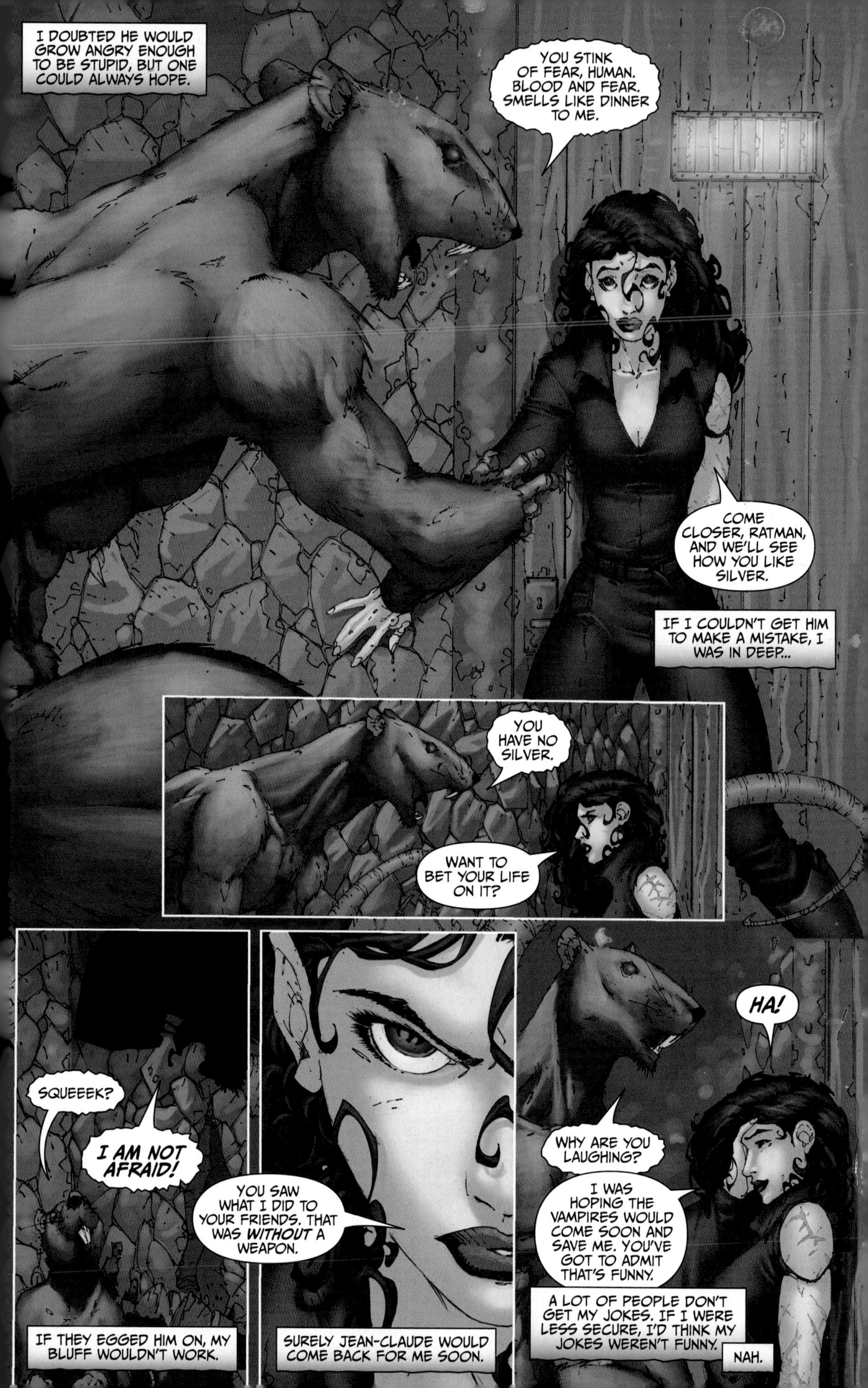
I DOUBTED HE WOULD GROW ANGRY ENOUGH TO BE STUPID, BUT ONE COULD ALWAYS HOPE.
YOU STINK OF FEAR, HUMAN. BLOOD AND FEAR. SMELLS LIKE DINNER TO ME.
COME CLOSER, RATMAN, AND WE'LL SEE HOW YOU LIKE SILVER.
IF I COULDN'T GET HIM TO MAKE A MISTAKE, I WAS IN DEEP...
YOU HAVE NO SILVER.
WANT TO BET YOUR LIFE ON IT?
SQUEEEK?
I AM NOT AFRAID!
IF THEY EGGED HIM ON, MY BLUFF WOULDN'T WORK.
YOU SAW WHAT I DID TO YOUR FRIENDS. THAT WAS WITHOUT A WEAPON.
SURELY JEAN-CLAUDE WOULD COME BACK FOR ME SOON.
HA!
WHY ARE YOU LAUGHING?
I WAS HOPING THE VAMPIRES WOULD COME SOON AND SAVE ME. YOU'VE GOT TO ADMIT THAT'S FUNNY.
A LOT OF PEOPLE DON'T GET MY JOKES. IF I WERE LESS SECURE, I'D THINK MY JOKES WEREN'T FUNNY.
NAH.

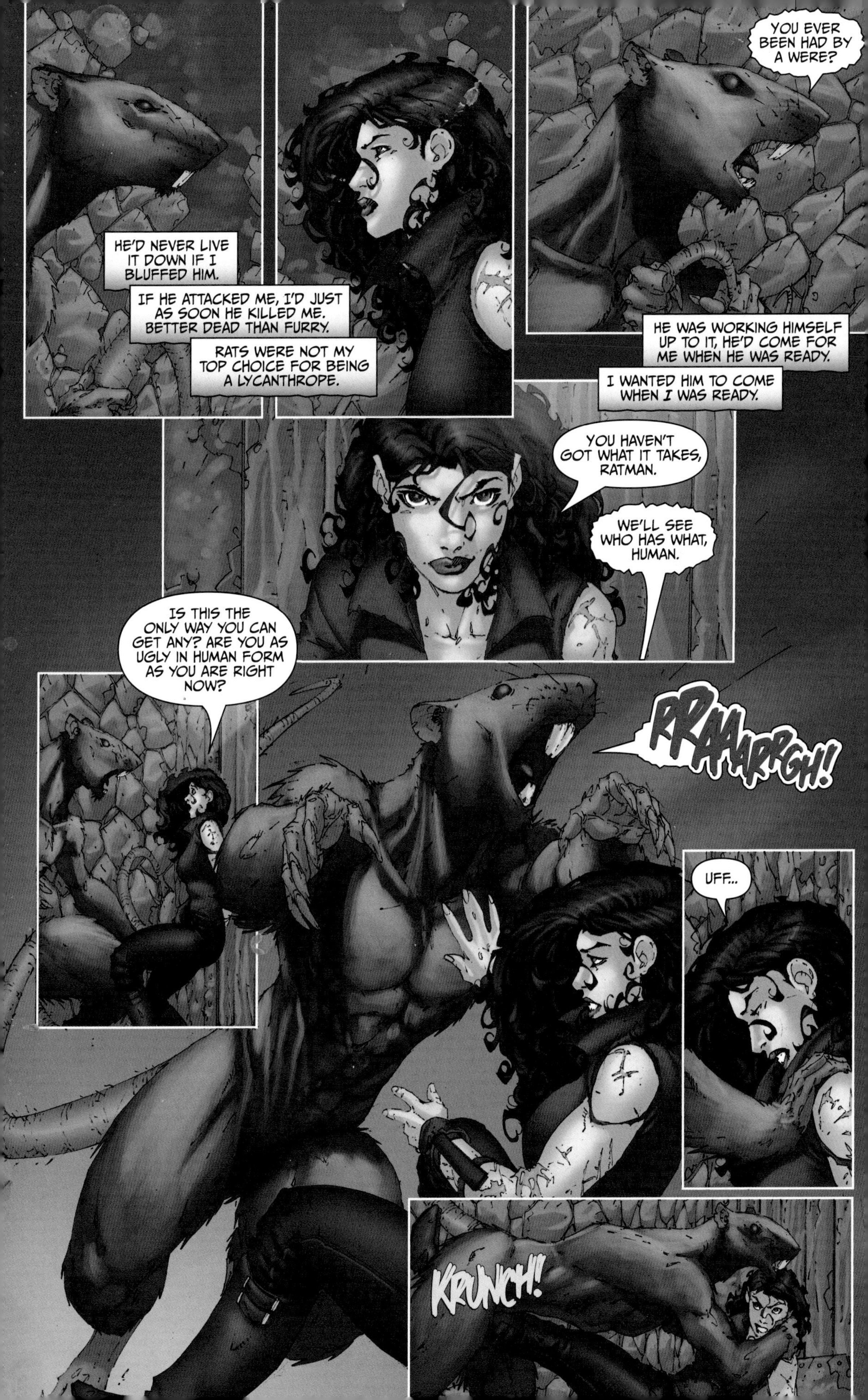
HE'D NEVER LIVE IT DOWN IF I BLUFFED HIM.
IF HE ATTACKED ME, I'D JUST AS SOON HE KILLED ME. BETTER DEAD THAN FURRY.
RATS WERE NOT MY TOP CHOICE FOR BEING A LYCANTHROPE.
YOU EVER BEEN HAD BY A WERE?
HE WAS WORKING HIMSELF UP TO IT, HE'D COME FOR ME WHEN HE WAS READY.
I WANTED HIM TO COME WHEN I WAS READY.
YOU HAVEN'T GOT WHAT IT TAKES, RATMAN.
WE'LL SEE WHO HAS WHAT, HUMAN.
IS THIS THE ONLY WAY YOU CAN GET ANY? ARE YOU AS UGLY IN HUMAN FORM AS YOU ARE RIGHT NOW?
RRAAAARRGH!
UFF...
KRUNCH!

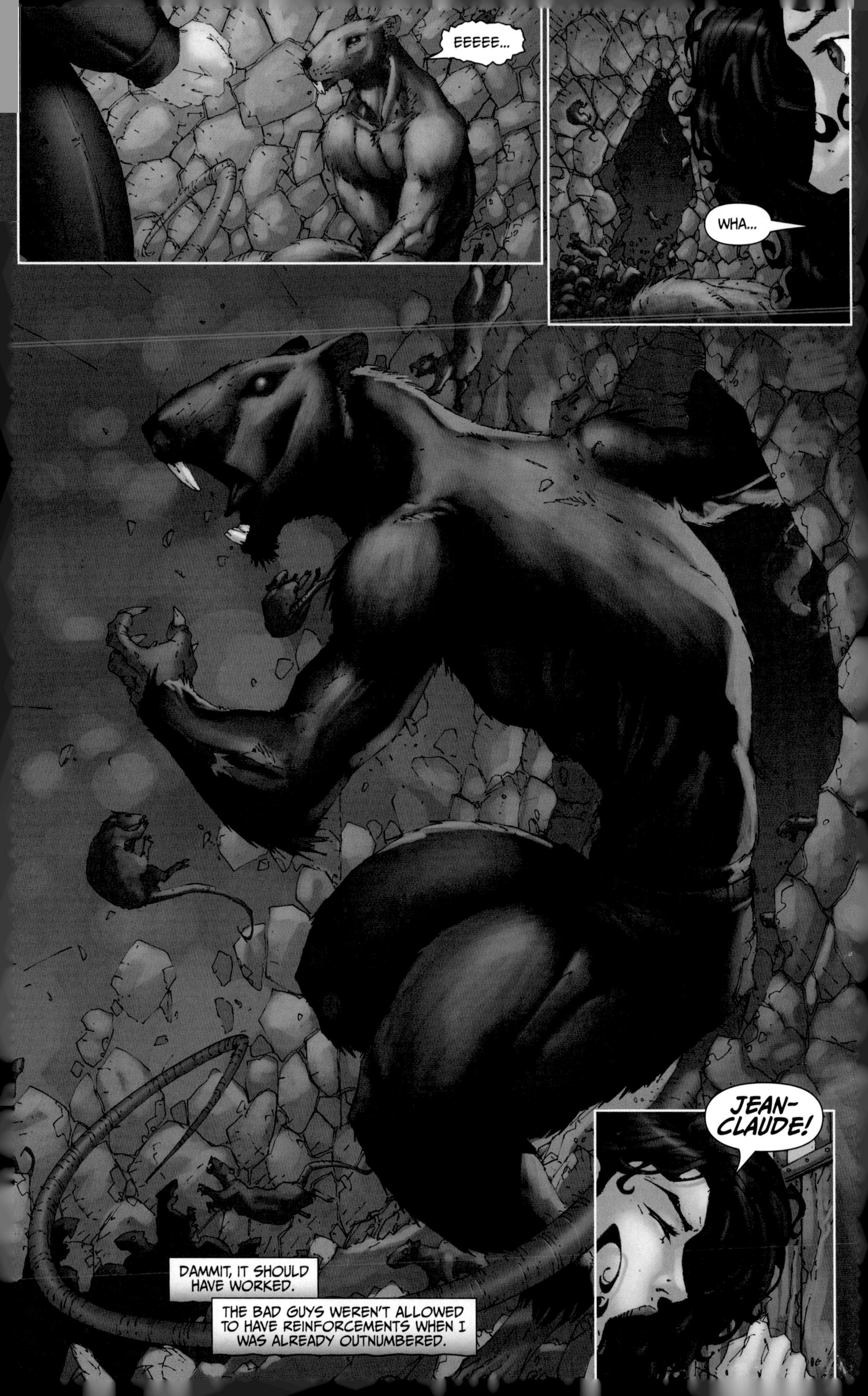
EEEEE...
WHA...
JEAN-CLAUDE!
DAMMIT, IT SHOULD HAVE WORKED.
THE BAD GUYS WEREN'T ALLOWED TO HAVE REINFORCEMENTS WHEN I WAS ALREADY OUTNUMBERED.

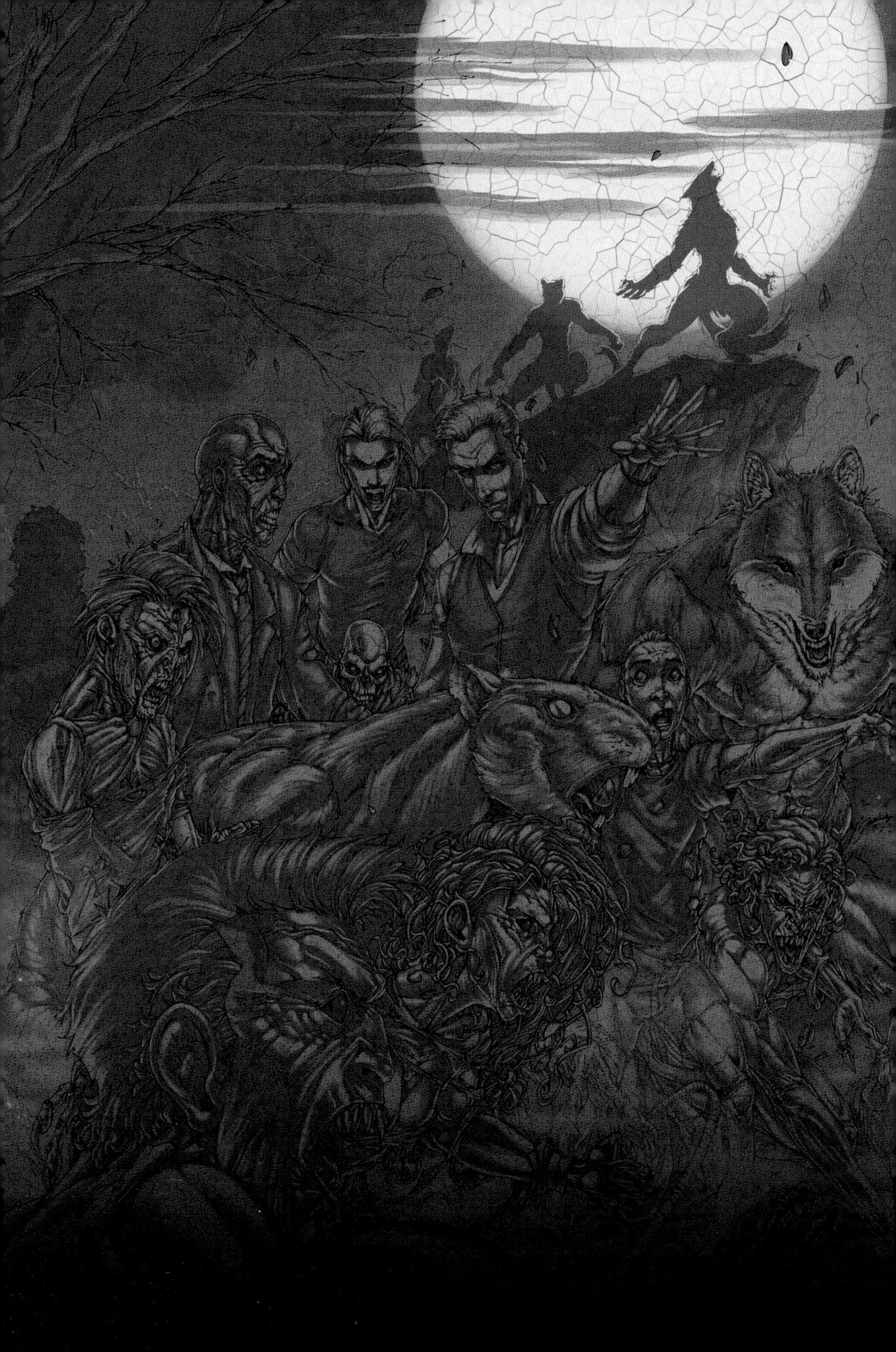

CHAPTER THREE

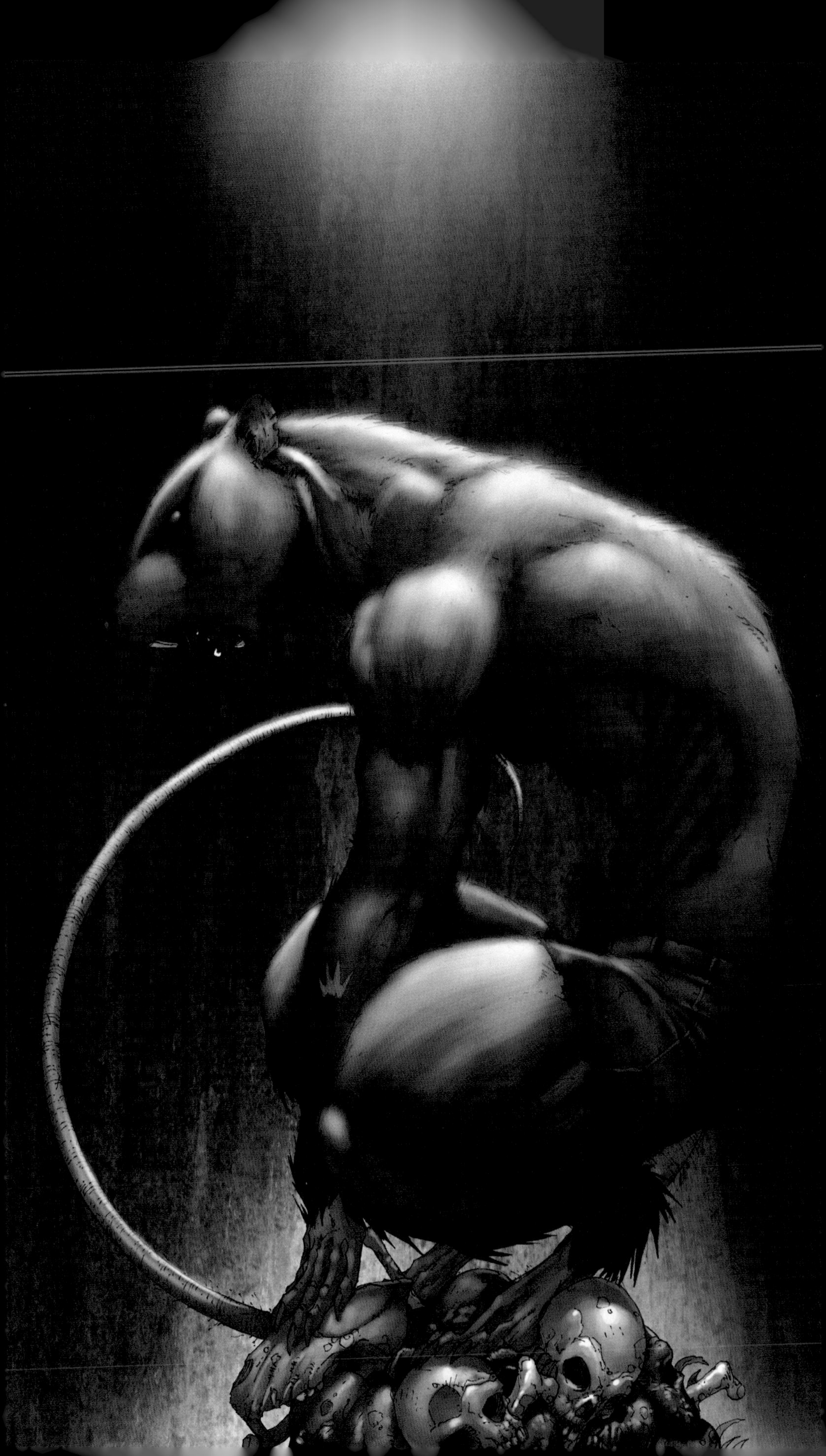

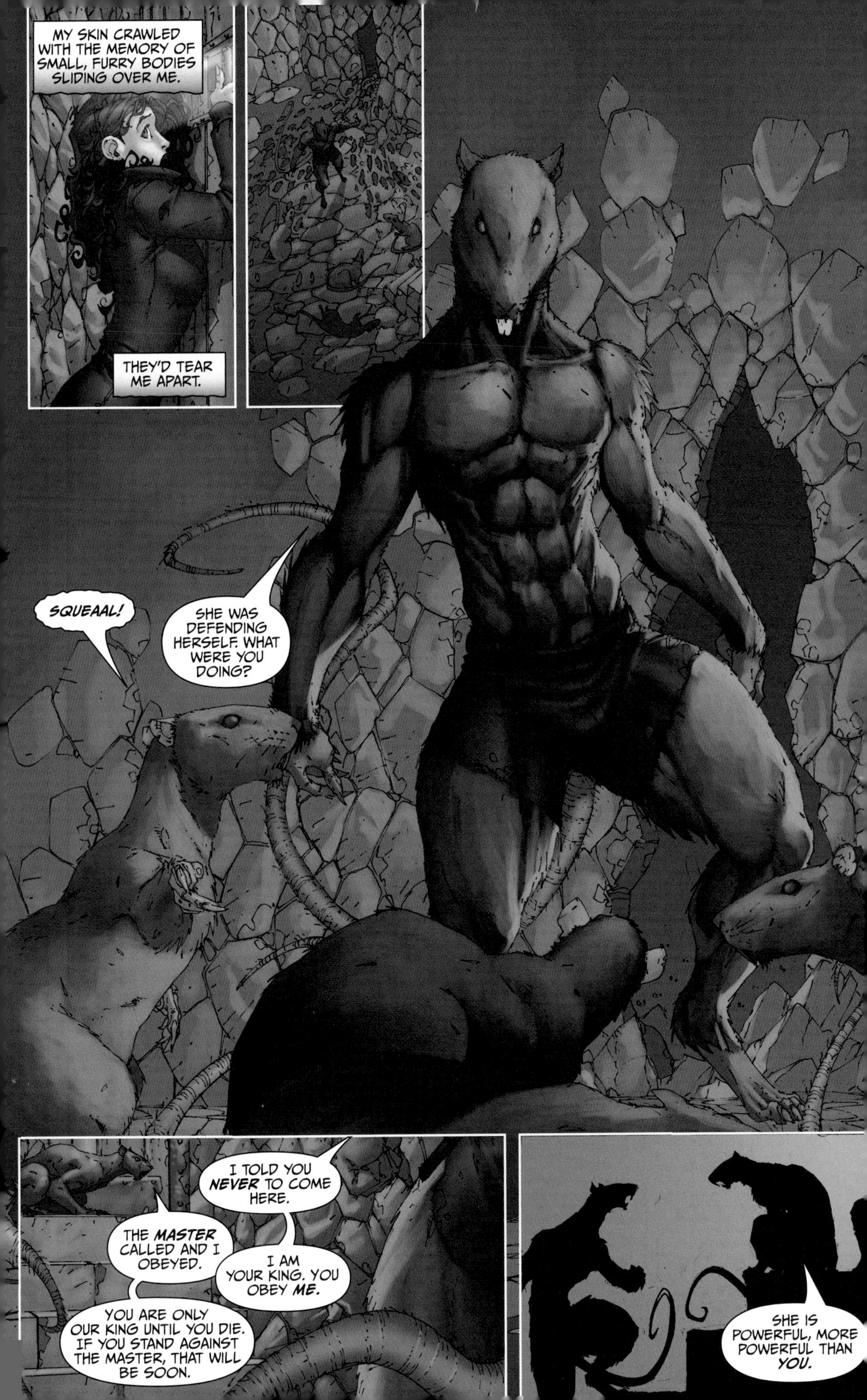
MY SKIN CRAWLED WITH THE MEMORY OF SMALL, FURRY BODIES SLIDING OVER ME.
THEY'D TEAR ME APART.
SQUEAAL!
SHE WAS DEFENDING HERSELF. WHAT WERE YOU DOING?
I TOLD YOU NEVER TO COME HERE.
THE MASTER CALLED AND I OBEYED.
I AM YOUR KING. YOU OBEY ME.
YOU ARE ONLY OUR KING UNTIL YOU DIE. IF YOU STAND AGAINST THE MASTER, THAT WILL BE SOON.
SHE IS POWERFUL, MORE POWERFUL THAN YOU.

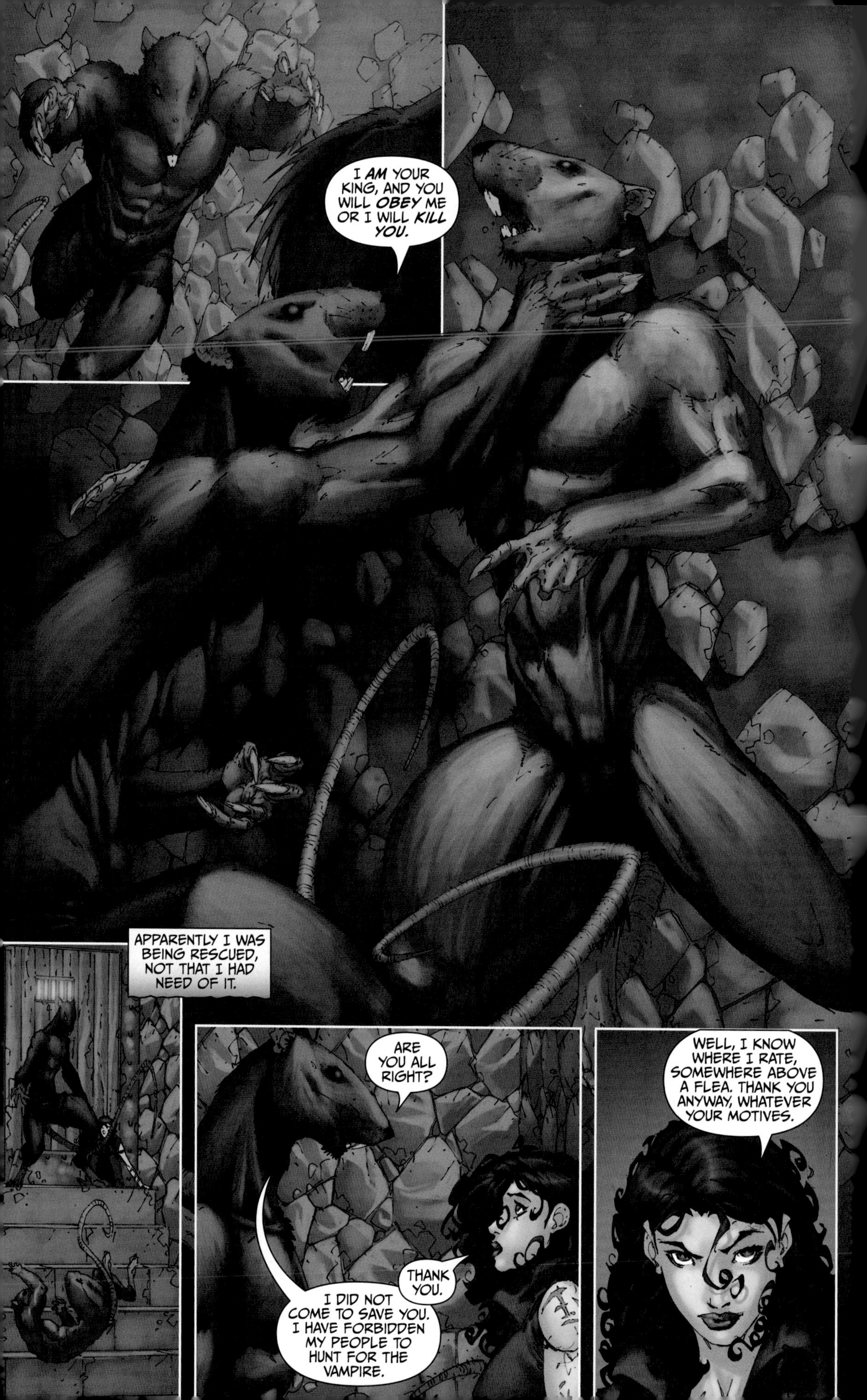
I AM YOUR KING, AND YOU WILL OBEY ME OR I WILL KILL YOU.
APPARENTLY I WAS BEING RESCUED, NOT THAT I HAD NEED OF IT.
ARE YOU ALL RIGHT?
THANK YOU.
I DID NOT COME TO SAVE YOU. I HAVE FORBIDDEN MY PEOPLE TO HUNT FOR THE VAMPIRE.
WELL, I KNOW WHERE I RATE, SOMEWHERE ABOVE A FLEA. THANK YOU ANYWAY, WHATEVER YOUR MOTIVES.

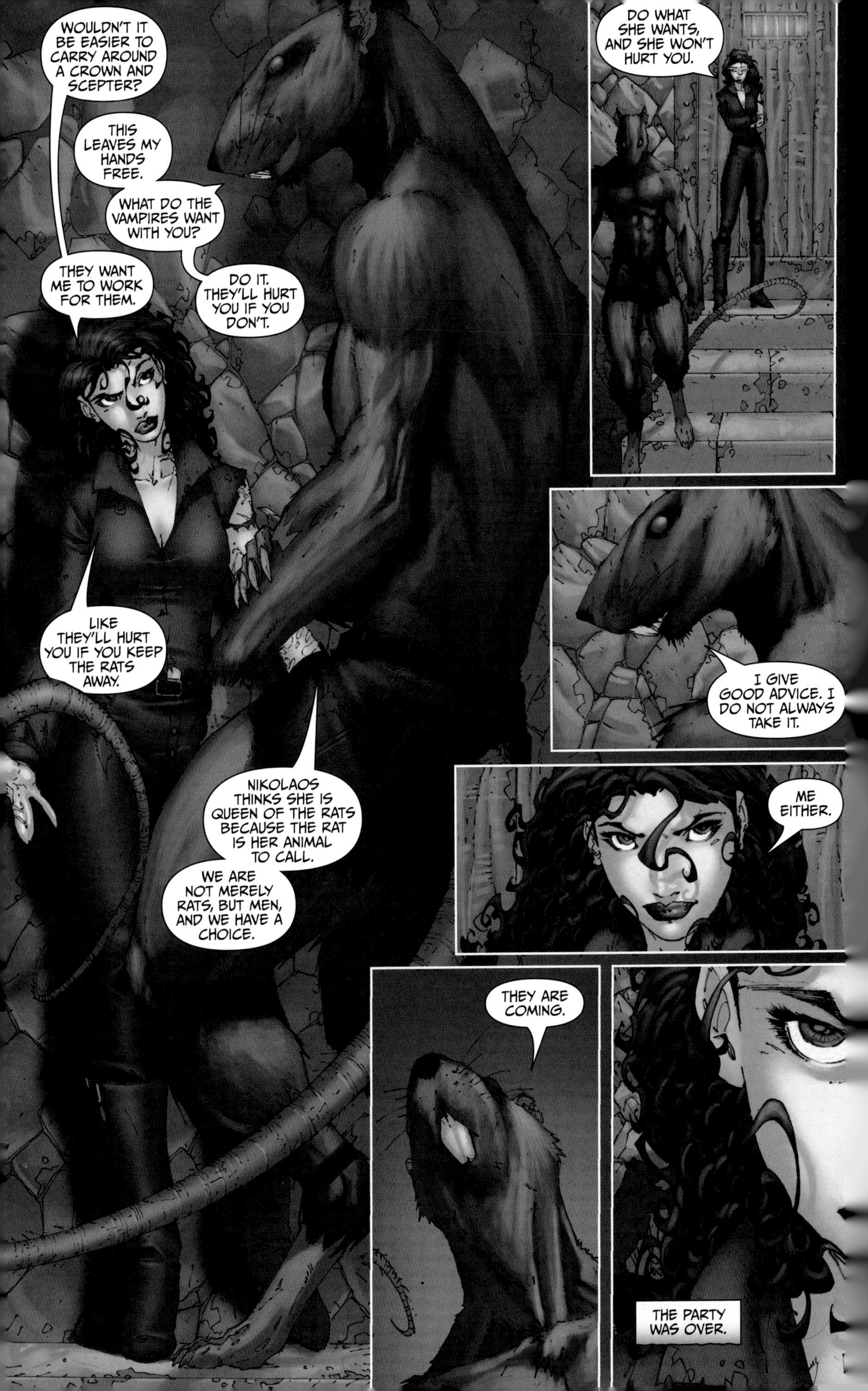
WOULDN'T IT BE EASIER TO CARRY AROUND A CROWN AND SCEPTER?
THIS LEAVES MY HANDS FREE.
WHAT DO THE VAMPIRES WANT WITH YOU?
THEY WANT ME TO WORK FOR THEM.
DO IT. THEY'LL HURT YOU IF YOU DON'T.
LIKE THEY'LL HURT YOU IF YOU KEEP THE RATS AWAY.
NIKOLAOS THINKS SHE IS QUEEN OF THE RATS BECAUSE THE RAT IS HER ANIMAL TO CALL.
WE ARE NOT MERELY RATS, BUT MEN, AND WE HAVE A CHOICE.
DO WHAT SHE WANTS, AND SHE WON'T HURT YOU.
I GIVE GOOD ADVICE. I DO NOT ALWAYS TAKE IT.
ME EITHER.
THEY ARE COMING.
THE PARTY WAS OVER.

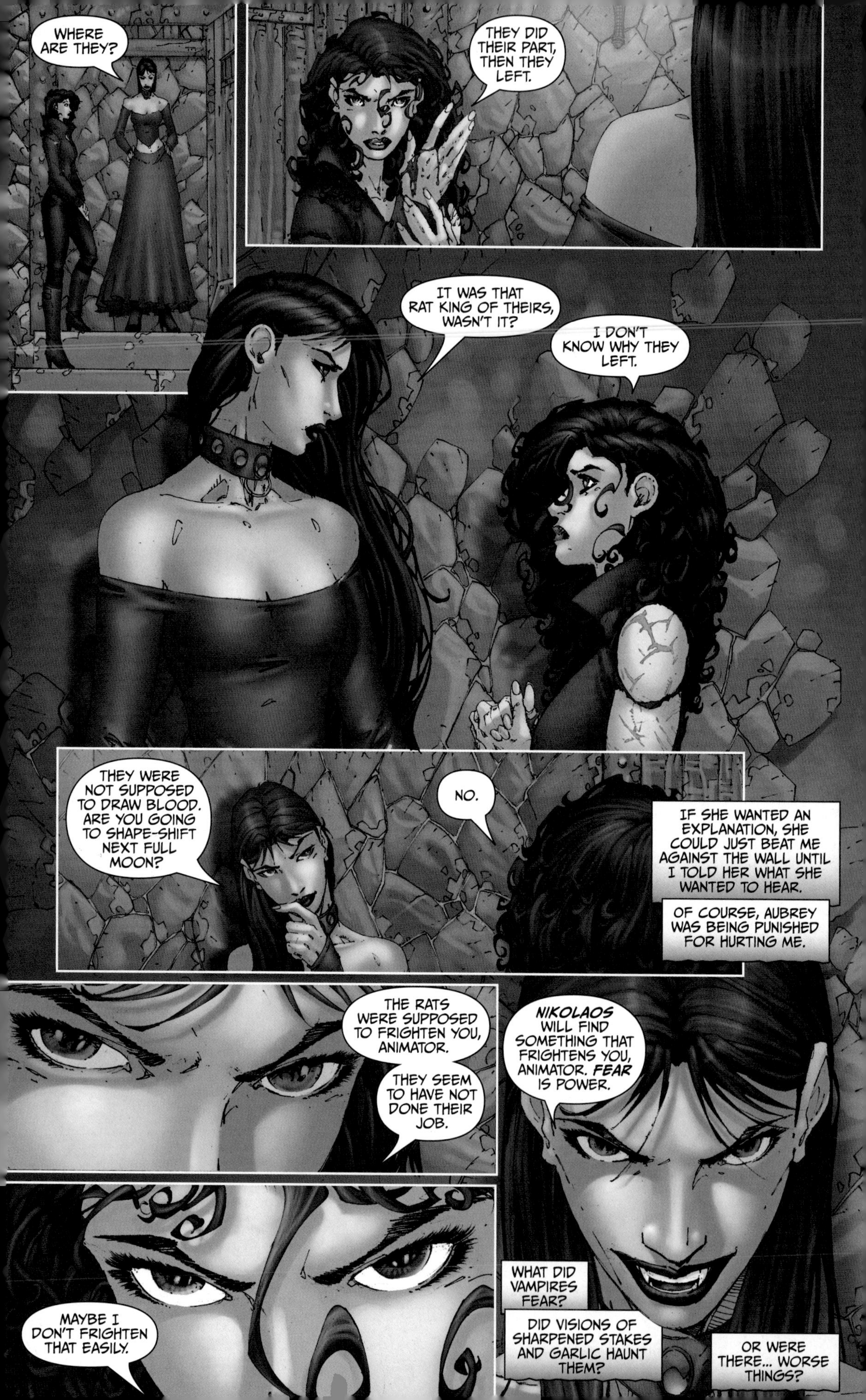

WHERE ARE THEY?
THEY DID THEIR PART, THEN THEY LEFT.
IT WAS THAT RAT KING OF THEIRS, WASN'T IT?
I DON'T KNOW WHY THEY LEFT.
THEY WERE NOT SUPPOSED TO DRAW BLOOD. ARE YOU GOING TO SHAPE-SHIFT NEXT FULL MOON?
NO.
IF SHE WANTED AN EXPLANATION, SHE COULD JUST BEAT ME AGAINST THE WALL UNTIL I TOLD HER WHAT SHE WANTED TO HEAR.
OF COURSE, AUBREY WAS BEING PUNISHED FOR HURTING ME.
THE RATS WERE SUPPOSED TO FRIGHTEN YOU, ANIMATOR.
THEY SEEM TO HAVE NOT DONE THEIR JOB.
NIKOLAOS WILL FIND SOMETHING THAT FRIGHTENS YOU, ANIMATOR. FEAR IS POWER.
MAYBE I DON'T FRIGHTEN THAT EASILY.
WHAT DID VAMPIRES FEAR?
DID VISIONS OF SHARPENED STAKES AND GARLIC HAUNT THEM?
OR WERE THERE... WORSE THINGS?

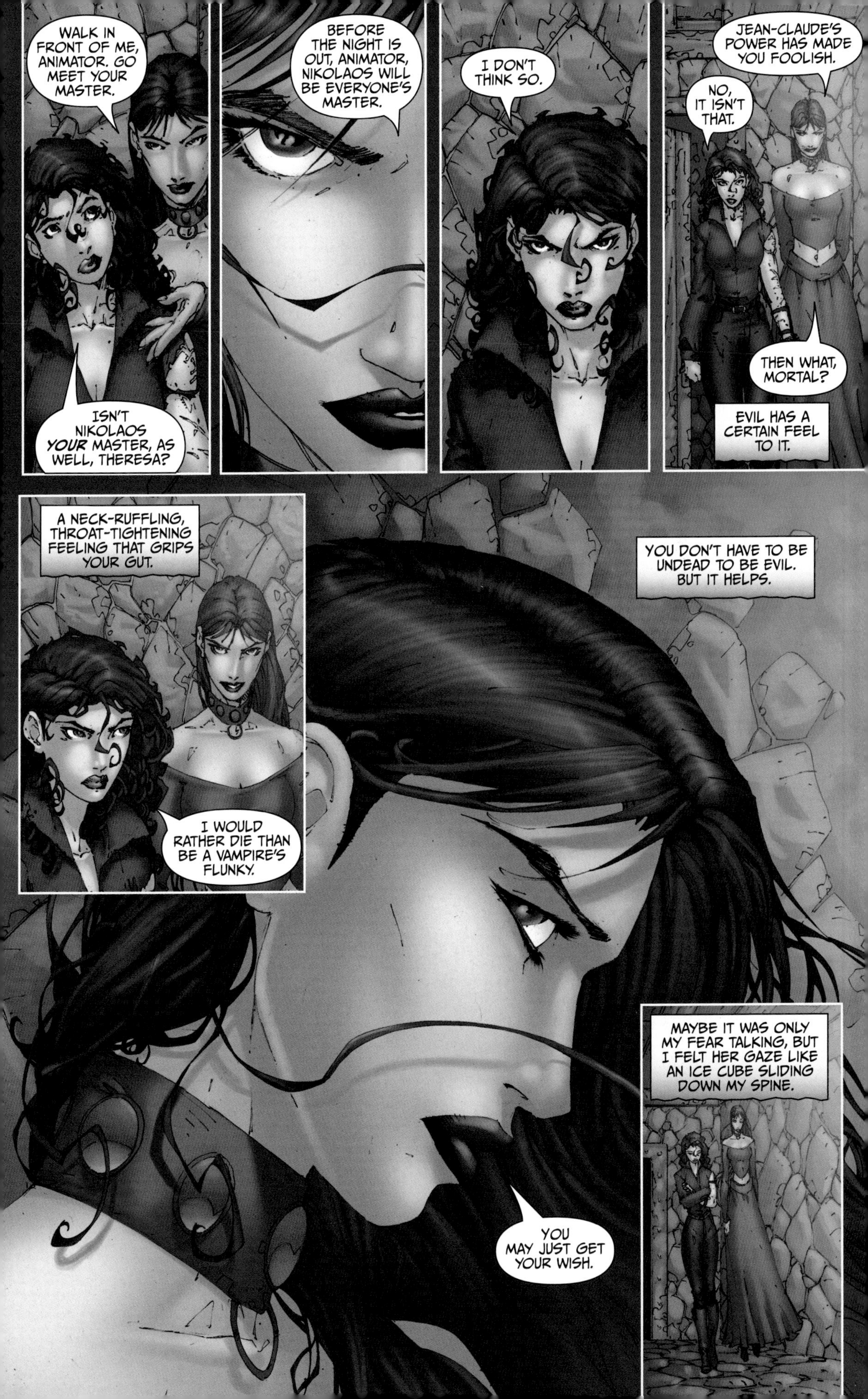
WALK IN FRONT OF ME, ANIMATOR. GO MEET YOUR MASTER.
ISN'T NIKOLAOS *YOUR* MASTER, AS WELL, THERESA?
BEFORE THE NIGHT IS OUT, ANIMATOR, NIKOLAOS WILL BE EVERYONE'S MASTER.
I DON'T THINK SO.
JEAN-CLAUDE'S POWER HAS MADE YOU FOOLISH.
NO, IT ISN'T THAT.
THEN WHAT, MORTAL?
EVIL HAS A CERTAIN FEEL TO IT.
A NECK-RUFFLING, THROAT-TIGHTENING FEELING THAT GRIPS YOUR GUT.
I WOULD RATHER DIE THAN BE A VAMPIRE'S FLUNKY.
YOU DON'T HAVE TO BE UNDEAD TO BE EVIL. BUT IT HELPS.
YOU MAY JUST GET YOUR WISH.
MAYBE IT WAS ONLY MY FEAR TALKING, BUT I FELT HER GAZE LIKE AN ICE CUBE SLIDING DOWN MY SPINE.

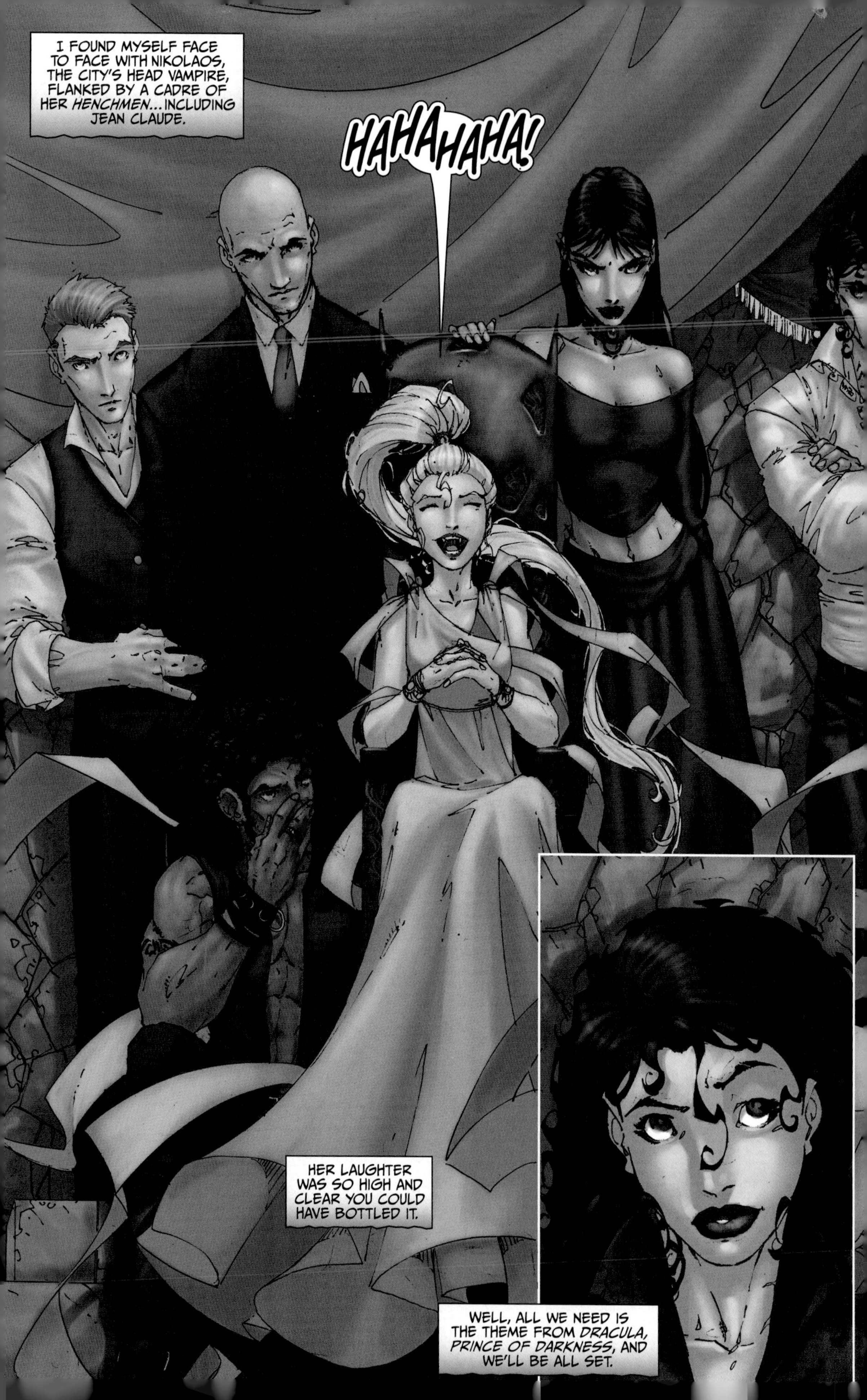
I FOUND MYSELF FACE TO FACE WITH NIKOLAOS, THE CITY'S HEAD VAMPIRE, FLANKED BY A CADRE OF HER *HENCHMEN*...INCLUDING JEAN CLAUDE.
HAHAHAHA!
HER LAUGHTER WAS SO HIGH AND CLEAR YOU COULD HAVE BOTTLED IT.
WELL, ALL WE NEED IS THE THEME FROM *DRACULA, PRINCE OF DARKNESS,* AND WE'LL BE ALL SET.

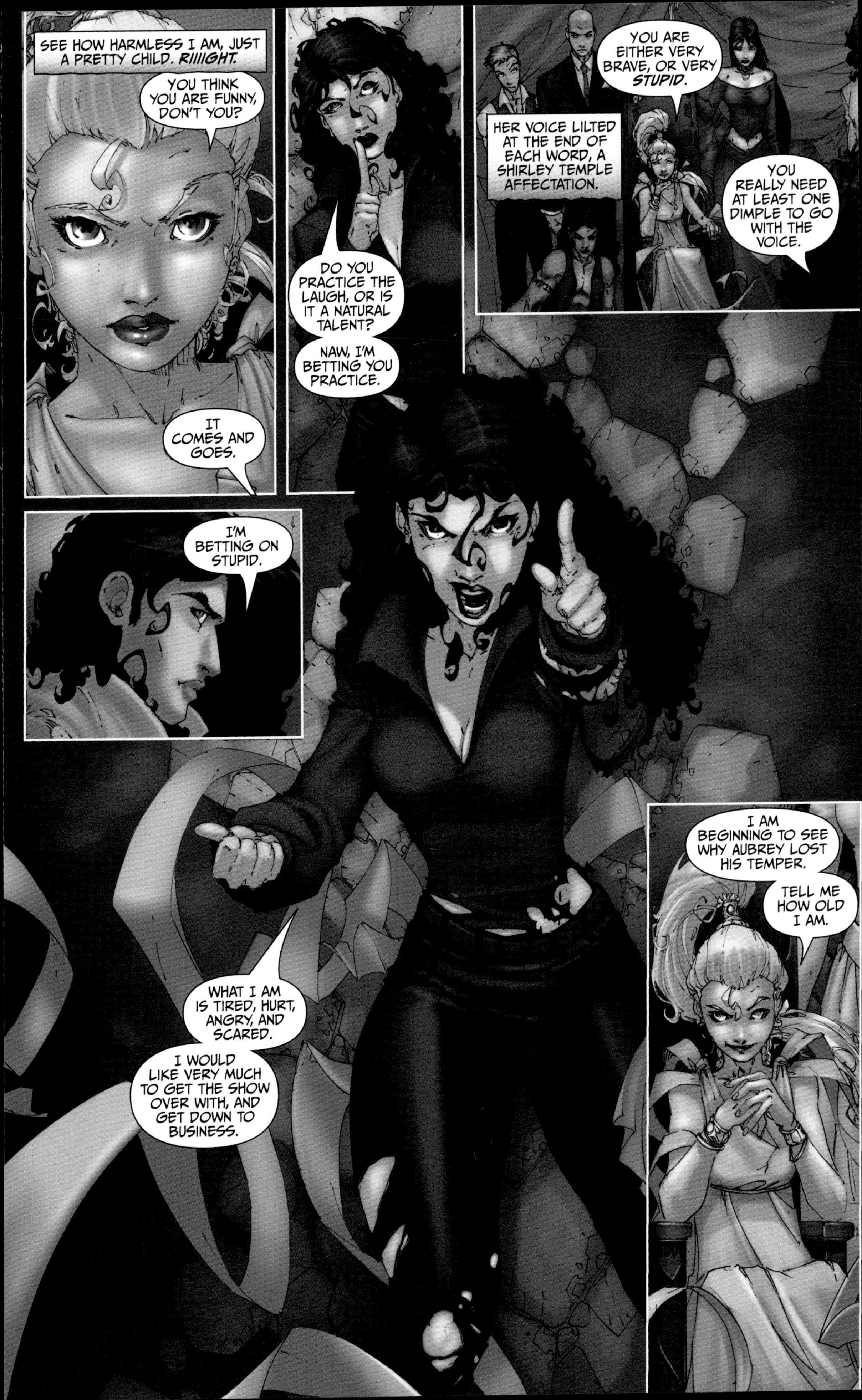
SEE HOW HARMLESS I AM, JUST A PRETTY CHILD. *RIIIGHT.*
YOU THINK YOU ARE FUNNY, DON'T YOU?
IT COMES AND GOES.
DO YOU PRACTICE THE LAUGH, OR IS IT A NATURAL TALENT?
NAW, I'M BETTING YOU PRACTICE.
YOU ARE EITHER VERY BRAVE, OR VERY *STUPID*.
HER VOICE LILTED AT THE END OF EACH WORD, A SHIRLEY TEMPLE AFFECTATION.
YOU REALLY NEED AT LEAST ONE DIMPLE TO GO WITH THE VOICE.
I'M BETTING ON STUPID.
WHAT I AM IS TIRED, HURT, ANGRY, AND SCARED.
I WOULD LIKE VERY MUCH TO GET THE SHOW OVER WITH, AND GET DOWN TO BUSINESS.
I AM BEGINNING TO SEE WHY AUBREY LOST HIS TEMPER.
TELL ME HOW OLD I AM.

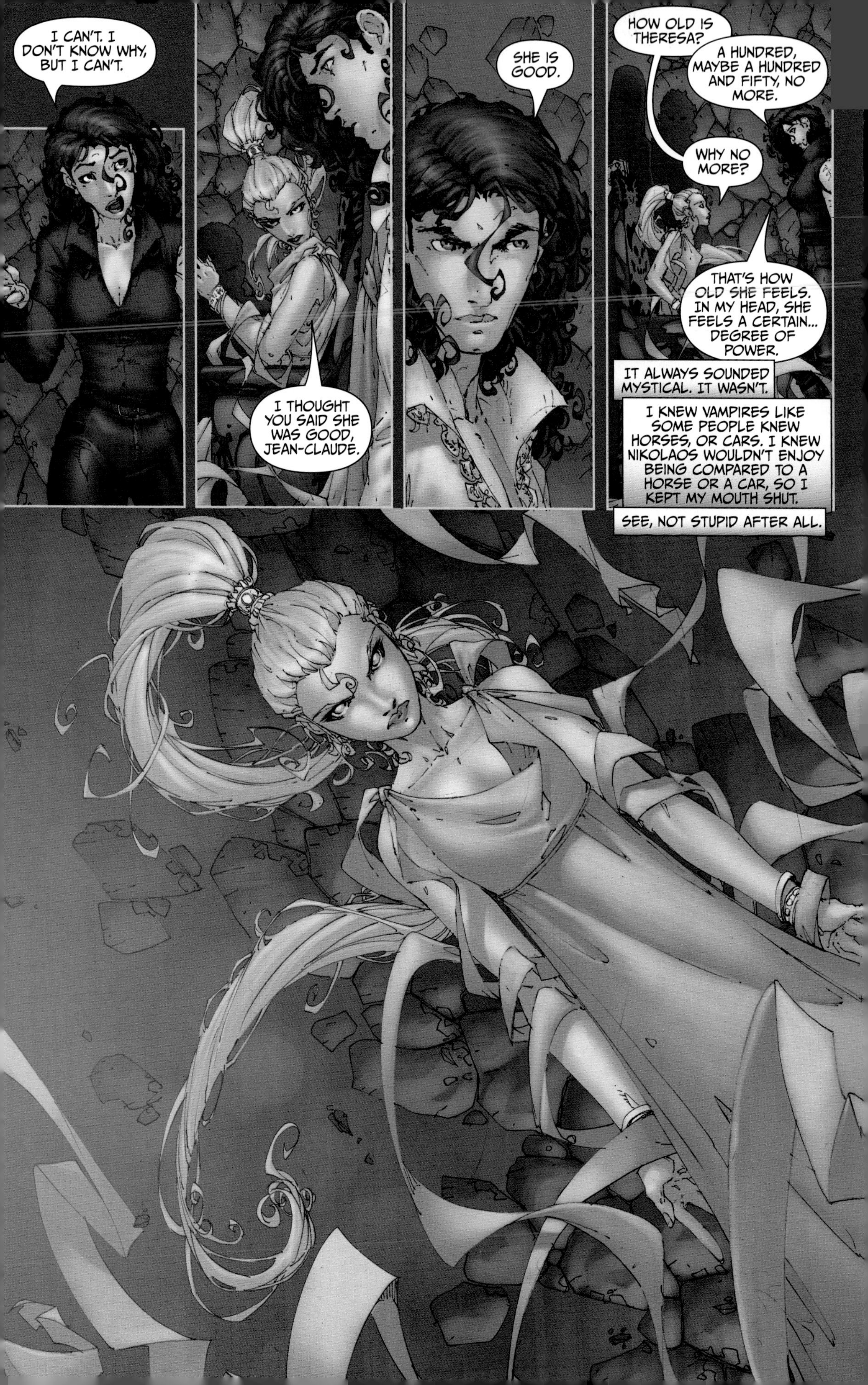
I CAN'T. I DON'T KNOW WHY, BUT I CAN'T.
I THOUGHT YOU SAID SHE WAS GOOD, JEAN-CLAUDE.
SHE IS GOOD.
HOW OLD IS THERESA?
A HUNDRED, MAYBE A HUNDRED AND FIFTY, NO MORE.
WHY NO MORE?
THAT'S HOW OLD SHE FEELS. IN MY HEAD, SHE FEELS A CERTAIN... DEGREE OF POWER.
IT ALWAYS SOUNDED MYSTICAL. IT WASN'T.
I KNEW VAMPIRES LIKE SOME PEOPLE KNEW HORSES, OR CARS. I KNEW NIKOLAOS WOULDN'T ENJOY BEING COMPARED TO A HORSE OR A CAR, SO I KEPT MY MOUTH SHUT.
SEE, NOT STUPID AFTER ALL.

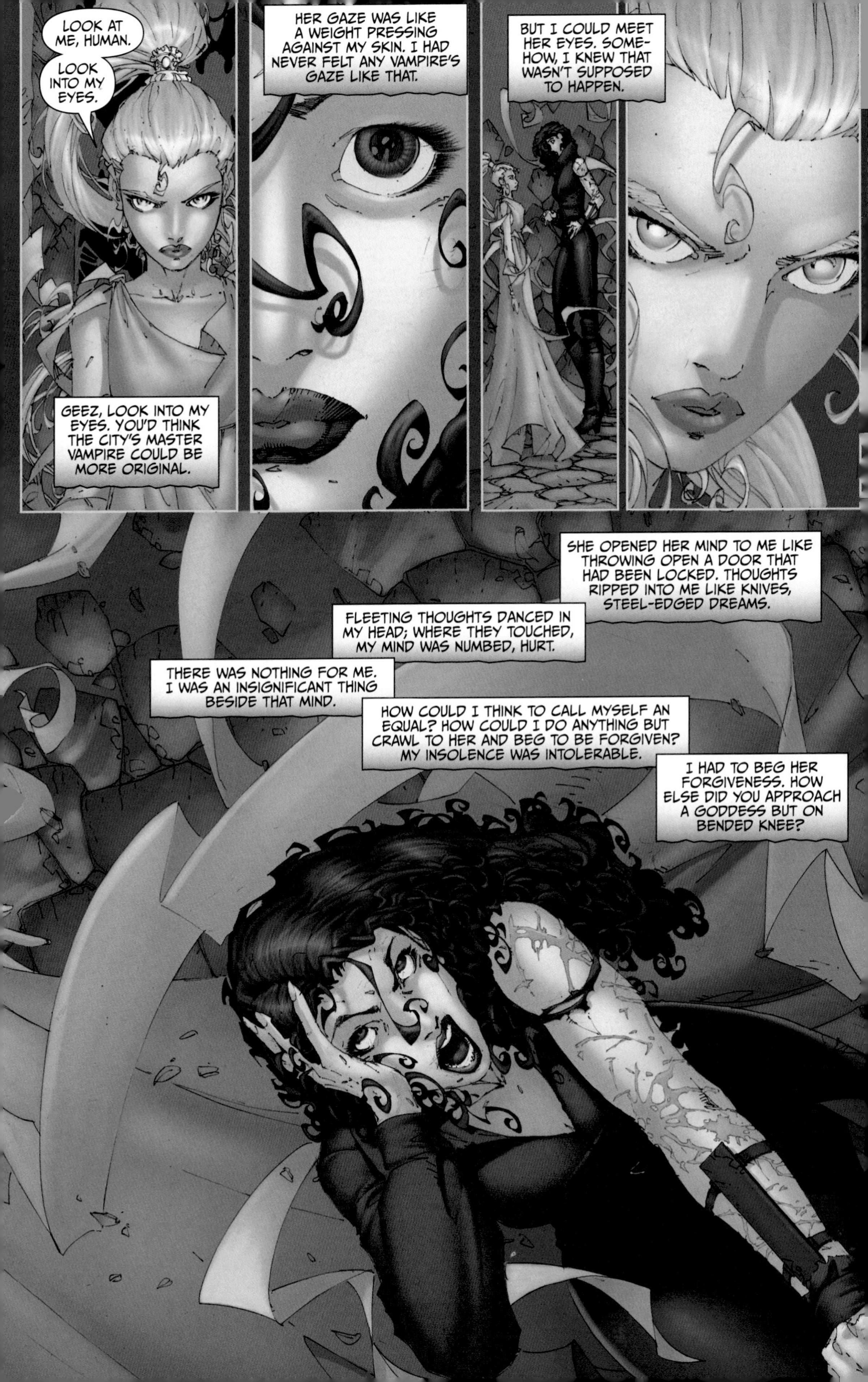

LOOK AT ME, HUMAN.
LOOK INTO MY EYES.
GEEZ, LOOK INTO MY EYES. YOU'D THINK THE CITY'S MASTER VAMPIRE COULD BE MORE ORIGINAL.
HER GAZE WAS LIKE A WEIGHT PRESSING AGAINST MY SKIN. I HAD NEVER FELT ANY VAMPIRE'S GAZE LIKE THAT.
BUT I COULD MEET HER EYES. SOME-HOW, I KNEW THAT WASN'T SUPPOSED TO HAPPEN.
SHE OPENED HER MIND TO ME LIKE THROWING OPEN A DOOR THAT HAD BEEN LOCKED. THOUGHTS RIPPED INTO ME LIKE KNIVES, STEEL-EDGED DREAMS.
FLEETING THOUGHTS DANCED IN MY HEAD; WHERE THEY TOUCHED, MY MIND WAS NUMBED, HURT.
THERE WAS NOTHING FOR ME. I WAS AN INSIGNIFICANT THING BESIDE THAT MIND.
HOW COULD I THINK TO CALL MYSELF AN EQUAL? HOW COULD I DO ANYTHING BUT CRAWL TO HER AND BEG TO BE FORGIVEN? MY INSOLENCE WAS INTOLERABLE.
I HAD TO BEG HER FORGIVENESS. HOW ELSE DID YOU APPROACH A GODDESS BUT ON BENDED KNEE?

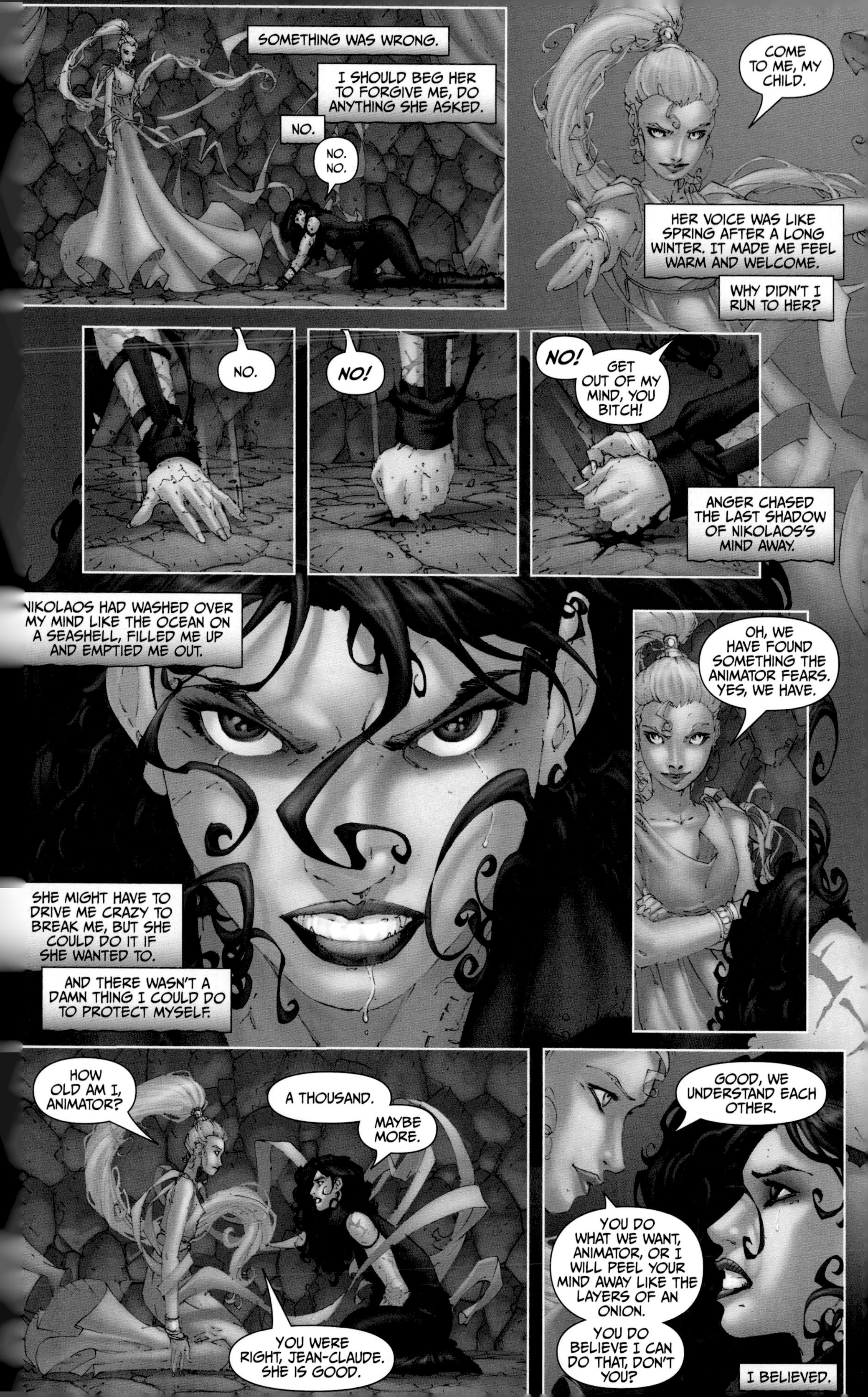
SOMETHING WAS WRONG.
I SHOULD BEG HER TO FORGIVE ME, DO ANYTHING SHE ASKED.
NO.
NO. NO.
COME TO ME, MY CHILD.
HER VOICE WAS LIKE SPRING AFTER A LONG WINTER. IT MADE ME FEEL WARM AND WELCOME.
WHY DIDN'T I RUN TO HER?
NO.
NO!
NO!
GET OUT OF MY MIND, YOU BITCH!
ANGER CHASED THE LAST SHADOW OF NIKOLAOS'S MIND AWAY.
NIKOLAOS HAD WASHED OVER MY MIND LIKE THE OCEAN ON A SEASHELL, FILLED ME UP AND EMPTIED ME OUT.
OH, WE HAVE FOUND SOMETHING THE ANIMATOR FEARS. YES, WE HAVE.
SHE MIGHT HAVE TO DRIVE ME CRAZY TO BREAK ME, BUT SHE COULD DO IT IF SHE WANTED TO.
AND THERE WASN'T A DAMN THING I COULD DO TO PROTECT MYSELF.
HOW OLD AM I, ANIMATOR?
A THOUSAND.
MAYBE MORE.
YOU WERE RIGHT, JEAN-CLAUDE. SHE IS GOOD.
GOOD, WE UNDERSTAND EACH OTHER.
YOU DO WHAT WE WANT, ANIMATOR, OR I WILL PEEL YOUR MIND AWAY LIKE THE LAYERS OF AN ONION.
YOU DO BELIEVE I CAN DO THAT, DON'T YOU?
I BELIEVED.

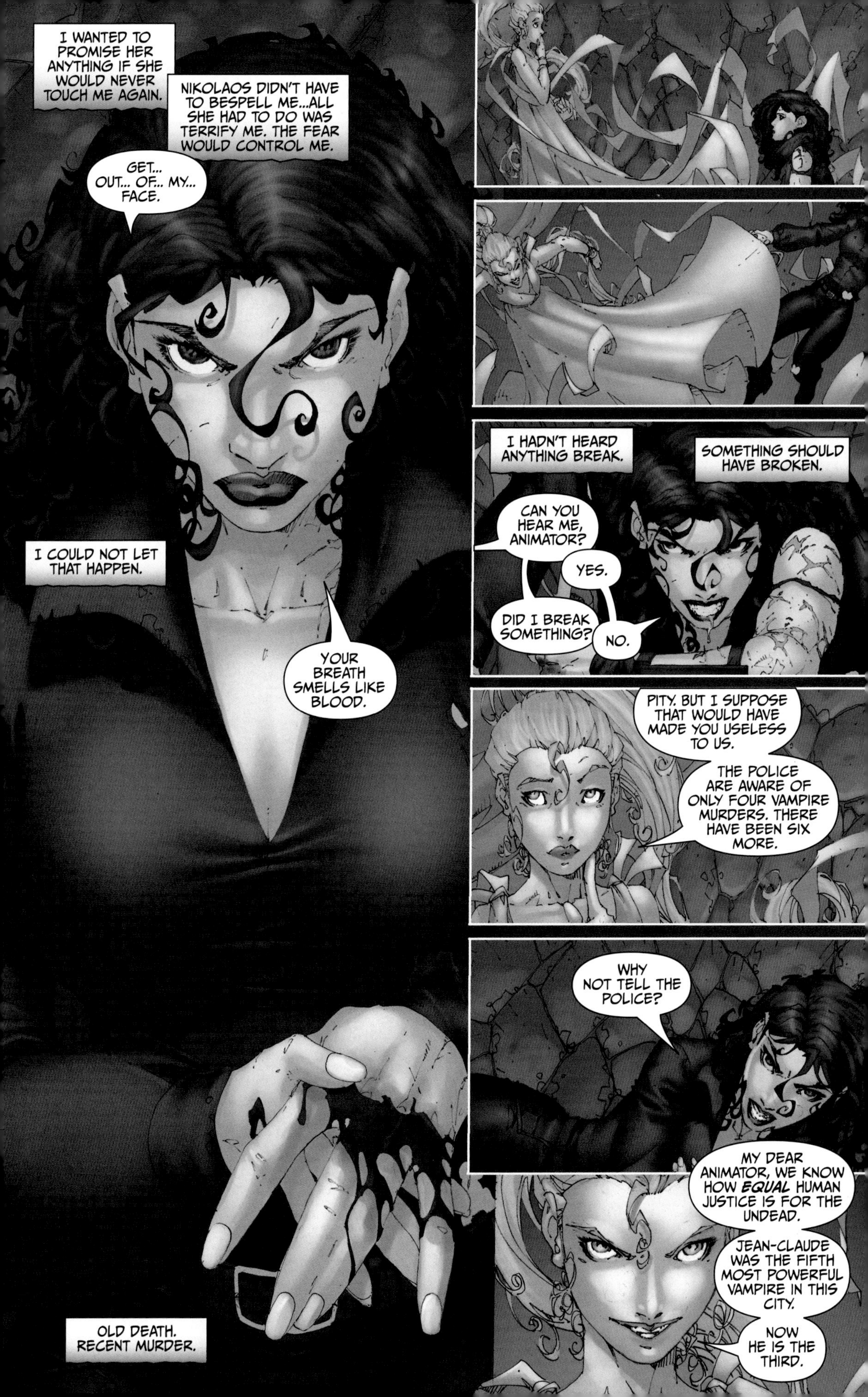
I WANTED TO PROMISE HER ANYTHING IF SHE WOULD NEVER TOUCH ME AGAIN.
NIKOLAOS DIDN'T HAVE TO BESPELL ME...ALL SHE HAD TO DO WAS TERRIFY ME. THE FEAR WOULD CONTROL ME.
GET... OUT... OF... MY... FACE.
I COULD NOT LET THAT HAPPEN.
YOUR BREATH SMELLS LIKE BLOOD.
OLD DEATH. RECENT MURDER.
I HADN'T HEARD ANYTHING BREAK.
SOMETHING SHOULD HAVE BROKEN.
CAN YOU HEAR ME, ANIMATOR?
YES.
DID I BREAK SOMETHING?
NO.
PITY. BUT I SUPPOSE THAT WOULD HAVE MADE YOU USELESS TO US.
THE POLICE ARE AWARE OF ONLY FOUR VAMPIRE MURDERS. THERE HAVE BEEN SIX MORE.
WHY NOT TELL THE POLICE?
MY DEAR ANIMATOR, WE KNOW HOW *EQUAL* HUMAN JUSTICE IS FOR THE UNDEAD.
JEAN-CLAUDE WAS THE FIFTH MOST POWERFUL VAMPIRE IN THIS CITY.
NOW HE IS THE THIRD.

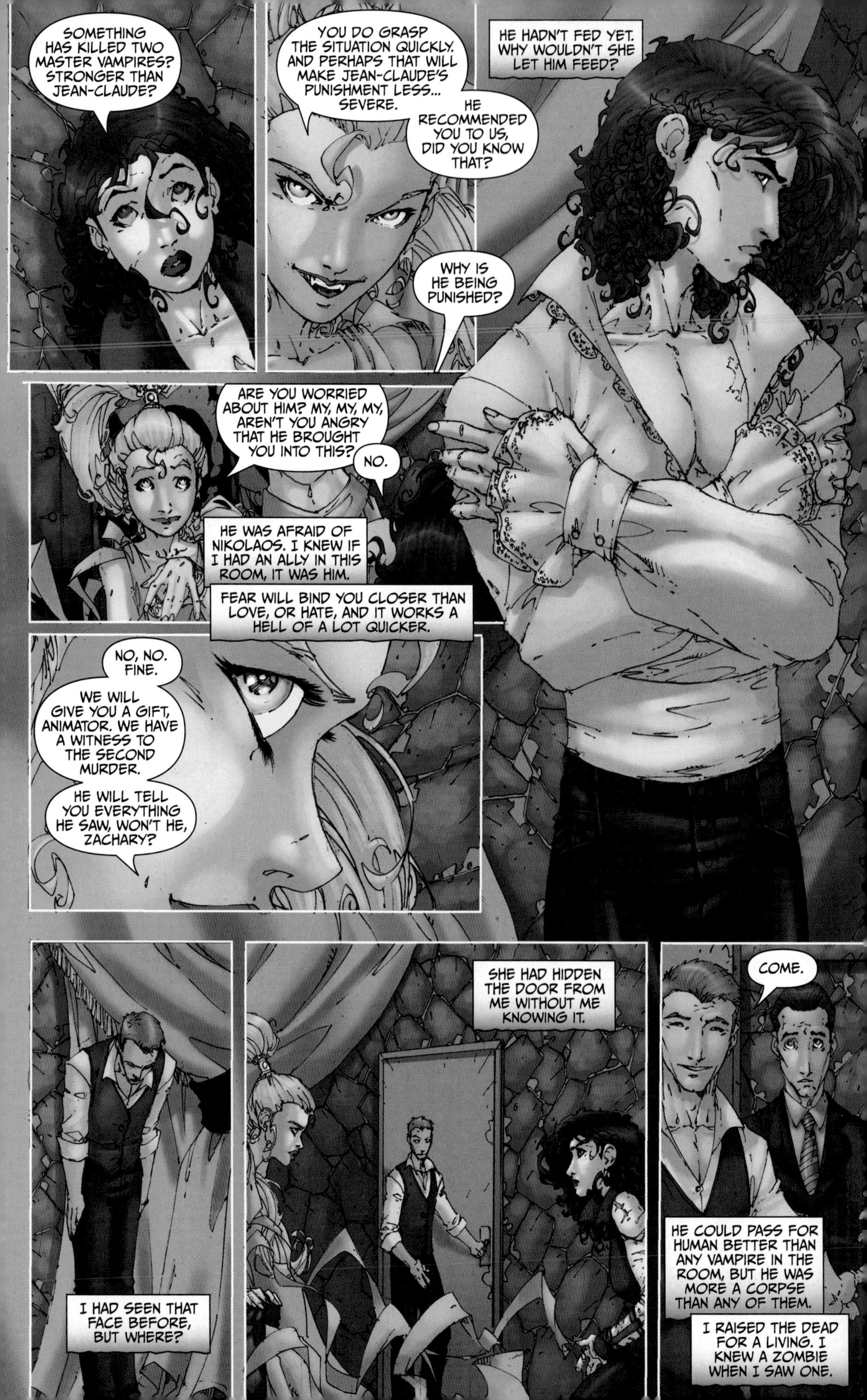
SOMETHING HAS KILLED TWO MASTER VAMPIRES? STRONGER THAN JEAN-CLAUDE?
YOU DO GRASP THE SITUATION QUICKLY. AND PERHAPS THAT WILL MAKE JEAN-CLAUDE'S PUNISHMENT LESS... SEVERE.
HE RECOMMENDED YOU TO US, DID YOU KNOW THAT?
WHY IS HE BEING PUNISHED?
HE HADN'T FED YET. WHY WOULDN'T SHE LET HIM FEED?
ARE YOU WORRIED ABOUT HIM? MY, MY, MY, AREN'T YOU ANGRY THAT HE BROUGHT YOU INTO THIS?
NO.
HE WAS AFRAID OF NIKOLAOS. I KNEW IF I HAD AN ALLY IN THIS ROOM, IT WAS HIM.
FEAR WILL BIND YOU CLOSER THAN LOVE, OR HATE, AND IT WORKS A HELL OF A LOT QUICKER.
NO, NO. FINE.
WE WILL GIVE YOU A GIFT, ANIMATOR. WE HAVE A WITNESS TO THE SECOND MURDER.
HE WILL TELL YOU EVERYTHING HE SAW, WON'T HE, ZACHARY?
I HAD SEEN THAT FACE BEFORE, BUT WHERE?
SHE HAD HIDDEN THE DOOR FROM ME WITHOUT ME KNOWING IT.
COME.
HE COULD PASS FOR HUMAN BETTER THAN ANY VAMPIRE IN THE ROOM, BUT HE WAS MORE A CORPSE THAN ANY OF THEM.
I RAISED THE DEAD FOR A LIVING. I KNEW A ZOMBIE WHEN I SAW ONE.

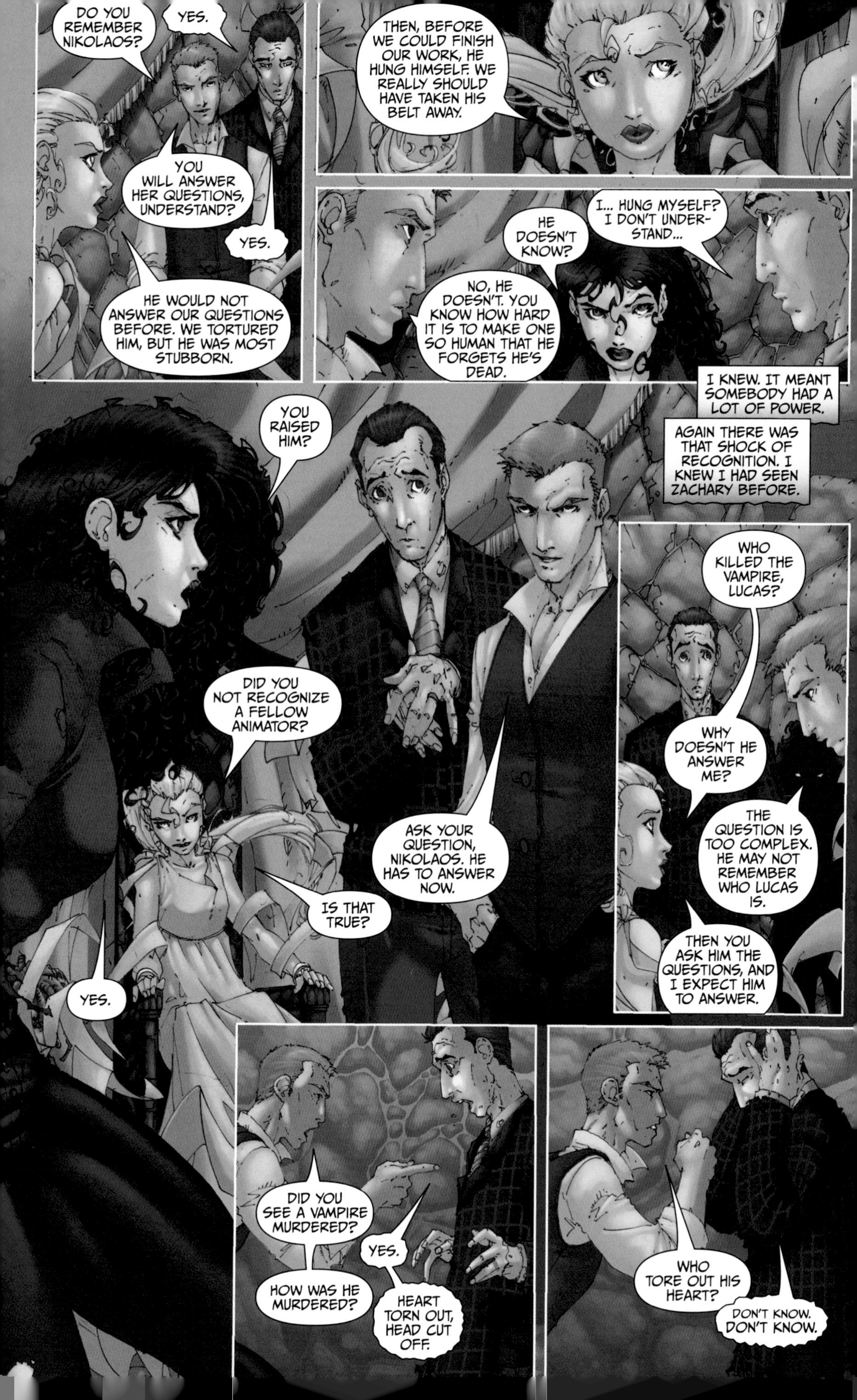

DO YOU REMEMBER NIKOLAOS?
YES.
YOU WILL ANSWER HER QUESTIONS, UNDERSTAND?
YES.
HE WOULD NOT ANSWER OUR QUESTIONS BEFORE. WE TORTURED HIM, BUT HE WAS MOST STUBBORN.
THEN, BEFORE WE COULD FINISH OUR WORK, HE HUNG HIMSELF. WE REALLY SHOULD HAVE TAKEN HIS BELT AWAY.
I... HUNG MYSELF? I DON'T UNDERSTAND...
HE DOESN'T KNOW?
NO, HE DOESN'T. YOU KNOW HOW HARD IT IS TO MAKE ONE SO HUMAN THAT HE FORGETS HE'S DEAD.
I KNEW. IT MEANT SOMEBODY HAD A LOT OF POWER.
AGAIN THERE WAS THAT SHOCK OF RECOGNITION. I KNEW I HAD SEEN ZACHARY BEFORE.
YOU RAISED HIM?
DID YOU NOT RECOGNIZE A FELLOW ANIMATOR?
ASK YOUR QUESTION, NIKOLAOS. HE HAS TO ANSWER NOW.
IS THAT TRUE?
YES.
WHO KILLED THE VAMPIRE, LUCAS?
WHY DOESN'T HE ANSWER ME?
THE QUESTION IS TOO COMPLEX. HE MAY NOT REMEMBER WHO LUCAS IS.
THEN YOU ASK HIM THE QUESTIONS, AND I EXPECT HIM TO ANSWER.
DID YOU SEE A VAMPIRE MURDERED?
YES.
HOW WAS HE MURDERED?
HEART TORN OUT, HEAD CUT OFF.
WHO TORE OUT HIS HEART?
DON'T KNOW. DON'T KNOW.

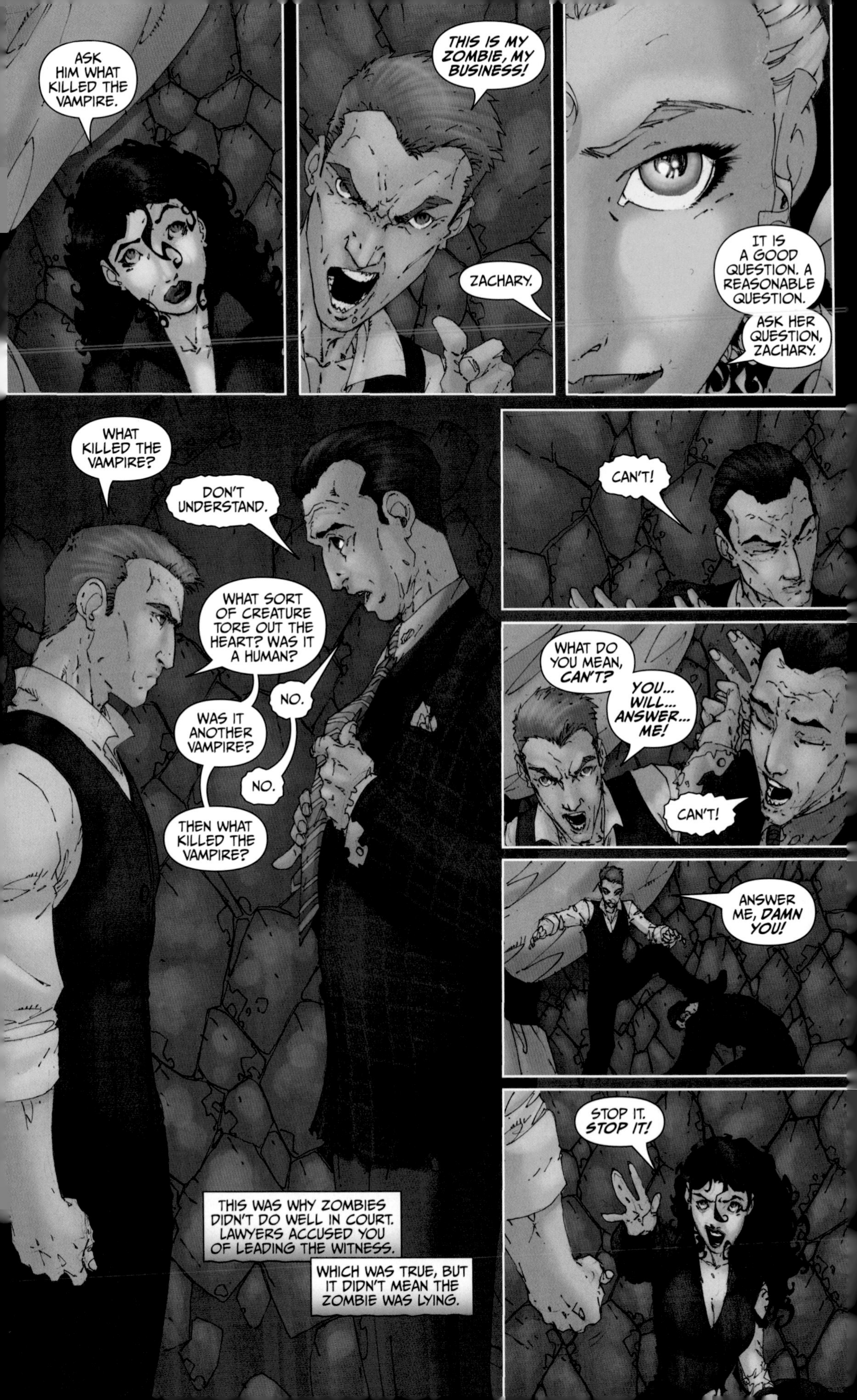
ASK HIM WHAT KILLED THE VAMPIRE.
THIS IS MY ZOMBIE, MY BUSINESS!
ZACHARY.
IT IS A GOOD QUESTION. A REASONABLE QUESTION.
ASK HER QUESTION, ZACHARY.
WHAT KILLED THE VAMPIRE?
DON'T UNDERSTAND.
WHAT SORT OF CREATURE TORE OUT THE HEART? WAS IT A HUMAN?
NO.
WAS IT ANOTHER VAMPIRE?
NO.
THEN WHAT KILLED THE VAMPIRE?
THIS WAS WHY ZOMBIES DIDN'T DO WELL IN COURT. LAWYERS ACCUSED YOU OF LEADING THE WITNESS.
WHICH WAS TRUE, BUT IT DIDN'T MEAN THE ZOMBIE WAS LYING.
CAN'T!
WHAT DO YOU MEAN, CAN'T?
YOU... WILL... ANSWER... ME!
CAN'T!
ANSWER ME, DAMN YOU!
STOP IT. STOP IT!

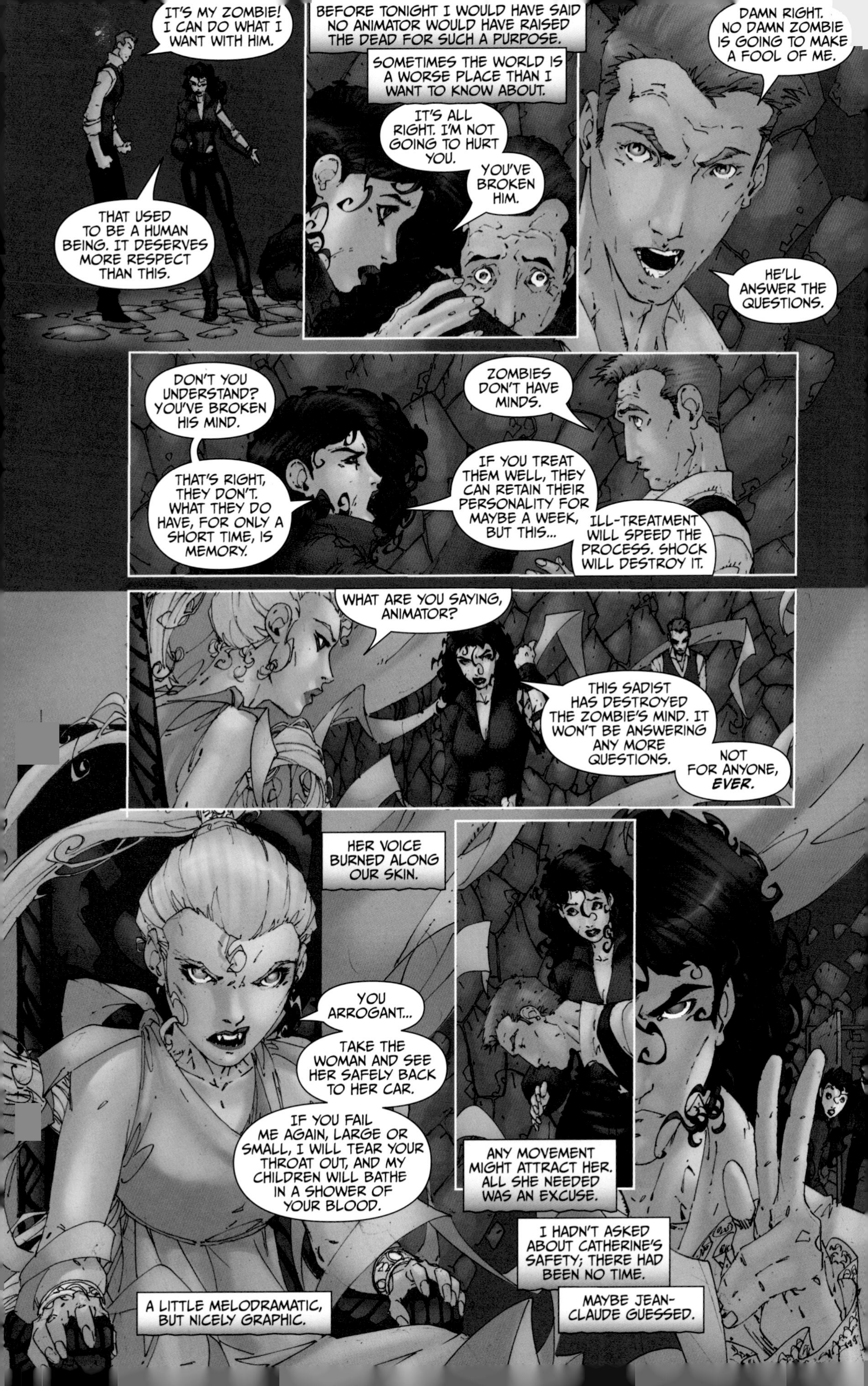
IT'S MY ZOMBIE! I CAN DO WHAT I WANT WITH HIM.
THAT USED TO BE A HUMAN BEING. IT DESERVES MORE RESPECT THAN THIS.
BEFORE TONIGHT I WOULD HAVE SAID NO ANIMATOR WOULD HAVE RAISED THE DEAD FOR SUCH A PURPOSE.
SOMETIMES THE WORLD IS A WORSE PLACE THAN I WANT TO KNOW ABOUT.
IT'S ALL RIGHT. I'M NOT GOING TO HURT YOU.
YOU'VE BROKEN HIM.
DAMN RIGHT. NO DAMN ZOMBIE IS GOING TO MAKE A FOOL OF ME.
HE'LL ANSWER THE QUESTIONS.
DON'T YOU UNDERSTAND? YOU'VE BROKEN HIS MIND.
ZOMBIES DON'T HAVE MINDS.
THAT'S RIGHT, THEY DON'T. WHAT THEY DO HAVE, FOR ONLY A SHORT TIME, IS MEMORY.
IF YOU TREAT THEM WELL, THEY CAN RETAIN THEIR PERSONALITY FOR MAYBE A WEEK, BUT THIS...
ILL-TREATMENT WILL SPEED THE PROCESS. SHOCK WILL DESTROY IT.
WHAT ARE YOU SAYING, ANIMATOR?
THIS SADIST HAS DESTROYED THE ZOMBIE'S MIND. IT WON'T BE ANSWERING ANY MORE QUESTIONS.
NOT FOR ANYONE, *EVER.*
HER VOICE BURNED ALONG OUR SKIN.
YOU ARROGANT...
TAKE THE WOMAN AND SEE HER SAFELY BACK TO HER CAR.
IF YOU FAIL ME AGAIN, LARGE OR SMALL, I WILL TEAR YOUR THROAT OUT, AND MY CHILDREN WILL BATHE IN A SHOWER OF YOUR BLOOD.
A LITTLE MELODRAMATIC, BUT NICELY GRAPHIC.
ANY MOVEMENT MIGHT ATTRACT HER. ALL SHE NEEDED WAS AN EXCUSE.
I HADN'T ASKED ABOUT CATHERINE'S SAFETY; THERE HAD BEEN NO TIME.
MAYBE JEAN-CLAUDE GUESSED.

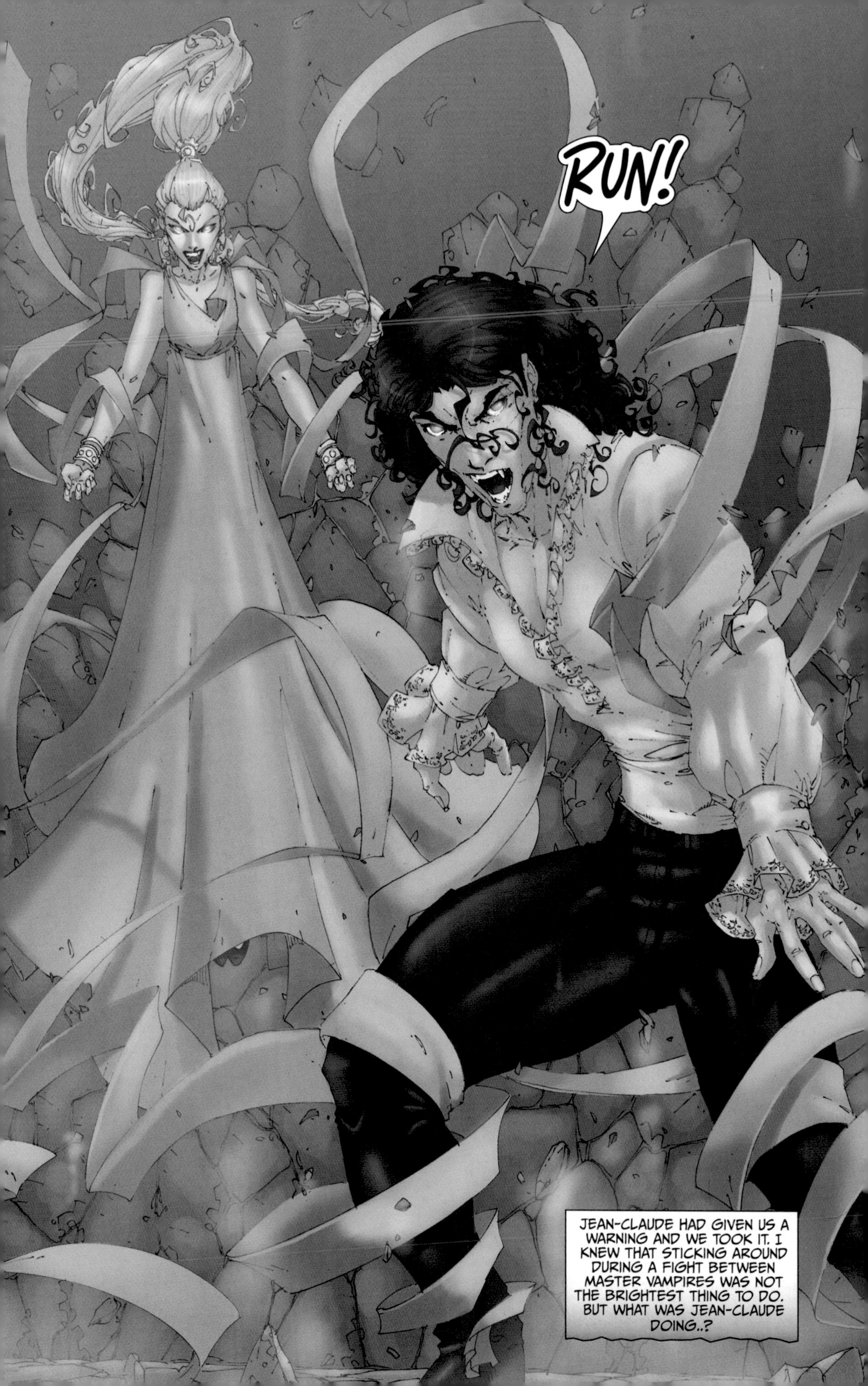
RUN!
JEAN-CLAUDE HAD GIVEN US A WARNING AND WE TOOK IT. I KNEW THAT STICKING AROUND DURING A FIGHT BETWEEN MASTER VAMPIRES WAS NOT THE BRIGHTEST THING TO DO. BUT WHAT WAS JEAN-CLAUDE DOING..?

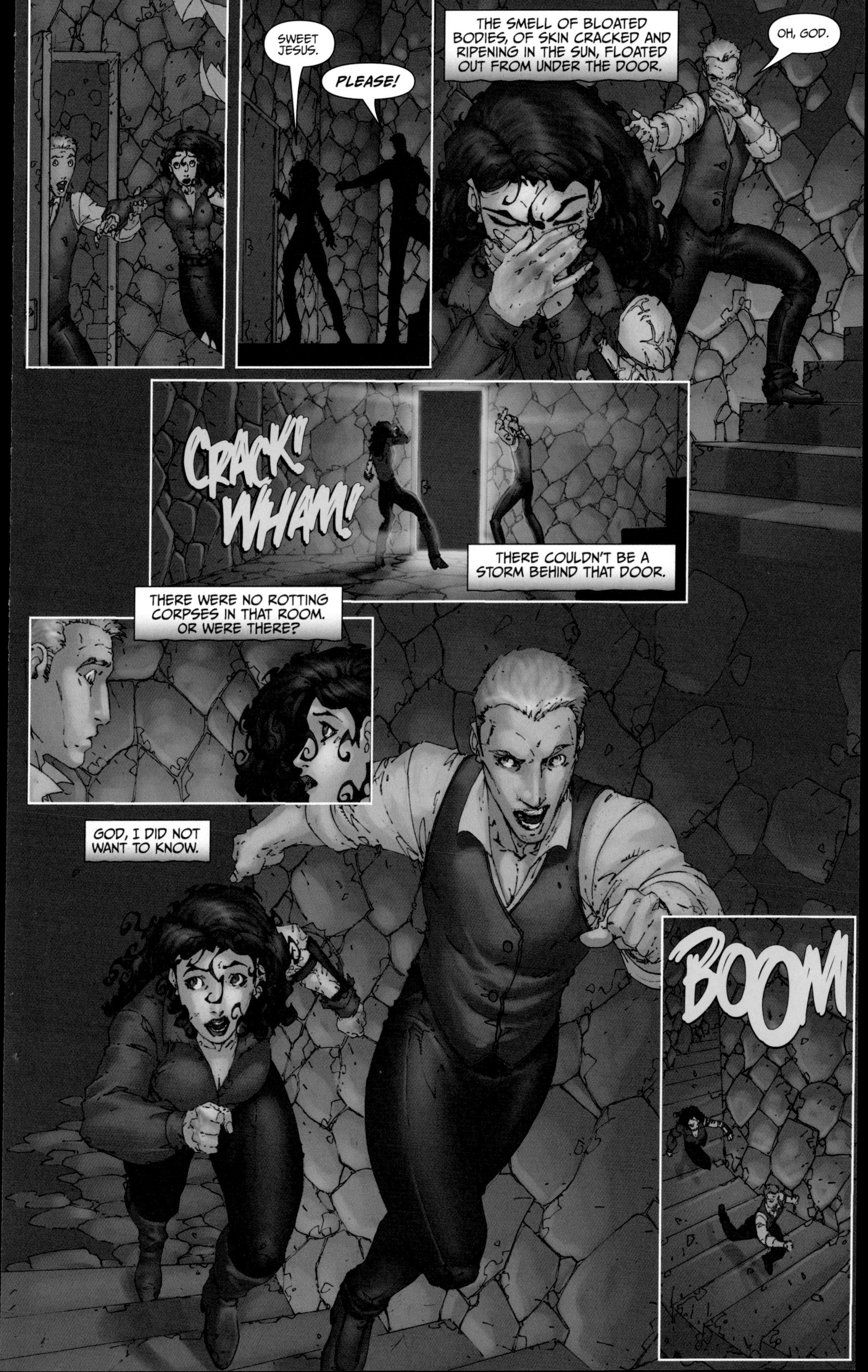
SWEET JESUS.
PLEASE!
THE SMELL OF BLOATED BODIES, OF SKIN CRACKED AND RIPENING IN THE SUN, FLOATED OUT FROM UNDER THE DOOR.
OH, GOD.
CRACK!
WHAM!
THERE COULDN'T BE A STORM BEHIND THAT DOOR.
THERE WERE NO ROTTING CORPSES IN THAT ROOM. OR WERE THERE?
GOD, I DID NOT WANT TO KNOW.
BOOM

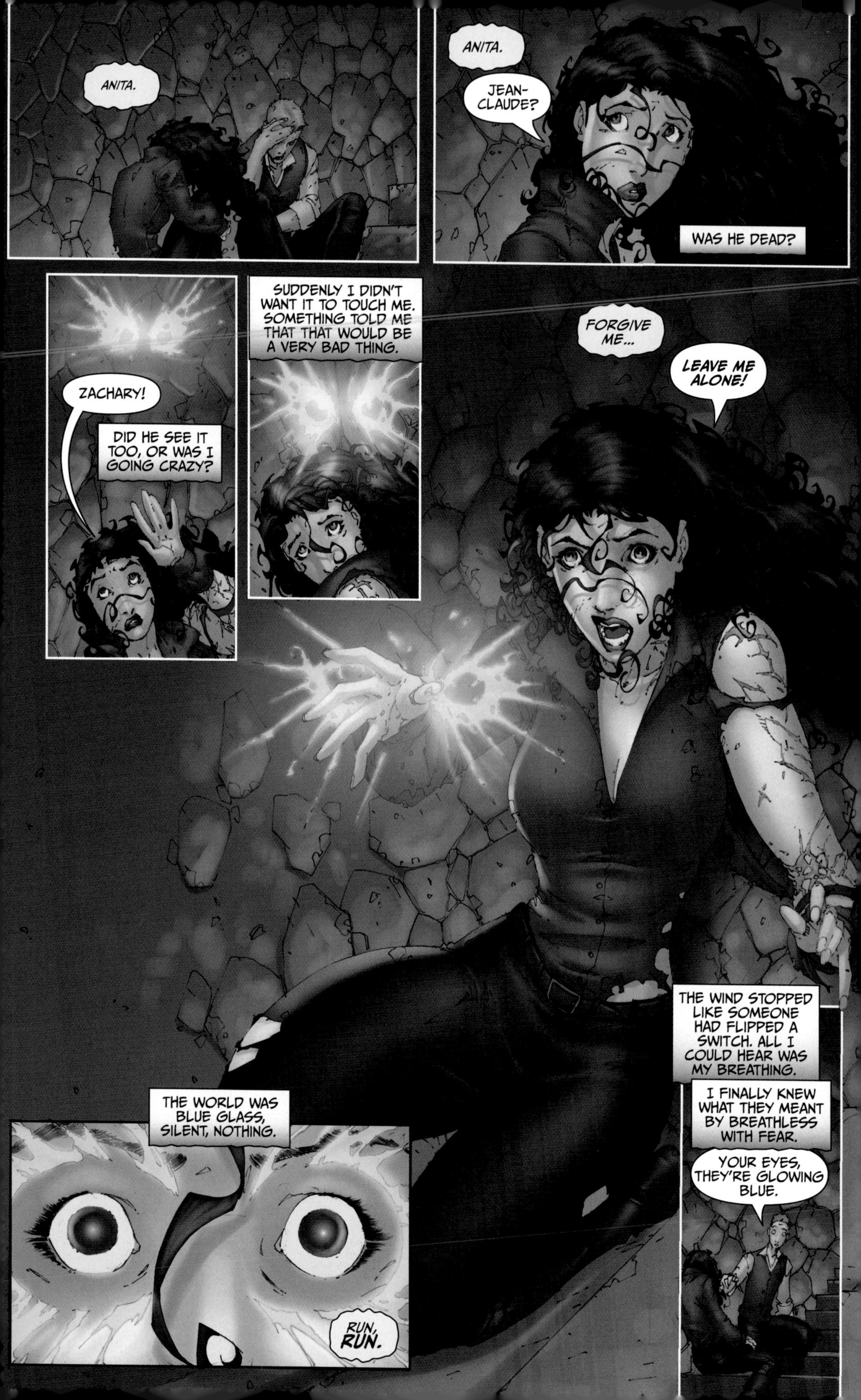
ANITA.
ANITA.
JEAN-CLAUDE?
WAS HE DEAD?
ZACHARY!
DID HE SEE IT TOO, OR WAS I GOING CRAZY?
SUDDENLY I DIDN'T WANT IT TO TOUCH ME. SOMETHING TOLD ME THAT THAT WOULD BE A VERY BAD THING.
FORGIVE ME...
LEAVE ME ALONE!
THE WIND STOPPED LIKE SOMEONE HAD FLIPPED A SWITCH. ALL I COULD HEAR WAS MY BREATHING.
I FINALLY KNEW WHAT THEY MEANT BY BREATHLESS WITH FEAR.
YOUR EYES, THEY'RE GLOWING BLUE.
THE WORLD WAS BLUE GLASS, SILENT, NOTHING.
RUN, RUN.

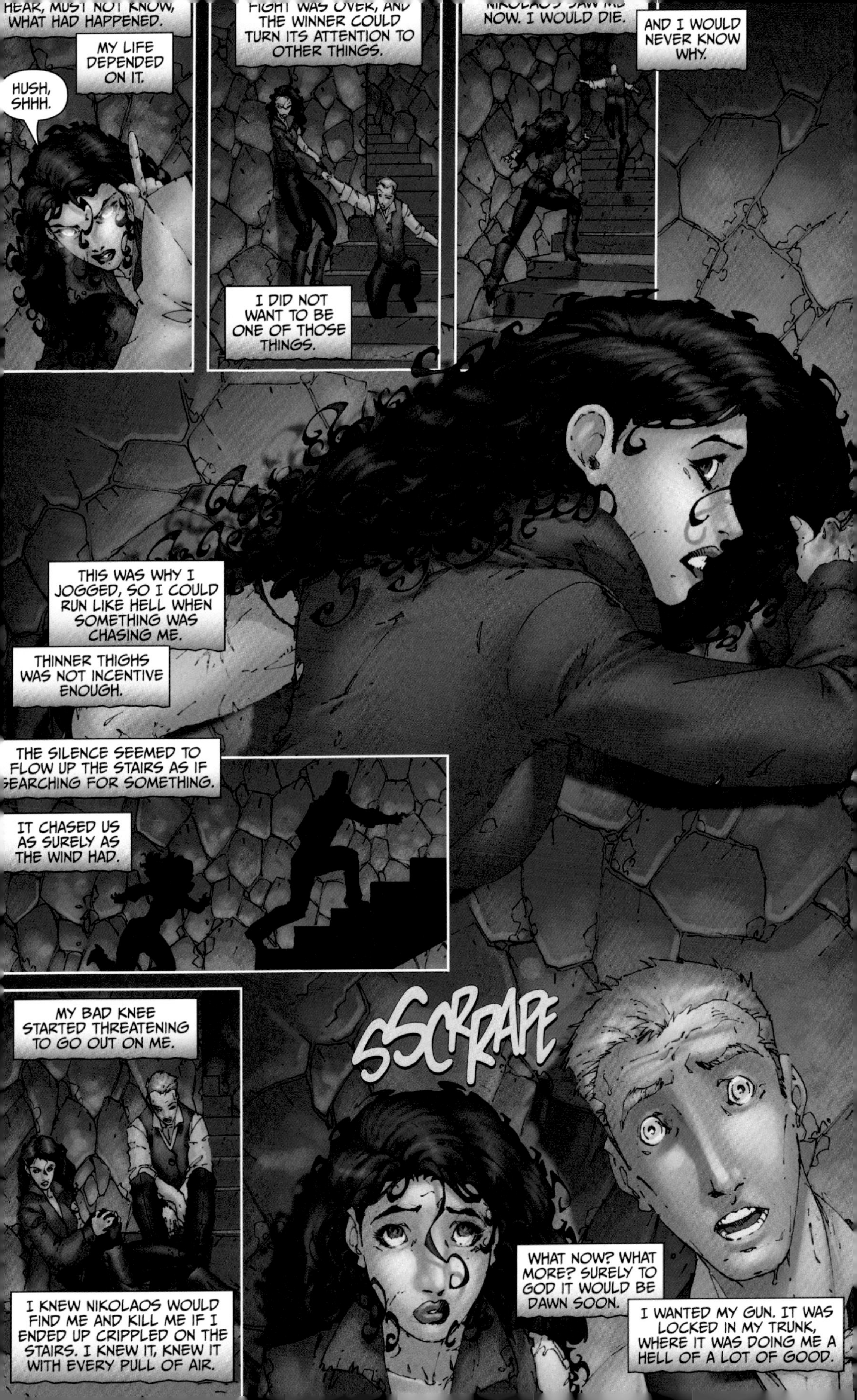

HEAR, MUST NOT KNOW, WHAT HAD HAPPENED.
MY LIFE DEPENDED ON IT.
HUSH, SHHH.
FIGHT WAS OVER, AND THE WINNER COULD TURN ITS ATTENTION TO OTHER THINGS.
I DID NOT WANT TO BE ONE OF THOSE THINGS.
NIKOLAOS SAW ME NOW. I WOULD DIE.
AND I WOULD NEVER KNOW WHY.
THIS WAS WHY I JOGGED, SO I COULD RUN LIKE HELL WHEN SOMETHING WAS CHASING ME.
THINNER THIGHS WAS NOT INCENTIVE ENOUGH.
THE SILENCE SEEMED TO FLOW UP THE STAIRS AS IF SEARCHING FOR SOMETHING.
IT CHASED US AS SURELY AS THE WIND HAD.
MY BAD KNEE STARTED THREATENING TO GO OUT ON ME.
I KNEW NIKOLAOS WOULD FIND ME AND KILL ME IF I ENDED UP CRIPPLED ON THE STAIRS. I KNEW IT, KNEW IT WITH EVERY PULL OF AIR.
SSCRAPE
WHAT NOW? WHAT MORE? SURELY TO GOD IT WOULD BE DAWN SOON.
I WANTED MY GUN. IT WAS LOCKED IN MY TRUNK, WHERE IT WAS DOING ME A HELL OF A LOT OF GOOD.

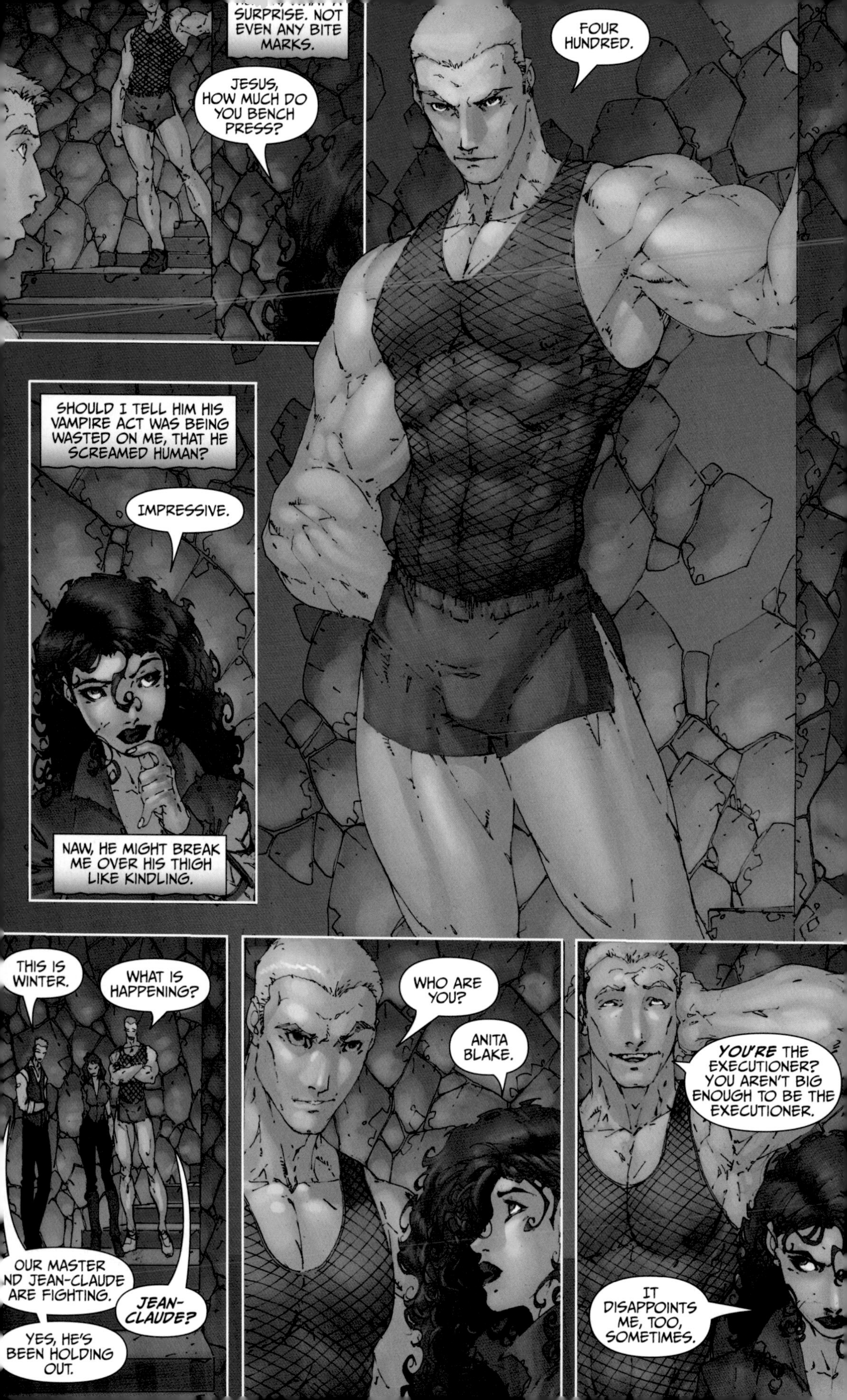

SURPRISE. NOT EVEN ANY BITE MARKS.
JESUS, HOW MUCH DO YOU BENCH PRESS?
FOUR HUNDRED.
SHOULD I TELL HIM HIS VAMPIRE ACT WAS BEING WASTED ON ME, THAT HE SCREAMED HUMAN?
IMPRESSIVE.
NAW, HE MIGHT BREAK ME OVER HIS THIGH LIKE KINDLING.
THIS IS WINTER.
WHAT IS HAPPENING?
OUR MASTER ND JEAN-CLAUDE ARE FIGHTING.
JEAN-CLAUDE?
YES, HE'S BEEN HOLDING OUT.
WHO ARE YOU?
ANITA BLAKE.
YOU'RE THE EXECUTIONER? YOU AREN'T BIG ENOUGH TO BE THE EXECUTIONER.
IT DISAPPOINTS ME, TOO, SOMETIMES.

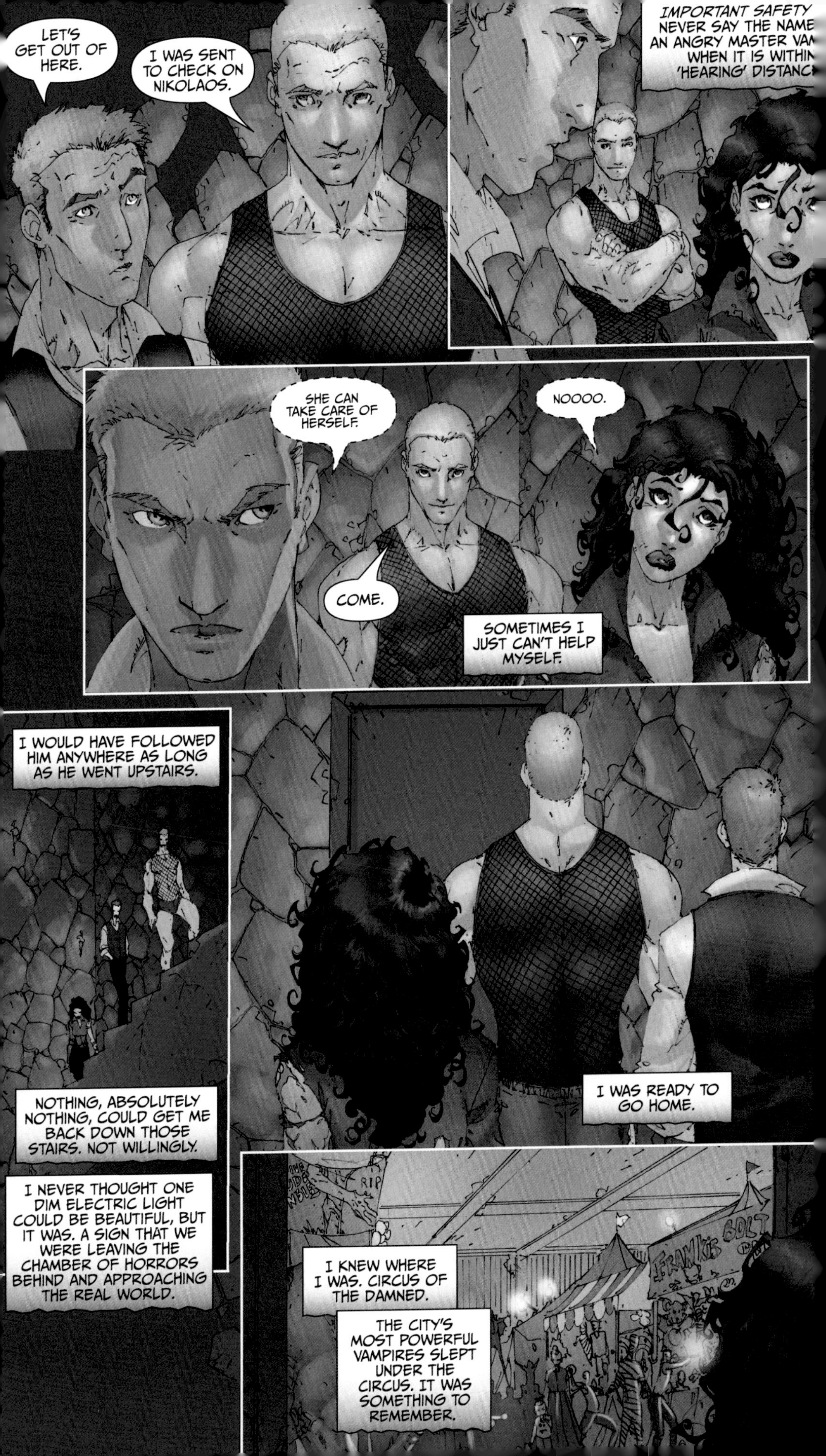
LET'S GET OUT OF HERE.
I WAS SENT TO CHECK ON NIKOLAOS.
IMPORTANT SAFETY
NEVER SAY THE NAME
AN ANGRY MASTER VAM
WHEN IT IS WITHIN
'HEARING' DISTANC
SHE CAN TAKE CARE OF HERSELF.
NOOOO.
COME.
SOMETIMES I JUST CAN'T HELP MYSELF.
I WOULD HAVE FOLLOWED HIM ANYWHERE AS LONG AS HE WENT UPSTAIRS.
NOTHING, ABSOLUTELY NOTHING, COULD GET ME BACK DOWN THOSE STAIRS. NOT WILLINGLY.
I NEVER THOUGHT ONE DIM ELECTRIC LIGHT COULD BE BEAUTIFUL, BUT IT WAS. A SIGN THAT WE WERE LEAVING THE CHAMBER OF HORRORS BEHIND AND APPROACHING THE REAL WORLD.
I WAS READY TO GO HOME.
I KNEW WHERE I WAS. CIRCUS OF THE DAMNED.
THE CITY'S MOST POWERFUL VAMPIRES SLEPT UNDER THE CIRCUS. IT WAS SOMETHING TO REMEMBER.

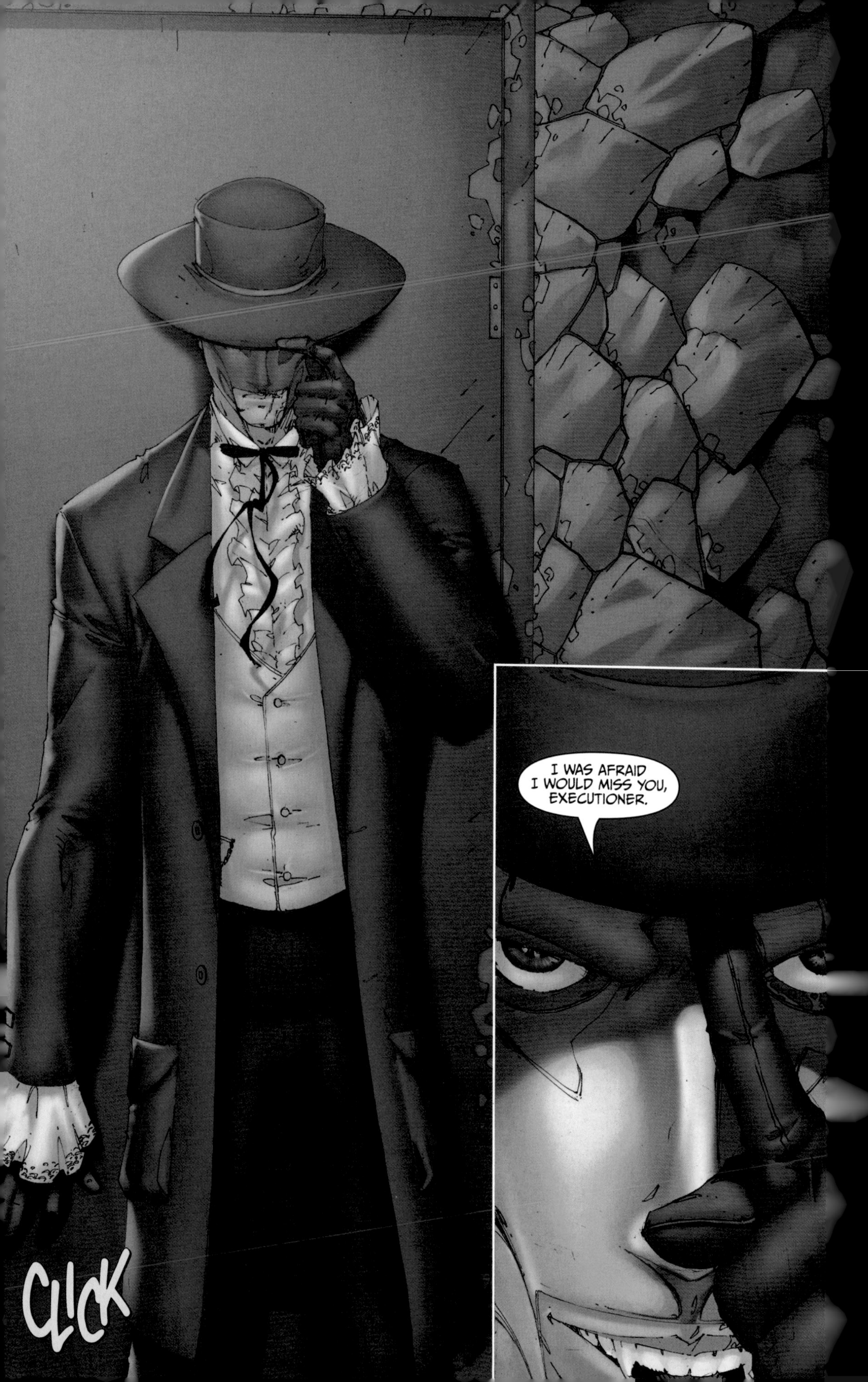
CLICK
I WAS AFRAID I WOULD MISS YOU, EXECUTIONER.

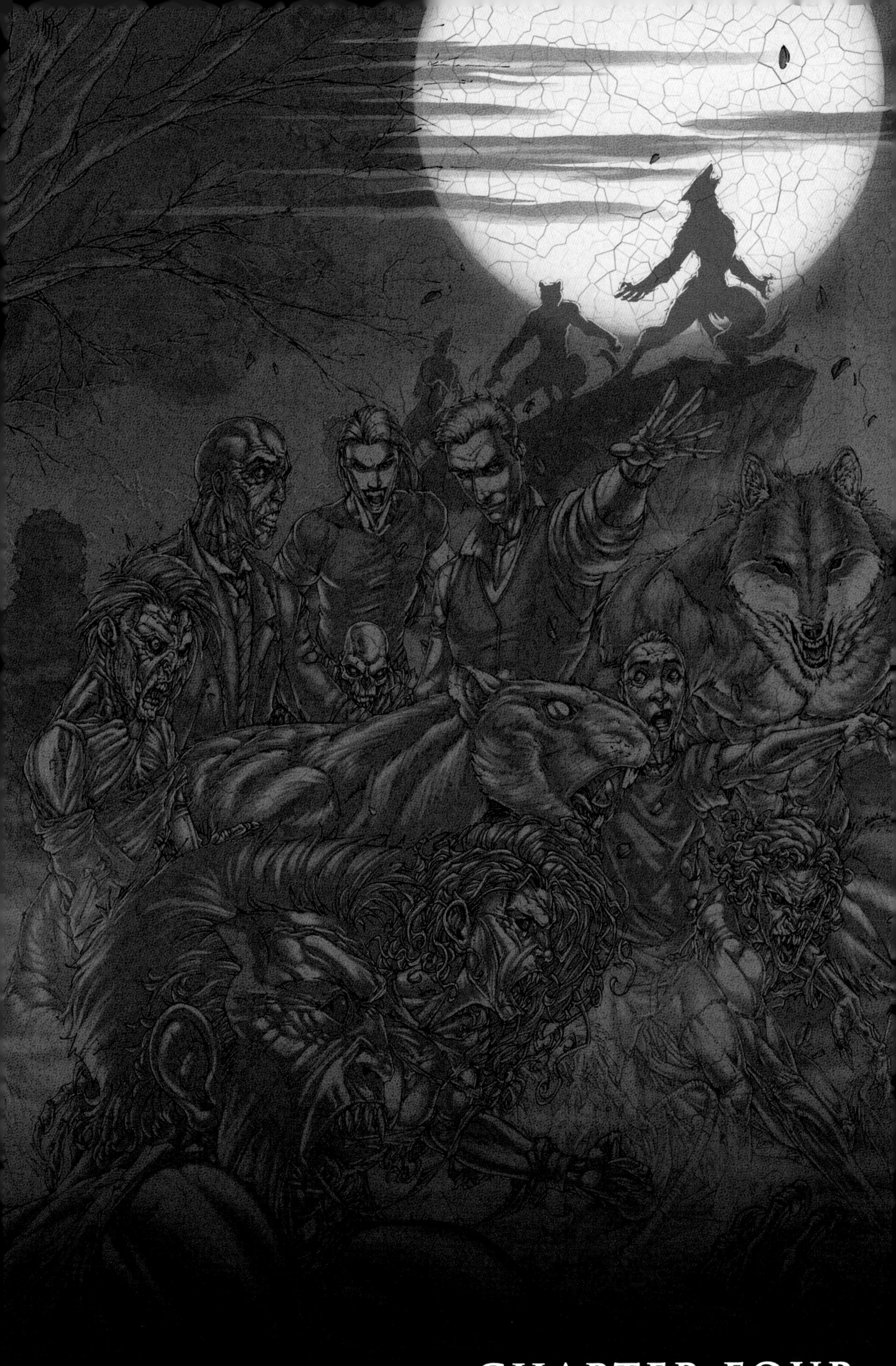

CHAPTER FOUR

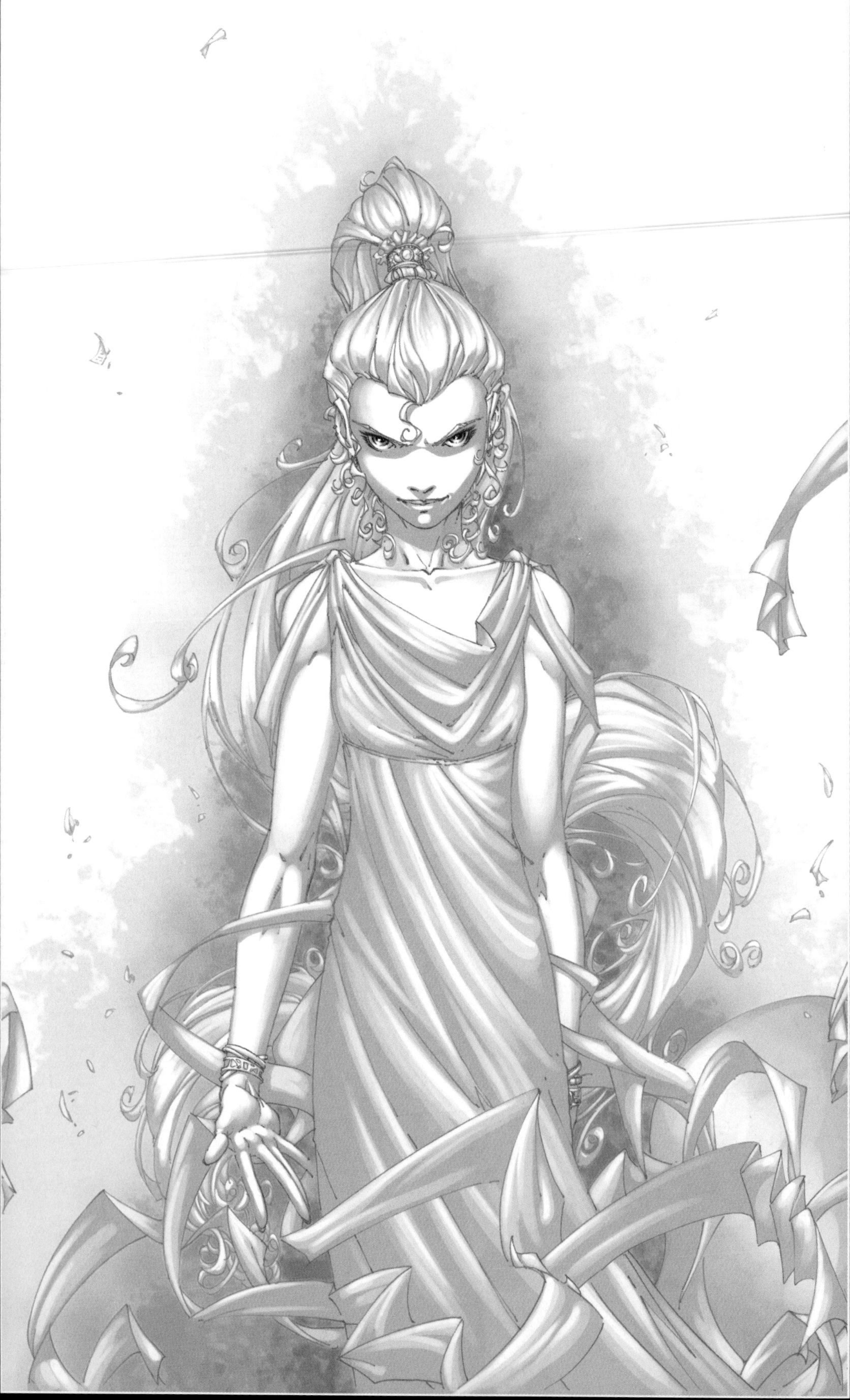

COVER BY: BRETT BOOTH & JESS RUFFNER-BOOTH

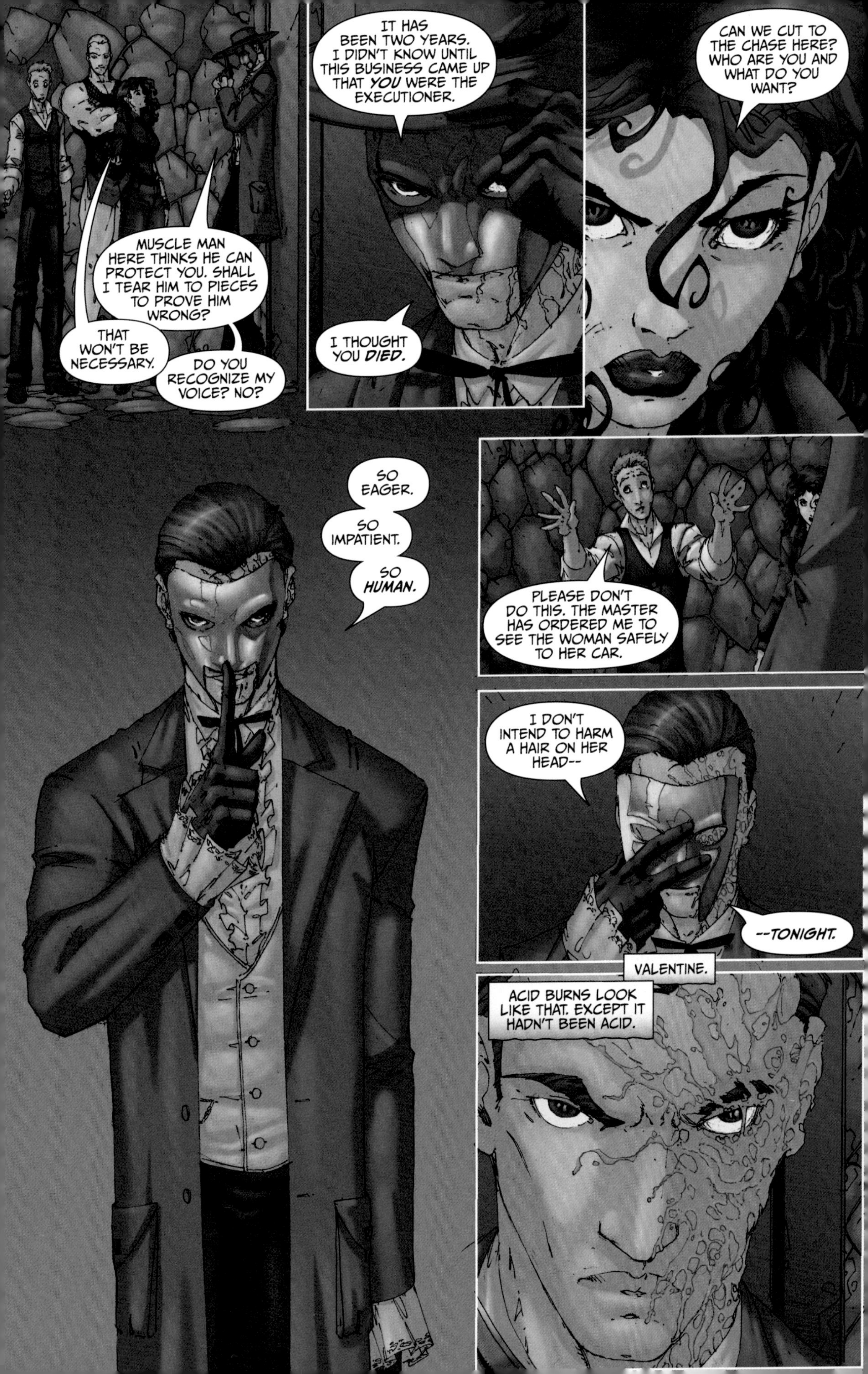

MUSCLE MAN HERE THINKS HE CAN PROTECT YOU. SHALL I TEAR HIM TO PIECES TO PROVE HIM WRONG?
THAT WON'T BE NECESSARY.
DO YOU RECOGNIZE MY VOICE? NO?
IT HAS BEEN TWO YEARS. I DIDN'T KNOW UNTIL THIS BUSINESS CAME UP THAT *YOU* WERE THE EXECUTIONER.
I THOUGHT YOU *DIED.*
CAN WE CUT TO THE CHASE HERE? WHO ARE YOU AND WHAT DO YOU WANT?
SO EAGER.
SO IMPATIENT.
SO *HUMAN.*
PLEASE DON'T DO THIS. THE MASTER HAS ORDERED ME TO SEE THE WOMAN SAFELY TO HER CAR.
I DON'T INTEND TO HARM A HAIR ON HER HEAD--
--TONIGHT.
VALENTINE.
ACID BURNS LOOK LIKE THAT. EXCEPT IT HADN'T BEEN ACID.

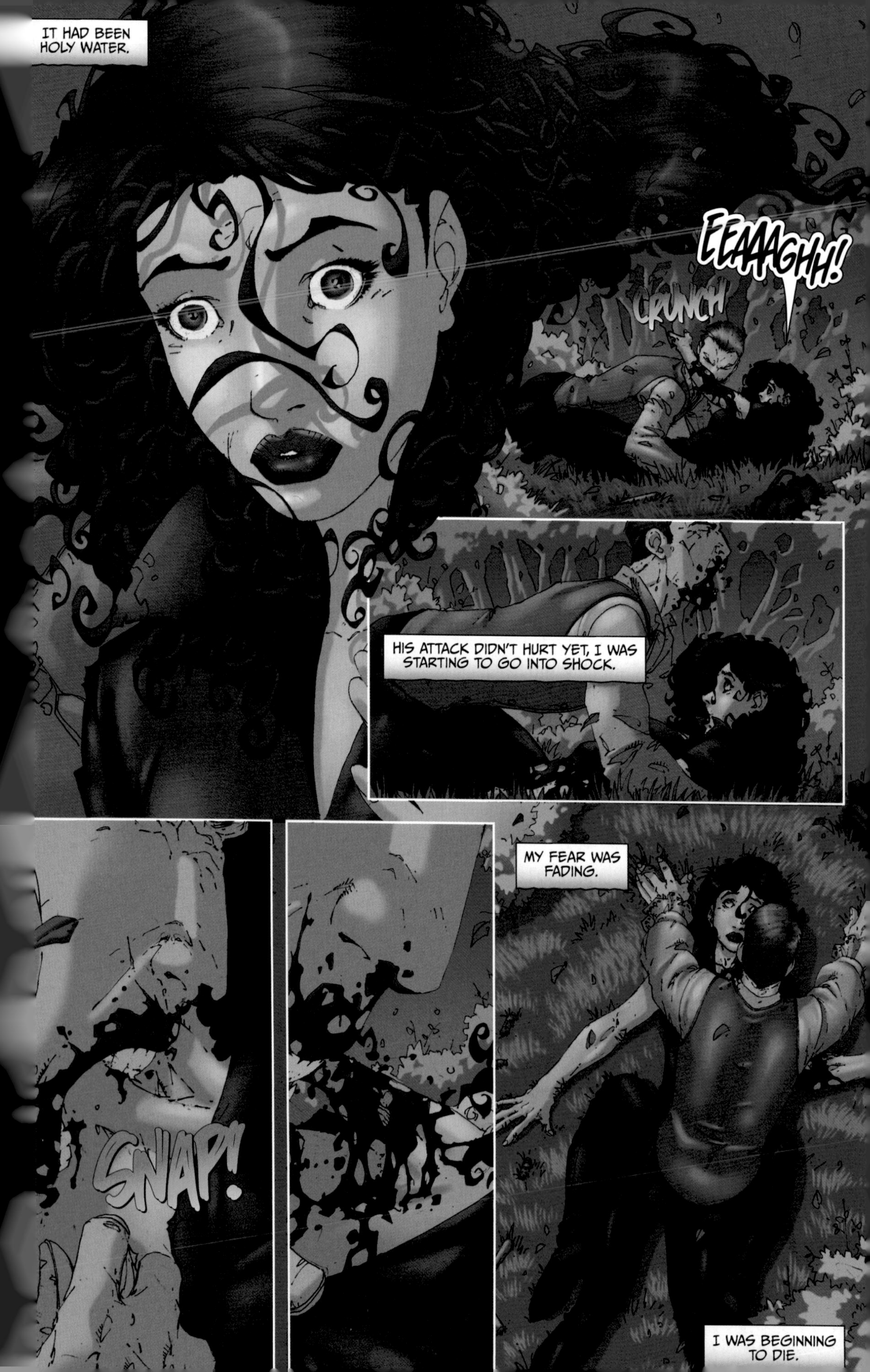
IT HAD BEEN HOLY WATER.
EEAAAGHH!
CRUNCH
HIS ATTACK DIDN'T HURT YET, I WAS STARTING TO GO INTO SHOCK.
SNAP!
MY FEAR WAS FADING.
I WAS BEGINNING TO DIE.

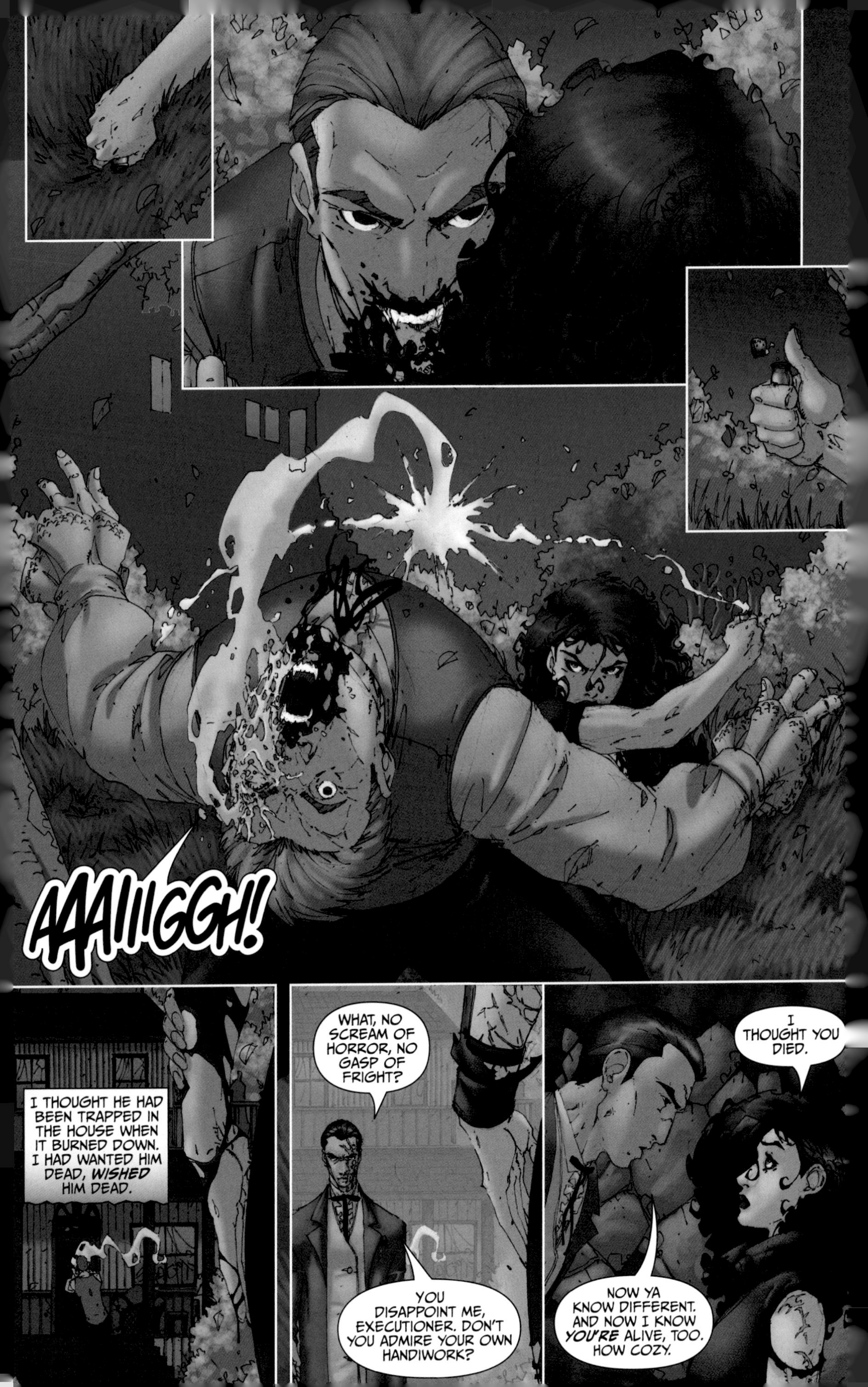
AAAIIIGGH!
I THOUGHT HE HAD BEEN TRAPPED IN THE HOUSE WHEN IT BURNED DOWN. I HAD WANTED HIM DEAD, *WISHED* HIM DEAD.
WHAT, NO SCREAM OF HORROR, NO GASP OF FRIGHT?
YOU DISAPPOINT ME, EXECUTIONER. DON'T YOU ADMIRE YOUR OWN HANDIWORK?
I THOUGHT YOU DIED.
NOW YA KNOW DIFFERENT. AND NOW I KNOW *YOU'RE* ALIVE, TOO. HOW COZY.

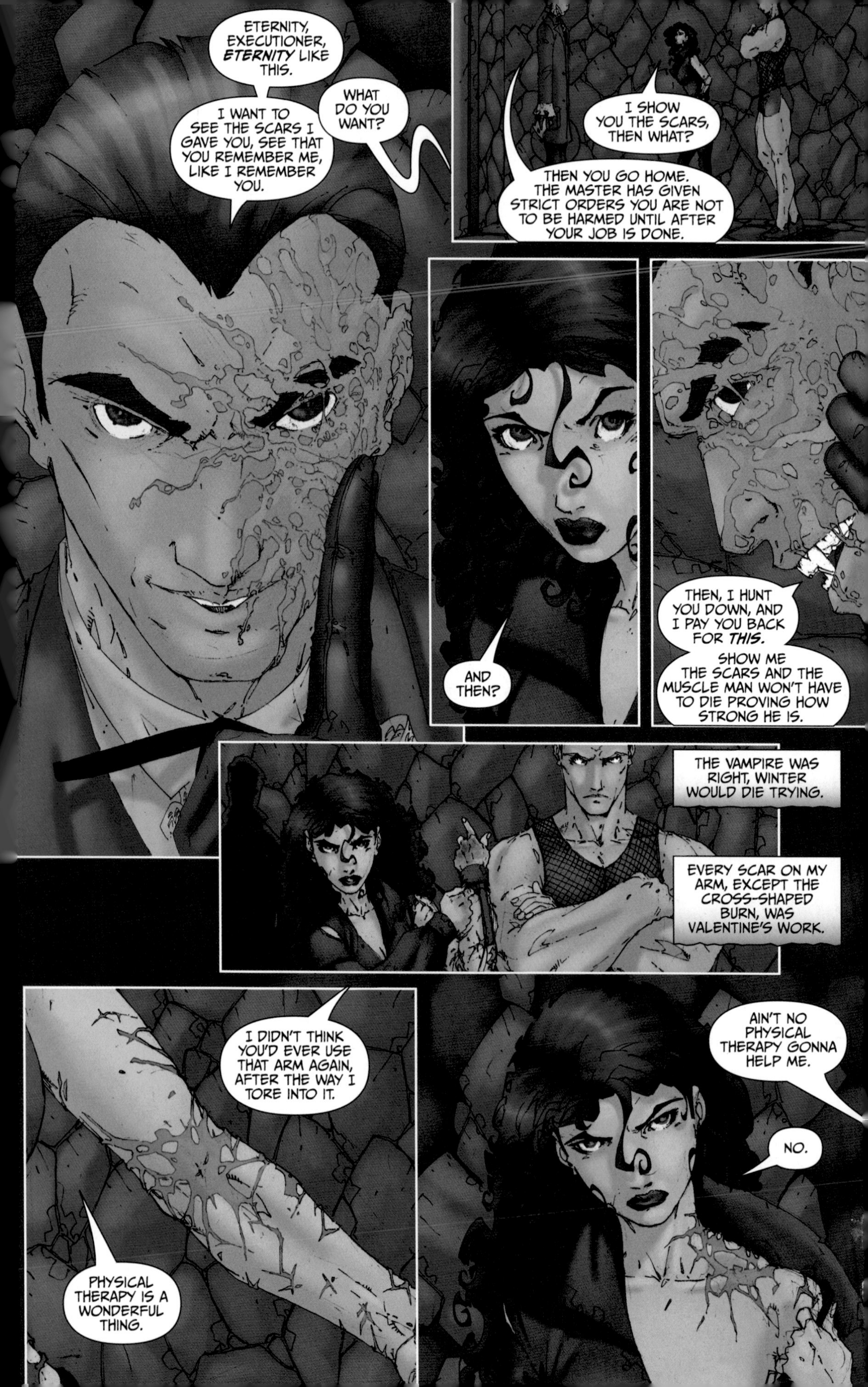
ETERNITY, EXECUTIONER, ETERNITY LIKE THIS.
I WANT TO SEE THE SCARS I GAVE YOU, SEE THAT YOU REMEMBER ME, LIKE I REMEMBER YOU.
WHAT DO YOU WANT?
I SHOW YOU THE SCARS, THEN WHAT?
THEN YOU GO HOME. THE MASTER HAS GIVEN STRICT ORDERS YOU ARE NOT TO BE HARMED UNTIL AFTER YOUR JOB IS DONE.
AND THEN?
THEN, I HUNT YOU DOWN, AND I PAY YOU BACK FOR THIS.
SHOW ME THE SCARS AND THE MUSCLE MAN WON'T HAVE TO DIE PROVING HOW STRONG HE IS.
THE VAMPIRE WAS RIGHT, WINTER WOULD DIE TRYING.
EVERY SCAR ON MY ARM, EXCEPT THE CROSS-SHAPED BURN, WAS VALENTINE'S WORK.
I DIDN'T THINK YOU'D EVER USE THAT ARM AGAIN, AFTER THE WAY I TORE INTO IT.
PHYSICAL THERAPY IS A WONDERFUL THING.
AIN'T NO PHYSICAL THERAPY GONNA HELP ME.
NO.

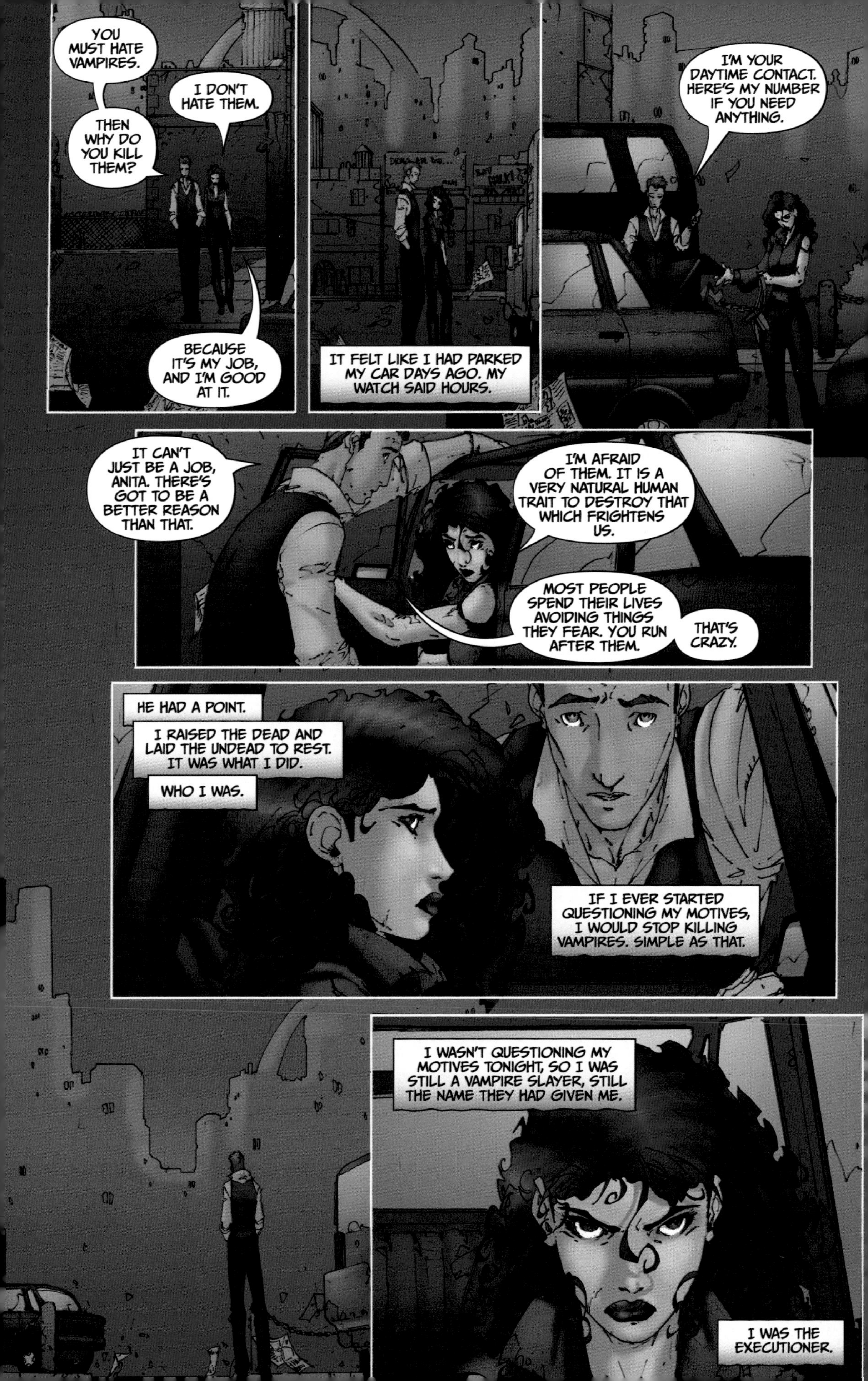
YOU MUST HATE VAMPIRES.
I DON'T HATE THEM.
THEN WHY DO YOU KILL THEM?
BECAUSE IT'S MY JOB, AND I'M GOOD AT IT.
IT FELT LIKE I HAD PARKED MY CAR DAYS AGO. MY WATCH SAID HOURS.
I'M YOUR DAYTIME CONTACT. HERE'S MY NUMBER IF YOU NEED ANYTHING.
IT CAN'T JUST BE A JOB, ANITA. THERE'S GOT TO BE A BETTER REASON THAN THAT.
I'M AFRAID OF THEM. IT IS A VERY NATURAL HUMAN TRAIT TO DESTROY THAT WHICH FRIGHTENS US.
MOST PEOPLE SPEND THEIR LIVES AVOIDING THINGS THEY FEAR. YOU RUN AFTER THEM.
THAT'S CRAZY.
HE HAD A POINT.
I RAISED THE DEAD AND LAID THE UNDEAD TO REST. IT WAS WHAT I DID.
WHO I WAS.
IF I EVER STARTED QUESTIONING MY MOTIVES, I WOULD STOP KILLING VAMPIRES. SIMPLE AS THAT.
I WASN'T QUESTIONING MY MOTIVES TONIGHT, SO I WAS STILL A VAMPIRE SLAYER, STILL THE NAME THEY HAD GIVEN ME.
I WAS THE EXECUTIONER.

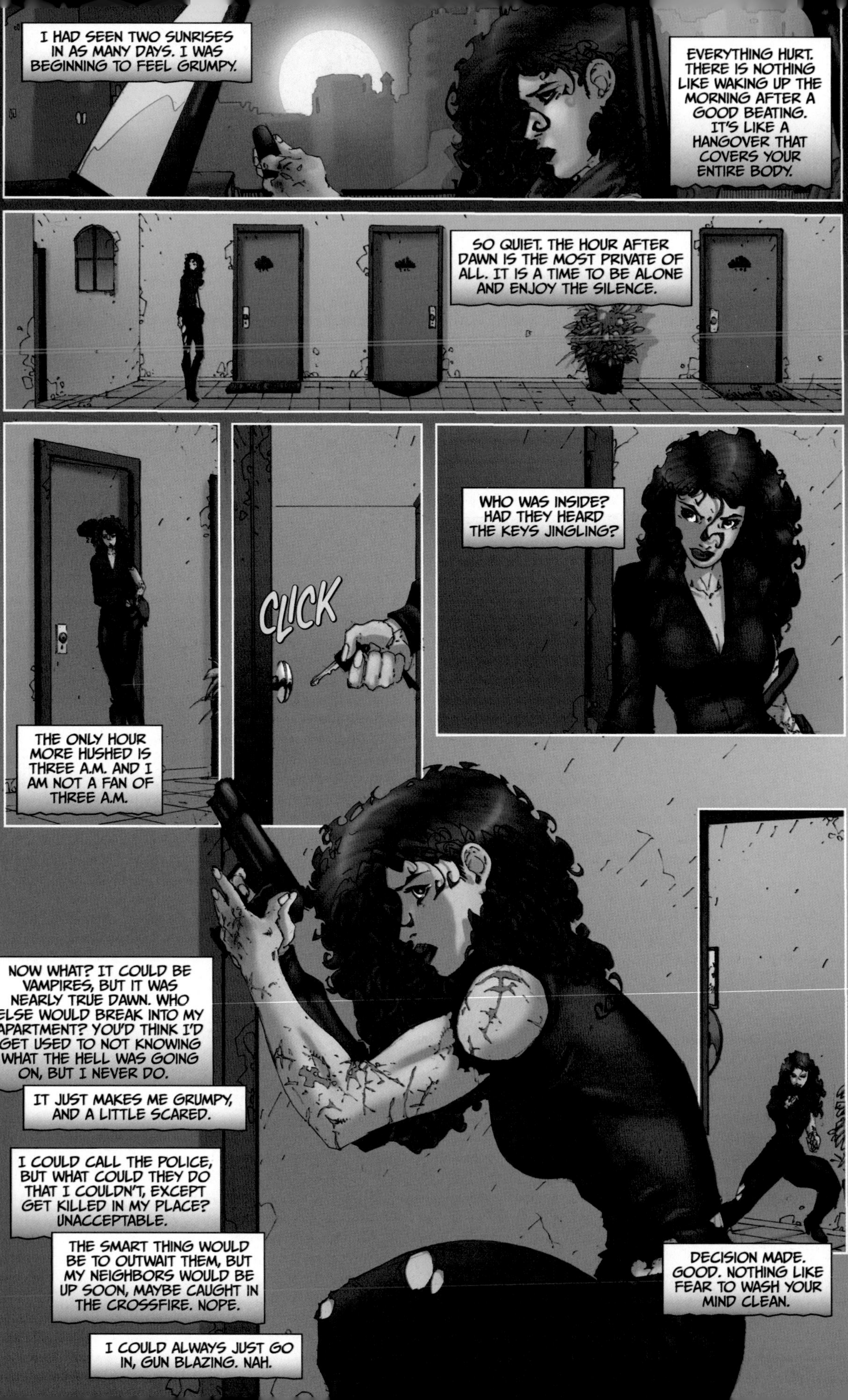
I HAD SEEN TWO SUNRISES IN AS MANY DAYS. I WAS BEGINNING TO FEEL GRUMPY.
EVERYTHING HURT. THERE IS NOTHING LIKE WAKING UP THE MORNING AFTER A GOOD BEATING. IT'S LIKE A HANGOVER THAT COVERS YOUR ENTIRE BODY.
SO QUIET. THE HOUR AFTER DAWN IS THE MOST PRIVATE OF ALL. IT IS A TIME TO BE ALONE AND ENJOY THE SILENCE.
THE ONLY HOUR MORE HUSHED IS THREE A.M. AND I AM NOT A FAN OF THREE A.M.
CLICK
WHO WAS INSIDE? HAD THEY HEARD THE KEYS JINGLING?
NOW WHAT? IT COULD BE VAMPIRES, BUT IT WAS NEARLY TRUE DAWN. WHO ELSE WOULD BREAK INTO MY APARTMENT? YOU'D THINK I'D GET USED TO NOT KNOWING WHAT THE HELL WAS GOING ON, BUT I NEVER DO.
IT JUST MAKES ME GRUMPY, AND A LITTLE SCARED.
I COULD CALL THE POLICE, BUT WHAT COULD THEY DO THAT I COULDN'T, EXCEPT GET KILLED IN MY PLACE? UNACCEPTABLE.
THE SMART THING WOULD BE TO OUTWAIT THEM, BUT MY NEIGHBORS WOULD BE UP SOON, MAYBE CAUGHT IN THE CROSSFIRE. NOPE.
I COULD ALWAYS JUST GO IN, GUN BLAZING. NAH.
DECISION MADE. GOOD. NOTHING LIKE FEAR TO WASH YOUR MIND CLEAN.

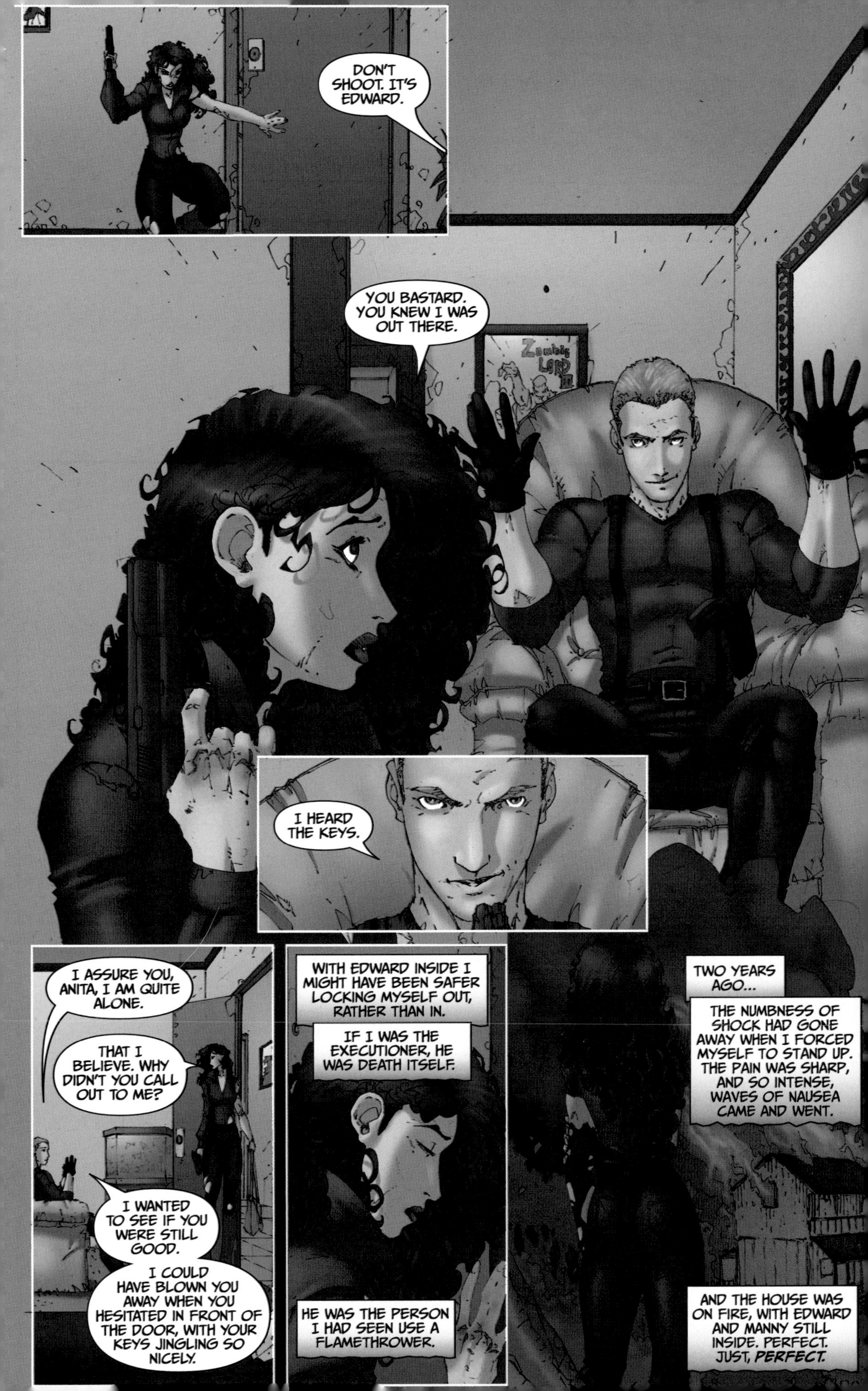
DON'T SHOOT. IT'S EDWARD.
YOU BASTARD. YOU KNEW I WAS OUT THERE.
I HEARD THE KEYS.
I ASSURE YOU, ANITA, I AM QUITE ALONE.
THAT I BELIEVE. WHY DIDN'T YOU CALL OUT TO ME?
I WANTED TO SEE IF YOU WERE STILL GOOD.
I COULD HAVE BLOWN YOU AWAY WHEN YOU HESITATED IN FRONT OF THE DOOR, WITH YOUR KEYS JINGLING SO NICELY.
WITH EDWARD INSIDE I MIGHT HAVE BEEN SAFER LOCKING MYSELF OUT, RATHER THAN IN.
IF I WAS THE EXECUTIONER, HE WAS DEATH ITSELF.
HE WAS THE PERSON I HAD SEEN USE A FLAMETHROWER.
TWO YEARS AGO...
THE NUMBNESS OF SHOCK HAD GONE AWAY WHEN I FORCED MYSELF TO STAND UP. THE PAIN WAS SHARP, AND SO INTENSE, WAVES OF NAUSEA CAME AND WENT.
AND THE HOUSE WAS ON FIRE, WITH EDWARD AND MANNY STILL INSIDE. PERFECT. JUST, *PERFECT.*

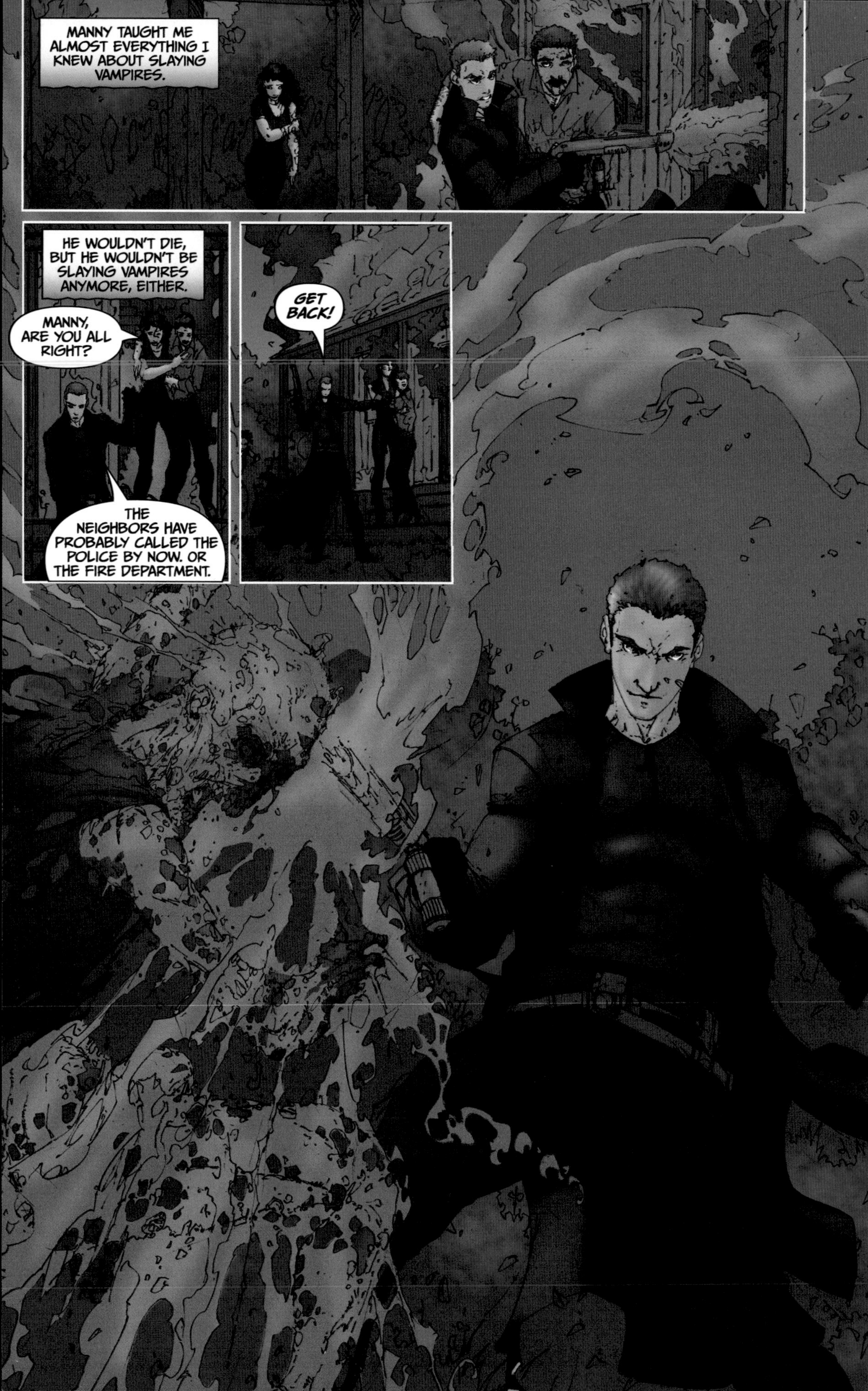
MANNY TAUGHT ME ALMOST EVERYTHING I KNEW ABOUT SLAYING VAMPIRES.
HE WOULDN'T DIE, BUT HE WOULDN'T BE SLAYING VAMPIRES ANYMORE, EITHER.
MANNY, ARE YOU ALL RIGHT?
THE NEIGHBORS HAVE PROBABLY CALLED THE POLICE BY NOW. OR THE FIRE DEPARTMENT.
GET BACK!

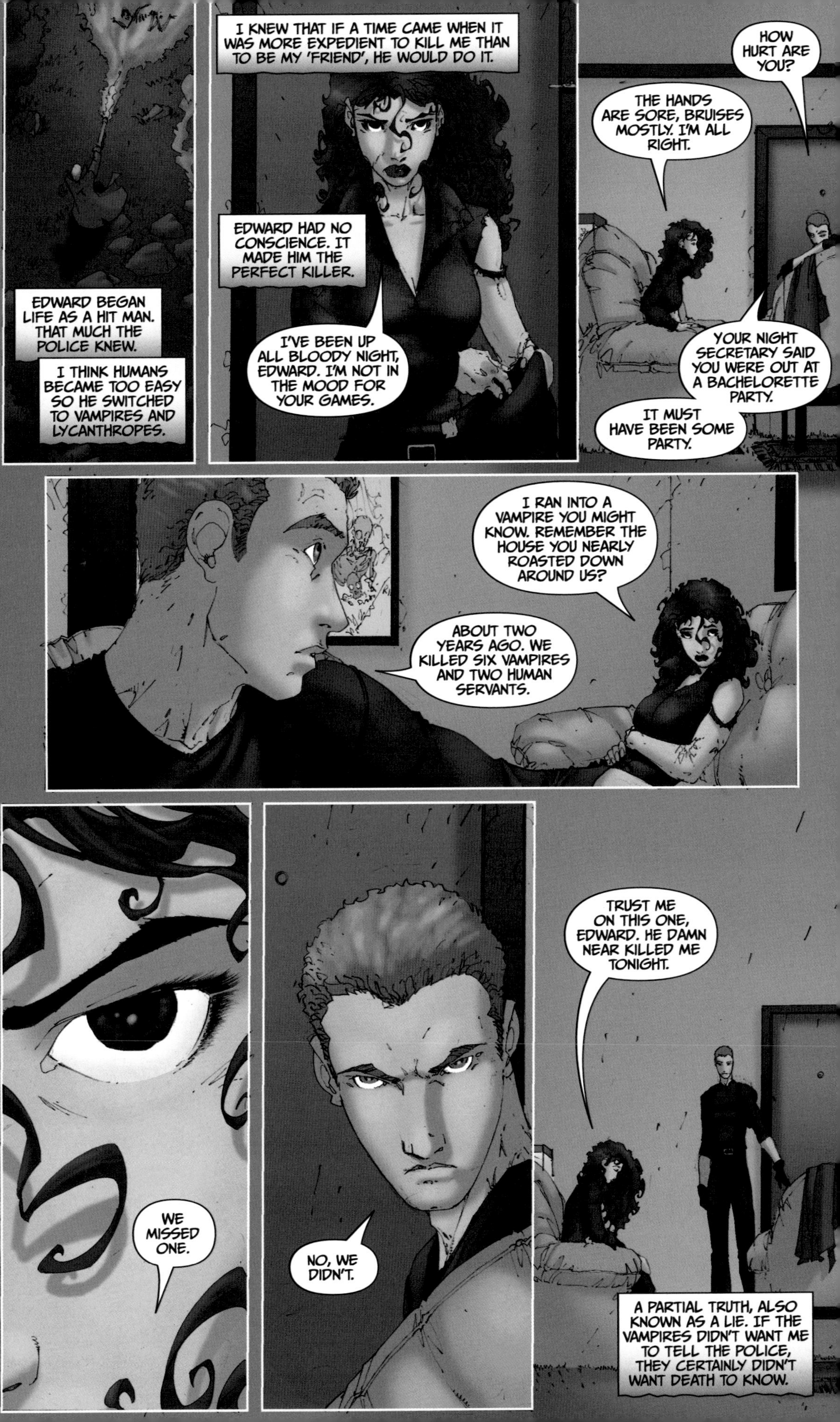
EDWARD BEGAN LIFE AS A HIT MAN. THAT MUCH THE POLICE KNEW.
I THINK HUMANS BECAME TOO EASY SO HE SWITCHED TO VAMPIRES AND LYCANTHROPES.
I KNEW THAT IF A TIME CAME WHEN IT WAS MORE EXPEDIENT TO KILL ME THAN TO BE MY 'FRIEND', HE WOULD DO IT.
EDWARD HAD NO CONSCIENCE. IT MADE HIM THE PERFECT KILLER.
I'VE BEEN UP ALL BLOODY NIGHT, EDWARD. I'M NOT IN THE MOOD FOR YOUR GAMES.
HOW HURT ARE YOU?
THE HANDS ARE SORE, BRUISES MOSTLY. I'M ALL RIGHT.
YOUR NIGHT SECRETARY SAID YOU WERE OUT AT A BACHELORETTE PARTY.
IT MUST HAVE BEEN SOME PARTY.
I RAN INTO A VAMPIRE YOU MIGHT KNOW. REMEMBER THE HOUSE YOU NEARLY ROASTED DOWN AROUND US?
ABOUT TWO YEARS AGO. WE KILLED SIX VAMPIRES AND TWO HUMAN SERVANTS.
WE MISSED ONE.
NO, WE DIDN'T.
TRUST ME ON THIS ONE, EDWARD. HE DAMN NEAR KILLED ME TONIGHT.
A PARTIAL TRUTH, ALSO KNOWN AS A LIE. IF THE VAMPIRES DIDN'T WANT ME TO TELL THE POLICE, THEY CERTAINLY DIDN'T WANT DEATH TO KNOW.

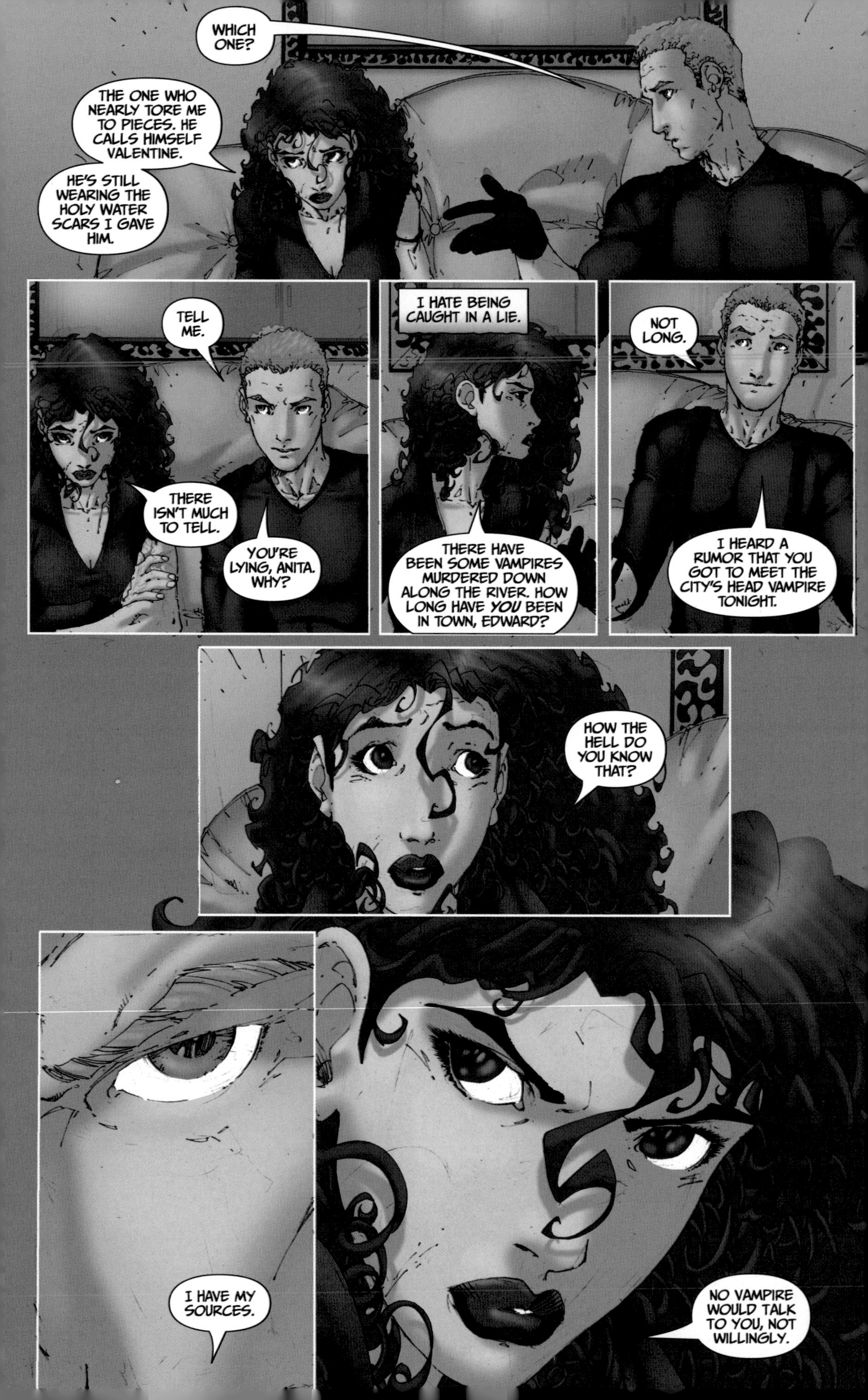
WHICH ONE?
THE ONE WHO NEARLY TORE ME TO PIECES. HE CALLS HIMSELF VALENTINE.
HE'S STILL WEARING THE HOLY WATER SCARS I GAVE HIM.
TELL ME.
THERE ISN'T MUCH TO TELL.
YOU'RE LYING, ANITA. WHY?
I HATE BEING CAUGHT IN A LIE.
THERE HAVE BEEN SOME VAMPIRES MURDERED DOWN ALONG THE RIVER. HOW LONG HAVE *YOU* BEEN IN TOWN, EDWARD?
NOT LONG.
I HEARD A RUMOR THAT YOU GOT TO MEET THE CITY'S HEAD VAMPIRE TONIGHT.
HOW THE HELL DO YOU KNOW THAT?
I HAVE MY SOURCES.
NO VAMPIRE WOULD TALK TO YOU, NOT WILLINGLY.

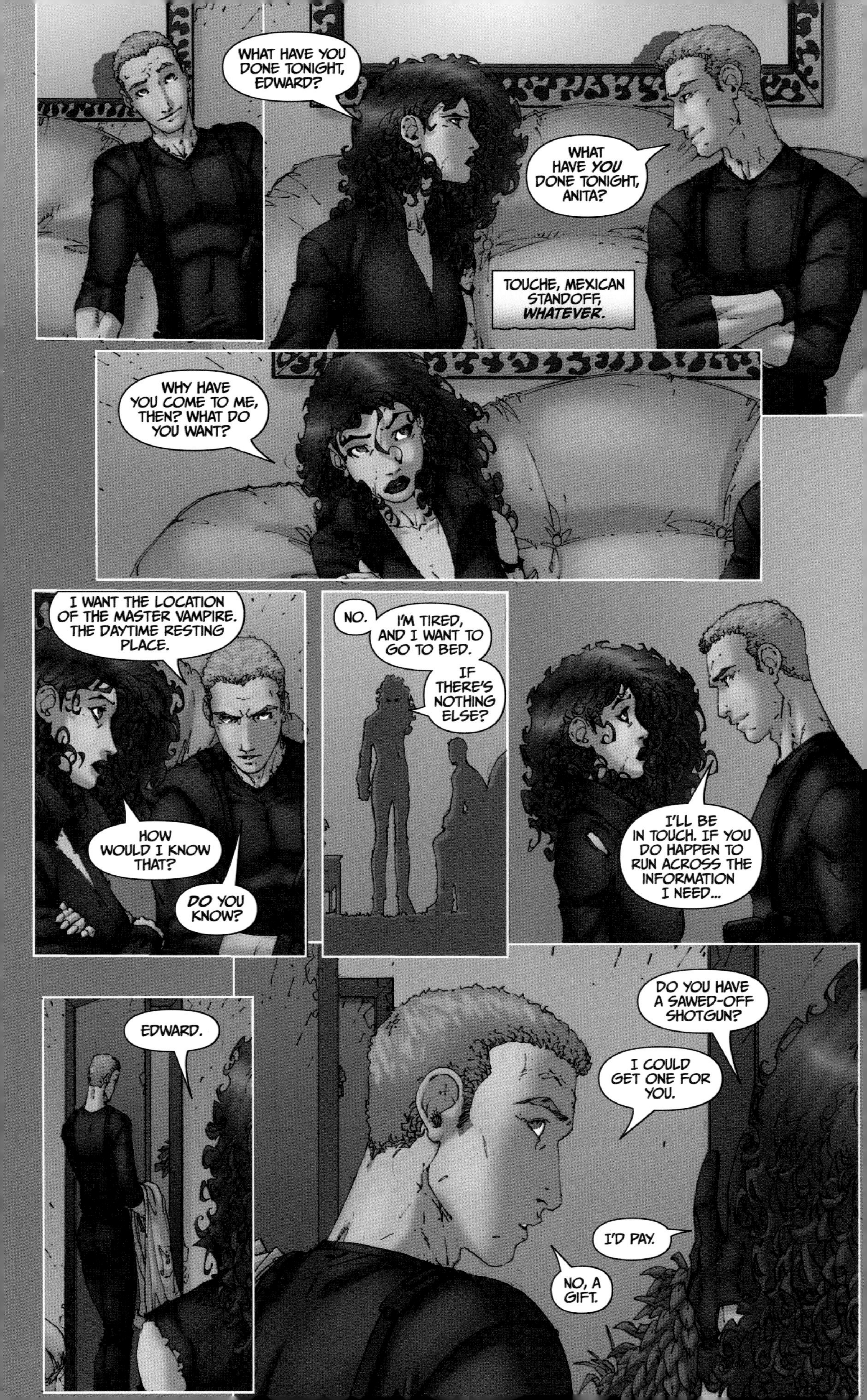
WHAT HAVE YOU DONE TONIGHT, EDWARD?
WHAT HAVE *YOU* DONE TONIGHT, ANITA?
TOUCHE, MEXICAN STANDOFF, *WHATEVER.*
WHY HAVE YOU COME TO ME, THEN? WHAT DO YOU WANT?
I WANT THE LOCATION OF THE MASTER VAMPIRE. THE DAYTIME RESTING PLACE.
HOW WOULD I KNOW THAT?
DO YOU KNOW?
NO.
I'M TIRED, AND I WANT TO GO TO BED.
IF THERE'S NOTHING ELSE?
I'LL BE IN TOUCH. IF YOU DO HAPPEN TO RUN ACROSS THE INFORMATION I NEED...
EDWARD.
DO YOU HAVE A SAWED-OFF SHOTGUN?
I COULD GET ONE FOR YOU.
I'D PAY.
NO, A GIFT.

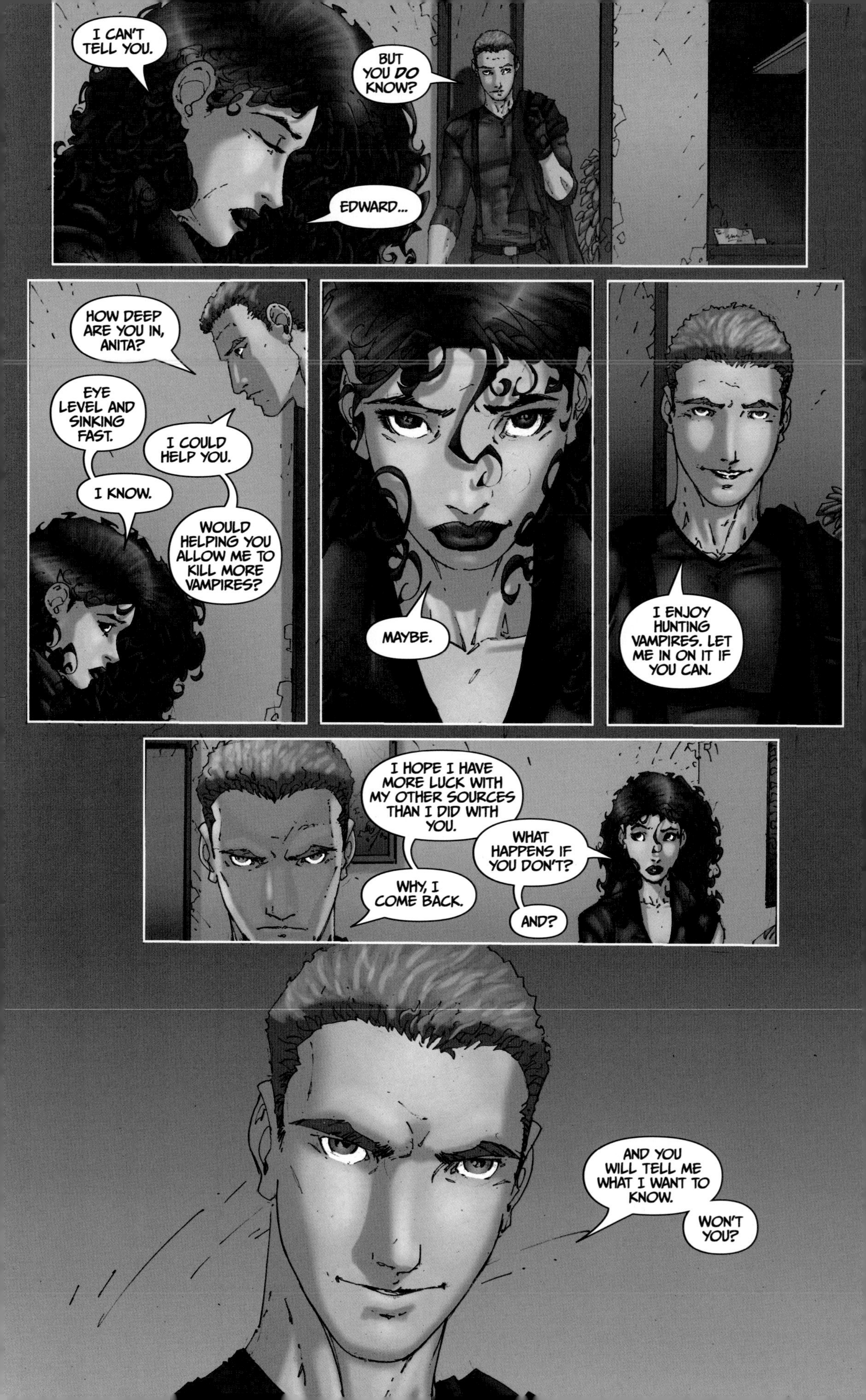
I CAN'T TELL YOU.
BUT YOU DO KNOW?
EDWARD...
HOW DEEP ARE YOU IN, ANITA?
EYE LEVEL AND SINKING FAST.
I COULD HELP YOU.
I KNOW.
WOULD HELPING YOU ALLOW ME TO KILL MORE VAMPIRES?
MAYBE.
I ENJOY HUNTING VAMPIRES. LET ME IN ON IT IF YOU CAN.
I HOPE I HAVE MORE LUCK WITH MY OTHER SOURCES THAN I DID WITH YOU.
WHAT HAPPENS IF YOU DON'T?
WHY, I COME BACK.
AND?
AND YOU WILL TELL ME WHAT I WANT TO KNOW.
WON'T YOU?

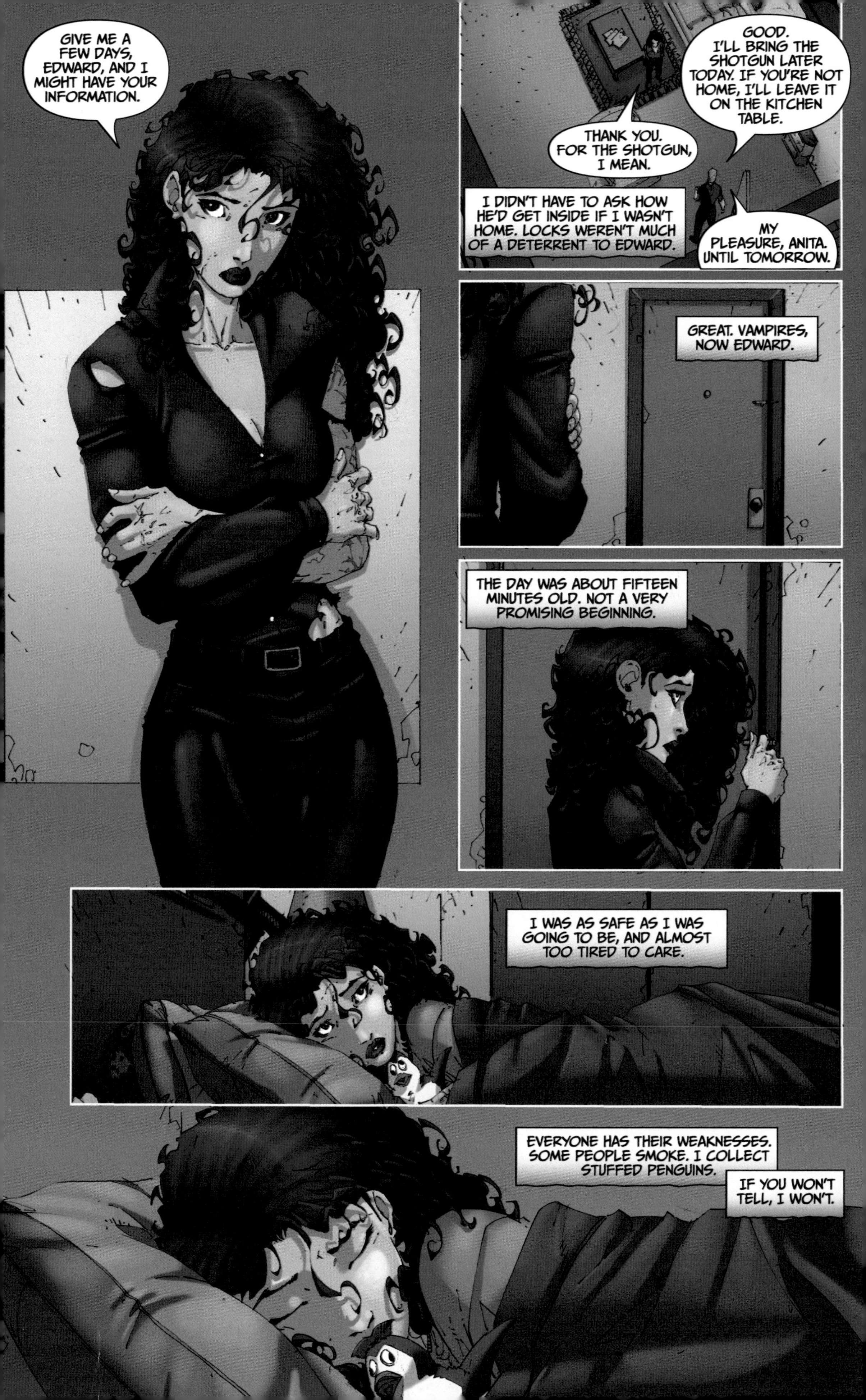
GIVE ME A FEW DAYS, EDWARD, AND I MIGHT HAVE YOUR INFORMATION.
GOOD. I'LL BRING THE SHOTGUN LATER TODAY. IF YOU'RE NOT HOME, I'LL LEAVE IT ON THE KITCHEN TABLE.
THANK YOU. FOR THE SHOTGUN, I MEAN.
I DIDN'T HAVE TO ASK HOW HE'D GET INSIDE IF I WASN'T HOME. LOCKS WEREN'T MUCH OF A DETERRENT TO EDWARD.
MY PLEASURE, ANITA. UNTIL TOMORROW.
GREAT. VAMPIRES, NOW EDWARD.
THE DAY WAS ABOUT FIFTEEN MINUTES OLD. NOT A VERY PROMISING BEGINNING.
I WAS AS SAFE AS I WAS GOING TO BE, AND ALMOST TOO TIRED TO CARE.
EVERYONE HAS THEIR WEAKNESSES. SOME PEOPLE SMOKE. I COLLECT STUFFED PENGUINS.
IF YOU WON'T TELL, I WON'T.

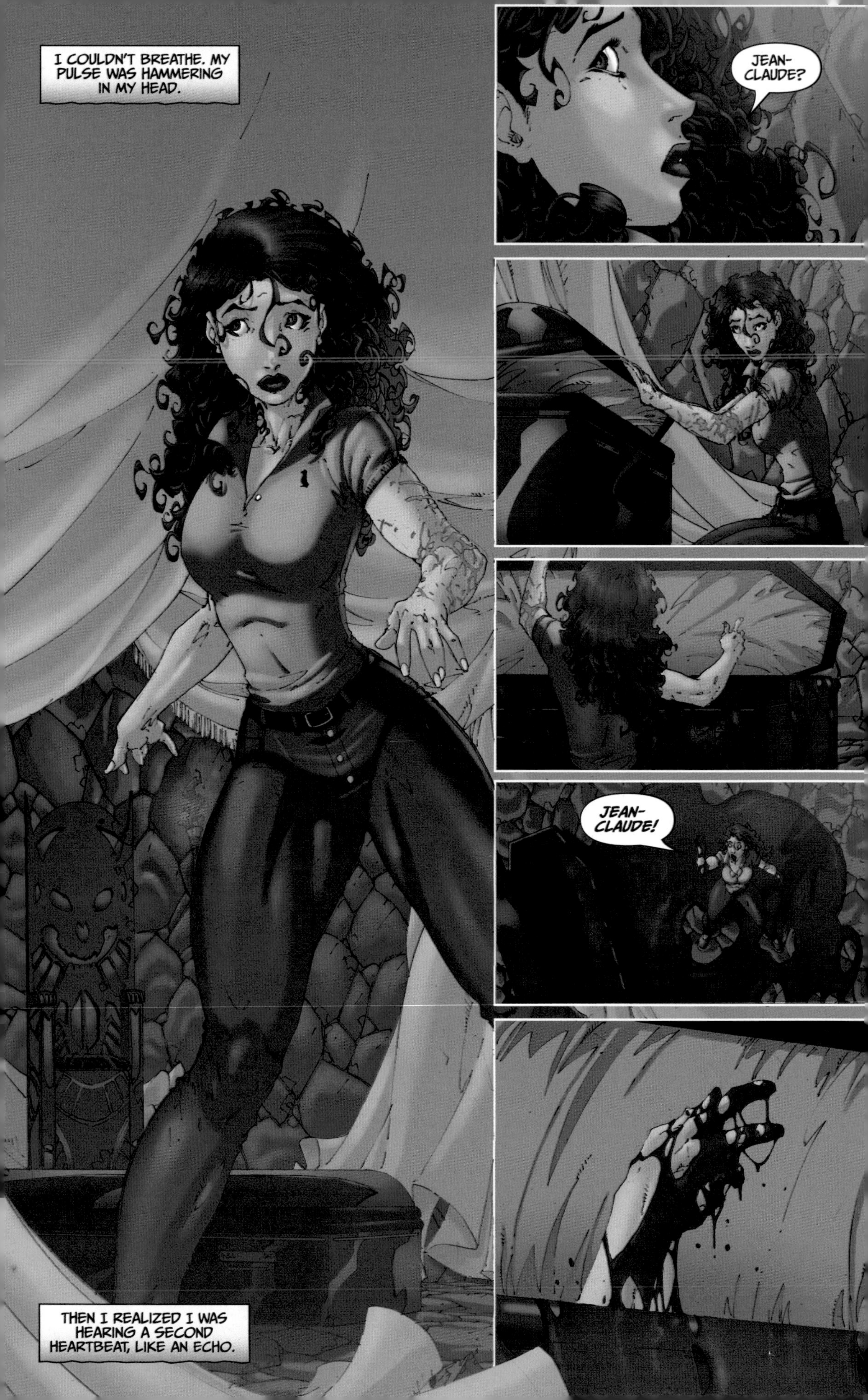
I COULDN'T BREATHE. MY PULSE WAS HAMMERING IN MY HEAD.
THEN I REALIZED I WAS HEARING A SECOND HEARTBEAT, LIKE AN ECHO.
JEAN-CLAUDE?
JEAN-CLAUDE!

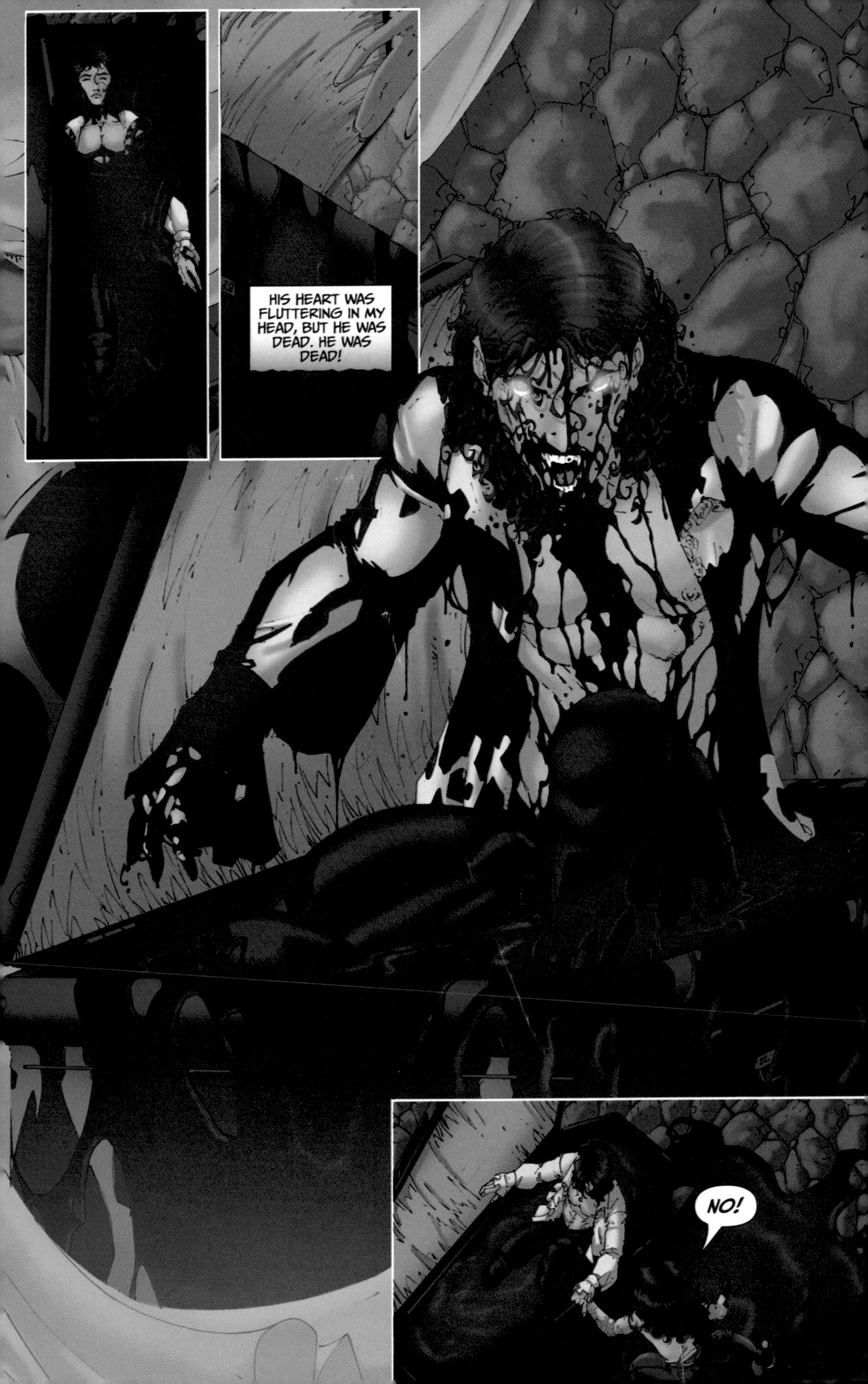
HIS HEART WAS FLUTTERING IN MY HEAD, BUT HE WAS DEAD. HE WAS DEAD!
NO!

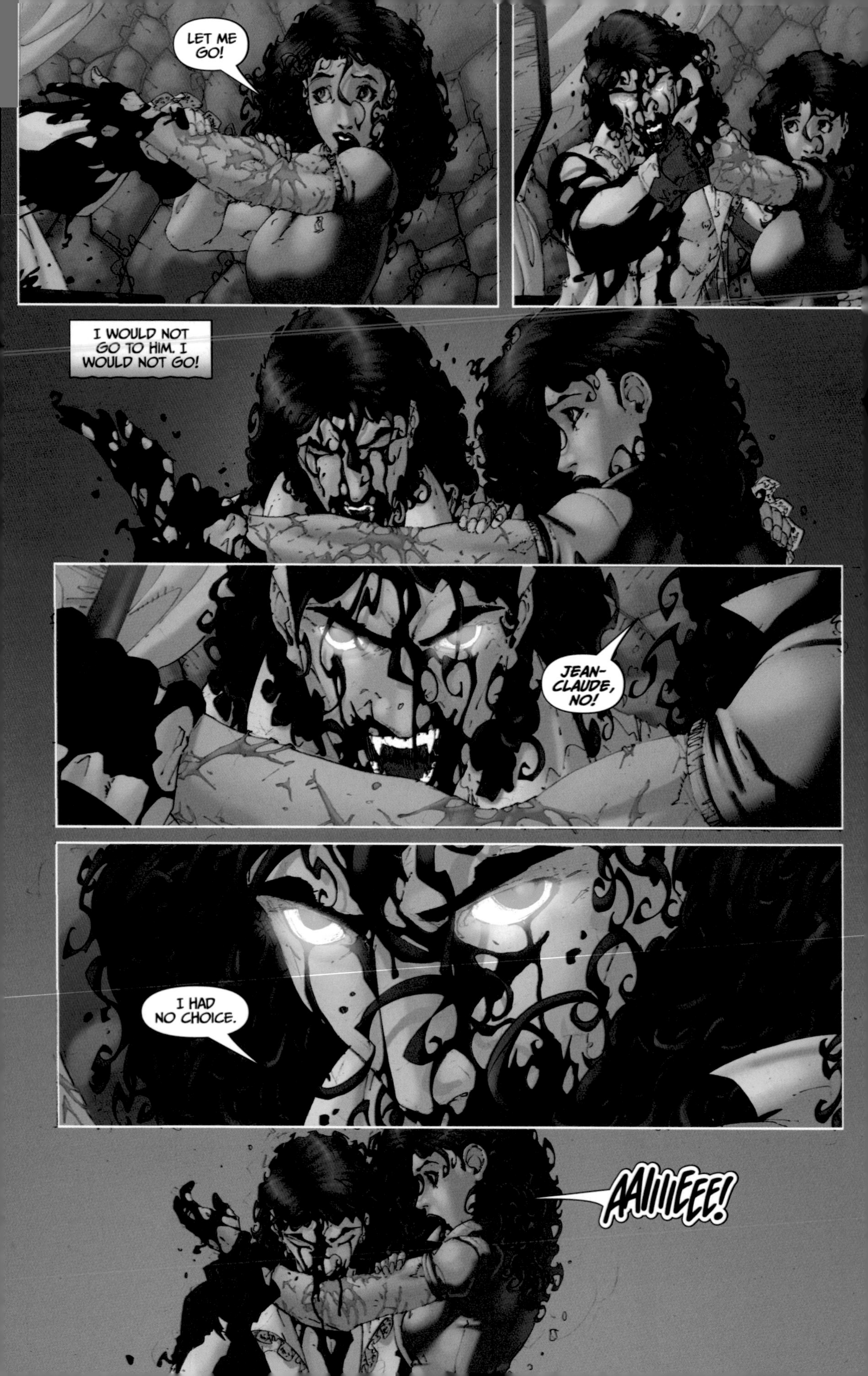
LET ME GO!
I WOULD NOT GO TO HIM. I WOULD NOT GO!
JEAN-CLAUDE, NO!
I HAD NO CHOICE.
AAIIIIEEE!

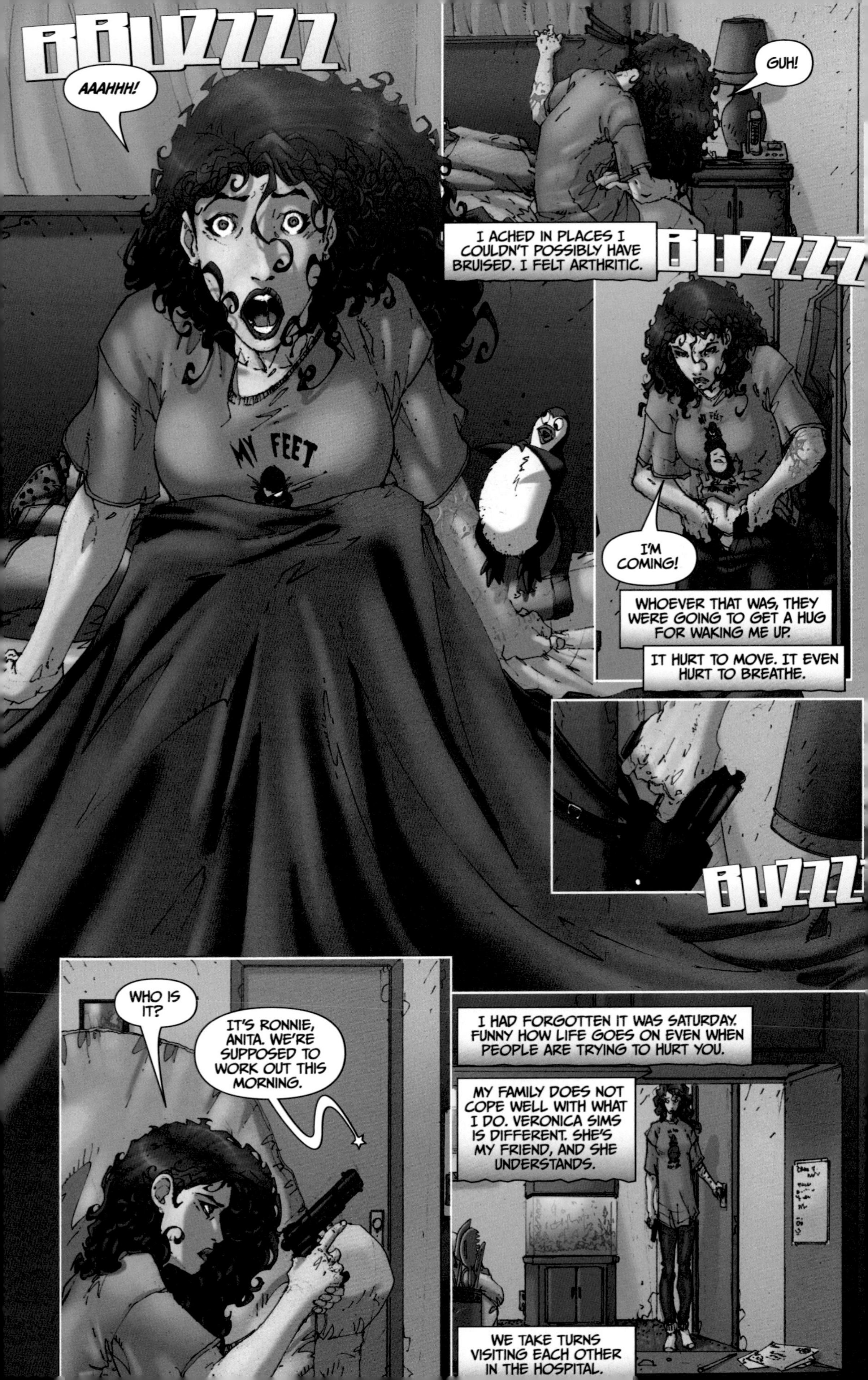
BRUZZZZ
AAAHHH!
MY FEET
GUH!
I ACHED IN PLACES I COULDN'T POSSIBLY HAVE BRUISED. I FELT ARTHRITIC.
BUZZZZ
I'M COMING!
WHOEVER THAT WAS, THEY WERE GOING TO GET A HUG FOR WAKING ME UP.
IT HURT TO MOVE. IT EVEN HURT TO BREATHE.
BUZZZ
WHO IS IT?
IT'S RONNIE, ANITA. WE'RE SUPPOSED TO WORK OUT THIS MORNING.
I HAD FORGOTTEN IT WAS SATURDAY. FUNNY HOW LIFE GOES ON EVEN WHEN PEOPLE ARE TRYING TO HURT YOU.
MY FAMILY DOES NOT COPE WELL WITH WHAT I DO. VERONICA SIMS IS DIFFERENT. SHE'S MY FRIEND, AND SHE UNDERSTANDS.
WE TAKE TURNS VISITING EACH OTHER IN THE HOSPITAL.

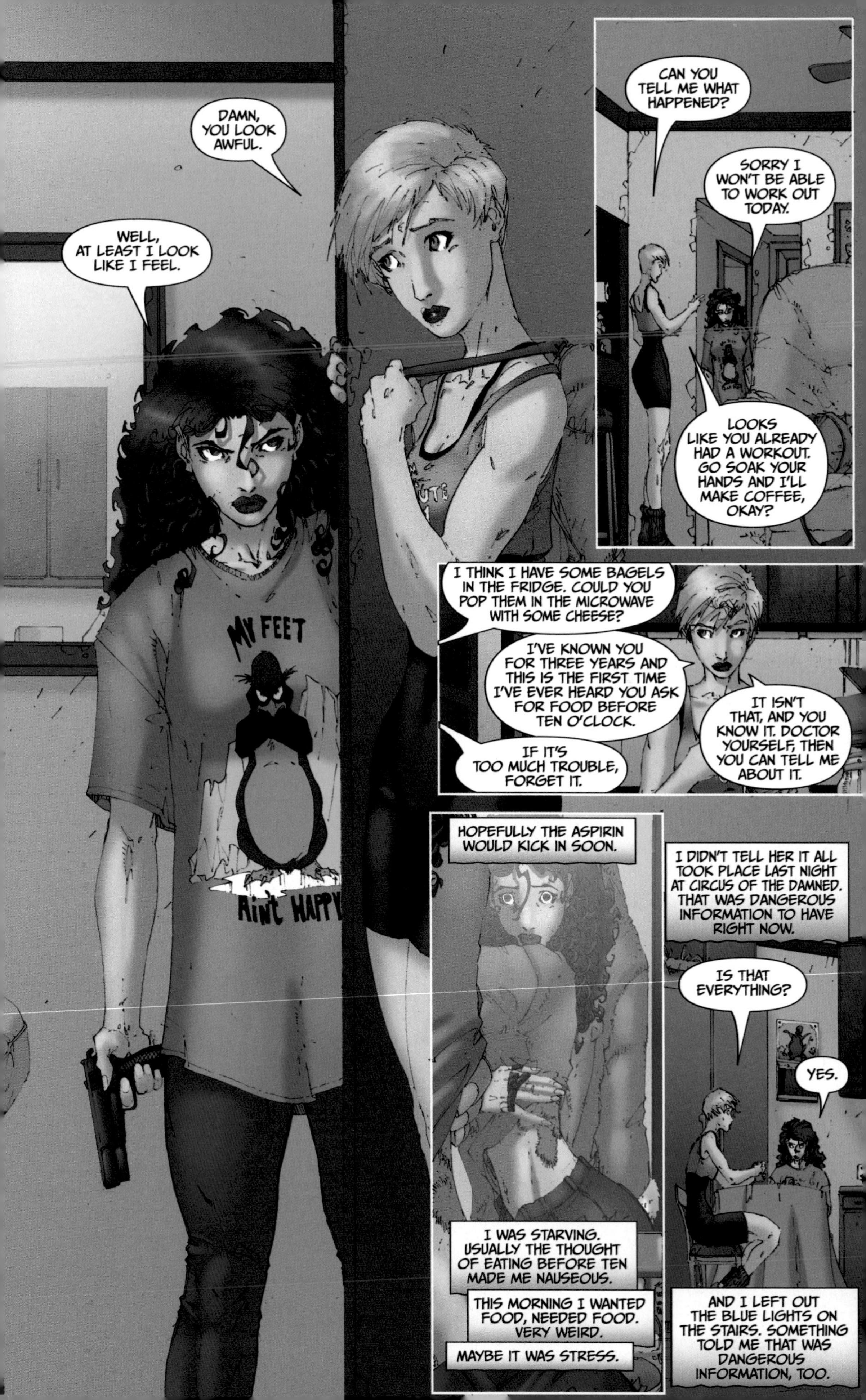
DAMN, YOU LOOK AWFUL.
WELL, AT LEAST I LOOK LIKE I FEEL.
MY FEET AIN'T HAPPY
CAN YOU TELL ME WHAT HAPPENED?
SORRY I WON'T BE ABLE TO WORK OUT TODAY.
LOOKS LIKE YOU ALREADY HAD A WORKOUT. GO SOAK YOUR HANDS AND I'LL MAKE COFFEE, OKAY?
I THINK I HAVE SOME BAGELS IN THE FRIDGE. COULD YOU POP THEM IN THE MICROWAVE WITH SOME CHEESE?
I'VE KNOWN YOU FOR THREE YEARS AND THIS IS THE FIRST TIME I'VE EVER HEARD YOU ASK FOR FOOD BEFORE TEN O'CLOCK.
IF IT'S TOO MUCH TROUBLE, FORGET IT.
IT ISN'T THAT, AND YOU KNOW IT. DOCTOR YOURSELF, THEN YOU CAN TELL ME ABOUT IT.
HOPEFULLY THE ASPIRIN WOULD KICK IN SOON.
I WAS STARVING. USUALLY THE THOUGHT OF EATING BEFORE TEN MADE ME NAUSEOUS.
THIS MORNING I WANTED FOOD, NEEDED FOOD. VERY WEIRD.
MAYBE IT WAS STRESS.
I DIDN'T TELL HER IT ALL TOOK PLACE LAST NIGHT AT CIRCUS OF THE DAMNED. THAT WAS DANGEROUS INFORMATION TO HAVE RIGHT NOW.
IS THAT EVERYTHING?
YES.
AND I LEFT OUT THE BLUE LIGHTS ON THE STAIRS. SOMETHING TOLD ME THAT WAS DANGEROUS INFORMATION, TOO.

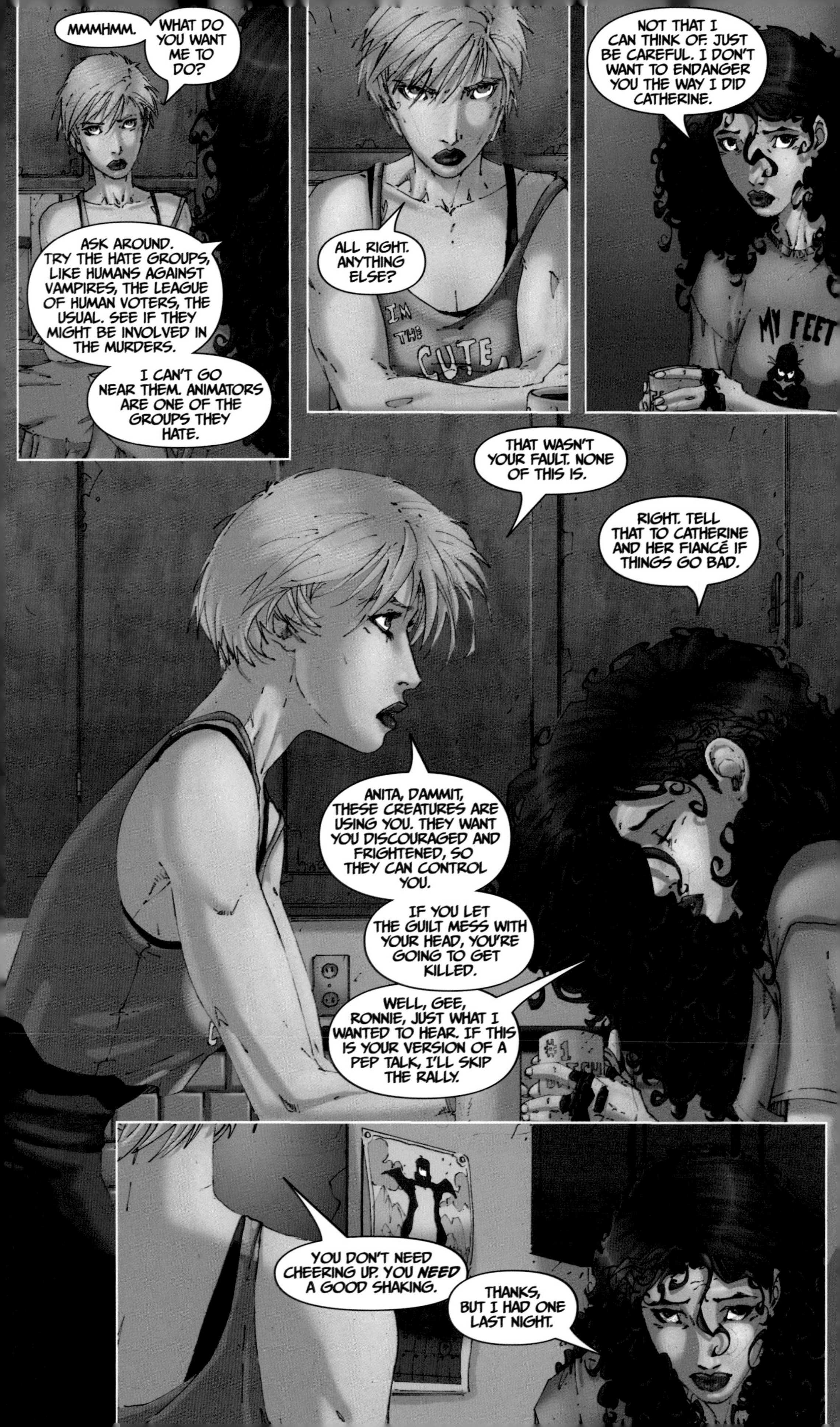
MMMHMM.
WHAT DO YOU WANT ME TO DO?
ASK AROUND. TRY THE HATE GROUPS, LIKE HUMANS AGAINST VAMPIRES, THE LEAGUE OF HUMAN VOTERS, THE USUAL. SEE IF THEY MIGHT BE INVOLVED IN THE MURDERS.
I CAN'T GO NEAR THEM. ANIMATORS ARE ONE OF THE GROUPS THEY HATE.
ALL RIGHT. ANYTHING ELSE?
I'M THE CUTE
NOT THAT I CAN THINK OF. JUST BE CAREFUL. I DON'T WANT TO ENDANGER YOU THE WAY I DID CATHERINE.
MY FEET
THAT WASN'T YOUR FAULT. NONE OF THIS IS.
RIGHT. TELL THAT TO CATHERINE AND HER FIANCÉ IF THINGS GO BAD.
ANITA, DAMMIT, THESE CREATURES ARE USING YOU. THEY WANT YOU DISCOURAGED AND FRIGHTENED, SO THEY CAN CONTROL YOU.
IF YOU LET THE GUILT MESS WITH YOUR HEAD, YOU'RE GOING TO GET KILLED.
WELL, GEE, RONNIE, JUST WHAT I WANTED TO HEAR. IF THIS IS YOUR VERSION OF A PEP TALK, I'LL SKIP THE RALLY.
YOU DON'T NEED CHEERING UP. YOU *NEED* A GOOD SHAKING.
THANKS, BUT I HAD ONE LAST NIGHT.

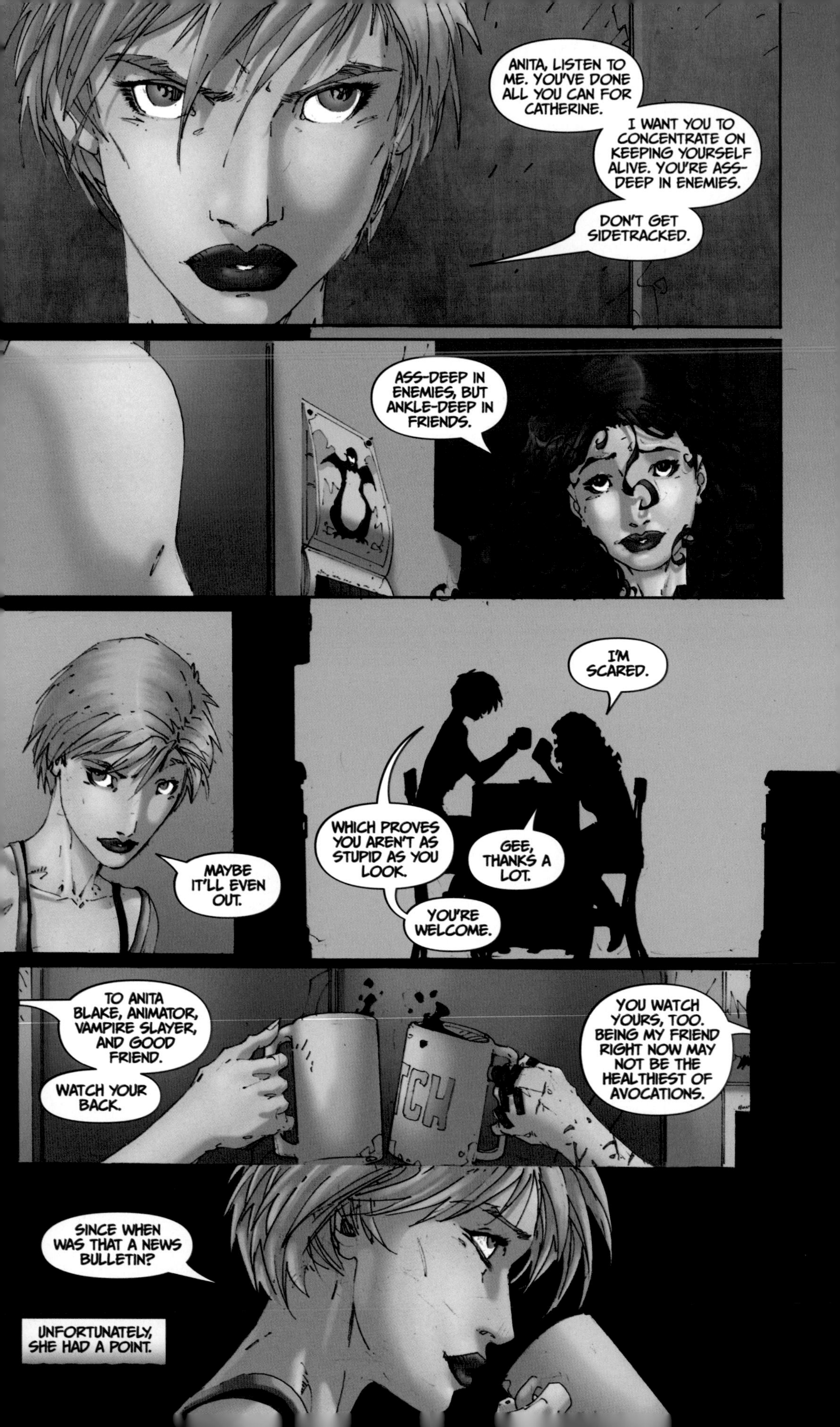
ANITA, LISTEN TO ME. YOU'VE DONE ALL YOU CAN FOR CATHERINE.
I WANT YOU TO CONCENTRATE ON KEEPING YOURSELF ALIVE. YOU'RE ASS-DEEP IN ENEMIES.
DON'T GET SIDETRACKED.
ASS-DEEP IN ENEMIES, BUT ANKLE-DEEP IN FRIENDS.
MAYBE IT'LL EVEN OUT.
I'M SCARED.
WHICH PROVES YOU AREN'T AS STUPID AS YOU LOOK.
GEE, THANKS A LOT.
YOU'RE WELCOME.
TO ANITA BLAKE, ANIMATOR, VAMPIRE SLAYER, AND GOOD FRIEND.
WATCH YOUR BACK.
YOU WATCH YOURS, TOO. BEING MY FRIEND RIGHT NOW MAY NOT BE THE HEALTHIEST OF AVOCATIONS.
SINCE WHEN WAS THAT A NEWS BULLETIN?
UNFORTUNATELY, SHE HAD A POINT.

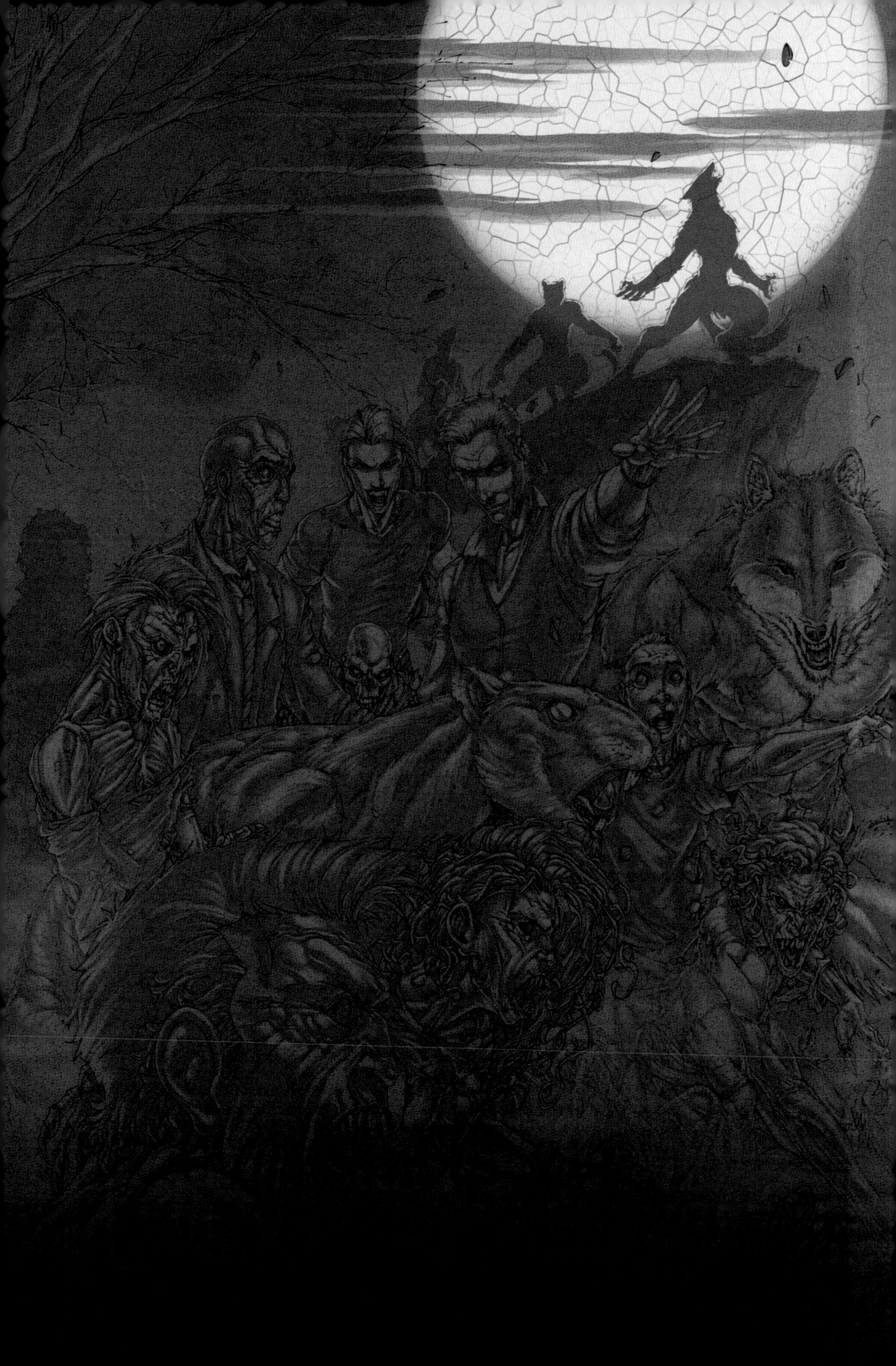

CHAPTER FIVE

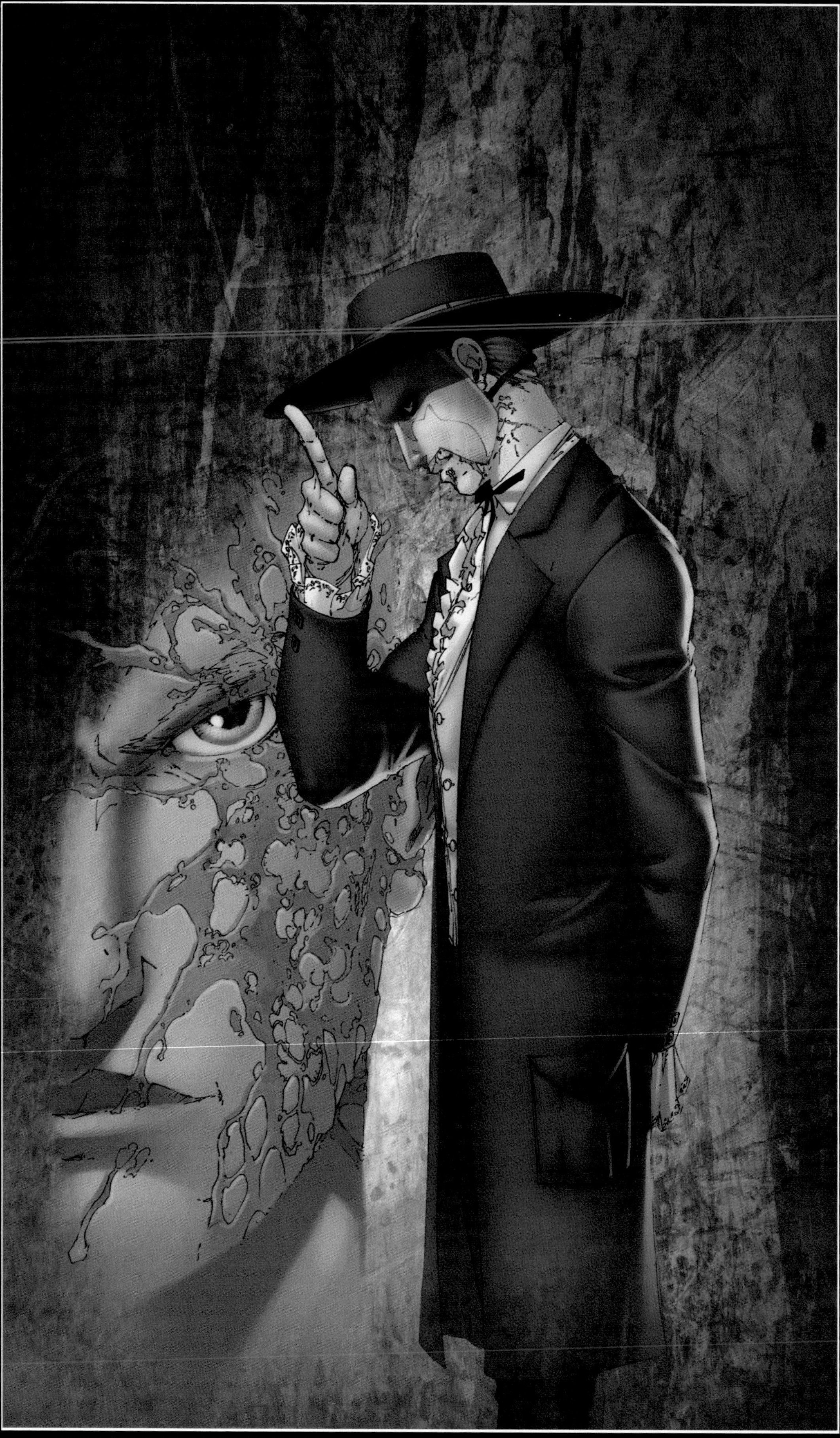

COVER BY: BRETT BOOTH & IMAGINARY FRIENDS STUDIO

I HAD TWO CHOICES AFTER MY FRIEND RONNIE LEFT:

I COULD GO BACK TO SLEEP, OR I COULD START SOLVING THE CASE EVERYONE WAS SO EAGER FOR ME TO WORK ON.

I COULD GET BY ON FOUR HOURS' SLEEP, BUT I WOULD NOT LAST NEARLY AS LONG IF NIKOLAOS'S LIEUTENANT, AUBREY, TORE MY THROAT OUT.

GUESS I WOULD GO TO WORK.

IT'S HARD TO WEAR A GUN IN ST. LOUIS IN THE SUMMERTIME. IF YOU WEAR A JACKET TO COVER THE GUN, YOU MELT.

IF YOU KEEP THE GUN IN YOUR PURSE, YOU GET KILLED, BECAUSE NO WOMAN CAN FIND ANYTHING IN HER PURSE IN UNDER TWELVE MINUTES.

I HAD BEEN KIDNAPPED AND NEARLY KILLED. I DID NOT PLAN ON IT HAPPENING AGAIN WITHOUT A FIGHT.

I COULD BENCH PRESS A HUNDRED POUNDS, BUT VAMPIRES, WELL, UNLESS I COULD BENCH PRESS TRUCKS, I WAS OUTCLASSED.

SO I NEEDED TO CARRY A GUN.

I HAD A SECOND GUN FOR COMFORT AND CONCEALABILITY: A FIRESTAR 9MM.

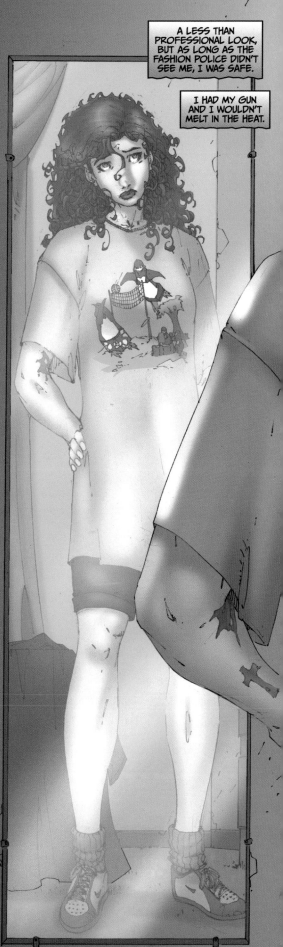

A LESS THAN PROFESSIONAL LOOK, BUT AS LONG AS THE FASHION POLICE DIDN'T SEE ME, I WAS SAFE.

I HAD MY GUN AND I WOULDN'T MELT IN THE HEAT.

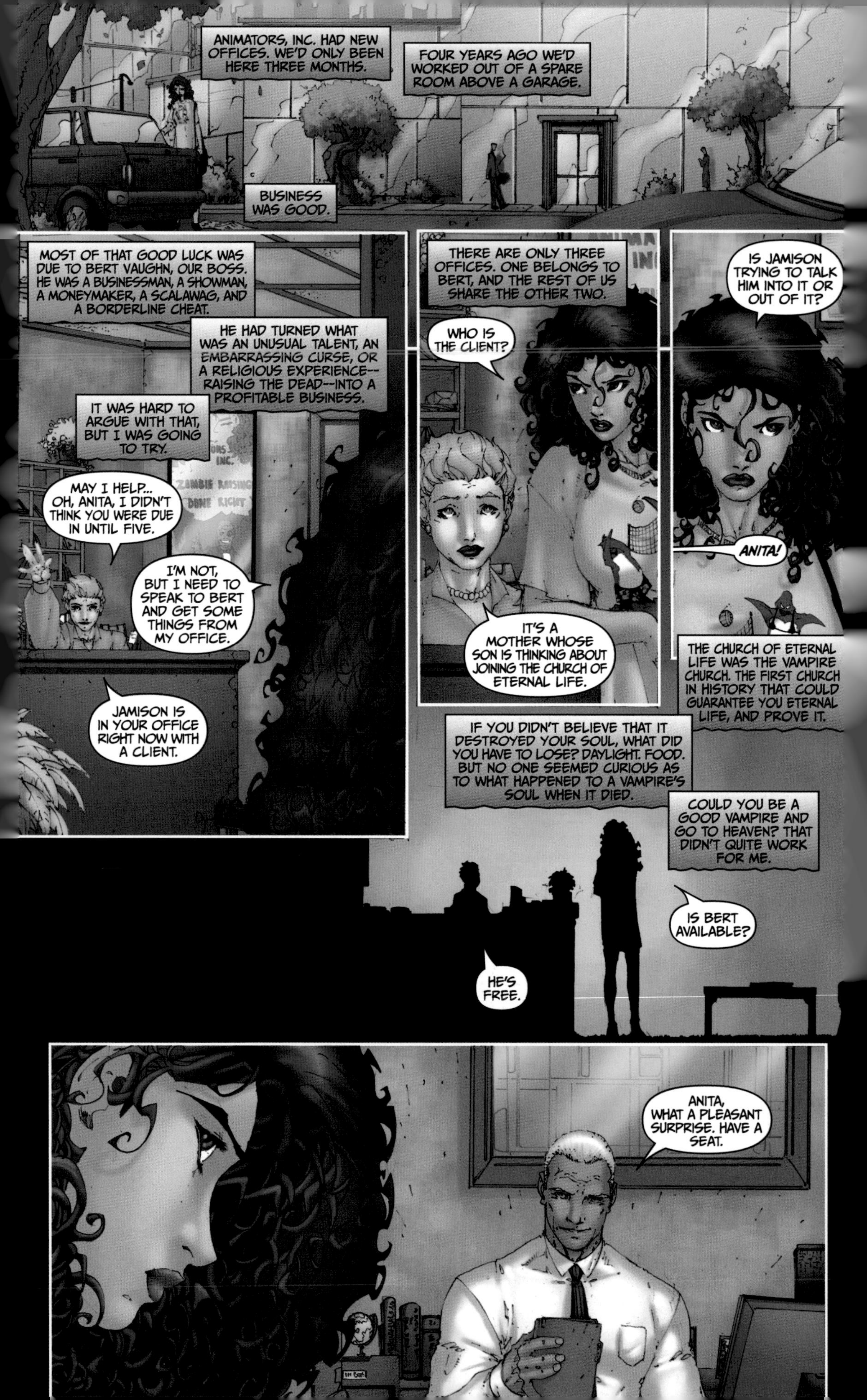
ANIMATORS, INC. HAD NEW OFFICES. WE'D ONLY BEEN HERE THREE MONTHS.
FOUR YEARS AGO WE'D WORKED OUT OF A SPARE ROOM ABOVE A GARAGE.
BUSINESS WAS GOOD.
MOST OF THAT GOOD LUCK WAS DUE TO BERT VAUGHN, OUR BOSS. HE WAS A BUSINESSMAN, A SHOWMAN, A MONEYMAKER, A SCALAWAG, AND A BORDERLINE CHEAT.
HE HAD TURNED WHAT WAS AN UNUSUAL TALENT, AN EMBARRASSING CURSE, OR A RELIGIOUS EXPERIENCE--RAISING THE DEAD--INTO A PROFITABLE BUSINESS.
IT WAS HARD TO ARGUE WITH THAT, BUT I WAS GOING TO TRY.
MAY I HELP... OH, ANITA, I DIDN'T THINK YOU WERE DUE IN UNTIL FIVE.
I'M NOT, BUT I NEED TO SPEAK TO BERT AND GET SOME THINGS FROM MY OFFICE.
JAMISON IS IN YOUR OFFICE RIGHT NOW WITH A CLIENT.
THERE ARE ONLY THREE OFFICES. ONE BELONGS TO BERT, AND THE REST OF US SHARE THE OTHER TWO.
WHO IS THE CLIENT?
IT'S A MOTHER WHOSE SON IS THINKING ABOUT JOINING THE CHURCH OF ETERNAL LIFE.
IS JAMISON TRYING TO TALK HIM INTO IT OR OUT OF IT?
ANITA!
THE CHURCH OF ETERNAL LIFE WAS THE VAMPIRE CHURCH. THE FIRST CHURCH IN HISTORY THAT COULD GUARANTEE YOU ETERNAL LIFE, AND PROVE IT.
IF YOU DIDN'T BELIEVE THAT IT DESTROYED YOUR SOUL, WHAT DID YOU HAVE TO LOSE? DAYLIGHT. FOOD. BUT NO ONE SEEMED CURIOUS AS TO WHAT HAPPENED TO A VAMPIRE'S SOUL WHEN IT DIED.
COULD YOU BE A GOOD VAMPIRE AND GO TO HEAVEN? THAT DIDN'T QUITE WORK FOR ME.
IS BERT AVAILABLE?
HE'S FREE.
ANITA, WHAT A PLEASANT SURPRISE. HAVE A SEAT.

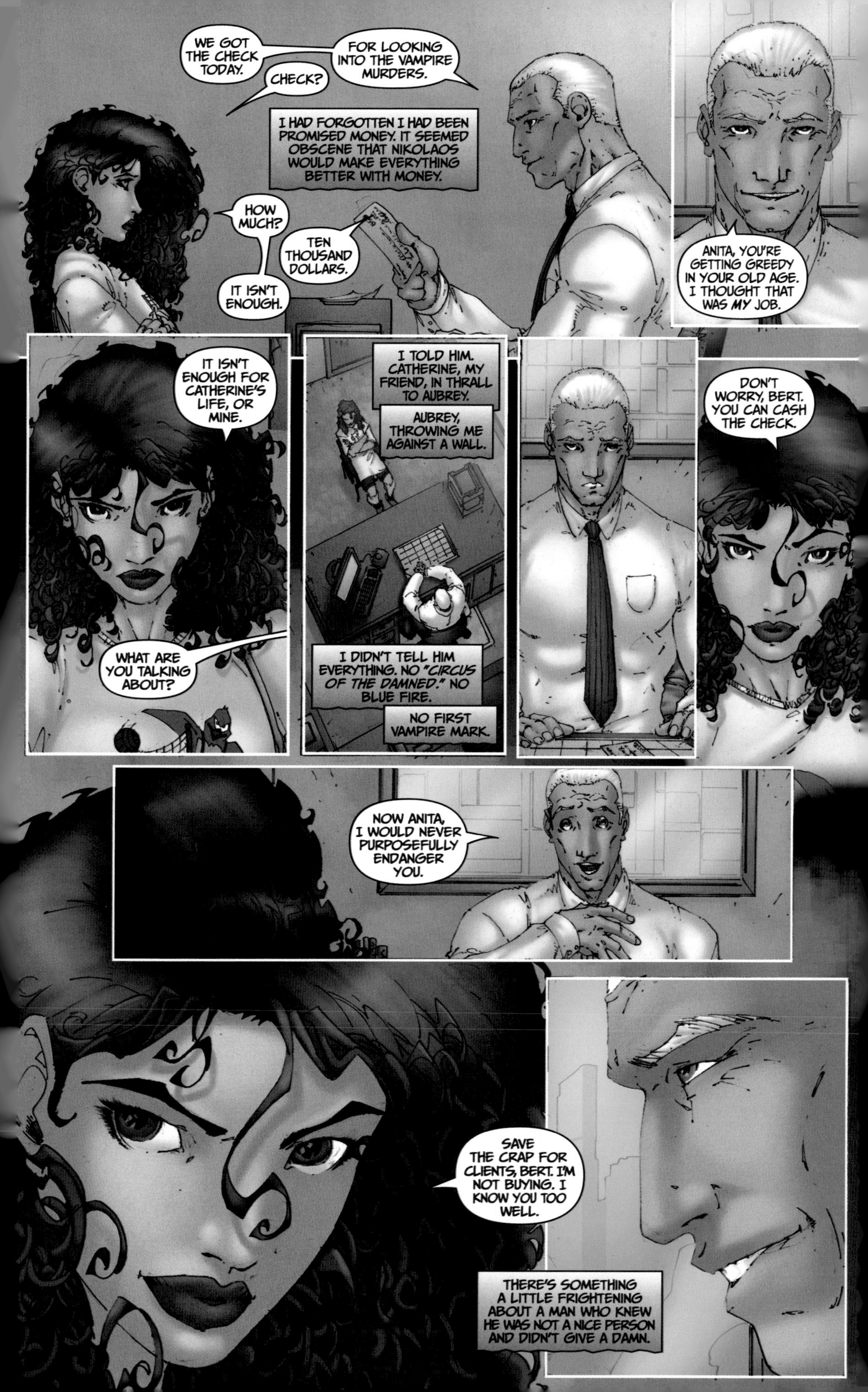
WE GOT THE CHECK TODAY.
FOR LOOKING INTO THE VAMPIRE MURDERS.
CHECK?
I HAD FORGOTTEN I HAD BEEN PROMISED MONEY. IT SEEMED OBSCENE THAT NIKOLAOS WOULD MAKE EVERYTHING BETTER WITH MONEY.
HOW MUCH?
TEN THOUSAND DOLLARS.
IT ISN'T ENOUGH.
ANITA, YOU'RE GETTING GREEDY IN YOUR OLD AGE. I THOUGHT THAT WAS MY JOB.
IT ISN'T ENOUGH FOR CATHERINE'S LIFE, OR MINE.
WHAT ARE YOU TALKING ABOUT?
I TOLD HIM. CATHERINE, MY FRIEND, IN THRALL TO AUBREY.
AUBREY, THROWING ME AGAINST A WALL.
I DIDN'T TELL HIM EVERYTHING. NO "CIRCUS OF THE DAMNED." NO BLUE FIRE.
NO FIRST VAMPIRE MARK.
DON'T WORRY, BERT. YOU CAN CASH THE CHECK.
NOW ANITA, I WOULD NEVER PURPOSEFULLY ENDANGER YOU.
SAVE THE CRAP FOR CLIENTS, BERT. I'M NOT BUYING. I KNOW YOU TOO WELL.
THERE'S SOMETHING A LITTLE FRIGHTENING ABOUT A MAN WHO KNEW HE WAS NOT A NICE PERSON AND DIDN'T GIVE A DAMN.

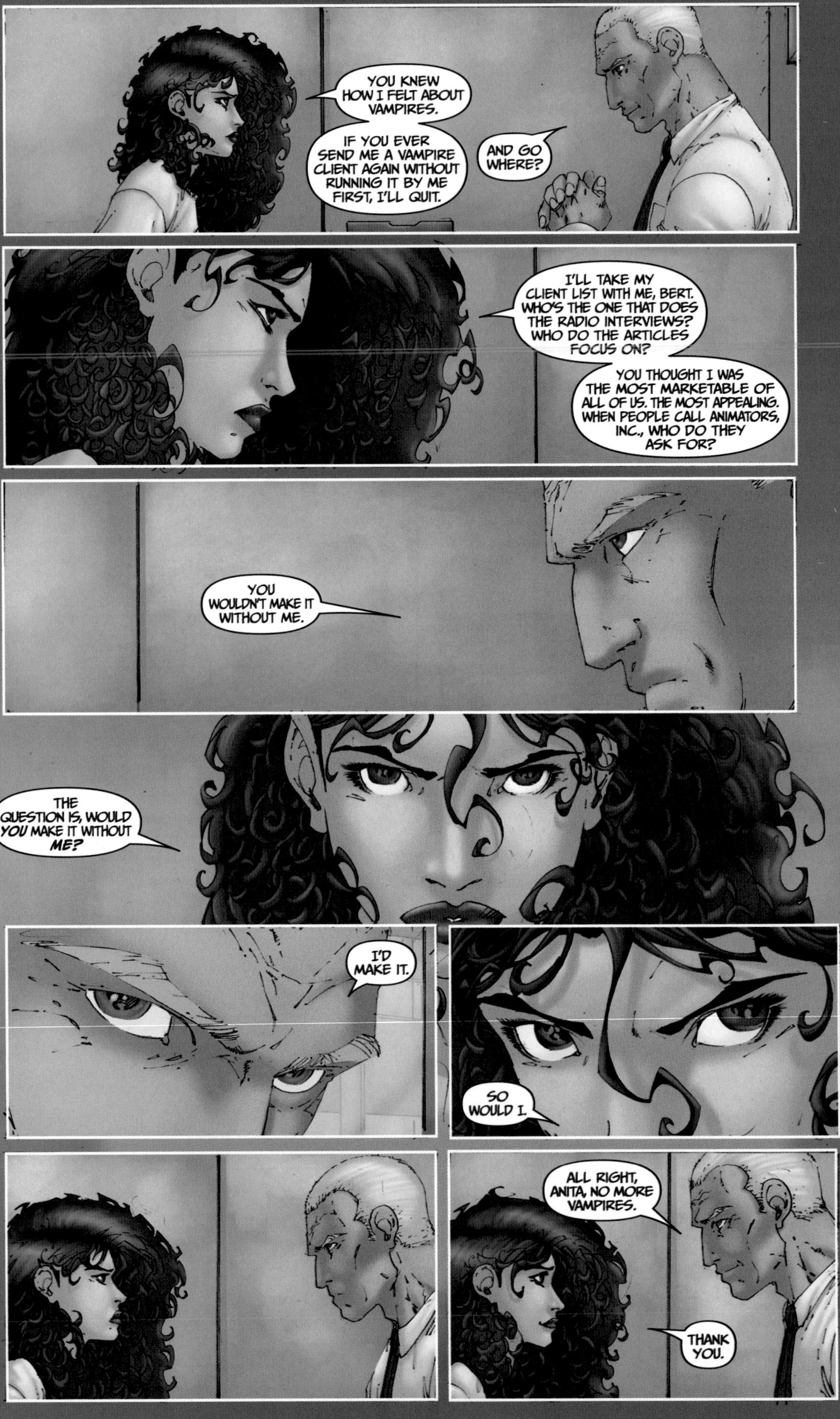
YOU KNEW HOW I FELT ABOUT VAMPIRES.
IF YOU EVER SEND ME A VAMPIRE CLIENT AGAIN WITHOUT RUNNING IT BY ME FIRST, I'LL QUIT.
AND GO WHERE?
I'LL TAKE MY CLIENT LIST WITH ME, BERT. WHO'S THE ONE THAT DOES THE RADIO INTERVIEWS? WHO DO THE ARTICLES FOCUS ON?
YOU THOUGHT I WAS THE MOST MARKETABLE OF ALL OF US. THE MOST APPEALING. WHEN PEOPLE CALL ANIMATORS, INC., WHO DO THEY ASK FOR?
YOU WOULDN'T MAKE IT WITHOUT ME.
THE QUESTION IS, WOULD *YOU* MAKE IT WITHOUT *ME?*
I'D MAKE IT.
SO WOULD I.
ALL RIGHT, ANITA, NO MORE VAMPIRES.
THANK YOU.

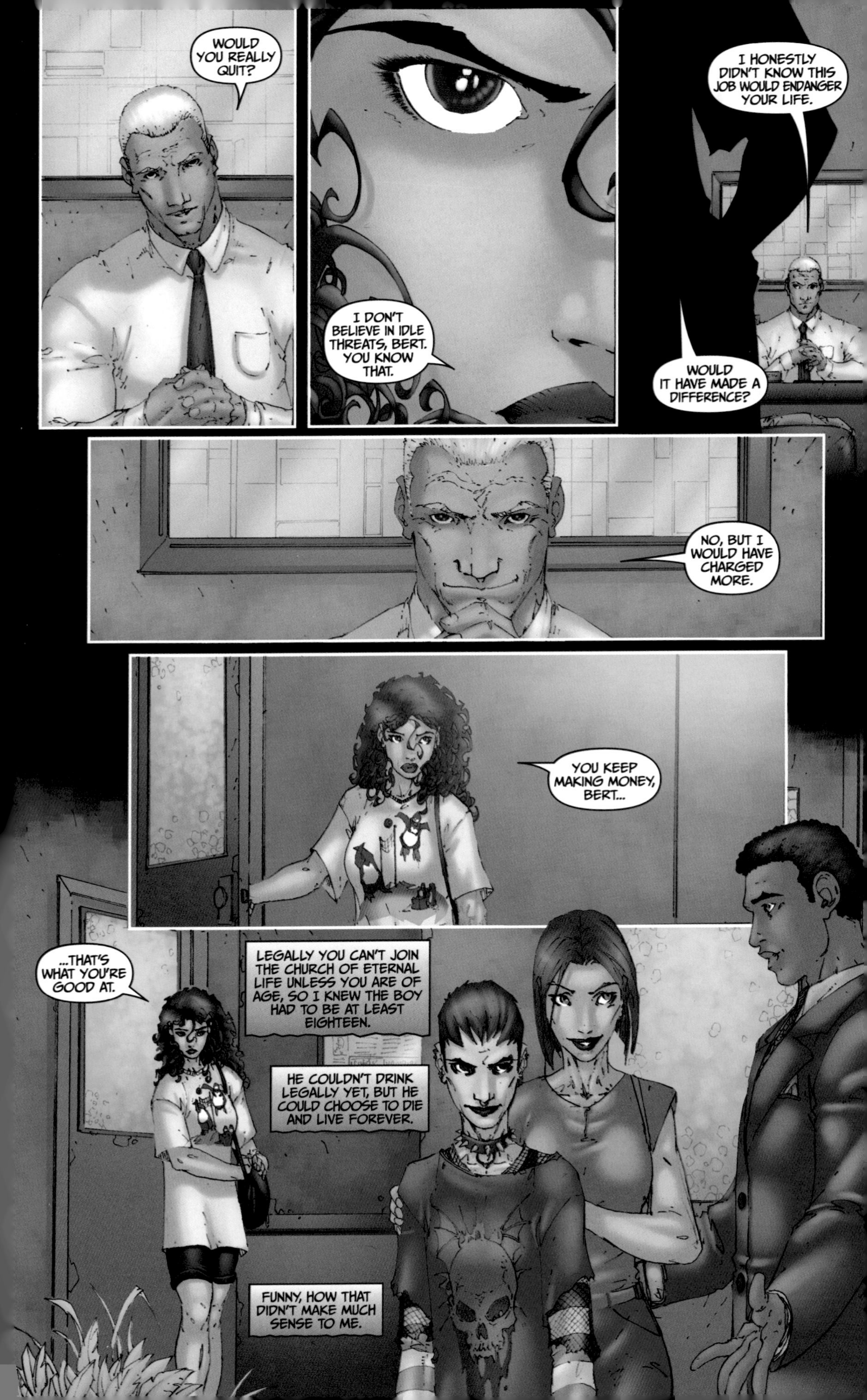

WOULD YOU REALLY QUIT?
I DON'T BELIEVE IN IDLE THREATS, BERT. YOU KNOW THAT.
I HONESTLY DIDN'T KNOW THIS JOB WOULD ENDANGER YOUR LIFE.
WOULD IT HAVE MADE A DIFFERENCE?
NO, BUT I WOULD HAVE CHARGED MORE.
YOU KEEP MAKING MONEY, BERT...
...THAT'S WHAT YOU'RE GOOD AT.
LEGALLY YOU CAN'T JOIN THE CHURCH OF ETERNAL LIFE UNLESS YOU ARE OF AGE, SO I KNEW THE BOY HAD TO BE AT LEAST EIGHTEEN.
HE COULDN'T DRINK LEGALLY YET, BUT HE COULD CHOOSE TO DIE AND LIVE FOREVER.
FUNNY, HOW THAT DIDN'T MAKE MUCH SENSE TO ME.

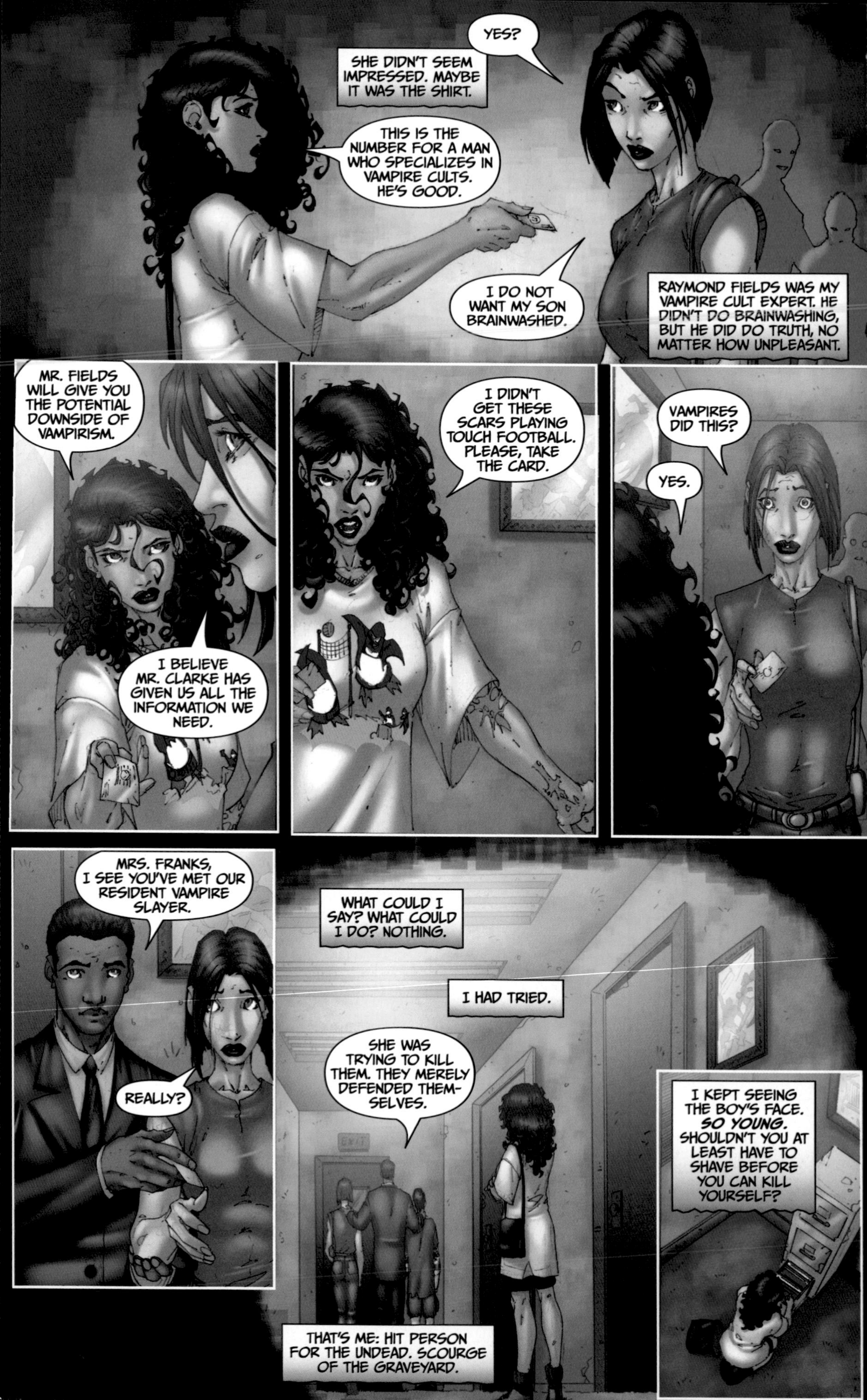
YES?
SHE DIDN'T SEEM IMPRESSED. MAYBE IT WAS THE SHIRT.
THIS IS THE NUMBER FOR A MAN WHO SPECIALIZES IN VAMPIRE CULTS. HE'S GOOD.
I DO NOT WANT MY SON BRAINWASHED.
RAYMOND FIELDS WAS MY VAMPIRE CULT EXPERT. HE DIDN'T DO BRAINWASHING, BUT HE DID DO TRUTH, NO MATTER HOW UNPLEASANT.
MR. FIELDS WILL GIVE YOU THE POTENTIAL DOWNSIDE OF VAMPIRISM.
I BELIEVE MR. CLARKE HAS GIVEN US ALL THE INFORMATION WE NEED.
I DIDN'T GET THESE SCARS PLAYING TOUCH FOOTBALL. PLEASE, TAKE THE CARD.
VAMPIRES DID THIS?
YES.
MRS. FRANKS, I SEE YOU'VE MET OUR RESIDENT VAMPIRE SLAYER.
REALLY?
WHAT COULD I SAY? WHAT COULD I DO? NOTHING.
I HAD TRIED.
SHE WAS TRYING TO KILL THEM. THEY MERELY DEFENDED THEMSELVES.
THAT'S ME: HIT PERSON FOR THE UNDEAD. SCOURGE OF THE GRAVEYARD.
I KEPT SEEING THE BOY'S FACE. **SO YOUNG.** SHOULDN'T YOU AT LEAST HAVE TO SHAVE BEFORE YOU CAN KILL YOURSELF?

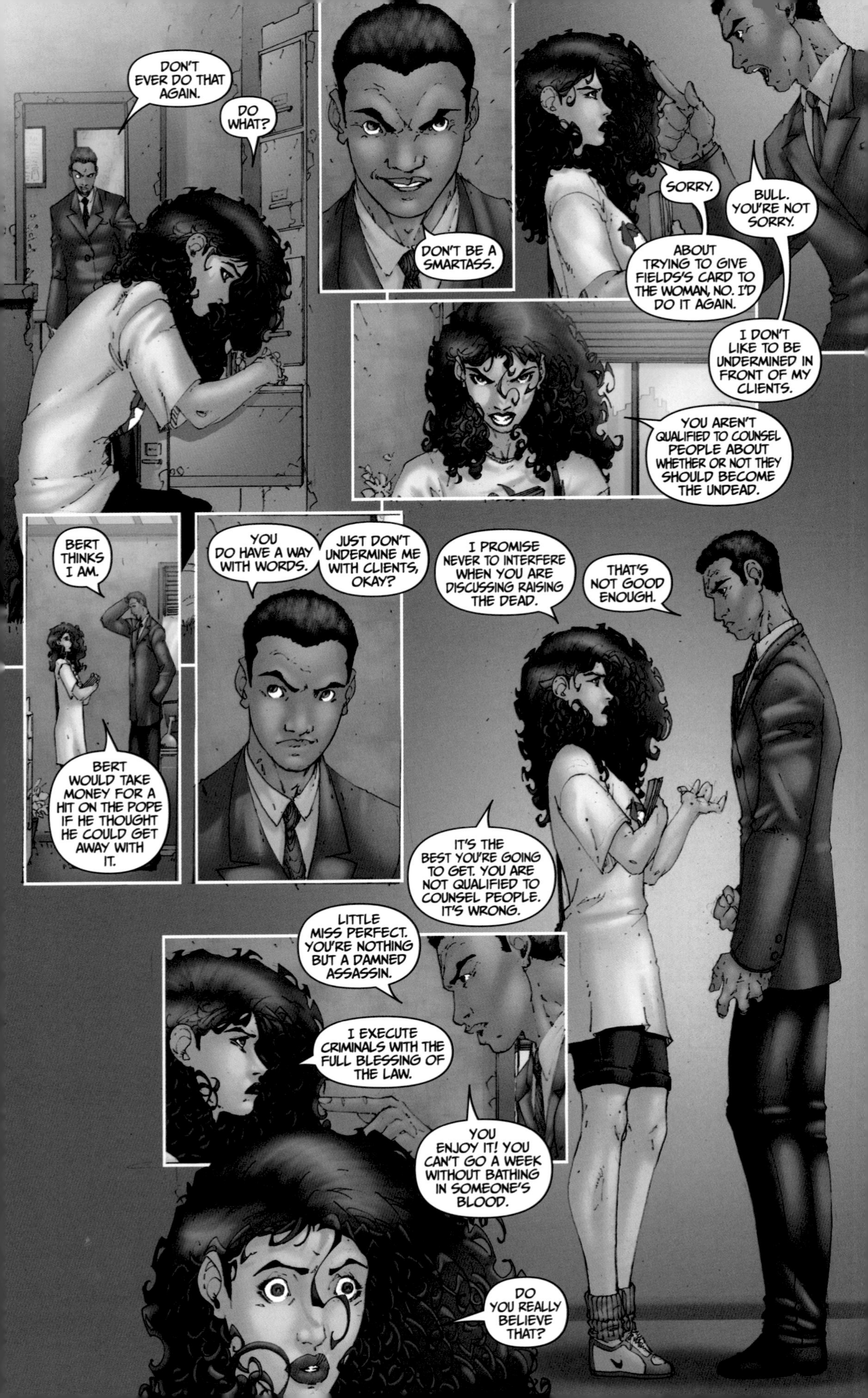
DON'T EVER DO THAT AGAIN.
DO WHAT?
DON'T BE A SMARTASS.
SORRY.
BULL. YOU'RE NOT SORRY.
ABOUT TRYING TO GIVE FIELDS'S CARD TO THE WOMAN, NO. I'D DO IT AGAIN.
I DON'T LIKE TO BE UNDERMINED IN FRONT OF MY CLIENTS.
YOU AREN'T QUALIFIED TO COUNSEL PEOPLE ABOUT WHETHER OR NOT THEY SHOULD BECOME THE UNDEAD.
BERT THINKS I AM.
BERT WOULD TAKE MONEY FOR A HIT ON THE POPE IF HE THOUGHT HE COULD GET AWAY WITH IT.
YOU DO HAVE A WAY WITH WORDS.
JUST DON'T UNDERMINE ME WITH CLIENTS, OKAY?
I PROMISE NEVER TO INTERFERE WHEN YOU ARE DISCUSSING RAISING THE DEAD.
THAT'S NOT GOOD ENOUGH.
IT'S THE BEST YOU'RE GOING TO GET. YOU ARE NOT QUALIFIED TO COUNSEL PEOPLE. IT'S WRONG.
LITTLE MISS PERFECT. YOU'RE NOTHING BUT A DAMNED ASSASSIN.
I EXECUTE CRIMINALS WITH THE FULL BLESSING OF THE LAW.
YOU ENJOY IT! YOU CAN'T GO A WEEK WITHOUT BATHING IN SOMEONE'S BLOOD.
DO YOU REALLY BELIEVE THAT?

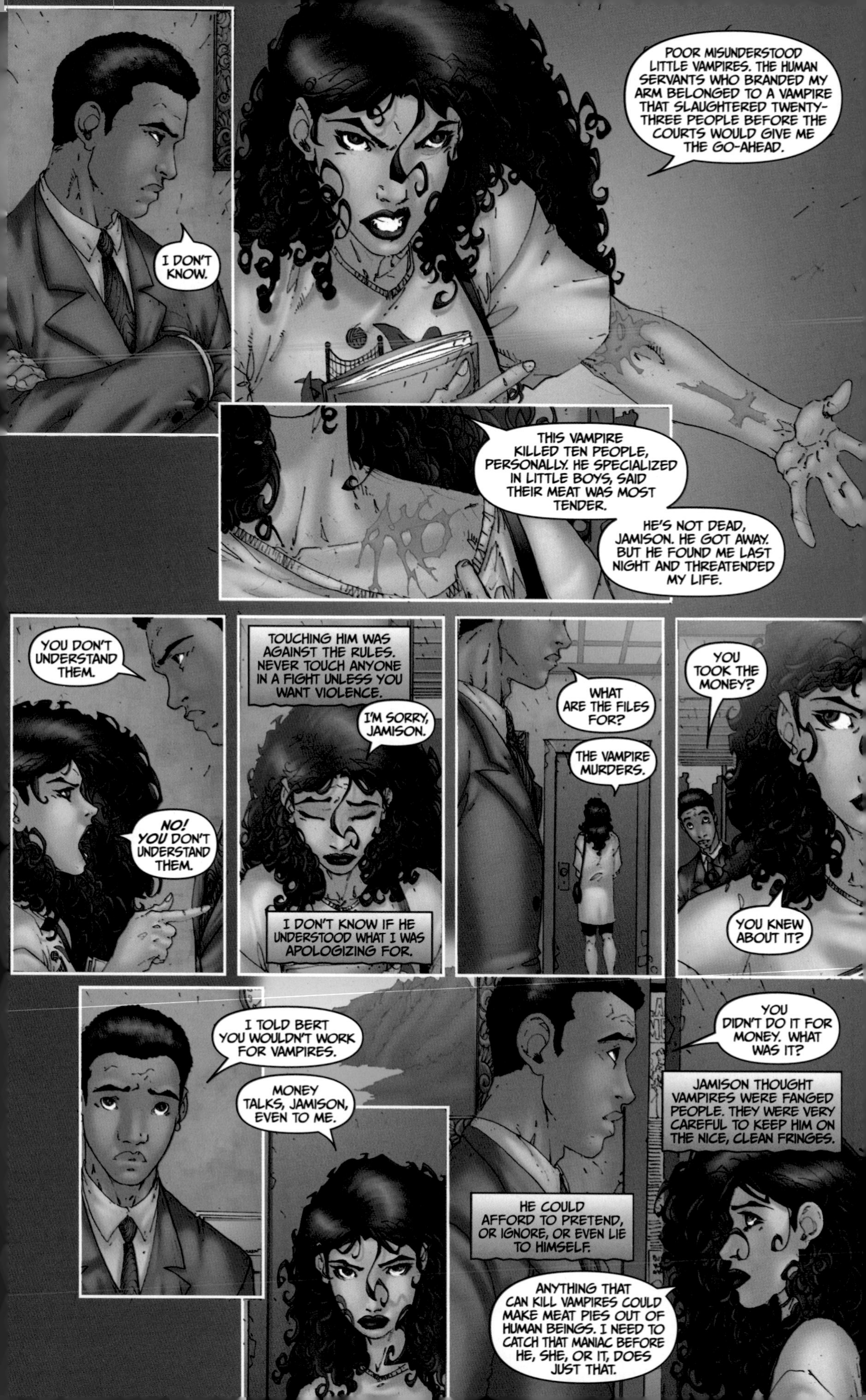
POOR MISUNDERSTOOD LITTLE VAMPIRES. THE HUMAN SERVANTS WHO BRANDED MY ARM BELONGED TO A VAMPIRE THAT SLAUGHTERED TWENTY-THREE PEOPLE BEFORE THE COURTS WOULD GIVE ME THE GO-AHEAD.
I DON'T KNOW.
THIS VAMPIRE KILLED TEN PEOPLE, PERSONALLY. HE SPECIALIZED IN LITTLE BOYS, SAID THEIR MEAT WAS MOST TENDER.
HE'S NOT DEAD, JAMISON. HE GOT AWAY. BUT HE FOUND ME LAST NIGHT AND THREATENDED MY LIFE.
YOU DON'T UNDERSTAND THEM.
NO! YOU DON'T UNDERSTAND THEM.
TOUCHING HIM WAS AGAINST THE RULES. NEVER TOUCH ANYONE IN A FIGHT UNLESS YOU WANT VIOLENCE.
I'M SORRY, JAMISON.
I DON'T KNOW IF HE UNDERSTOOD WHAT I WAS APOLOGIZING FOR.
WHAT ARE THE FILES FOR?
THE VAMPIRE MURDERS.
YOU TOOK THE MONEY?
YOU KNEW ABOUT IT?
I TOLD BERT YOU WOULDN'T WORK FOR VAMPIRES.
MONEY TALKS, JAMISON, EVEN TO ME.
YOU DIDN'T DO IT FOR MONEY. WHAT WAS IT?
JAMISON THOUGHT VAMPIRES WERE FANGED PEOPLE. THEY WERE VERY CAREFUL TO KEEP HIM ON THE NICE, CLEAN FRINGES.
HE COULD AFFORD TO PRETEND, OR IGNORE, OR EVEN LIE TO HIMSELF.
ANYTHING THAT CAN KILL VAMPIRES COULD MAKE MEAT PIES OUT OF HUMAN BEINGS. I NEED TO CATCH THAT MANIAC BEFORE HE, SHE, OR IT, DOES JUST THAT.

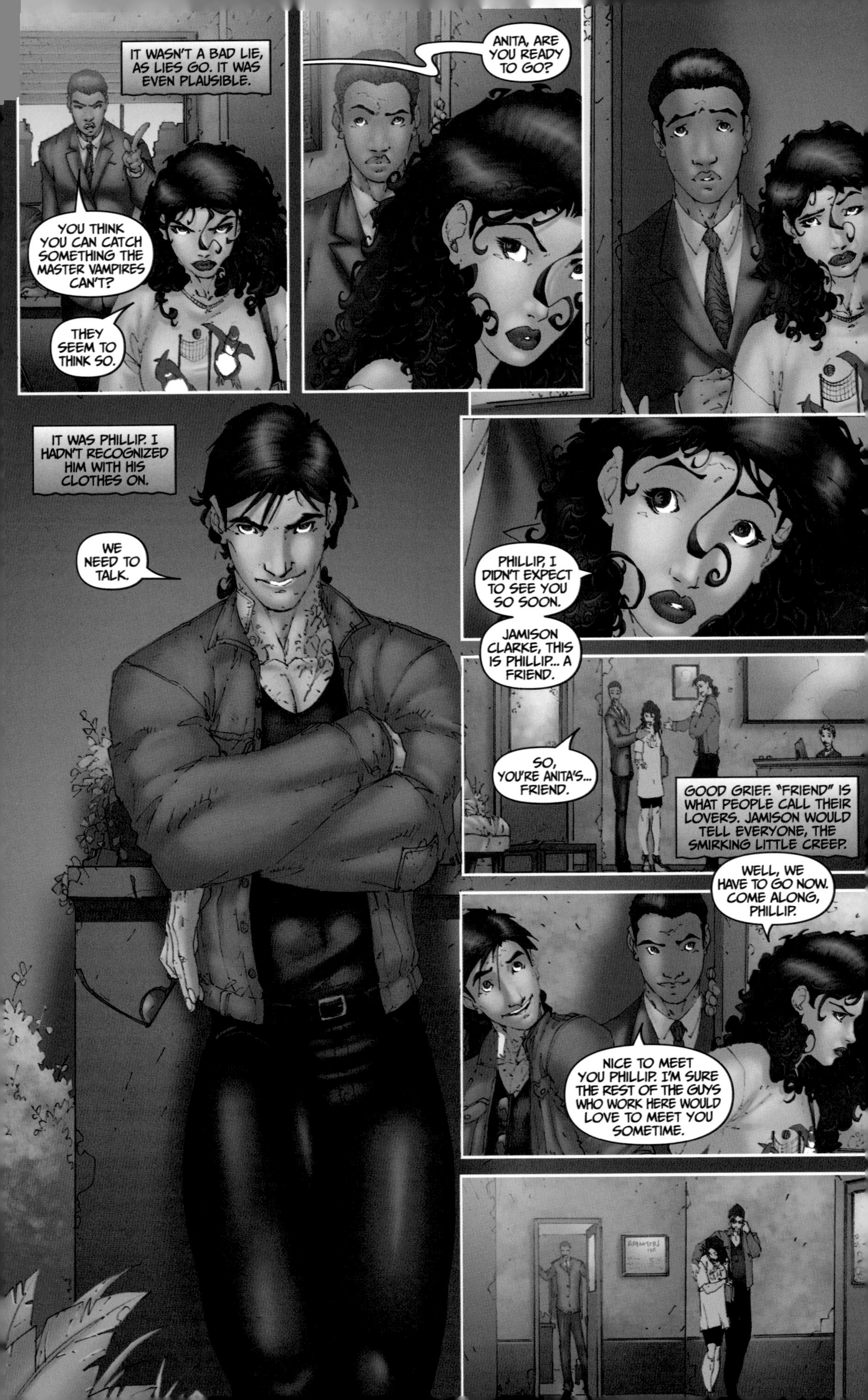
IT WASN'T A BAD LIE, AS LIES GO. IT WAS EVEN PLAUSIBLE.
YOU THINK YOU CAN CATCH SOMETHING THE MASTER VAMPIRES CAN'T?
THEY SEEM TO THINK SO.
ANITA, ARE YOU READY TO GO?
IT WAS PHILLIP. I HADN'T RECOGNIZED HIM WITH HIS CLOTHES ON.
WE NEED TO TALK.
PHILLIP, I DIDN'T EXPECT TO SEE YOU SO SOON.
JAMISON CLARKE, THIS IS PHILLIP... A FRIEND.
SO, YOU'RE ANITA'S... FRIEND.
GOOD GRIEF. "FRIEND" IS WHAT PEOPLE CALL THEIR LOVERS. JAMISON WOULD TELL EVERYONE, THE SMIRKING LITTLE CREEP.
WELL, WE HAVE TO GO NOW. COME ALONG, PHILLIP.
NICE TO MEET YOU PHILLIP. I'M SURE THE REST OF THE GUYS WHO WORK HERE WOULD LOVE TO MEET YOU SOMETIME.

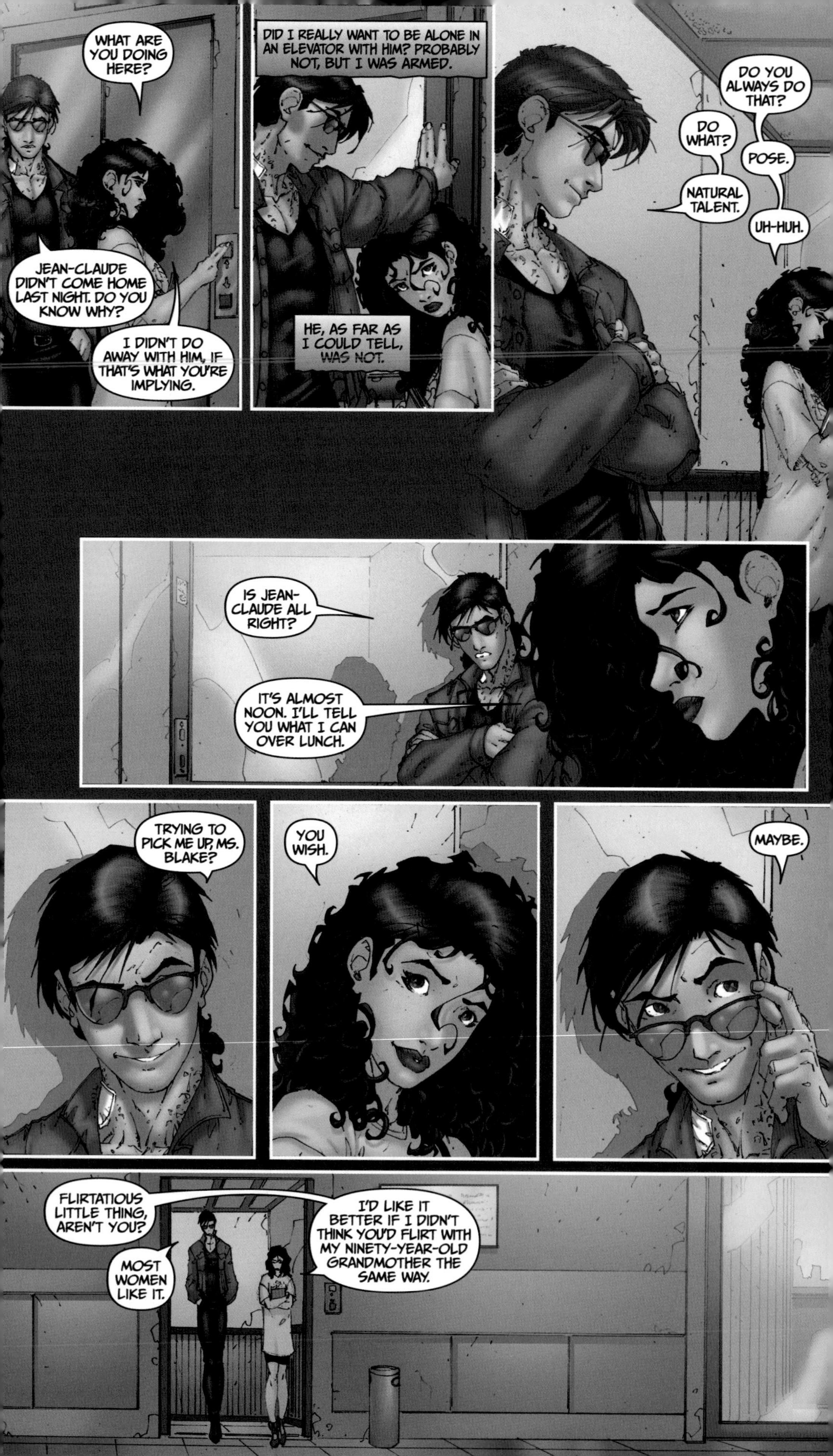
WHAT ARE YOU DOING HERE?
JEAN-CLAUDE DIDN'T COME HOME LAST NIGHT. DO YOU KNOW WHY?
I DIDN'T DO AWAY WITH HIM, IF THAT'S WHAT YOU'RE IMPLYING.
DID I REALLY WANT TO BE ALONE IN AN ELEVATOR WITH HIM? PROBABLY NOT, BUT I WAS ARMED.
HE, AS FAR AS I COULD TELL, WAS NOT.
DO YOU ALWAYS DO THAT?
DO WHAT?
POSE.
NATURAL TALENT.
UH-HUH.
IS JEAN-CLAUDE ALL RIGHT?
IT'S ALMOST NOON. I'LL TELL YOU WHAT I CAN OVER LUNCH.
TRYING TO PICK ME UP, MS. BLAKE?
YOU WISH.
MAYBE.
FLIRTATIOUS LITTLE THING, AREN'T YOU?
MOST WOMEN LIKE IT.
I'D LIKE IT BETTER IF I DIDN'T THINK YOU'D FLIRT WITH MY NINETY-YEAR-OLD GRANDMOTHER THE SAME WAY.

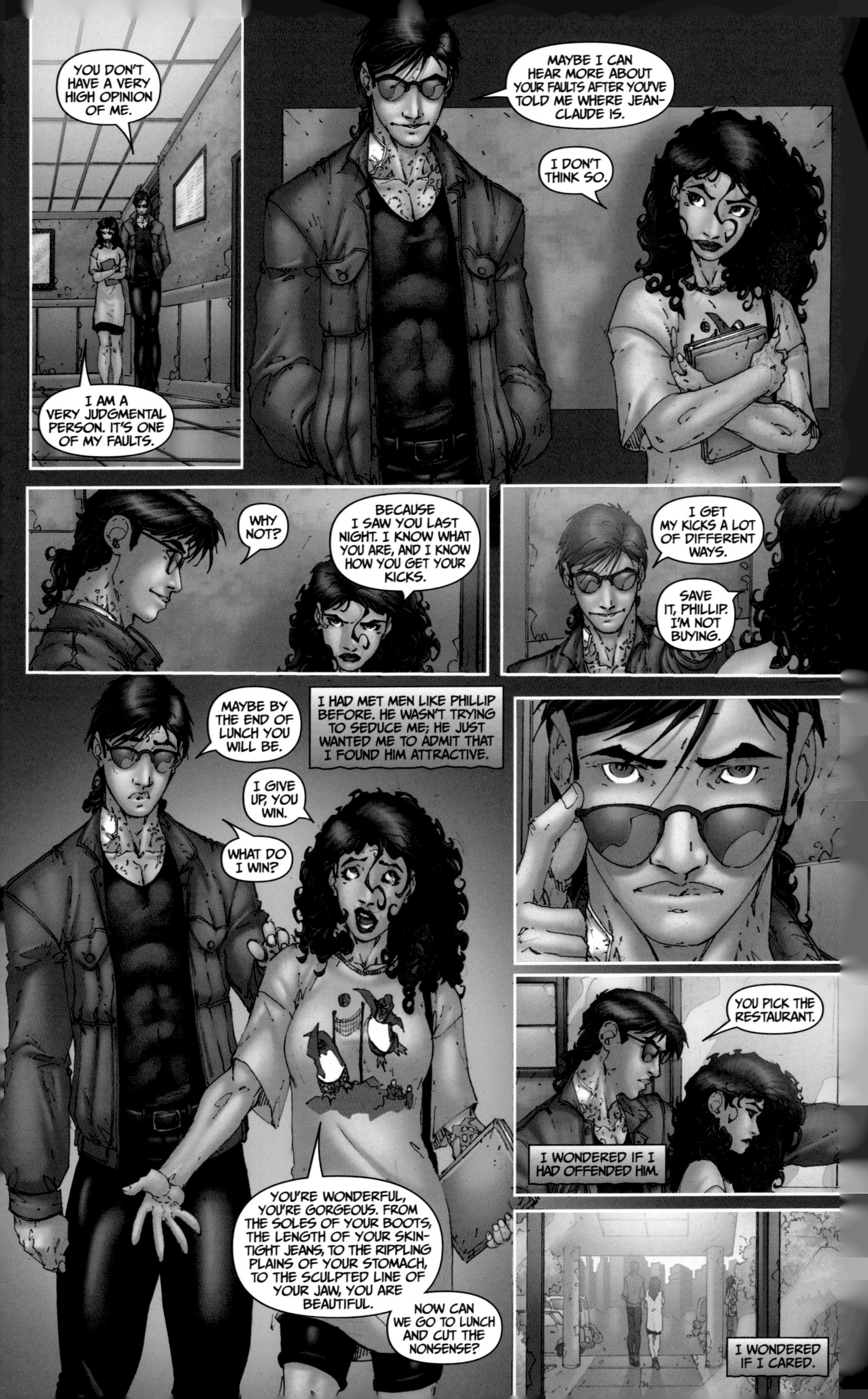

YOU DON'T HAVE A VERY HIGH OPINION OF ME.
I AM A VERY JUDGMENTAL PERSON. IT'S ONE OF MY FAULTS.
MAYBE I CAN HEAR MORE ABOUT YOUR FAULTS AFTER YOU'VE TOLD ME WHERE JEAN-CLAUDE IS.
I DON'T THINK SO.
WHY NOT?
BECAUSE I SAW YOU LAST NIGHT. I KNOW WHAT YOU ARE, AND I KNOW HOW YOU GET YOUR KICKS.
I GET MY KICKS A LOT OF DIFFERENT WAYS.
SAVE IT, PHILLIP. I'M NOT BUYING.
MAYBE BY THE END OF LUNCH YOU WILL BE.
I HAD MET MEN LIKE PHILLIP BEFORE. HE WASN'T TRYING TO SEDUCE ME; HE JUST WANTED ME TO ADMIT THAT I FOUND HIM ATTRACTIVE.
I GIVE UP, YOU WIN.
WHAT DO I WIN?
YOU'RE WONDERFUL, YOU'RE GORGEOUS. FROM THE SOLES OF YOUR BOOTS, THE LENGTH OF YOUR SKIN-TIGHT JEANS, TO THE RIPPLING PLAINS OF YOUR STOMACH, TO THE SCULPTED LINE OF YOUR JAW, YOU ARE BEAUTIFUL.
NOW CAN WE GO TO LUNCH AND CUT THE NONSENSE?
YOU PICK THE RESTAURANT.
I WONDERED IF I HAD OFFENDED HIM.
I WONDERED IF I CARED.

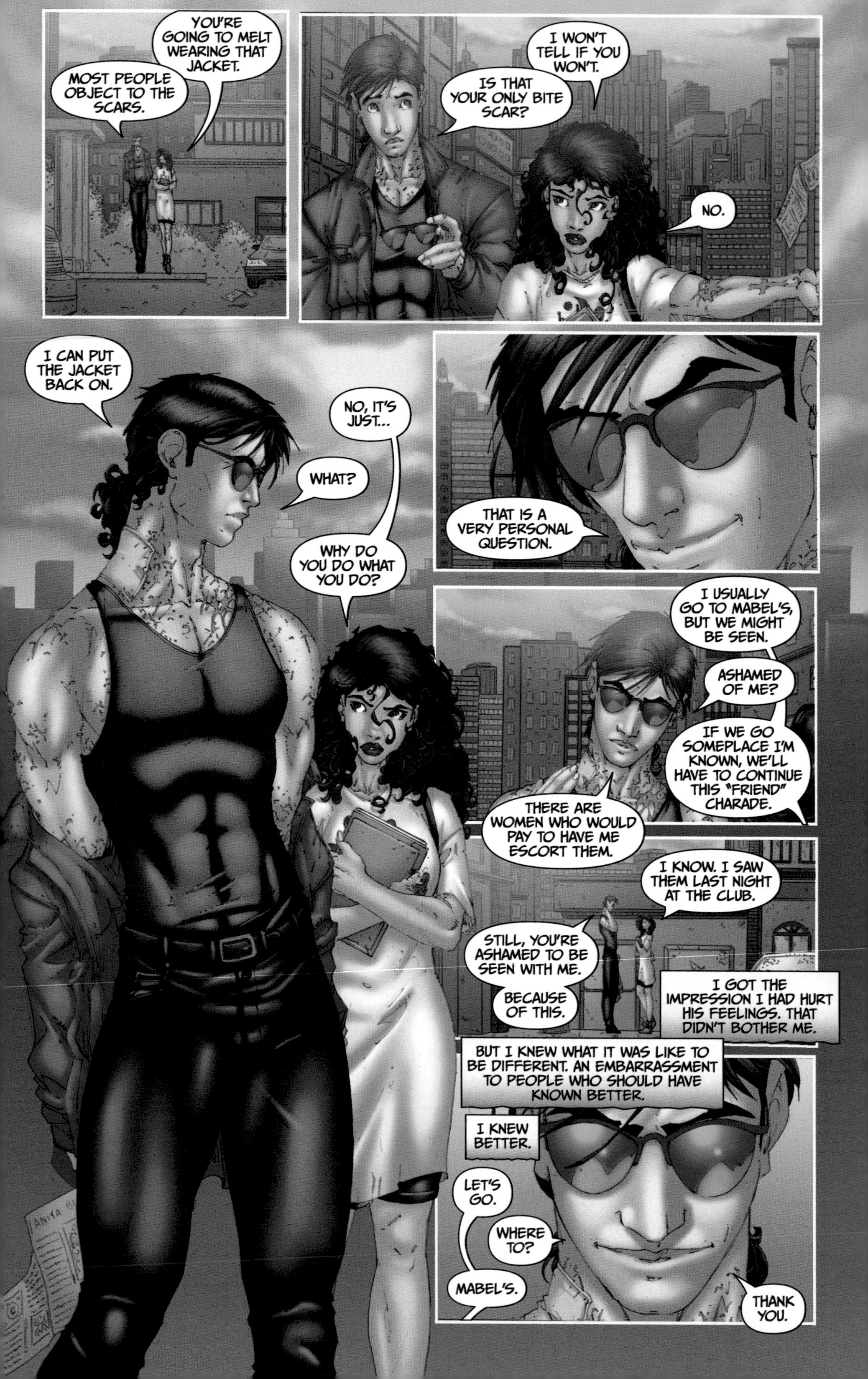
MOST PEOPLE OBJECT TO THE SCARS.
YOU'RE GOING TO MELT WEARING THAT JACKET.
I WON'T TELL IF YOU WON'T.
IS THAT YOUR ONLY BITE SCAR?
NO.
I CAN PUT THE JACKET BACK ON.
NO, IT'S JUST...
WHAT?
WHY DO YOU DO WHAT YOU DO?
THAT IS A VERY PERSONAL QUESTION.
I USUALLY GO TO MABEL'S, BUT WE MIGHT BE SEEN.
ASHAMED OF ME?
IF WE GO SOMEPLACE I'M KNOWN, WE'LL HAVE TO CONTINUE THIS "FRIEND" CHARADE.
THERE ARE WOMEN WHO WOULD PAY TO HAVE ME ESCORT THEM.
I KNOW. I SAW THEM LAST NIGHT AT THE CLUB.
STILL, YOU'RE ASHAMED TO BE SEEN WITH ME.
BECAUSE OF THIS.
I GOT THE IMPRESSION I HAD HURT HIS FEELINGS. THAT DIDN'T BOTHER ME.
BUT I KNEW WHAT IT WAS LIKE TO BE DIFFERENT. AN EMBARRASSMENT TO PEOPLE WHO SHOULD HAVE KNOWN BETTER.
I KNEW BETTER.
LET'S GO.
WHERE TO?
MABEL'S.
THANK YOU.

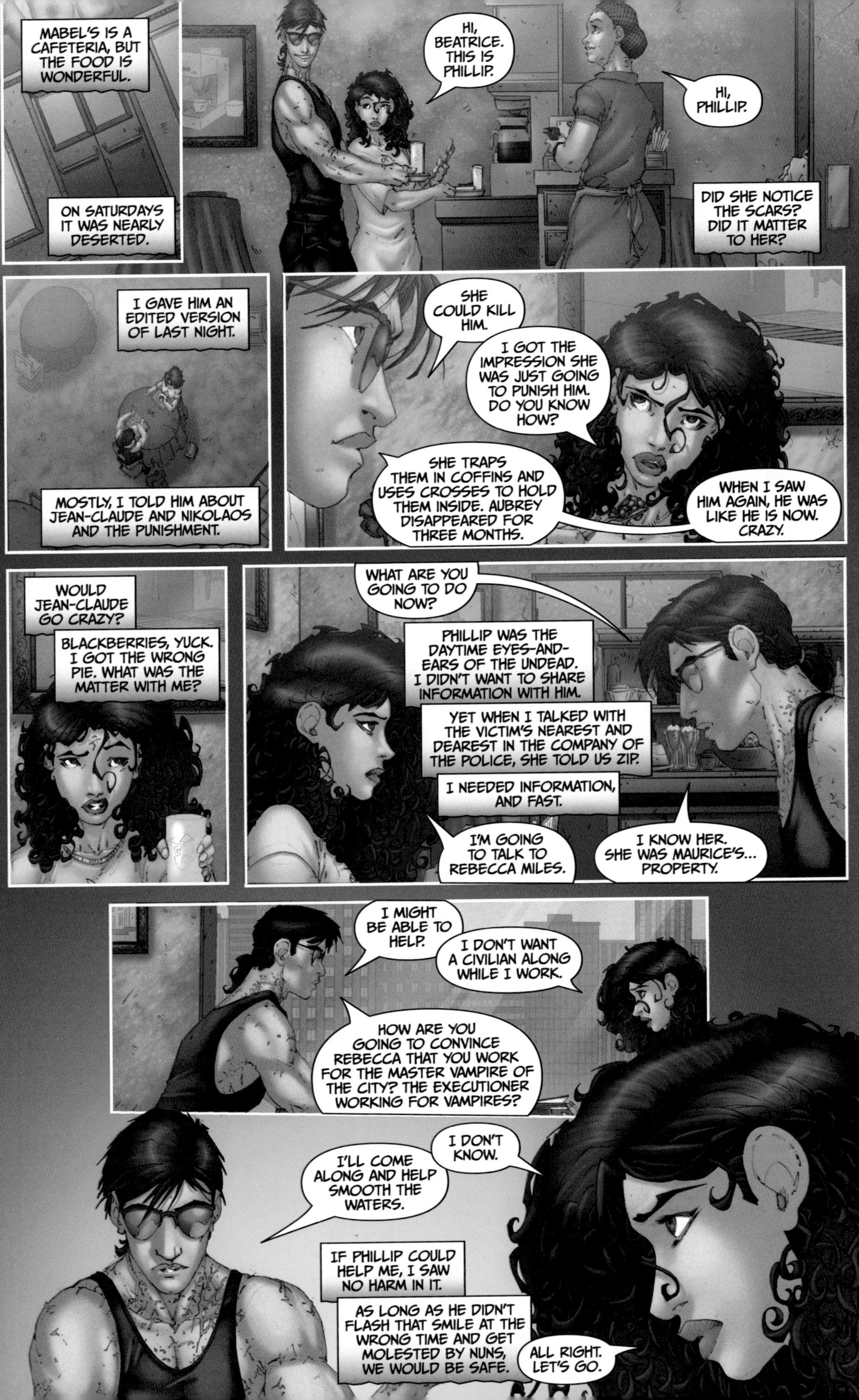

MABEL'S IS A CAFETERIA, BUT THE FOOD IS WONDERFUL.
HI, BEATRICE. THIS IS PHILLIP.
HI, PHILLIP.
ON SATURDAYS IT WAS NEARLY DESERTED.
DID SHE NOTICE THE SCARS? DID IT MATTER TO HER?
I GAVE HIM AN EDITED VERSION OF LAST NIGHT.
MOSTLY, I TOLD HIM ABOUT JEAN-CLAUDE AND NIKOLAOS AND THE PUNISHMENT.
SHE COULD KILL HIM.
I GOT THE IMPRESSION SHE WAS JUST GOING TO PUNISH HIM. DO YOU KNOW HOW?
SHE TRAPS THEM IN COFFINS AND USES CROSSES TO HOLD THEM INSIDE. AUBREY DISAPPEARED FOR THREE MONTHS.
WHEN I SAW HIM AGAIN, HE WAS LIKE HE IS NOW. CRAZY.
WOULD JEAN-CLAUDE GO CRAZY?
BLACKBERRIES, YUCK. I GOT THE WRONG PIE. WHAT WAS THE MATTER WITH ME?
WHAT ARE YOU GOING TO DO NOW?
PHILLIP WAS THE DAYTIME EYES-AND-EARS OF THE UNDEAD. I DIDN'T WANT TO SHARE INFORMATION WITH HIM.
YET WHEN I TALKED WITH THE VICTIM'S NEAREST AND DEAREST IN THE COMPANY OF THE POLICE, SHE TOLD US ZIP.
I NEEDED INFORMATION, AND FAST.
I'M GOING TO TALK TO REBECCA MILES.
I KNOW HER. SHE WAS MAURICE'S... PROPERTY.
I MIGHT BE ABLE TO HELP.
I DON'T WANT A CIVILIAN ALONG WHILE I WORK.
HOW ARE YOU GOING TO CONVINCE REBECCA THAT YOU WORK FOR THE MASTER VAMPIRE OF THE CITY? THE EXECUTIONER WORKING FOR VAMPIRES?
I DON'T KNOW.
I'LL COME ALONG AND HELP SMOOTH THE WATERS.
IF PHILLIP COULD HELP ME, I SAW NO HARM IN IT.
AS LONG AS HE DIDN'T FLASH THAT SMILE AT THE WRONG TIME AND GET MOLESTED BY NUNS, WE WOULD BE SAFE.
ALL RIGHT. LET'S GO.

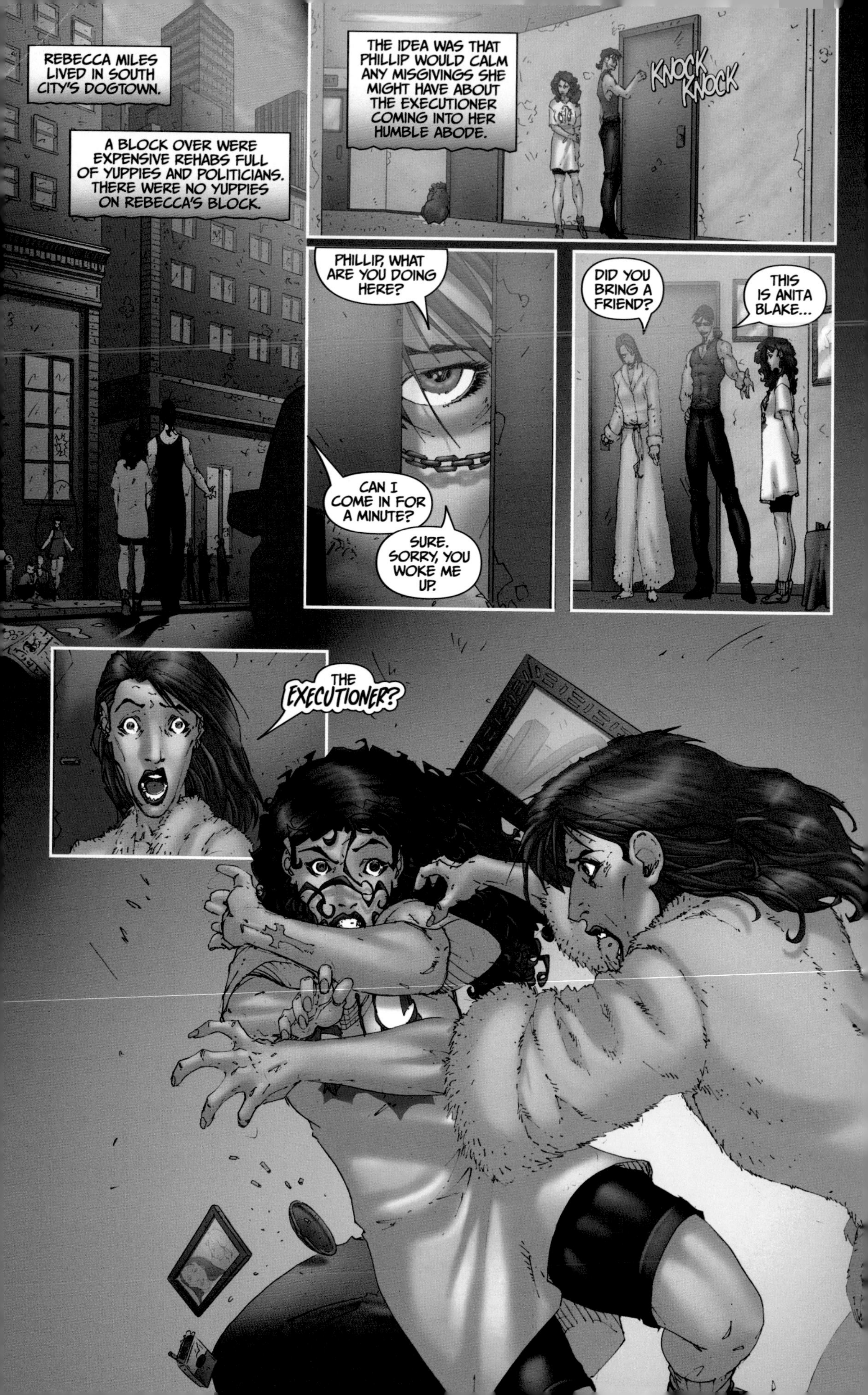
REBECCA MILES LIVED IN SOUTH CITY'S DOGTOWN.
A BLOCK OVER WERE EXPENSIVE REHABS FULL OF YUPPIES AND POLITICIANS. THERE WERE NO YUPPIES ON REBECCA'S BLOCK.
THE IDEA WAS THAT PHILLIP WOULD CALM ANY MISGIVINGS SHE MIGHT HAVE ABOUT THE EXECUTIONER COMING INTO HER HUMBLE ABODE.
KNOCK KNOCK
PHILLIP, WHAT ARE YOU DOING HERE?
CAN I COME IN FOR A MINUTE?
SURE. SORRY, YOU WOKE ME UP.
DID YOU BRING A FRIEND?
THIS IS ANITA BLAKE...
THE EXECUTIONER?

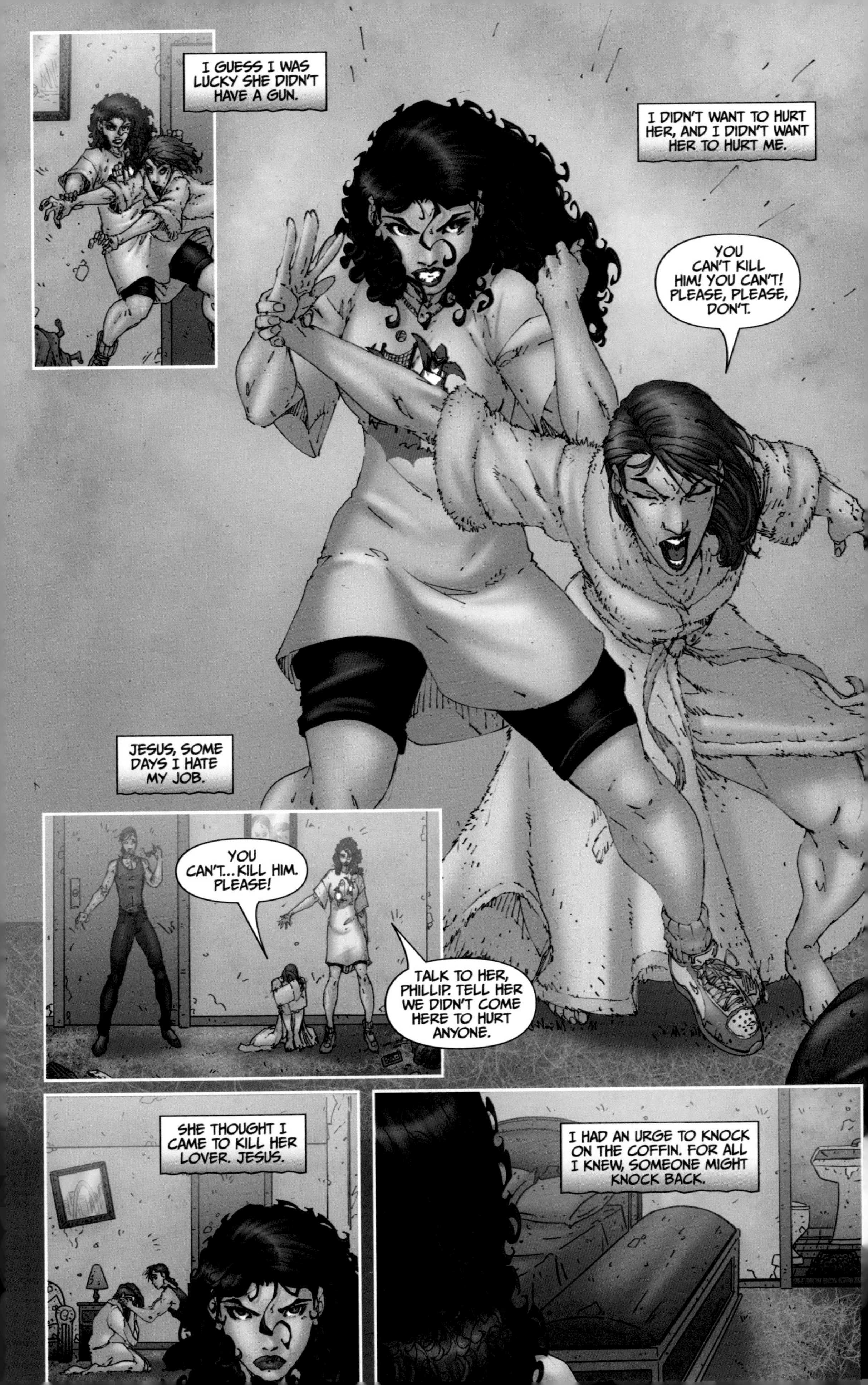
I GUESS I WAS LUCKY SHE DIDN'T HAVE A GUN.
I DIDN'T WANT TO HURT HER, AND I DIDN'T WANT HER TO HURT ME.
YOU CAN'T KILL HIM! YOU CAN'T! PLEASE, PLEASE, DON'T.
JESUS, SOME DAYS I HATE MY JOB.
YOU CAN'T... KILL HIM. PLEASE!
TALK TO HER, PHILLIP. TELL HER WE DIDN'T COME HERE TO HURT ANYONE.
SHE THOUGHT I CAME TO KILL HER LOVER. JESUS.
I HAD AN URGE TO KNOCK ON THE COFFIN. FOR ALL I KNEW, SOMEONE MIGHT KNOCK BACK.

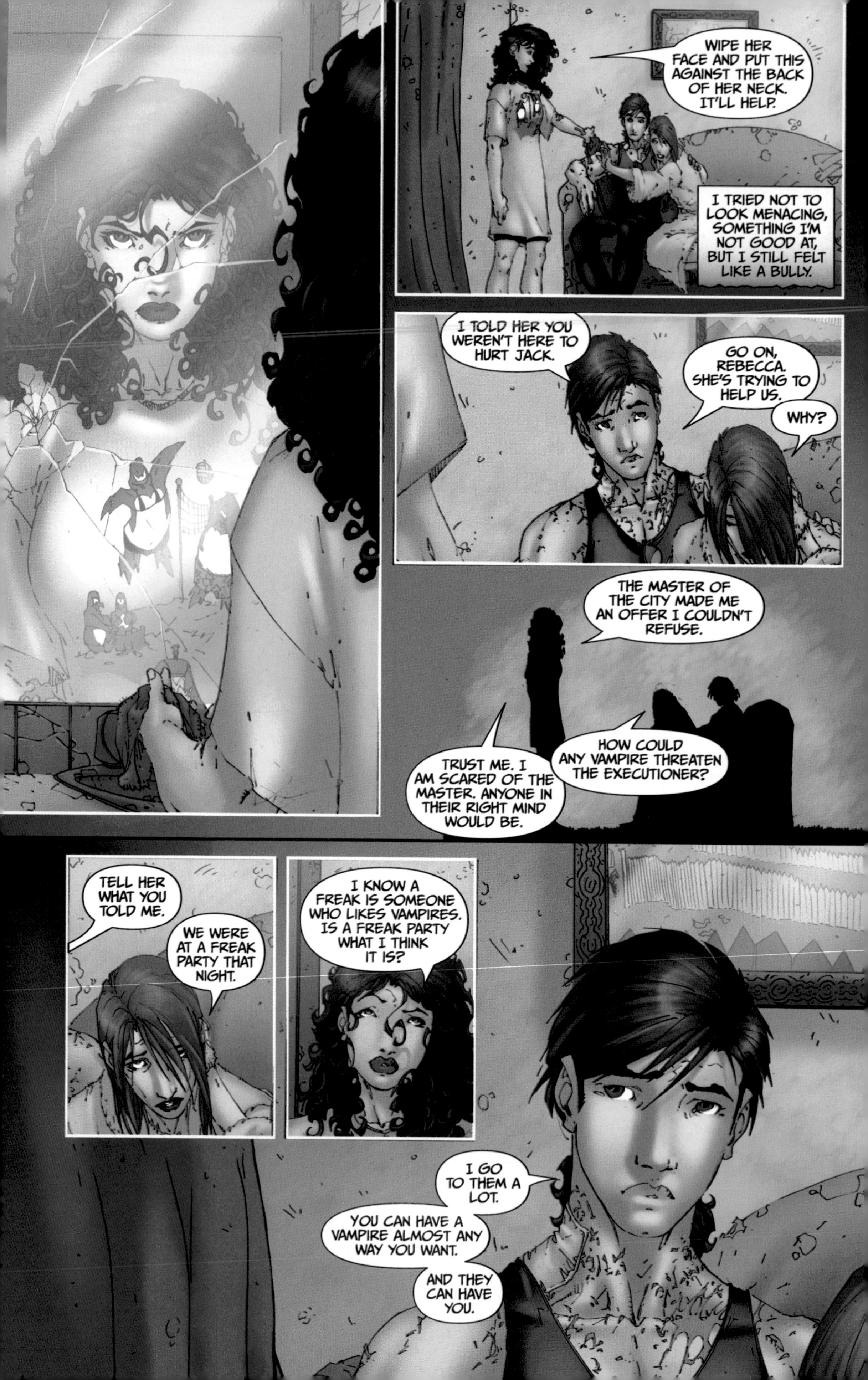
WIPE HER FACE AND PUT THIS AGAINST THE BACK OF HER NECK. IT'LL HELP.
I TRIED NOT TO LOOK MENACING, SOMETHING I'M NOT GOOD AT, BUT I STILL FELT LIKE A BULLY.
I TOLD HER YOU WEREN'T HERE TO HURT JACK.
GO ON, REBECCA. SHE'S TRYING TO HELP US.
WHY?
THE MASTER OF THE CITY MADE ME AN OFFER I COULDN'T REFUSE.
HOW COULD ANY VAMPIRE THREATEN THE EXECUTIONER?
TRUST ME. I AM SCARED OF THE MASTER. ANYONE IN THEIR RIGHT MIND WOULD BE.
TELL HER WHAT YOU TOLD ME.
WE WERE AT A FREAK PARTY THAT NIGHT.
I KNOW A FREAK IS SOMEONE WHO LIKES VAMPIRES. IS A FREAK PARTY WHAT I THINK IT IS?
I GO TO THEM A LOT.
YOU CAN HAVE A VAMPIRE ALMOST ANY WAY YOU WANT.
AND THEY CAN HAVE YOU.

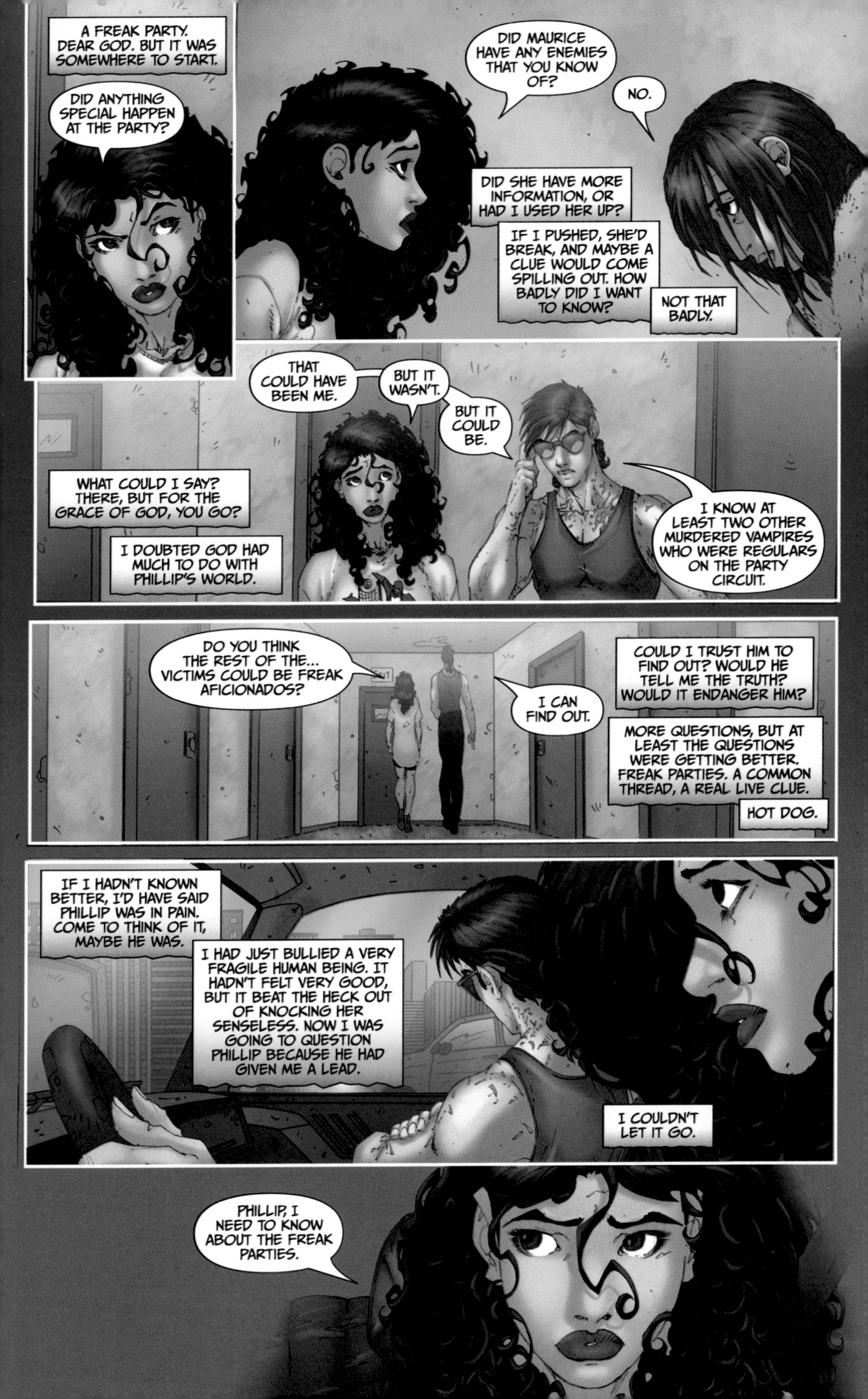
A FREAK PARTY. DEAR GOD. BUT IT WAS SOMEWHERE TO START.
DID ANYTHING SPECIAL HAPPEN AT THE PARTY?
DID MAURICE HAVE ANY ENEMIES THAT YOU KNOW OF?
NO.
DID SHE HAVE MORE INFORMATION, OR HAD I USED HER UP?
IF I PUSHED, SHE'D BREAK, AND MAYBE A CLUE WOULD COME SPILLING OUT. HOW BADLY DID I WANT TO KNOW?
NOT THAT BADLY.
THAT COULD HAVE BEEN ME.
BUT IT WASN'T.
BUT IT COULD BE.
WHAT COULD I SAY? THERE, BUT FOR THE GRACE OF GOD, YOU GO?
I DOUBTED GOD HAD MUCH TO DO WITH PHILLIP'S WORLD.
I KNOW AT LEAST TWO OTHER MURDERED VAMPIRES WHO WERE REGULARS ON THE PARTY CIRCUIT.
DO YOU THINK THE REST OF THE... VICTIMS COULD BE FREAK AFICIONADOS?
I CAN FIND OUT.
COULD I TRUST HIM TO FIND OUT? WOULD HE TELL ME THE TRUTH? WOULD IT ENDANGER HIM?
MORE QUESTIONS, BUT AT LEAST THE QUESTIONS WERE GETTING BETTER. FREAK PARTIES. A COMMON THREAD, A REAL LIVE CLUE.
HOT DOG.
IF I HADN'T KNOWN BETTER, I'D HAVE SAID PHILLIP WAS IN PAIN. COME TO THINK OF IT, MAYBE HE WAS.
I HAD JUST BULLIED A VERY FRAGILE HUMAN BEING. IT HADN'T FELT VERY GOOD, BUT IT BEAT THE HECK OUT OF KNOCKING HER SENSELESS. NOW I WAS GOING TO QUESTION PHILLIP BECAUSE HE HAD GIVEN ME A LEAD.
I COULDN'T LET IT GO.
PHILLIP, I NEED TO KNOW ABOUT THE FREAK PARTIES.

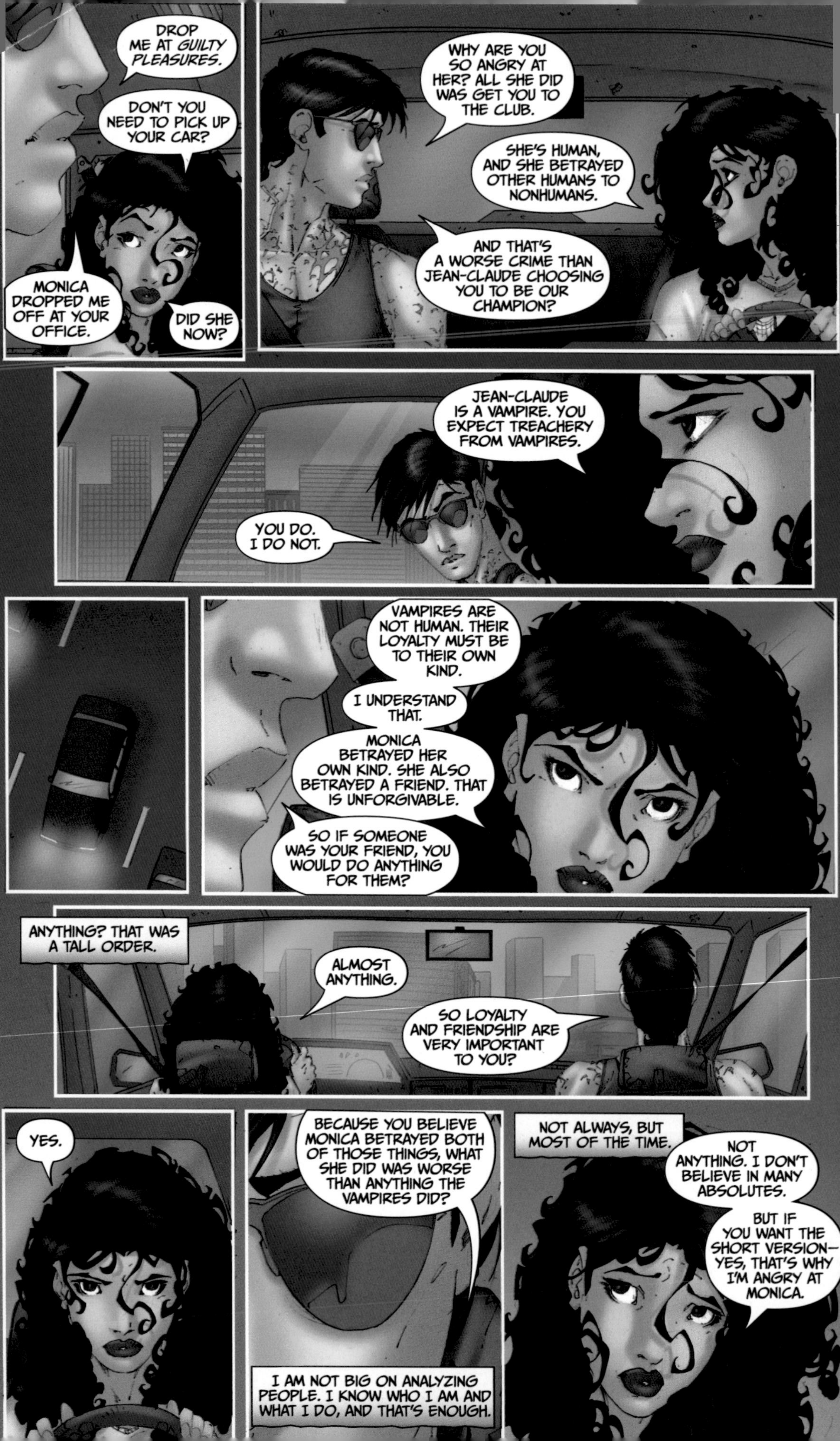
DROP ME AT GUILTY PLEASURES.
DON'T YOU NEED TO PICK UP YOUR CAR?
MONICA DROPPED ME OFF AT YOUR OFFICE.
DID SHE NOW?
WHY ARE YOU SO ANGRY AT HER? ALL SHE DID WAS GET YOU TO THE CLUB.
SHE'S HUMAN, AND SHE BETRAYED OTHER HUMANS TO NONHUMANS.
AND THAT'S A WORSE CRIME THAN JEAN-CLAUDE CHOOSING YOU TO BE OUR CHAMPION?
JEAN-CLAUDE IS A VAMPIRE. YOU EXPECT TREACHERY FROM VAMPIRES.
YOU DO. I DO NOT.
VAMPIRES ARE NOT HUMAN. THEIR LOYALTY MUST BE TO THEIR OWN KIND.
I UNDERSTAND THAT.
MONICA BETRAYED HER OWN KIND. SHE ALSO BETRAYED A FRIEND. THAT IS UNFORGIVABLE.
SO IF SOMEONE WAS YOUR FRIEND, YOU WOULD DO ANYTHING FOR THEM?
ANYTHING? THAT WAS A TALL ORDER.
ALMOST ANYTHING.
SO LOYALTY AND FRIENDSHIP ARE VERY IMPORTANT TO YOU?
YES.
BECAUSE YOU BELIEVE MONICA BETRAYED BOTH OF THOSE THINGS, WHAT SHE DID WAS WORSE THAN ANYTHING THE VAMPIRES DID?
I AM NOT BIG ON ANALYZING PEOPLE. I KNOW WHO I AM AND WHAT I DO, AND THAT'S ENOUGH.
NOT ALWAYS, BUT MOST OF THE TIME.
NOT ANYTHING. I DON'T BELIEVE IN MANY ABSOLUTES.
BUT IF YOU WANT THE SHORT VERSION— YES, THAT'S WHY I'M ANGRY AT MONICA.

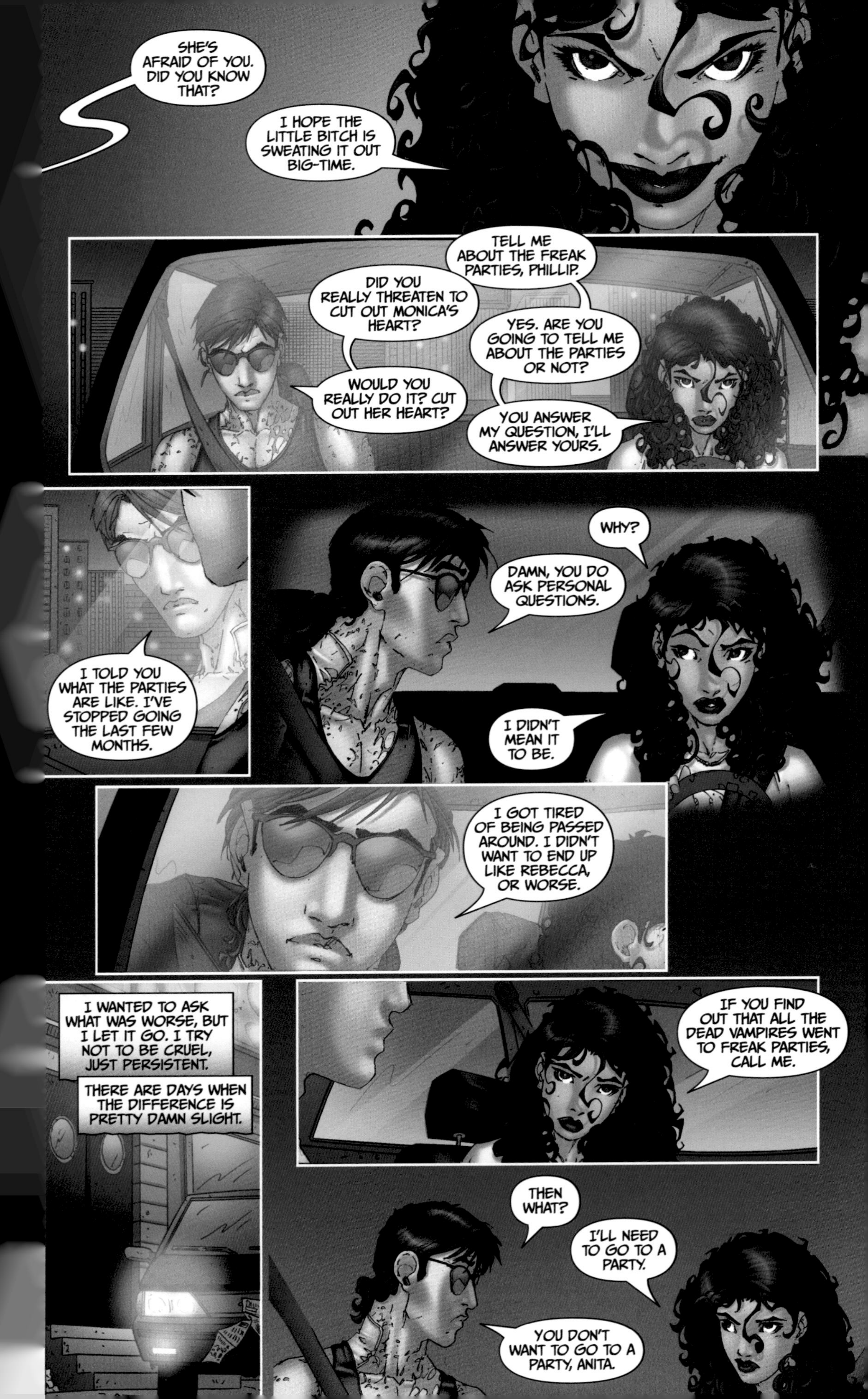
SHE'S AFRAID OF YOU. DID YOU KNOW THAT?
I HOPE THE LITTLE BITCH IS SWEATING IT OUT BIG-TIME.
TELL ME ABOUT THE FREAK PARTIES, PHILLIP.
DID YOU REALLY THREATEN TO CUT OUT MONICA'S HEART?
YES. ARE YOU GOING TO TELL ME ABOUT THE PARTIES OR NOT?
WOULD YOU REALLY DO IT? CUT OUT HER HEART?
YOU ANSWER MY QUESTION, I'LL ANSWER YOURS.
I TOLD YOU WHAT THE PARTIES ARE LIKE. I'VE STOPPED GOING THE LAST FEW MONTHS.
WHY?
DAMN, YOU DO ASK PERSONAL QUESTIONS.
I DIDN'T MEAN IT TO BE.
I GOT TIRED OF BEING PASSED AROUND. I DIDN'T WANT TO END UP LIKE REBECCA, OR WORSE.
I WANTED TO ASK WHAT WAS WORSE, BUT I LET IT GO. I TRY NOT TO BE CRUEL, JUST PERSISTENT.
THERE ARE DAYS WHEN THE DIFFERENCE IS PRETTY DAMN SLIGHT.
IF YOU FIND OUT THAT ALL THE DEAD VAMPIRES WENT TO FREAK PARTIES, CALL ME.
THEN WHAT?
I'LL NEED TO GO TO A PARTY.
YOU DON'T WANT TO GO TO A PARTY, ANITA.

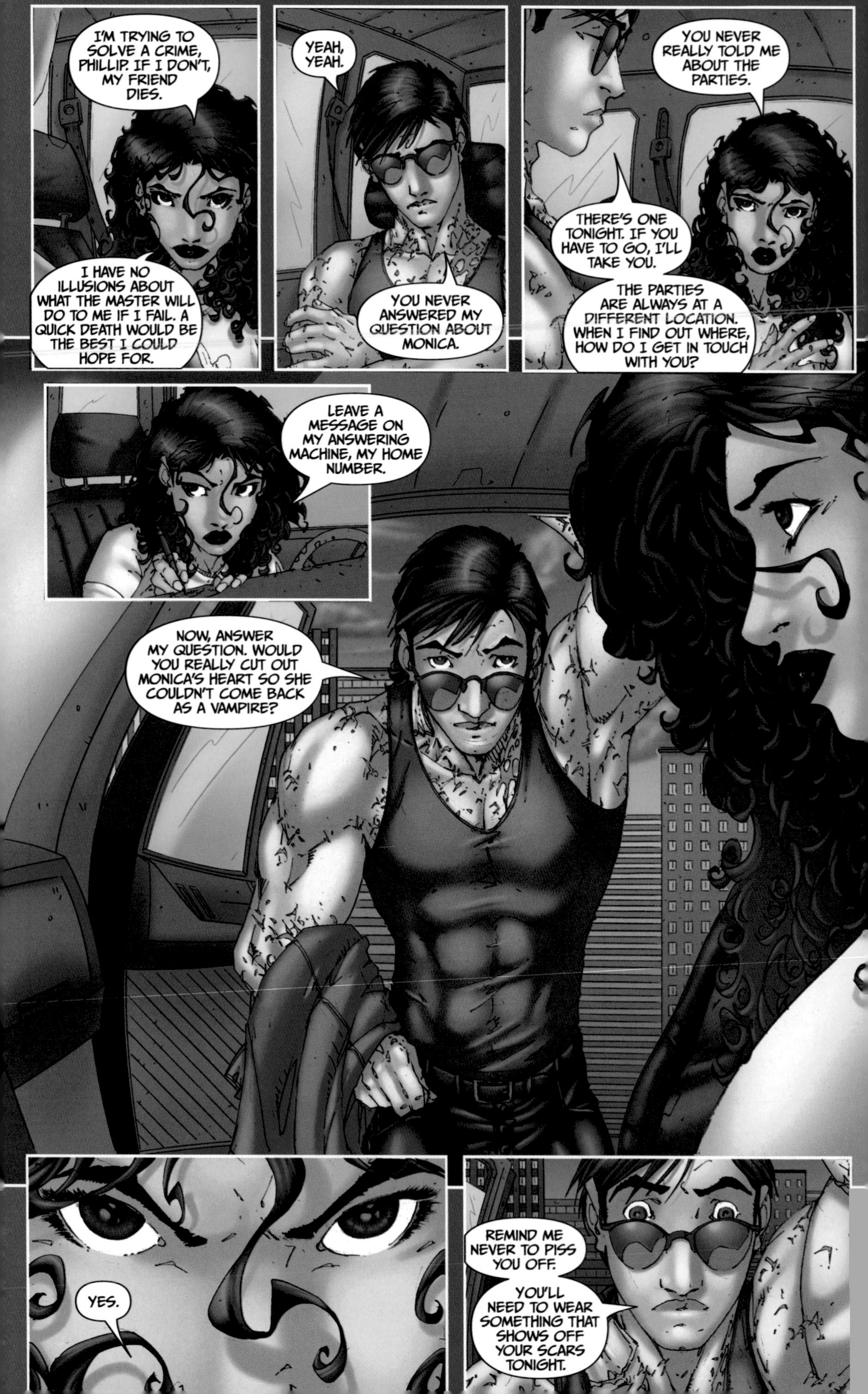
I'M TRYING TO SOLVE A CRIME, PHILLIP. IF I DON'T, MY FRIEND DIES.
I HAVE NO ILLUSIONS ABOUT WHAT THE MASTER WILL DO TO ME IF I FAIL. A QUICK DEATH WOULD BE THE BEST I COULD HOPE FOR.
YEAH, YEAH.
YOU NEVER ANSWERED MY QUESTION ABOUT MONICA.
YOU NEVER REALLY TOLD ME ABOUT THE PARTIES.
THERE'S ONE TONIGHT. IF YOU HAVE TO GO, I'LL TAKE YOU.
THE PARTIES ARE ALWAYS AT A DIFFERENT LOCATION. WHEN I FIND OUT WHERE, HOW DO I GET IN TOUCH WITH YOU?
LEAVE A MESSAGE ON MY ANSWERING MACHINE, MY HOME NUMBER.
NOW, ANSWER MY QUESTION. WOULD YOU REALLY CUT OUT MONICA'S HEART SO SHE COULDN'T COME BACK AS A VAMPIRE?
YES.
REMIND ME NEVER TO PISS YOU OFF.
YOU'LL NEED TO WEAR SOMETHING THAT SHOWS OFF YOUR SCARS TONIGHT.

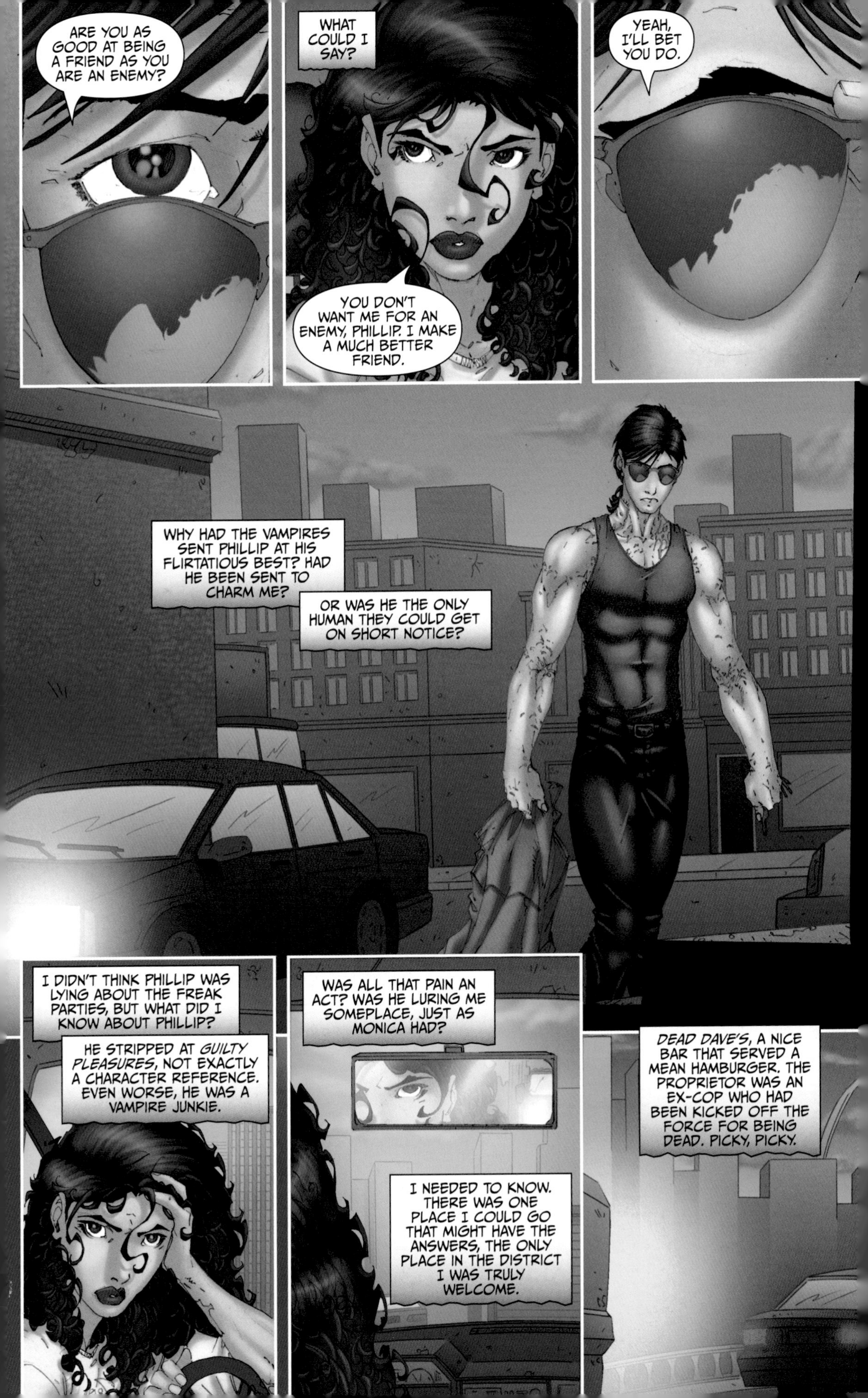
ARE YOU AS GOOD AT BEING A FRIEND AS YOU ARE AN ENEMY?
WHAT COULD I SAY?
YOU DON'T WANT ME FOR AN ENEMY, PHILLIP. I MAKE A MUCH BETTER FRIEND.
YEAH, I'LL BET YOU DO.
WHY HAD THE VAMPIRES SENT PHILLIP AT HIS FLIRTATIOUS BEST? HAD HE BEEN SENT TO CHARM ME?
OR WAS HE THE ONLY HUMAN THEY COULD GET ON SHORT NOTICE?
I DIDN'T THINK PHILLIP WAS LYING ABOUT THE FREAK PARTIES, BUT WHAT DID I KNOW ABOUT PHILLIP?
HE STRIPPED AT *GUILTY PLEASURES*, NOT EXACTLY A CHARACTER REFERENCE. EVEN WORSE, HE WAS A VAMPIRE JUNKIE.
WAS ALL THAT PAIN AN ACT? WAS HE LURING ME SOMEPLACE, JUST AS MONICA HAD?
I NEEDED TO KNOW. THERE WAS ONE PLACE I COULD GO THAT MIGHT HAVE THE ANSWERS, THE ONLY PLACE IN THE DISTRICT I WAS TRULY WELCOME.
DEAD DAVE'S, A NICE BAR THAT SERVED A MEAN HAMBURGER. THE PROPRIETOR WAS AN EX-COP WHO HAD BEEN KICKED OFF THE FORCE FOR BEING DEAD. PICKY, PICKY.

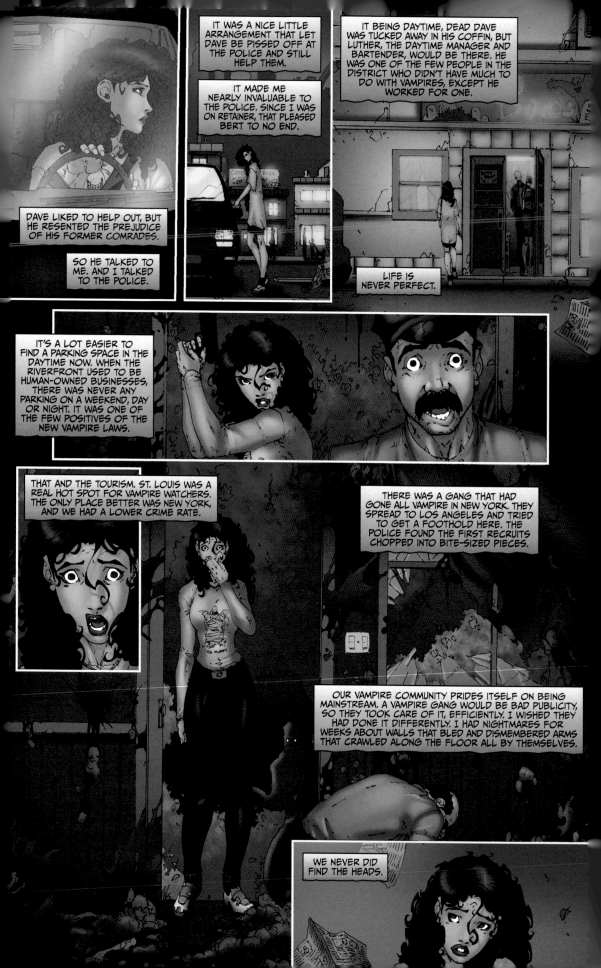

IT WAS A NICE LITTLE ARRANGEMENT THAT LET DAVE BE PISSED OFF AT THE POLICE AND STILL HELP THEM.

IT MADE ME NEARLY INVALUABLE TO THE POLICE. SINCE I WAS ON RETAINER, THAT PLEASED BERT TO NO END.

IT BEING DAYTIME, DEAD DAVE WAS TUCKED AWAY IN HIS COFFIN, BUT LUTHER, THE DAYTIME MANAGER AND BARTENDER, WOULD BE THERE. HE WAS ONE OF THE FEW PEOPLE IN THE DISTRICT WHO DIDN'T HAVE MUCH TO DO WITH VAMPIRES, EXCEPT HE WORKED FOR ONE.

DAVE LIKED TO HELP OUT, BUT HE RESENTED THE PREJUDICE OF HIS FORMER COMRADES.

SO HE TALKED TO ME. AND I TALKED TO THE POLICE.

LIFE IS NEVER PERFECT.

IT'S A LOT EASIER TO FIND A PARKING SPACE IN THE DAYTIME NOW. WHEN THE RIVERFRONT USED TO BE HUMAN-OWNED BUSINESSES, THERE WAS NEVER ANY PARKING ON A WEEKEND, DAY OR NIGHT. IT WAS ONE OF THE FEW POSITIVES OF THE NEW VAMPIRE LAWS.

THAT AND THE TOURISM. ST. LOUIS WAS A REAL HOT SPOT FOR VAMPIRE WATCHERS. THE ONLY PLACE BETTER WAS NEW YORK, AND WE HAD A LOWER CRIME RATE.

THERE WAS A GANG THAT HAD GONE ALL VAMPIRE IN NEW YORK. THEY SPREAD TO LOS ANGELES AND TRIED TO GET A FOOTHOLD HERE. THE POLICE FOUND THE FIRST RECRUITS CHOPPED INTO BITE-SIZED PIECES.

OUR VAMPIRE COMMUNITY PRIDES ITSELF ON BEING MAINSTREAM. A VAMPIRE GANG WOULD BE BAD PUBLICITY, SO THEY TOOK CARE OF IT, EFFICIENTLY. I WISHED THEY HAD DONE IT DIFFERENTLY. I HAD NIGHTMARES FOR WEEKS ABOUT WALLS THAT BLED AND DISMEMBERED ARMS THAT CRAWLED ALONG THE FLOOR ALL BY THEMSELVES.

WE NEVER DID FIND THE HEADS.

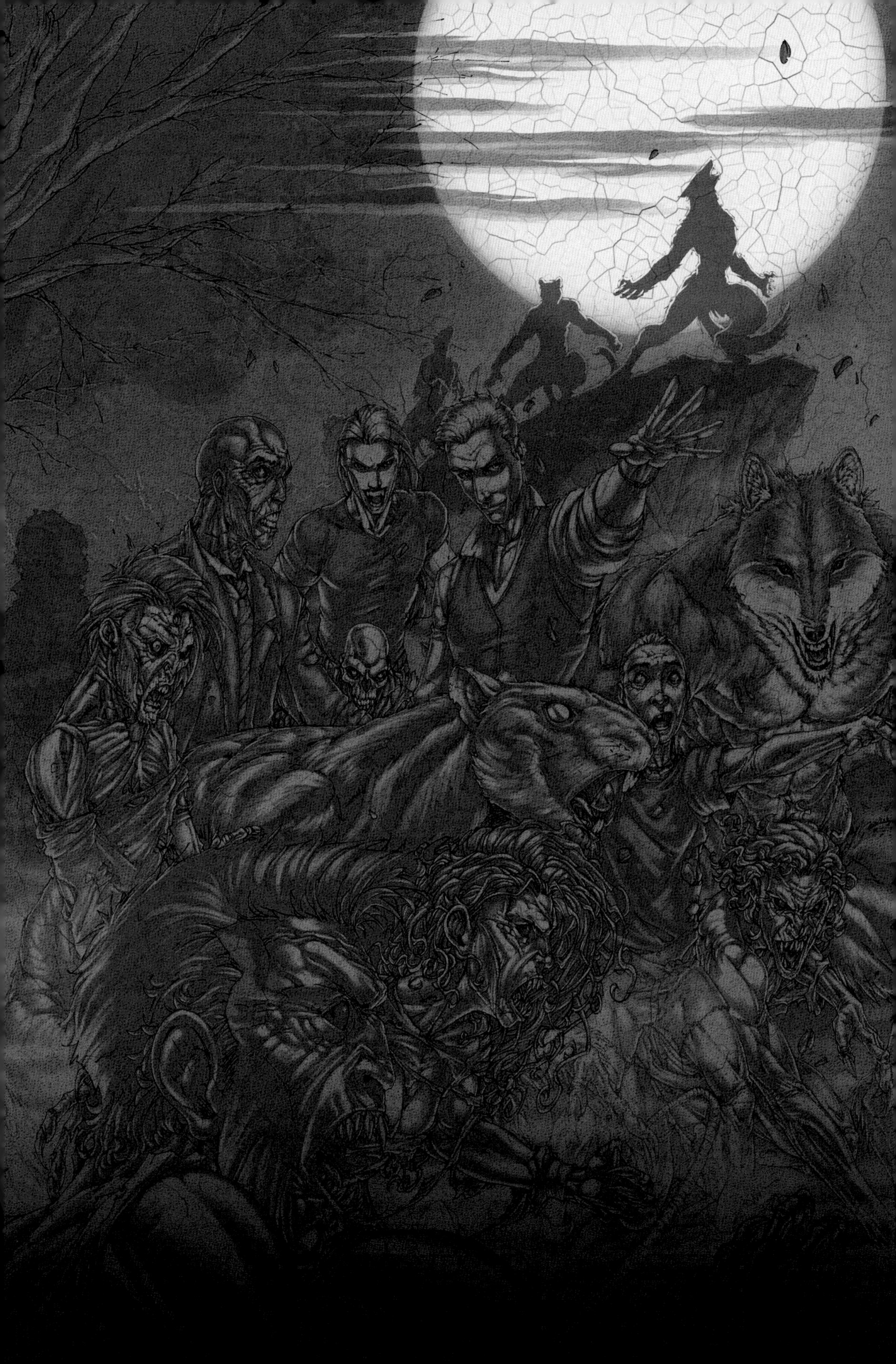

CHAPTER SIX

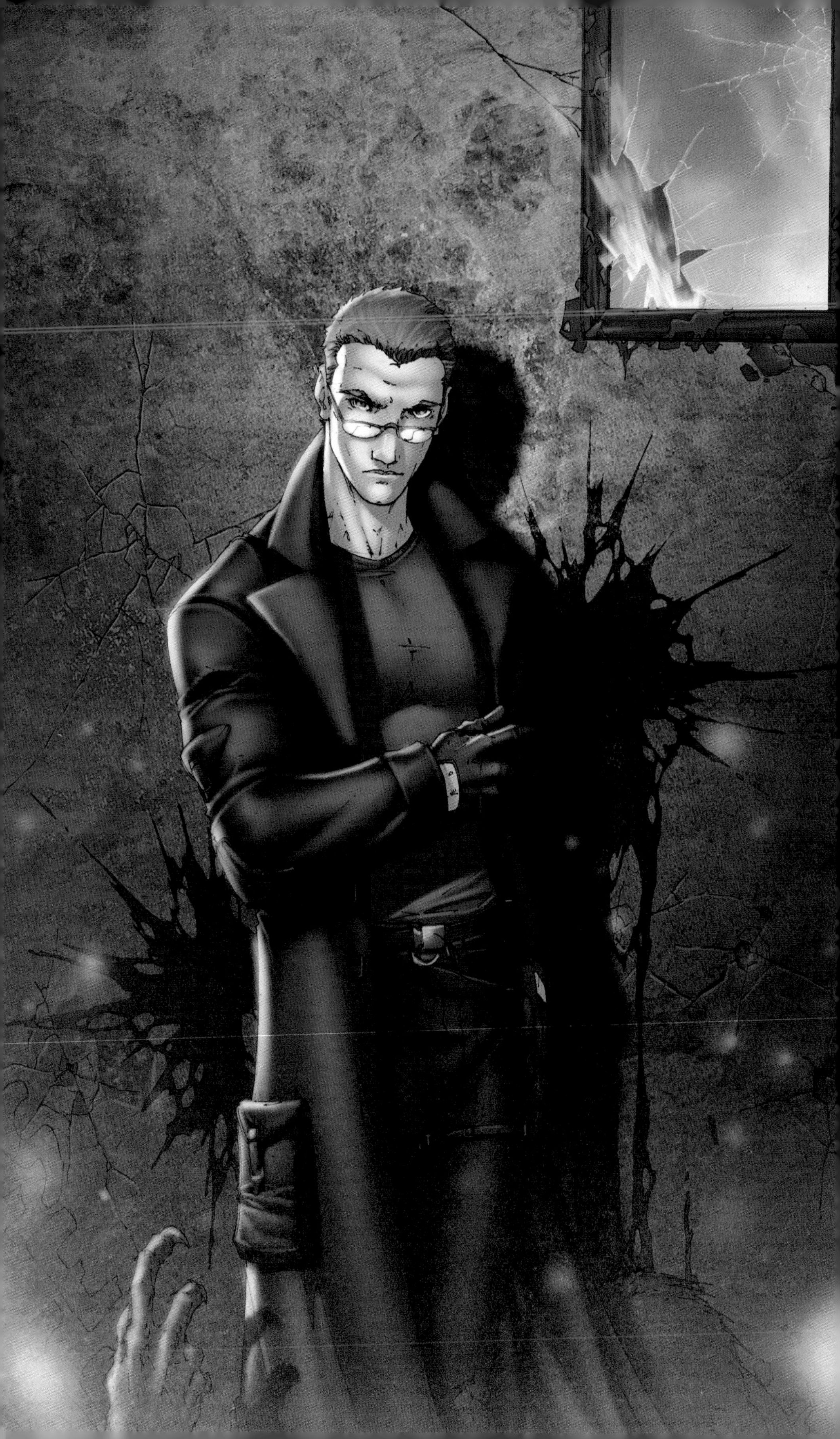

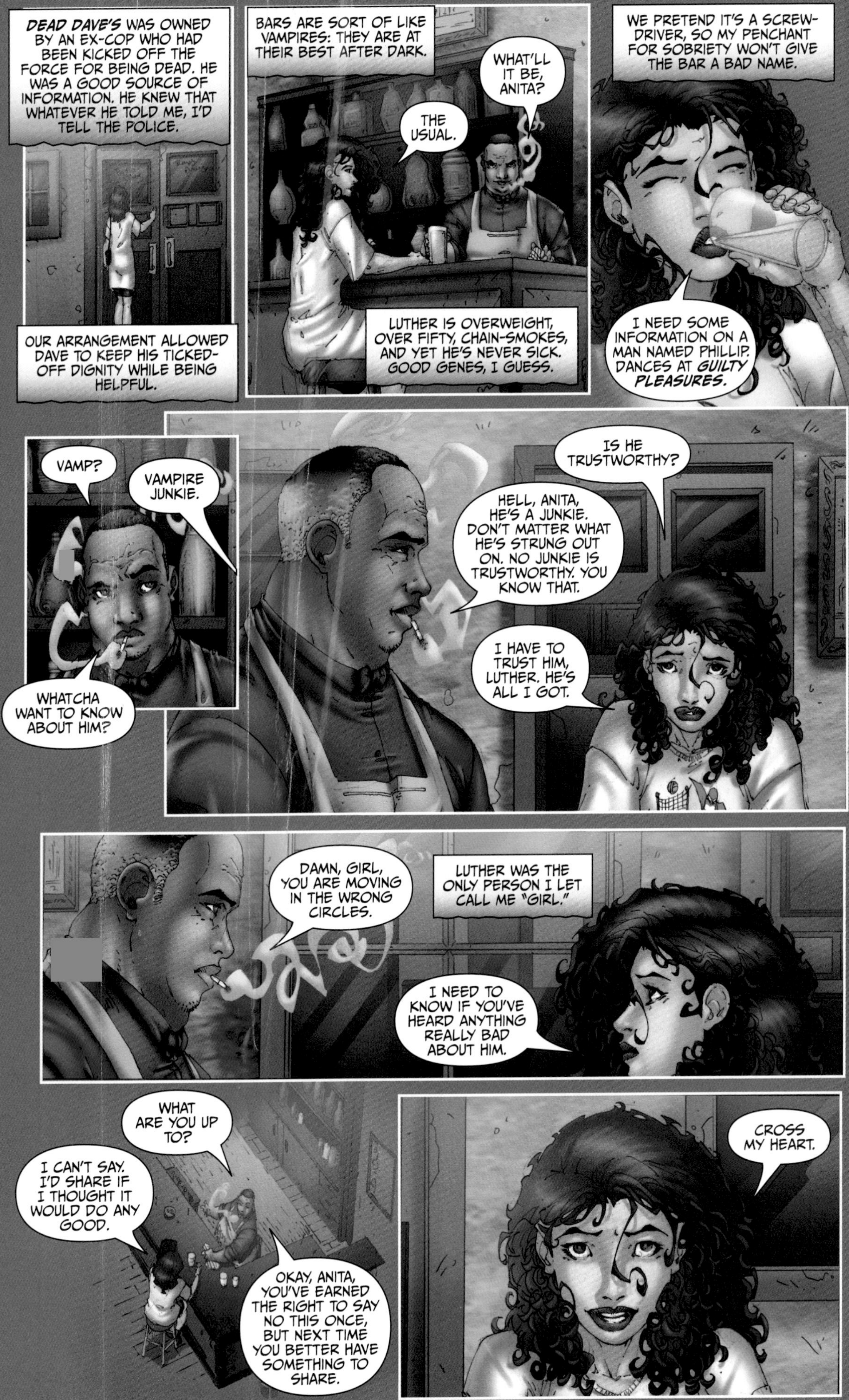
DEAD DAVE'S WAS OWNED BY AN EX-COP WHO HAD BEEN KICKED OFF THE FORCE FOR BEING DEAD. HE WAS A GOOD SOURCE OF INFORMATION. HE KNEW THAT WHATEVER HE TOLD ME, I'D TELL THE POLICE.
OUR ARRANGEMENT ALLOWED DAVE TO KEEP HIS TICKED-OFF DIGNITY WHILE BEING HELPFUL.
BARS ARE SORT OF LIKE VAMPIRES: THEY ARE AT THEIR BEST AFTER DARK.
WHAT'LL IT BE, ANITA?
THE USUAL.
LUTHER IS OVERWEIGHT, OVER FIFTY, CHAIN-SMOKES, AND YET HE'S NEVER SICK. GOOD GENES, I GUESS.
WE PRETEND IT'S A SCREW-DRIVER, SO MY PENCHANT FOR SOBRIETY WON'T GIVE THE BAR A BAD NAME.
I NEED SOME INFORMATION ON A MAN NAMED PHILLIP. DANCES AT GUILTY PLEASURES.
VAMP?
VAMPIRE JUNKIE.
WHATCHA WANT TO KNOW ABOUT HIM?
IS HE TRUSTWORTHY?
HELL, ANITA, HE'S A JUNKIE. DON'T MATTER WHAT HE'S STRUNG OUT ON. NO JUNKIE IS TRUSTWORTHY. YOU KNOW THAT.
I HAVE TO TRUST HIM, LUTHER. HE'S ALL I GOT.
DAMN, GIRL, YOU ARE MOVING IN THE WRONG CIRCLES.
LUTHER WAS THE ONLY PERSON I LET CALL ME "GIRL."
I NEED TO KNOW IF YOU'VE HEARD ANYTHING REALLY BAD ABOUT HIM.
WHAT ARE YOU UP TO?
I CAN'T SAY. I'D SHARE IF I THOUGHT IT WOULD DO ANY GOOD.
OKAY, ANITA, YOU'VE EARNED THE RIGHT TO SAY NO THIS ONCE, BUT NEXT TIME YOU BETTER HAVE SOMETHING TO SHARE.
CROSS MY HEART.

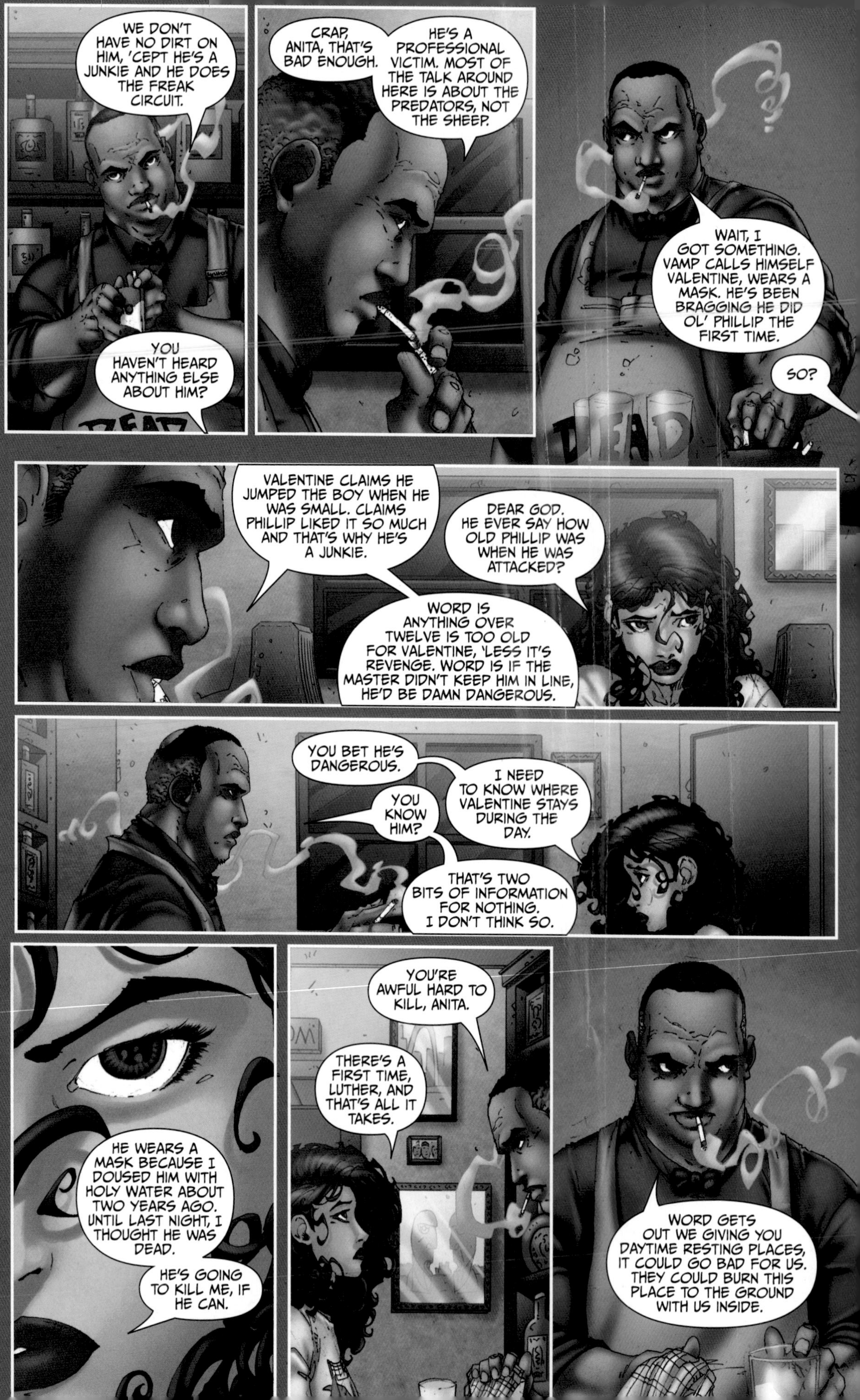
WE DON'T HAVE NO DIRT ON HIM, 'CEPT HE'S A JUNKIE AND HE DOES THE FREAK CIRCUIT.
YOU HAVEN'T HEARD ANYTHING ELSE ABOUT HIM?
CRAP, ANITA, THAT'S BAD ENOUGH.
HE'S A PROFESSIONAL VICTIM. MOST OF THE TALK AROUND HERE IS ABOUT THE PREDATORS, NOT THE SHEEP.
WAIT, I GOT SOMETHING. VAMP CALLS HIMSELF VALENTINE, WEARS A MASK. HE'S BEEN BRAGGING HE DID OL' PHILLIP THE FIRST TIME.
SO?
VALENTINE CLAIMS HE JUMPED THE BOY WHEN HE WAS SMALL. CLAIMS PHILLIP LIKED IT SO MUCH AND THAT'S WHY HE'S A JUNKIE.
DEAR GOD. HE EVER SAY HOW OLD PHILLIP WAS WHEN HE WAS ATTACKED?
WORD IS ANYTHING OVER TWELVE IS TOO OLD FOR VALENTINE, 'LESS IT'S REVENGE. WORD IS IF THE MASTER DIDN'T KEEP HIM IN LINE, HE'D BE DAMN DANGEROUS.
YOU BET HE'S DANGEROUS.
I NEED TO KNOW WHERE VALENTINE STAYS DURING THE DAY.
YOU KNOW HIM?
THAT'S TWO BITS OF INFORMATION FOR NOTHING. I DON'T THINK SO.
HE WEARS A MASK BECAUSE I DOUSED HIM WITH HOLY WATER ABOUT TWO YEARS AGO. UNTIL LAST NIGHT, I THOUGHT HE WAS DEAD.
HE'S GOING TO KILL ME, IF HE CAN.
YOU'RE AWFUL HARD TO KILL, ANITA.
THERE'S A FIRST TIME, LUTHER, AND THAT'S ALL IT TAKES.
WORD GETS OUT WE GIVING YOU DAYTIME RESTING PLACES, IT COULD GO BAD FOR US. THEY COULD BURN THIS PLACE TO THE GROUND WITH US INSIDE.

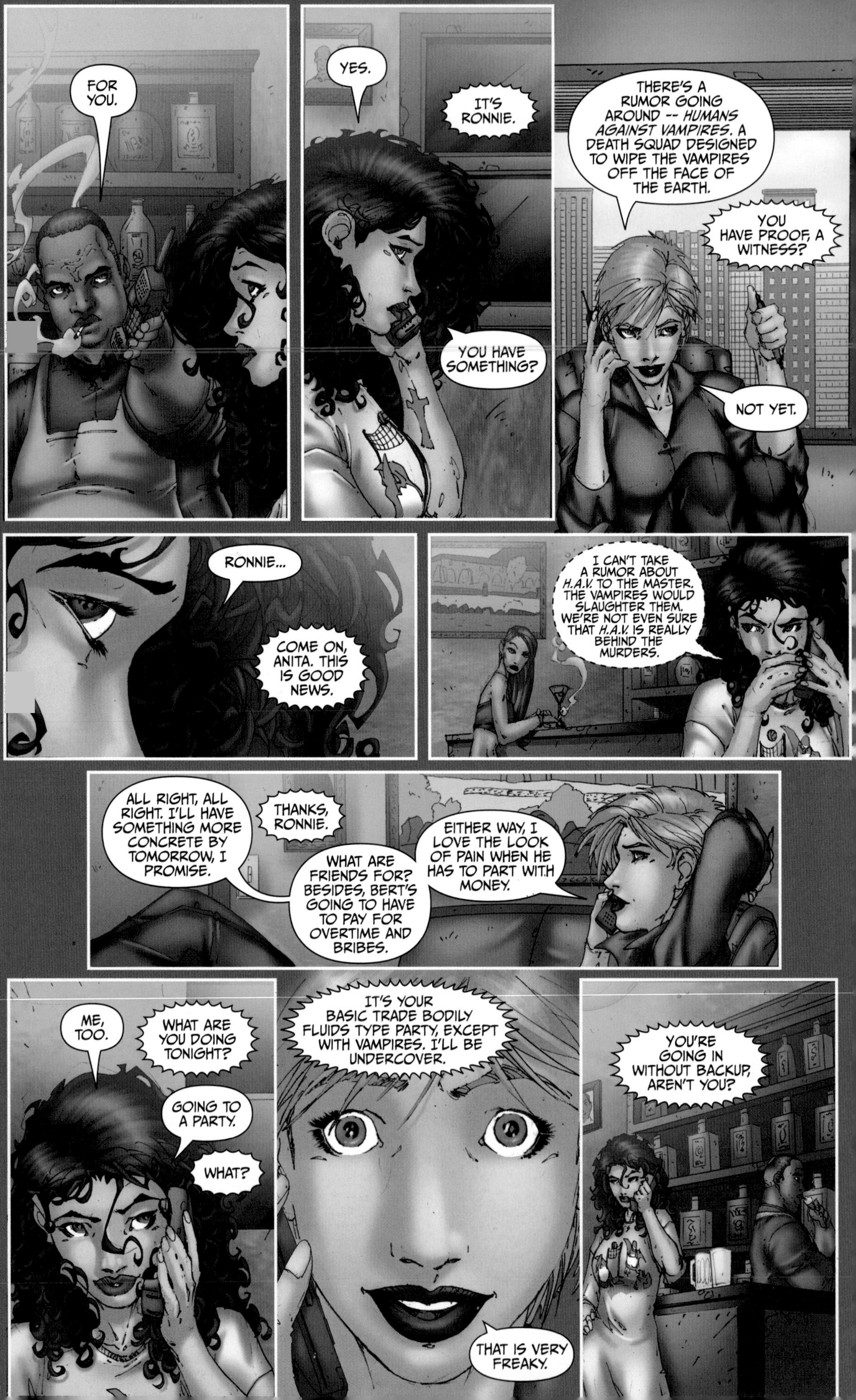
FOR YOU.
YES.
IT'S RONNIE.
YOU HAVE SOMETHING?
THERE'S A RUMOR GOING AROUND -- *HUMANS AGAINST VAMPIRES*. A DEATH SQUAD DESIGNED TO WIPE THE VAMPIRES OFF THE FACE OF THE EARTH.
YOU HAVE PROOF, A WITNESS?
NOT YET.
RONNIE...
COME ON, ANITA. THIS IS GOOD NEWS.
I CAN'T TAKE A RUMOR ABOUT *H.A.V.* TO THE MASTER. THE VAMPIRES WOULD SLAUGHTER THEM. WE'RE NOT EVEN SURE THAT *H.A.V.* IS REALLY BEHIND THE MURDERS.
ALL RIGHT, ALL RIGHT. I'LL HAVE SOMETHING MORE CONCRETE BY TOMORROW, I PROMISE.
THANKS, RONNIE.
WHAT ARE FRIENDS FOR? BESIDES, BERT'S GOING TO HAVE TO PAY FOR OVERTIME AND BRIBES.
EITHER WAY, I LOVE THE LOOK OF PAIN WHEN HE HAS TO PART WITH MONEY.
ME, TOO.
WHAT ARE YOU DOING TONIGHT?
GOING TO A PARTY.
WHAT?
IT'S YOUR BASIC TRADE BODILY FLUIDS TYPE PARTY, EXCEPT WITH VAMPIRES. I'LL BE UNDERCOVER.
THAT IS VERY FREAKY.
YOU'RE GOING IN WITHOUT BACKUP, AREN'T YOU?

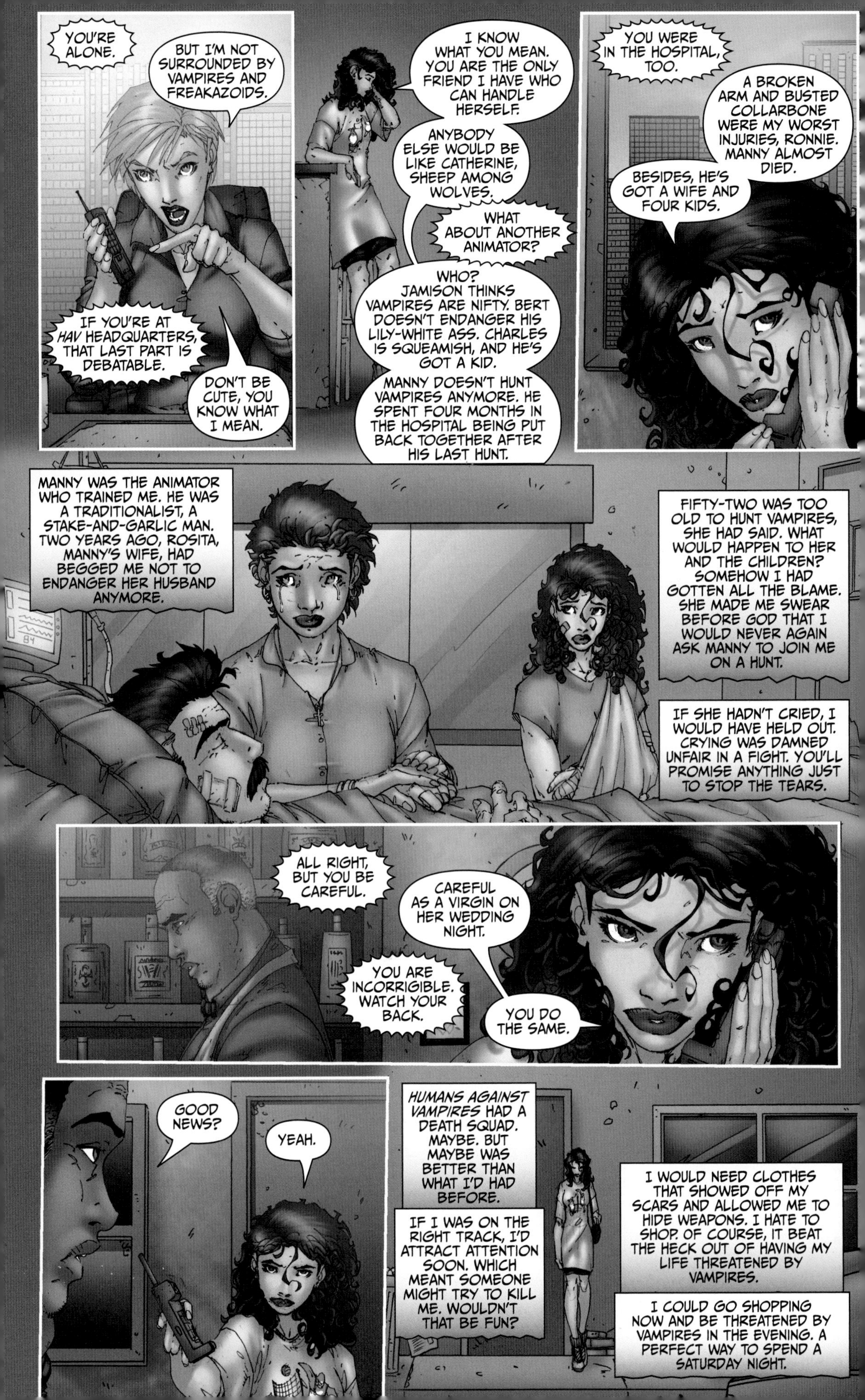
YOU'RE ALONE.
BUT I'M NOT SURROUNDED BY VAMPIRES AND FREAKAZOIDS.
IF YOU'RE AT *HAV* HEADQUARTERS, THAT LAST PART IS DEBATABLE.
DON'T BE CUTE, YOU KNOW WHAT I MEAN.
I KNOW WHAT YOU MEAN. YOU ARE THE ONLY FRIEND I HAVE WHO CAN HANDLE HERSELF.
ANYBODY ELSE WOULD BE LIKE CATHERINE, SHEEP AMONG WOLVES.
WHAT ABOUT ANOTHER ANIMATOR?
WHO? JAMISON THINKS VAMPIRES ARE NIFTY. BERT DOESN'T ENDANGER HIS LILY-WHITE ASS. CHARLES IS SQUEAMISH, AND HE'S GOT A KID.
MANNY DOESN'T HUNT VAMPIRES ANYMORE. HE SPENT FOUR MONTHS IN THE HOSPITAL BEING PUT BACK TOGETHER AFTER HIS LAST HUNT.
YOU WERE IN THE HOSPITAL, TOO.
A BROKEN ARM AND BUSTED COLLARBONE WERE MY WORST INJURIES, RONNIE. MANNY ALMOST DIED.
BESIDES, HE'S GOT A WIFE AND FOUR KIDS.
MANNY WAS THE ANIMATOR WHO TRAINED ME. HE WAS A TRADITIONALIST, A STAKE-AND-GARLIC MAN. TWO YEARS AGO, ROSITA, MANNY'S WIFE, HAD BEGGED ME NOT TO ENDANGER HER HUSBAND ANYMORE.
FIFTY-TWO WAS TOO OLD TO HUNT VAMPIRES, SHE HAD SAID. WHAT WOULD HAPPEN TO HER AND THE CHILDREN? SOMEHOW I HAD GOTTEN ALL THE BLAME. SHE MADE ME SWEAR BEFORE GOD THAT I WOULD NEVER AGAIN ASK MANNY TO JOIN ME ON A HUNT.
IF SHE HADN'T CRIED, I WOULD HAVE HELD OUT. CRYING WAS DAMNED UNFAIR IN A FIGHT. YOU'LL PROMISE ANYTHING JUST TO STOP THE TEARS.
ALL RIGHT, BUT YOU BE CAREFUL.
CAREFUL AS A VIRGIN ON HER WEDDING NIGHT.
YOU ARE INCORRIGIBLE. WATCH YOUR BACK.
YOU DO THE SAME.
GOOD NEWS?
YEAH.
HUMANS AGAINST VAMPIRES HAD A DEATH SQUAD. MAYBE. BUT MAYBE WAS BETTER THAN WHAT I'D HAD BEFORE.
IF I WAS ON THE RIGHT TRACK, I'D ATTRACT ATTENTION SOON. WHICH MEANT SOMEONE MIGHT TRY TO KILL ME. WOULDN'T THAT BE FUN?
I WOULD NEED CLOTHES THAT SHOWED OFF MY SCARS AND ALLOWED ME TO HIDE WEAPONS. I HATE TO SHOP. OF COURSE, IT BEAT THE HECK OUT OF HAVING MY LIFE THREATENED BY VAMPIRES.
I COULD GO SHOPPING NOW AND BE THREATENED BY VAMPIRES IN THE EVENING. A PERFECT WAY TO SPEND A SATURDAY NIGHT.

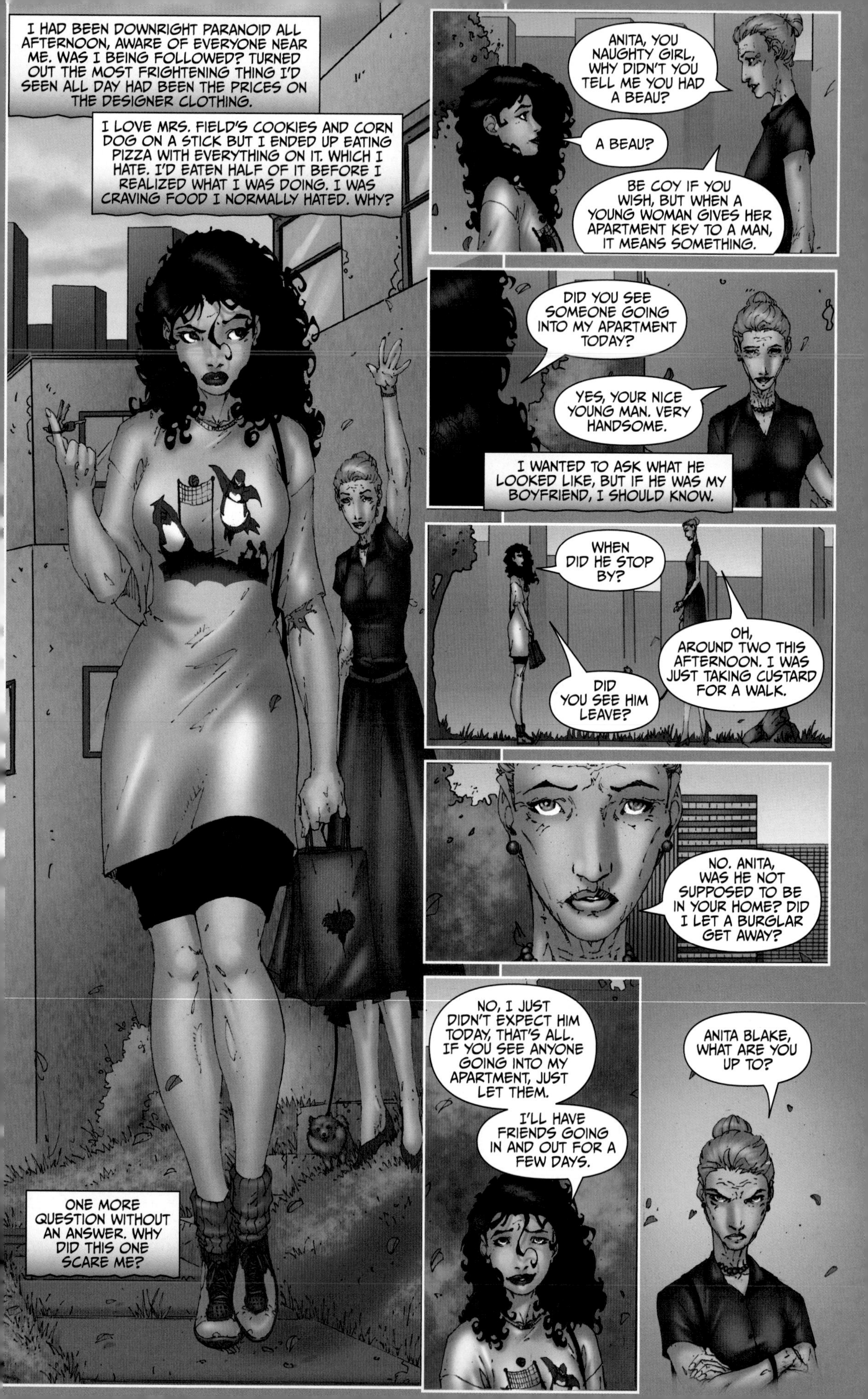
I HAD BEEN DOWNRIGHT PARANOID ALL AFTERNOON, AWARE OF EVERYONE NEAR ME. WAS I BEING FOLLOWED? TURNED OUT THE MOST FRIGHTENING THING I'D SEEN ALL DAY HAD BEEN THE PRICES ON THE DESIGNER CLOTHING.
I LOVE MRS. FIELD'S COOKIES AND CORN DOG ON A STICK BUT I ENDED UP EATING PIZZA WITH EVERYTHING ON IT. WHICH I HATE. I'D EATEN HALF OF IT BEFORE I REALIZED WHAT I WAS DOING. I WAS CRAVING FOOD I NORMALLY HATED. WHY?
ONE MORE QUESTION WITHOUT AN ANSWER. WHY DID THIS ONE SCARE ME?
ANITA, YOU NAUGHTY GIRL, WHY DIDN'T YOU TELL ME YOU HAD A BEAU?
A BEAU?
BE COY IF YOU WISH, BUT WHEN A YOUNG WOMAN GIVES HER APARTMENT KEY TO A MAN, IT MEANS SOMETHING.
DID YOU SEE SOMEONE GOING INTO MY APARTMENT TODAY?
YES, YOUR NICE YOUNG MAN. VERY HANDSOME.
I WANTED TO ASK WHAT HE LOOKED LIKE, BUT IF HE WAS MY BOYFRIEND, I SHOULD KNOW.
WHEN DID HE STOP BY?
OH, AROUND TWO THIS AFTERNOON. I WAS JUST TAKING CUSTARD FOR A WALK.
DID YOU SEE HIM LEAVE?
NO. ANITA, WAS HE NOT SUPPOSED TO BE IN YOUR HOME? DID I LET A BURGLAR GET AWAY?
NO, I JUST DIDN'T EXPECT HIM TODAY, THAT'S ALL. IF YOU SEE ANYONE GOING INTO MY APARTMENT, JUST LET THEM.
I'LL HAVE FRIENDS GOING IN AND OUT FOR A FEW DAYS.
ANITA BLAKE, WHAT ARE YOU UP TO?

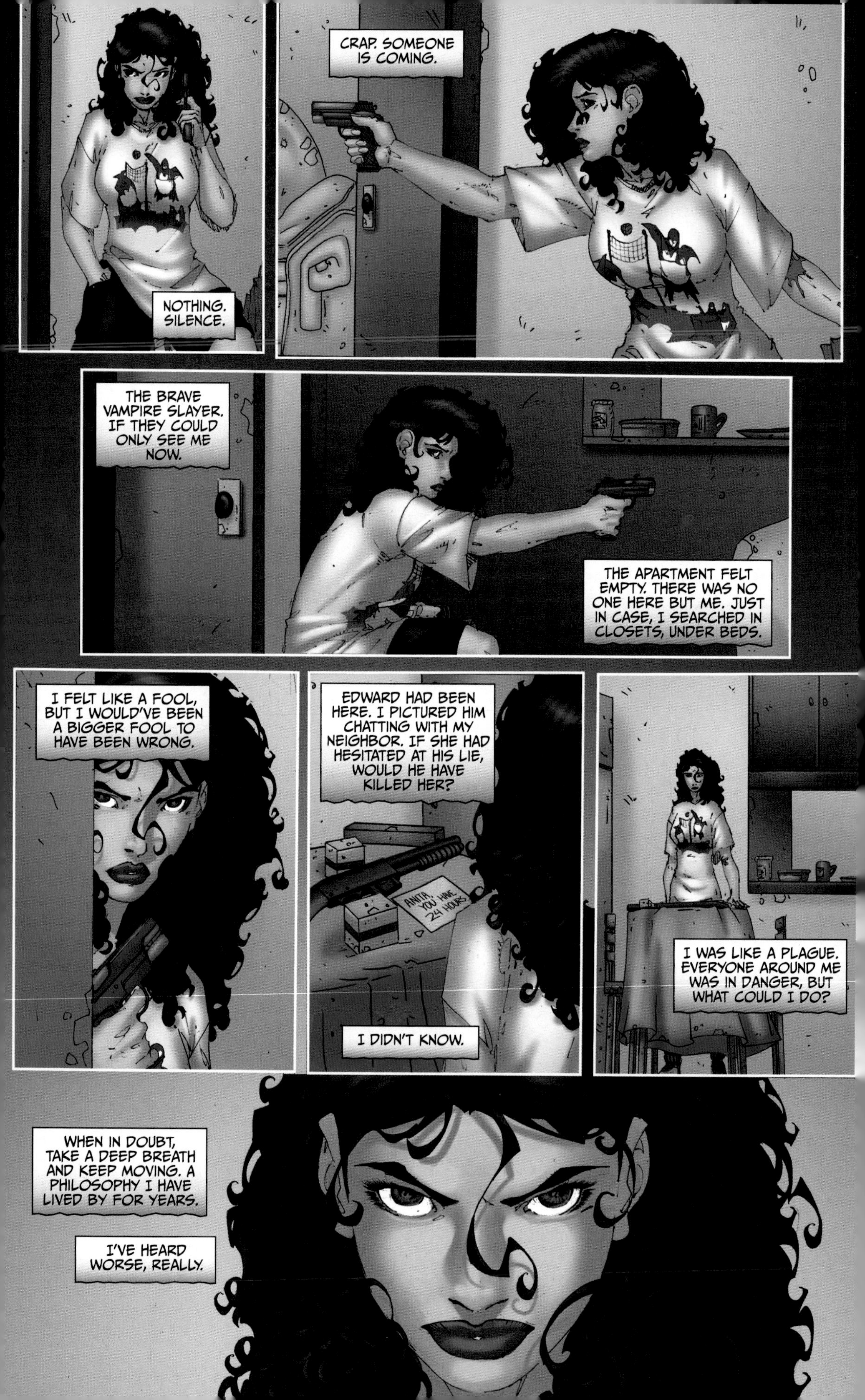
NOTHING. SILENCE.
CRAP. SOMEONE IS COMING.
THE BRAVE VAMPIRE SLAYER. IF THEY COULD ONLY SEE ME NOW.
THE APARTMENT FELT EMPTY. THERE WAS NO ONE HERE BUT ME. JUST IN CASE, I SEARCHED IN CLOSETS, UNDER BEDS.
I FELT LIKE A FOOL, BUT I WOULD'VE BEEN A BIGGER FOOL TO HAVE BEEN WRONG.
EDWARD HAD BEEN HERE. I PICTURED HIM CHATTING WITH MY NEIGHBOR. IF SHE HAD HESITATED AT HIS LIE, WOULD HE HAVE KILLED HER?
ANITA, YOU HAVE 24 HOURS
I DIDN'T KNOW.
I WAS LIKE A PLAGUE. EVERYONE AROUND ME WAS IN DANGER, BUT WHAT COULD I DO?
WHEN IN DOUBT, TAKE A DEEP BREATH AND KEEP MOVING. A PHILOSOPHY I HAVE LIVED BY FOR YEARS.
I'VE HEARD WORSE, REALLY.

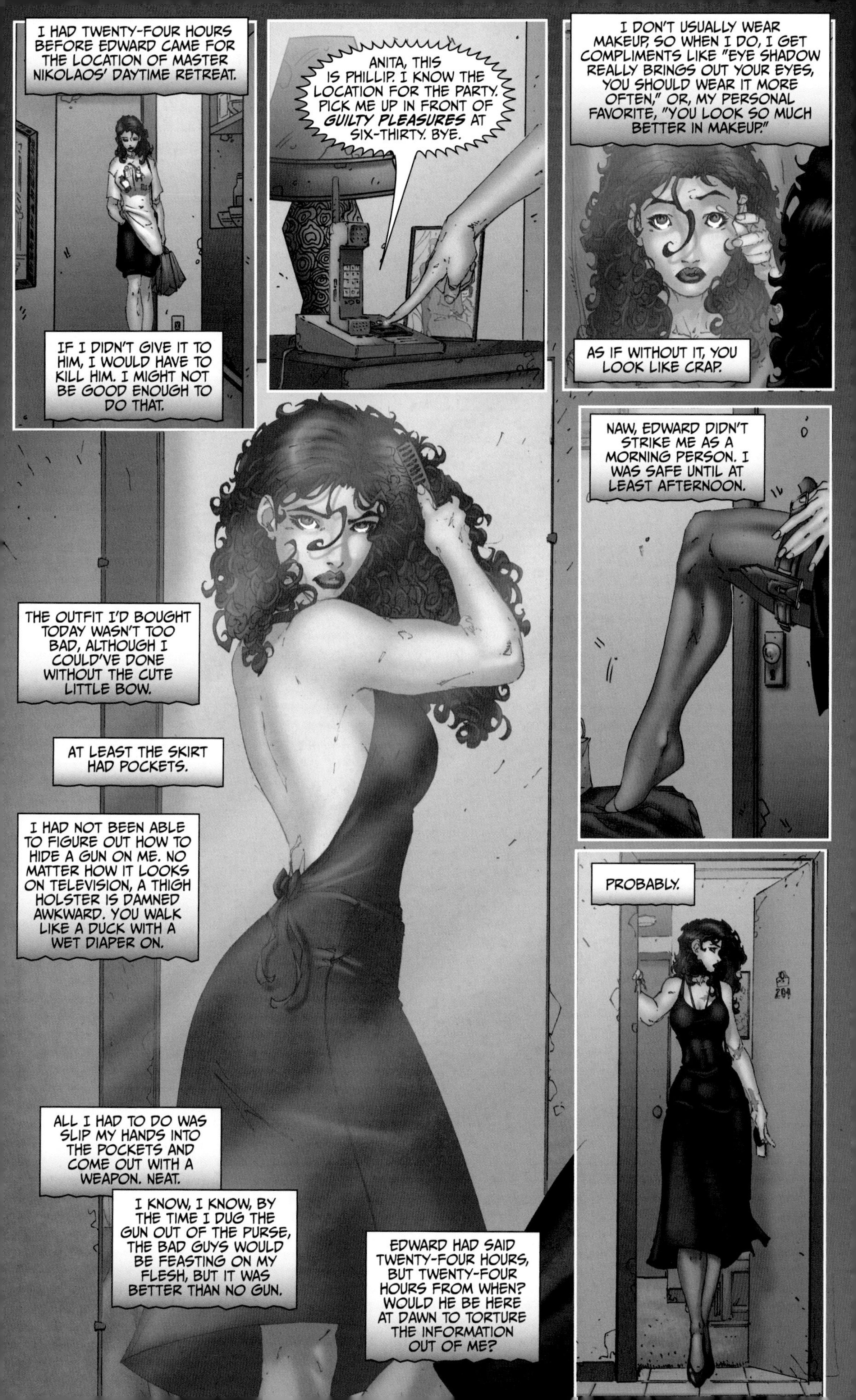

I HAD TWENTY-FOUR HOURS BEFORE EDWARD CAME FOR THE LOCATION OF MASTER NIKOLAOS' DAYTIME RETREAT.
IF I DIDN'T GIVE IT TO HIM, I WOULD HAVE TO KILL HIM. I MIGHT NOT BE GOOD ENOUGH TO DO THAT.
ANITA, THIS IS PHILLIP. I KNOW THE LOCATION FOR THE PARTY. PICK ME UP IN FRONT OF *GUILTY PLEASURES* AT SIX-THIRTY. BYE.
I DON'T USUALLY WEAR MAKEUP, SO WHEN I DO, I GET COMPLIMENTS LIKE "EYE SHADOW REALLY BRINGS OUT YOUR EYES, YOU SHOULD WEAR IT MORE OFTEN," OR, MY PERSONAL FAVORITE, "YOU LOOK SO MUCH BETTER IN MAKEUP."
AS IF WITHOUT IT, YOU LOOK LIKE CRAP.
THE OUTFIT I'D BOUGHT TODAY WASN'T TOO BAD, ALTHOUGH I COULD'VE DONE WITHOUT THE CUTE LITTLE BOW.
AT LEAST THE SKIRT HAD POCKETS.
I HAD NOT BEEN ABLE TO FIGURE OUT HOW TO HIDE A GUN ON ME. NO MATTER HOW IT LOOKS ON TELEVISION, A THIGH HOLSTER IS DAMNED AWKWARD. YOU WALK LIKE A DUCK WITH A WET DIAPER ON.
ALL I HAD TO DO WAS SLIP MY HANDS INTO THE POCKETS AND COME OUT WITH A WEAPON. NEAT.
I KNOW, I KNOW, BY THE TIME I DUG THE GUN OUT OF THE PURSE, THE BAD GUYS WOULD BE FEASTING ON MY FLESH, BUT IT WAS BETTER THAN NO GUN.
EDWARD HAD SAID TWENTY-FOUR HOURS, BUT TWENTY-FOUR HOURS FROM WHEN? WOULD HE BE HERE AT DAWN TO TORTURE THE INFORMATION OUT OF ME?
NAW, EDWARD DIDN'T STRIKE ME AS A MORNING PERSON. I WAS SAFE UNTIL AT LEAST AFTERNOON.
PROBABLY.

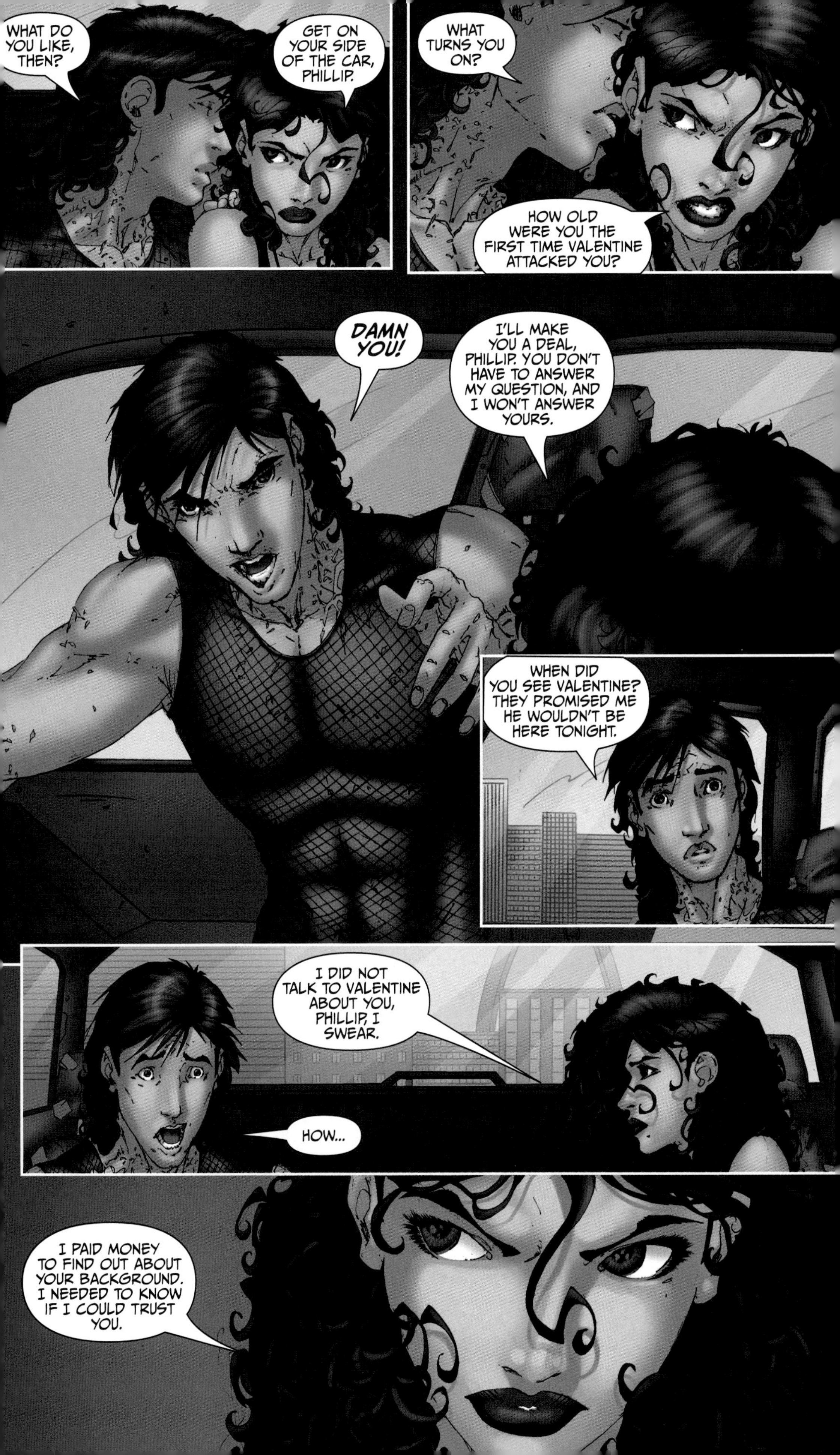
WHAT DO YOU LIKE, THEN?
GET ON YOUR SIDE OF THE CAR, PHILLIP.
WHAT TURNS YOU ON?
HOW OLD WERE YOU THE FIRST TIME VALENTINE ATTACKED YOU?
DAMN YOU!
I'LL MAKE YOU A DEAL, PHILLIP. YOU DON'T HAVE TO ANSWER MY QUESTION, AND I WON'T ANSWER YOURS.
WHEN DID YOU SEE VALENTINE? THEY PROMISED ME HE WOULDN'T BE HERE TONIGHT.
I DID NOT TALK TO VALENTINE ABOUT YOU, PHILLIP, I SWEAR.
HOW...
I PAID MONEY TO FIND OUT ABOUT YOUR BACKGROUND. I NEEDED TO KNOW IF I COULD TRUST YOU.

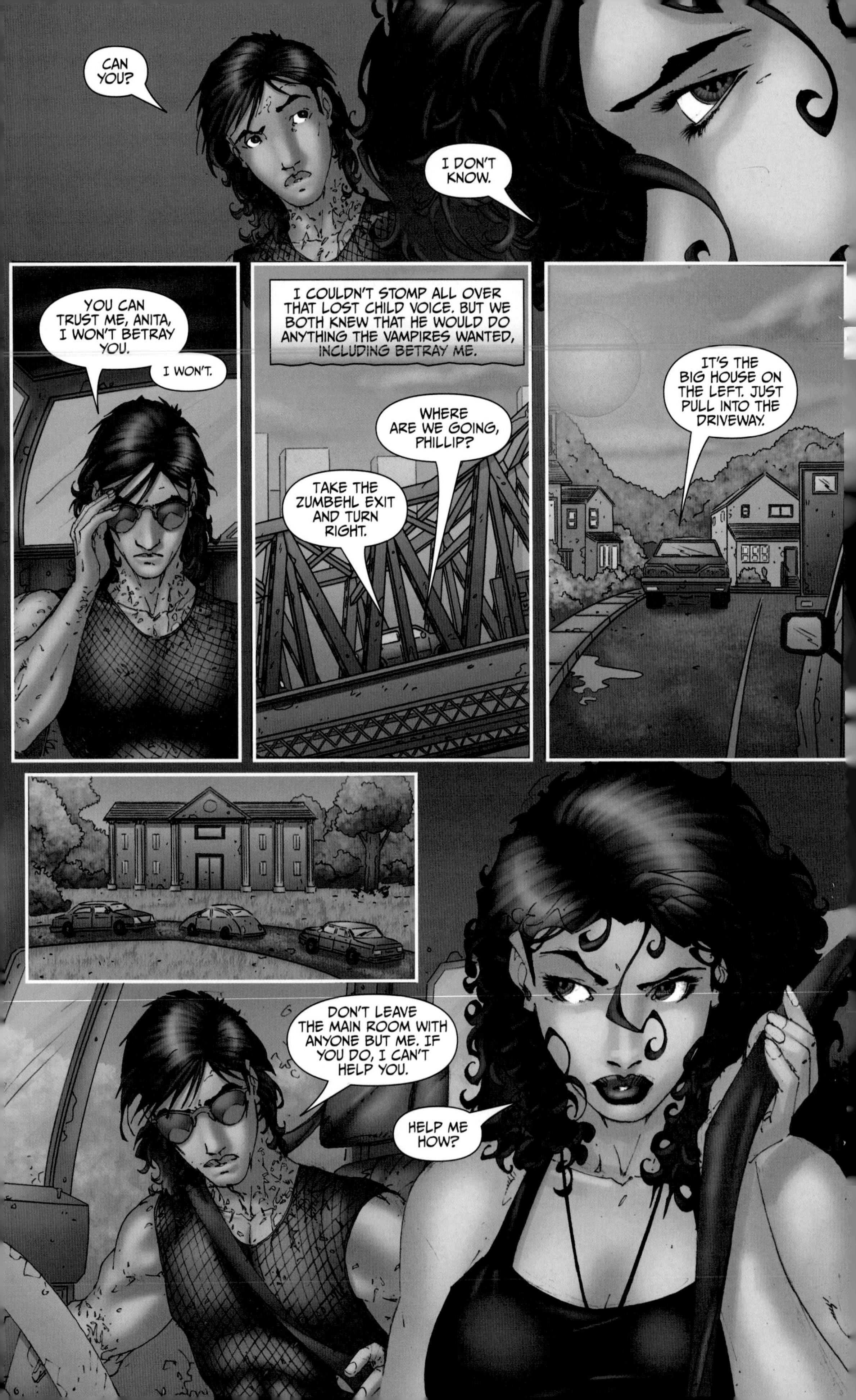
CAN YOU?
I DON'T KNOW.
YOU CAN TRUST ME, ANITA, I WON'T BETRAY YOU.
I WON'T.
I COULDN'T STOMP ALL OVER THAT LOST CHILD VOICE. BUT WE BOTH KNEW THAT HE WOULD DO ANYTHING THE VAMPIRES WANTED, INCLUDING BETRAY ME.
WHERE ARE WE GOING, PHILLIP?
TAKE THE ZUMBEHL EXIT AND TURN RIGHT.
IT'S THE BIG HOUSE ON THE LEFT. JUST PULL INTO THE DRIVEWAY.
DON'T LEAVE THE MAIN ROOM WITH ANYONE BUT ME. IF YOU DO, I CAN'T HELP YOU.
HELP ME HOW?

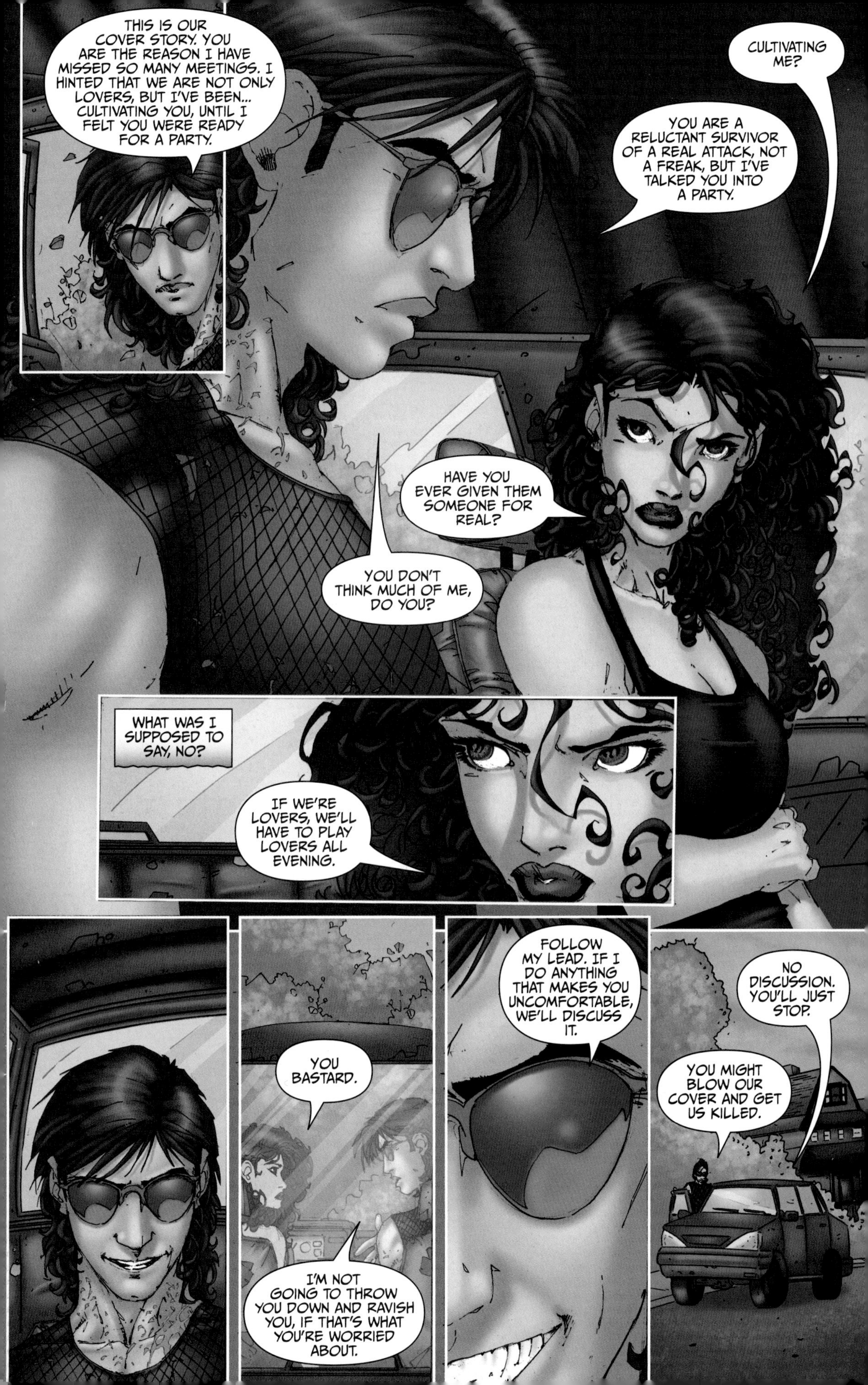
THIS IS OUR COVER STORY. YOU ARE THE REASON I HAVE MISSED SO MANY MEETINGS. I HINTED THAT WE ARE NOT ONLY LOVERS, BUT I'VE BEEN... CULTIVATING YOU, UNTIL I FELT YOU WERE READY FOR A PARTY.
CULTIVATING ME?
YOU ARE A RELUCTANT SURVIVOR OF A REAL ATTACK, NOT A FREAK, BUT I'VE TALKED YOU INTO A PARTY.
HAVE YOU EVER GIVEN THEM SOMEONE FOR REAL?
YOU DON'T THINK MUCH OF ME, DO YOU?
WHAT WAS I SUPPOSED TO SAY, NO?
IF WE'RE LOVERS, WE'LL HAVE TO PLAY LOVERS ALL EVENING.
YOU BASTARD.
I'M NOT GOING TO THROW YOU DOWN AND RAVISH YOU, IF THAT'S WHAT YOU'RE WORRIED ABOUT.
FOLLOW MY LEAD. IF I DO ANYTHING THAT MAKES YOU UNCOMFORTABLE, WE'LL DISCUSS IT.
NO DISCUSSION. YOU'LL JUST STOP.
YOU MIGHT BLOW OUR COVER AND GET US KILLED.

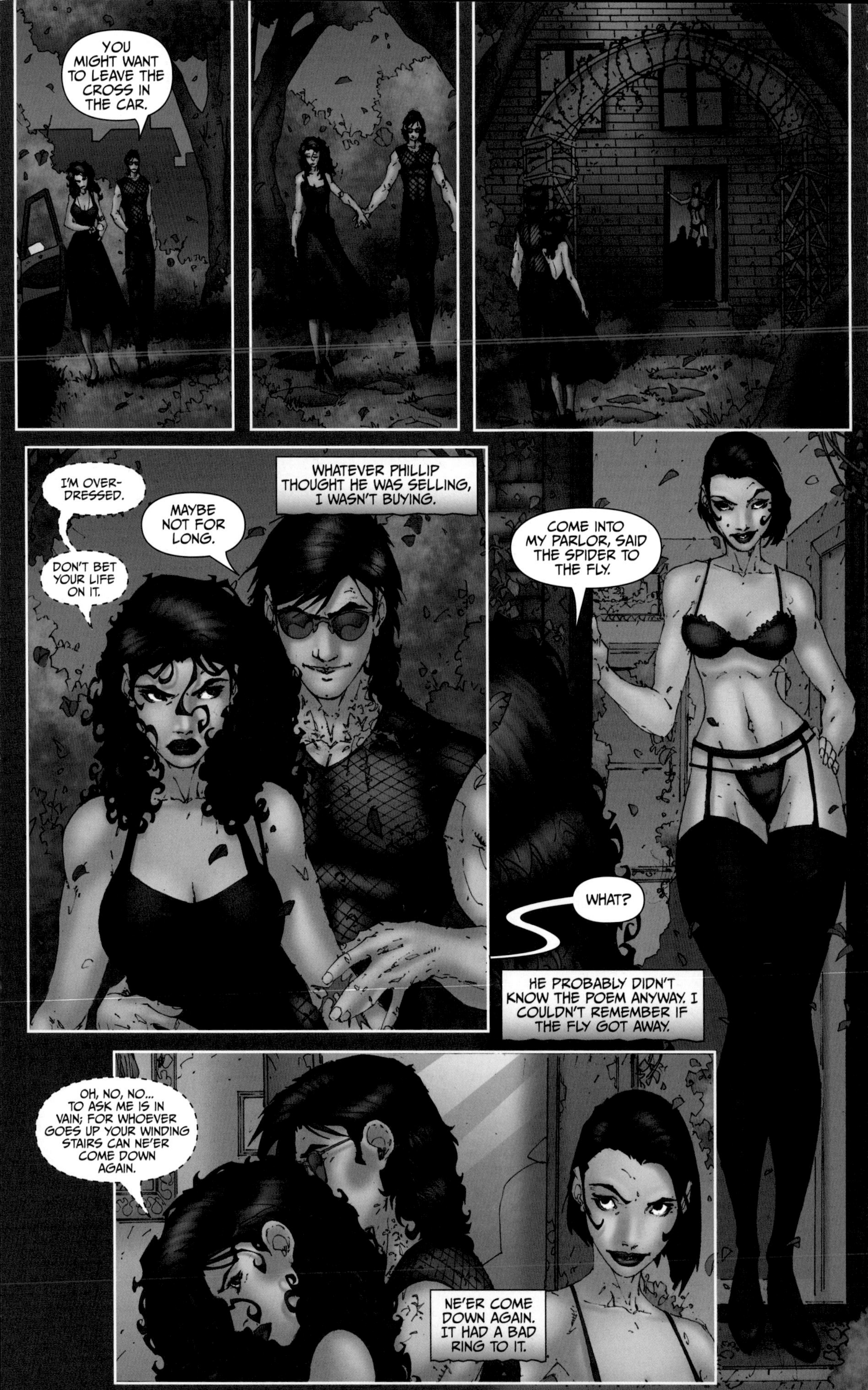
YOU MIGHT WANT TO LEAVE THE CROSS IN THE CAR.
WHATEVER PHILLIP THOUGHT HE WAS SELLING, I WASN'T BUYING.
I'M OVER-DRESSED.
MAYBE NOT FOR LONG.
DON'T BET YOUR LIFE ON IT.
COME INTO MY PARLOR, SAID THE SPIDER TO THE FLY.
WHAT?
HE PROBABLY DIDN'T KNOW THE POEM ANYWAY. I COULDN'T REMEMBER IF THE FLY GOT AWAY.
OH, NO, NO... TO ASK ME IS IN VAIN; FOR WHOEVER GOES UP YOUR WINDING STAIRS CAN NE'ER COME DOWN AGAIN.
NE'ER COME DOWN AGAIN. IT HAD A BAD RING TO IT.

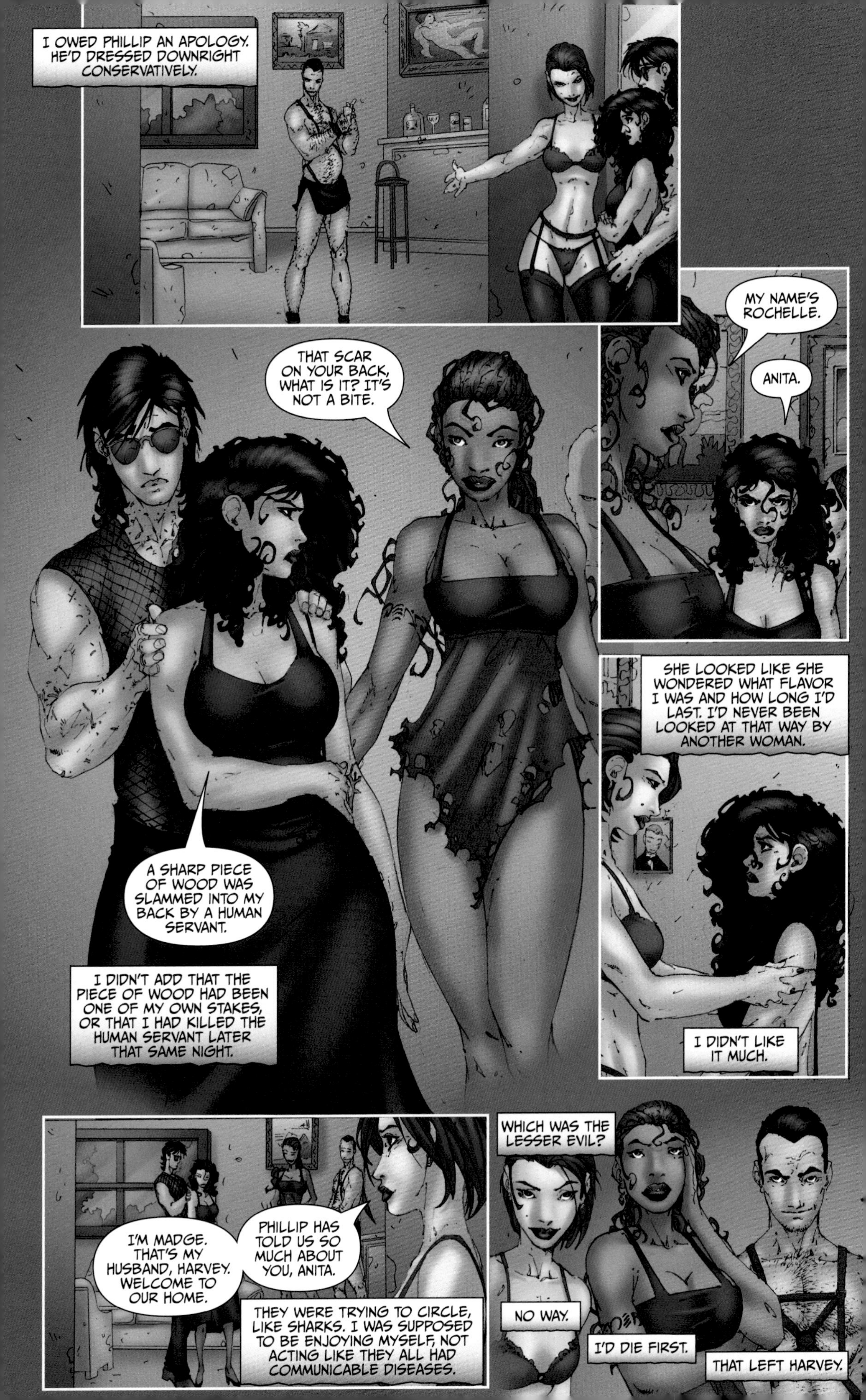
I OWED PHILLIP AN APOLOGY. HE'D DRESSED DOWNRIGHT CONSERVATIVELY.
MY NAME'S ROCHELLE.
ANITA.
THAT SCAR ON YOUR BACK, WHAT IS IT? IT'S NOT A BITE.
A SHARP PIECE OF WOOD WAS SLAMMED INTO MY BACK BY A HUMAN SERVANT.
I DIDN'T ADD THAT THE PIECE OF WOOD HAD BEEN ONE OF MY OWN STAKES, OR THAT I HAD KILLED THE HUMAN SERVANT LATER THAT SAME NIGHT.
SHE LOOKED LIKE SHE WONDERED WHAT FLAVOR I WAS AND HOW LONG I'D LAST. I'D NEVER BEEN LOOKED AT THAT WAY BY ANOTHER WOMAN.
I DIDN'T LIKE IT MUCH.
I'M MADGE. THAT'S MY HUSBAND, HARVEY. WELCOME TO OUR HOME.
PHILLIP HAS TOLD US SO MUCH ABOUT YOU, ANITA.
THEY WERE TRYING TO CIRCLE, LIKE SHARKS. I WAS SUPPOSED TO BE ENJOYING MYSELF, NOT ACTING LIKE THEY ALL HAD COMMUNICABLE DISEASES.
WHICH WAS THE LESSER EVIL?
NO WAY.
I'D DIE FIRST.
THAT LEFT HARVEY.

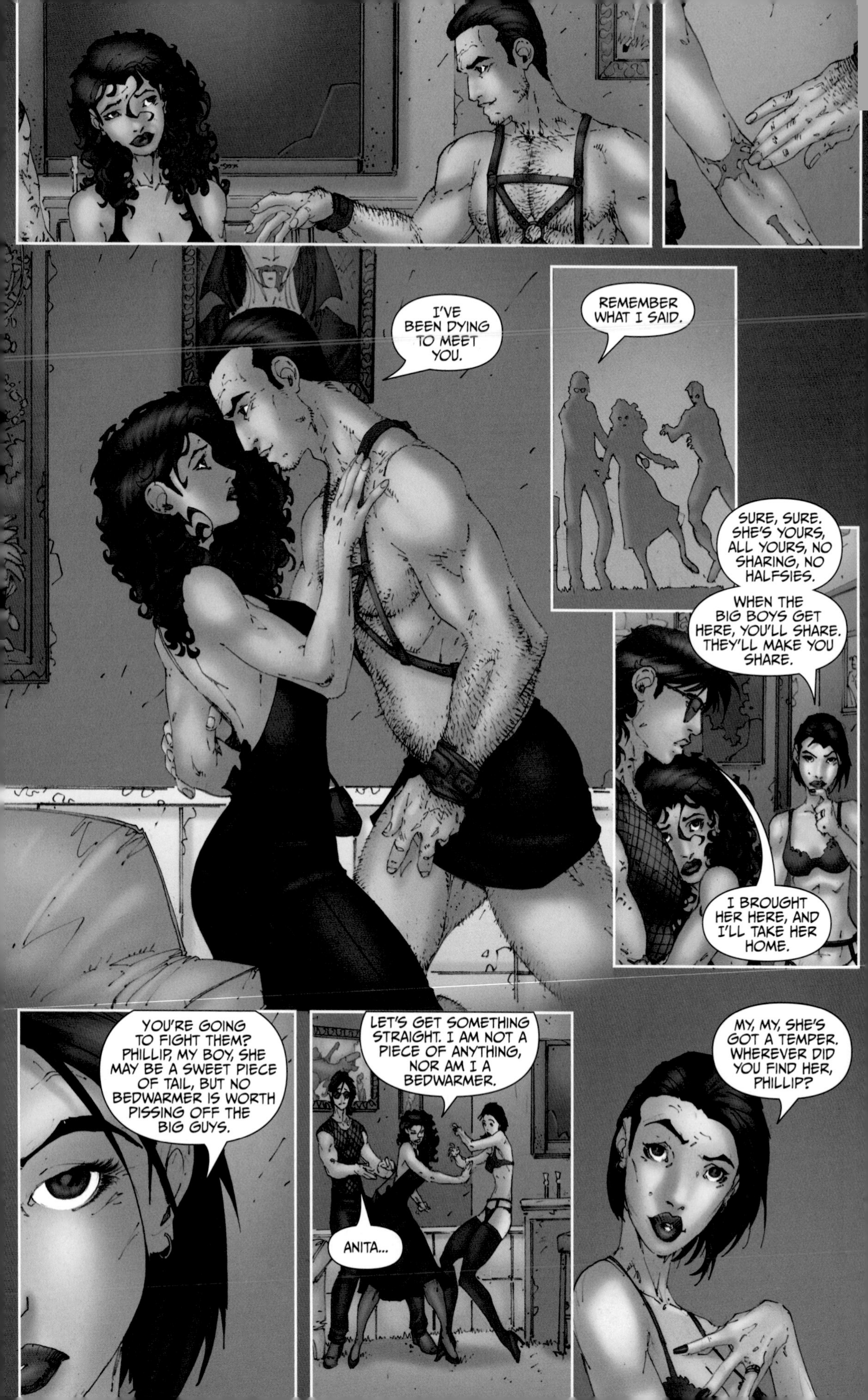
I'VE BEEN DYING TO MEET YOU.
REMEMBER WHAT I SAID.
SURE, SURE. SHE'S YOURS, ALL YOURS, NO SHARING, NO HALFSIES.
WHEN THE BIG BOYS GET HERE, YOU'LL SHARE. THEY'LL MAKE YOU SHARE.
I BROUGHT HER HERE, AND I'LL TAKE HER HOME.
YOU'RE GOING TO FIGHT THEM? PHILLIP, MY BOY, SHE MAY BE A SWEET PIECE OF TAIL, BUT NO BEDWARMER IS WORTH PISSING OFF THE BIG GUYS.
LET'S GET SOMETHING STRAIGHT. I AM NOT A PIECE OF ANYTHING, NOR AM I A BEDWARMER.
ANITA...
MY, MY, SHE'S GOT A TEMPER. WHEREVER DID YOU FIND HER, PHILLIP?

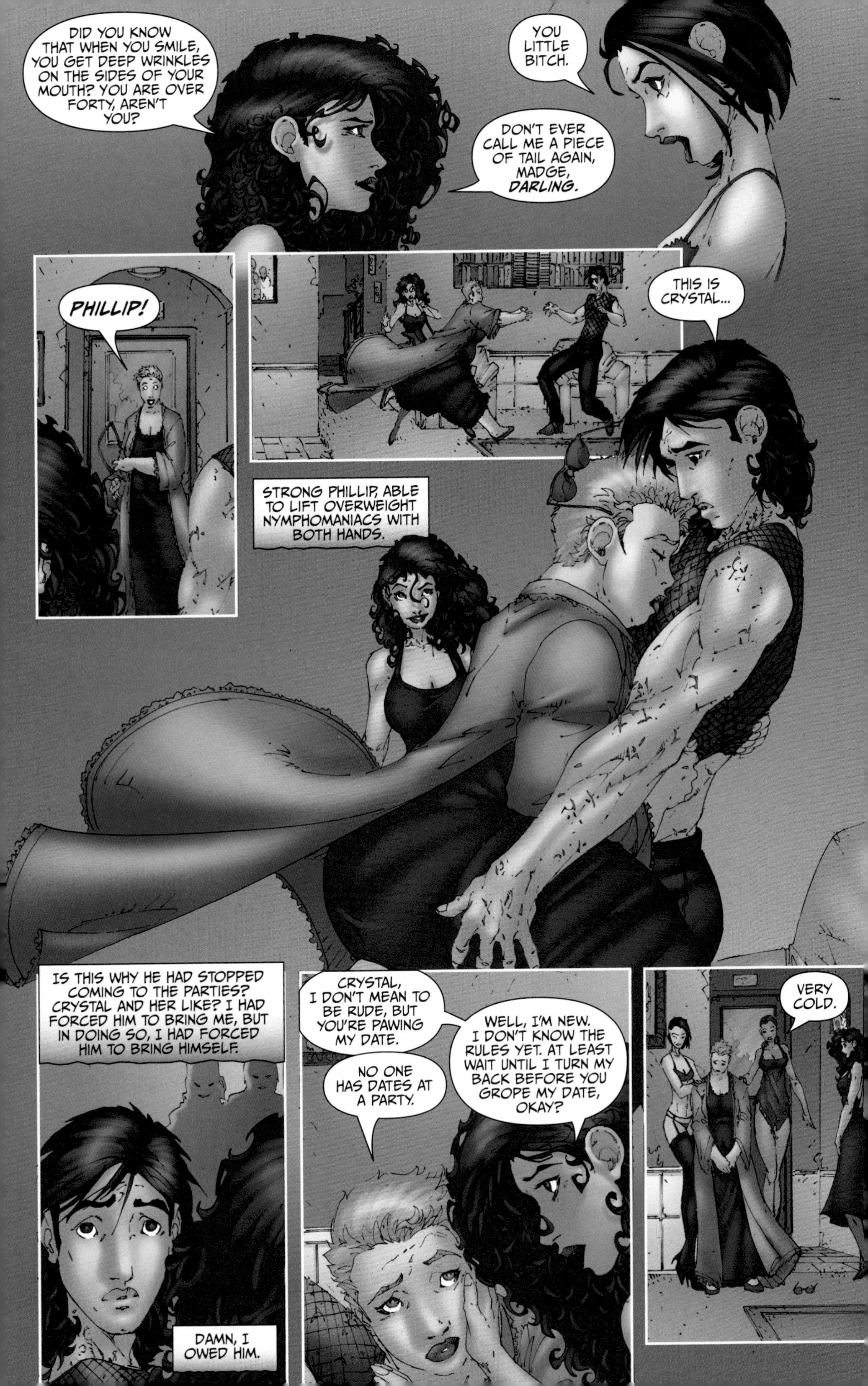
DID YOU KNOW THAT WHEN YOU SMILE, YOU GET DEEP WRINKLES ON THE SIDES OF YOUR MOUTH? YOU ARE OVER FORTY, AREN'T YOU?
YOU LITTLE BITCH.
DON'T EVER CALL ME A PIECE OF TAIL AGAIN, MADGE, *DARLING.*
PHILLIP!
THIS IS CRYSTAL...
STRONG PHILLIP, ABLE TO LIFT OVERWEIGHT NYMPHOMANIACS WITH BOTH HANDS.
IS THIS WHY HE HAD STOPPED COMING TO THE PARTIES? CRYSTAL AND HER LIKE? I HAD FORCED HIM TO BRING ME, BUT IN DOING SO, I HAD FORCED HIM TO BRING HIMSELF.
DAMN, I OWED HIM.
CRYSTAL, I DON'T MEAN TO BE RUDE, BUT YOU'RE PAWING MY DATE.
NO ONE HAS DATES AT A PARTY.
WELL, I'M NEW. I DON'T KNOW THE RULES YET. AT LEAST WAIT UNTIL I TURN MY BACK BEFORE YOU GROPE MY DATE, OKAY?
VERY COLD.

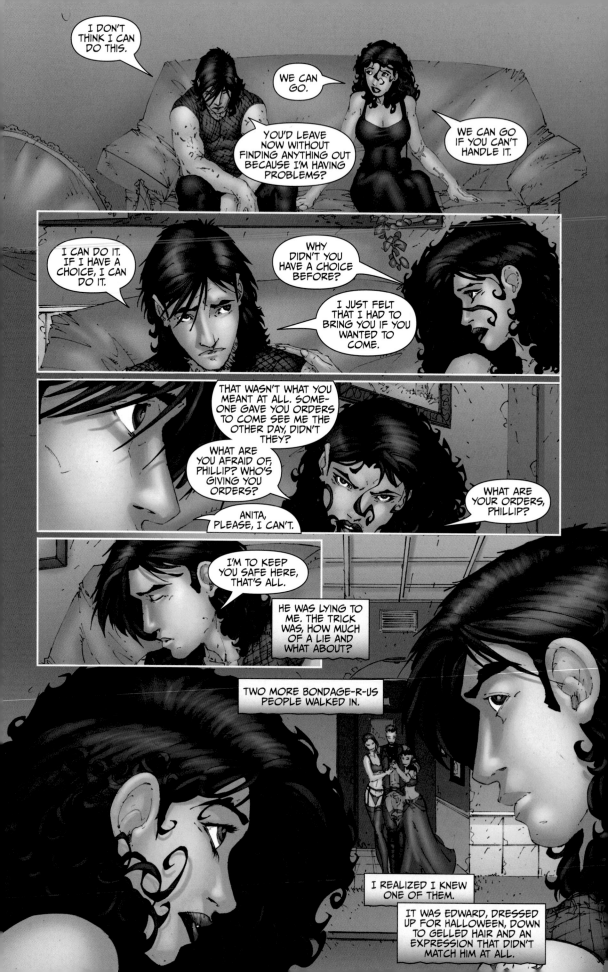

WHAT THE HELL WAS HE DOING HERE? I KNEW MY TWENTY-FOUR HOURS WERE NOT UP. EDWARD HAD DECIDED TO COME LOOKING FOR NIKOLAOS.

HAD HE FOLLOWED US? HAD HE LISTENED TO PHILLIP'S MESSAGE ON MY MACHINE?

WHAT'S WRONG?

WHAT'S WRONG? YOU ARE TAKING ORDERS FROM SOMEBODY, PROBABLY A VAMPIRE...

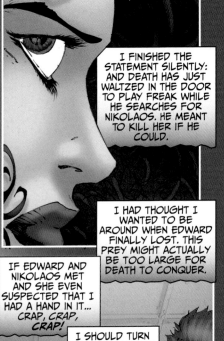

I FINISHED THE STATEMENT SILENTLY: AND DEATH HAS JUST WALTZED IN THE DOOR TO PLAY FREAK WHILE HE SEARCHES FOR NIKOLAOS. HE MEANT TO KILL HER IF HE COULD.

I HAD THOUGHT I WANTED TO BE AROUND WHEN EDWARD FINALLY LOST. THIS PREY MIGHT ACTUALLY BE TOO LARGE FOR DEATH TO CONQUER.

IF EDWARD AND NIKOLAOS MET AND SHE EVEN SUSPECTED THAT I HAD A HAND IN IT... CRAP, CRAP, CRAP!

I SHOULD TURN EDWARD IN. WHAT DID I OWE HIM? BUT I COULDN'T DO IT. A HUMAN DID NOT TURN ANOTHER HUMAN OVER TO THE MONSTERS.

I THINK I WAS THE CLOSEST THING THAT EDWARD HAD TO A REAL FRIEND. A PERSON WHO KNOWS WHO AND WHAT YOU ARE AND LIKES YOU ANYWAY. I DID LIKE HIM, EVEN THOUGH I KNEW HE'D KILL ME IF IT WORKED OUT THAT WAY.

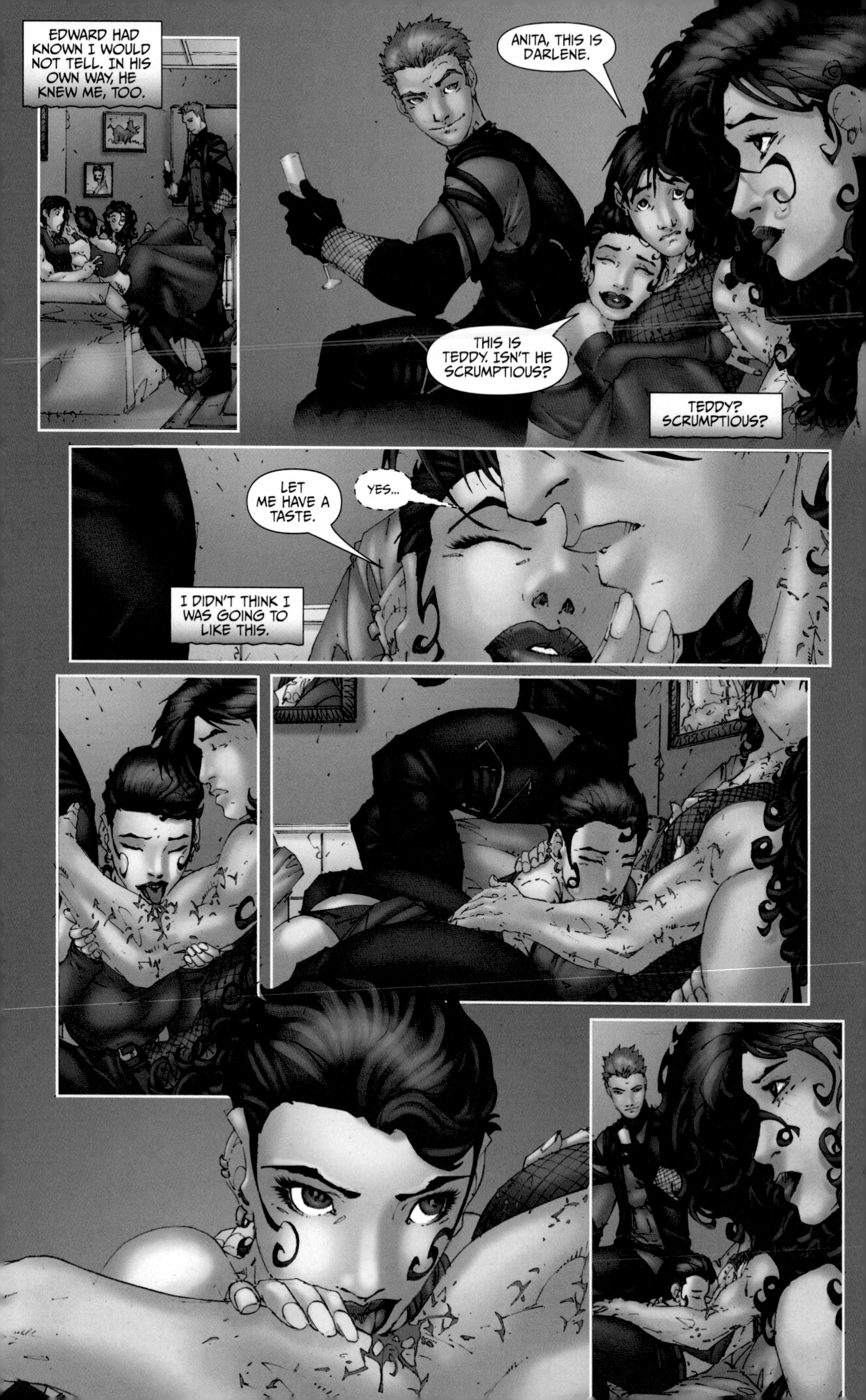
EDWARD HAD KNOWN I WOULD NOT TELL. IN HIS OWN WAY, HE KNEW ME, TOO.
ANITA, THIS IS DARLENE.
THIS IS TEDDY. ISN'T HE SCRUMPTIOUS?
TEDDY? SCRUMPTIOUS?
LET ME HAVE A TASTE.
YES...
I DIDN'T THINK I WAS GOING TO LIKE THIS.

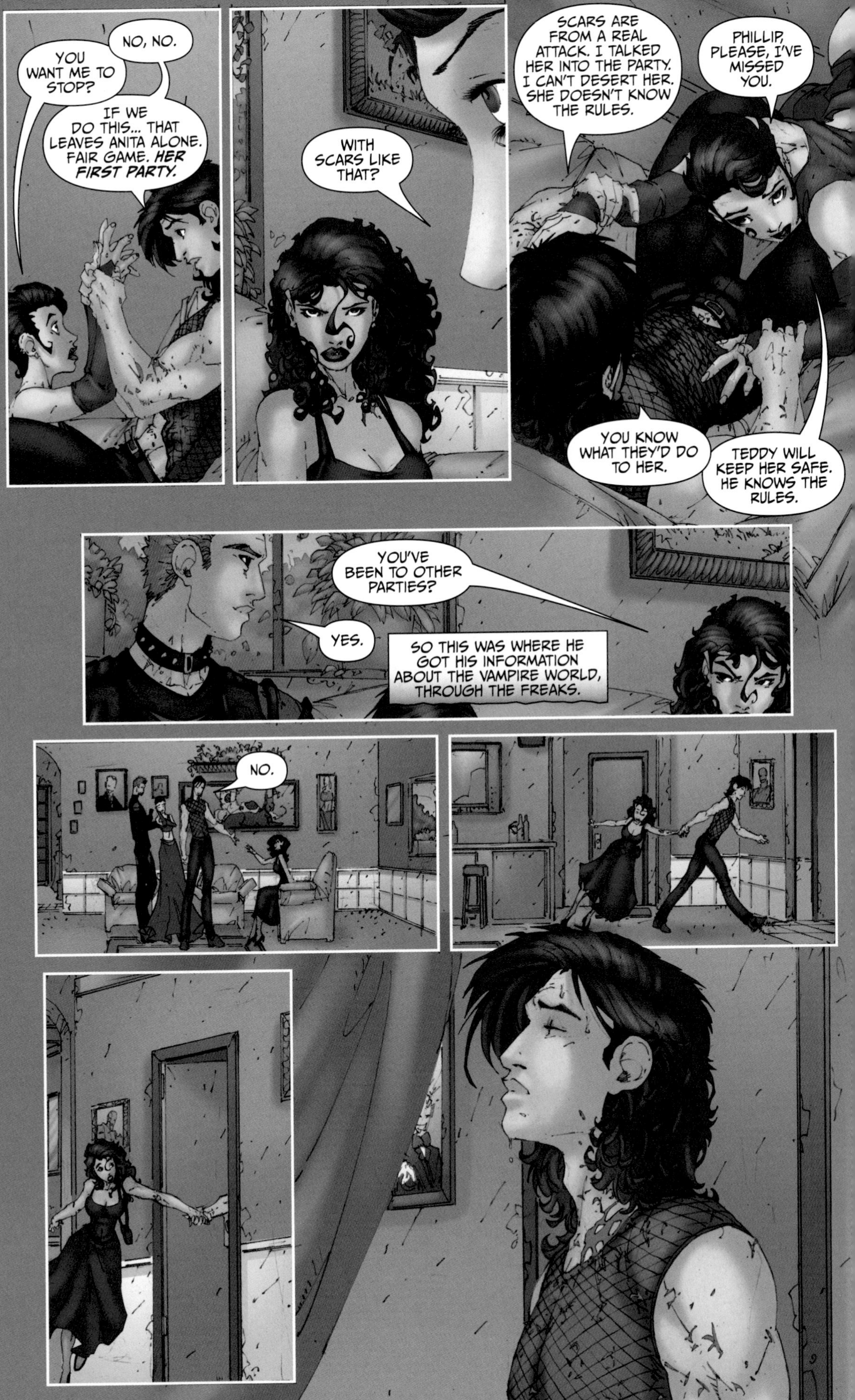
NO, NO.
YOU WANT ME TO STOP?
IF WE DO THIS... THAT LEAVES ANITA ALONE. FAIR GAME. *HER FIRST PARTY.*
WITH SCARS LIKE THAT?
SCARS ARE FROM A REAL ATTACK. I TALKED HER INTO THE PARTY. I CAN'T DESERT HER. SHE DOESN'T KNOW THE RULES.
PHILLIP, PLEASE, I'VE MISSED YOU.
YOU KNOW WHAT THEY'D DO TO HER.
TEDDY WILL KEEP HER SAFE. HE KNOWS THE RULES.
YOU'VE BEEN TO OTHER PARTIES?
YES.
SO THIS WAS WHERE HE GOT HIS INFORMATION ABOUT THE VAMPIRE WORLD, THROUGH THE FREAKS.
NO.

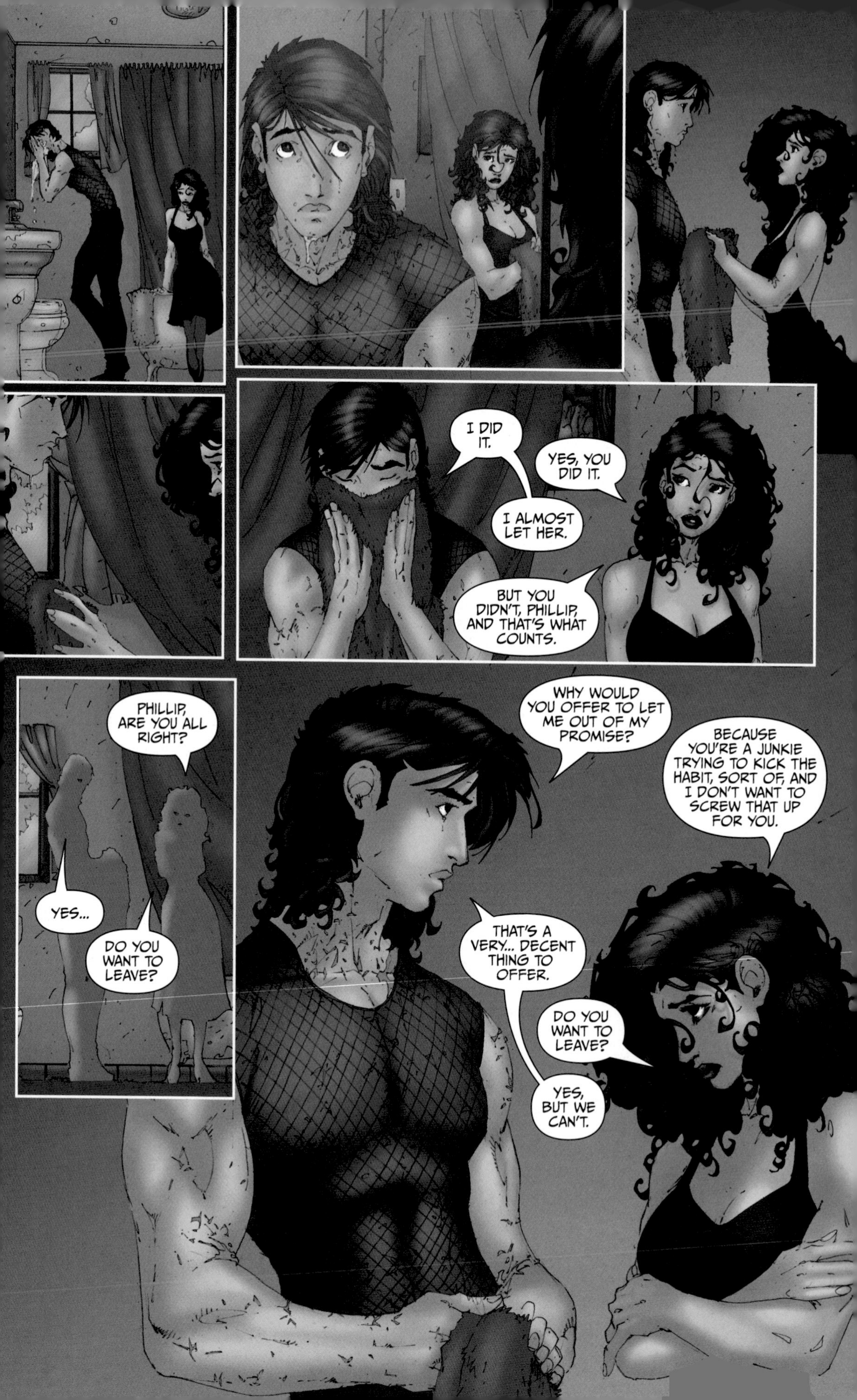
I DID IT.
YES, YOU DID IT.
I ALMOST LET HER.
BUT YOU DIDN'T, PHILLIP, AND THAT'S WHAT COUNTS.
PHILLIP, ARE YOU ALL RIGHT?
YES...
DO YOU WANT TO LEAVE?
WHY WOULD YOU OFFER TO LET ME OUT OF MY PROMISE?
BECAUSE YOU'RE A JUNKIE TRYING TO KICK THE HABIT, SORT OF, AND I DON'T WANT TO SCREW THAT UP FOR YOU.
THAT'S A VERY... DECENT THING TO OFFER.
DO YOU WANT TO LEAVE?
YES, BUT WE CAN'T.

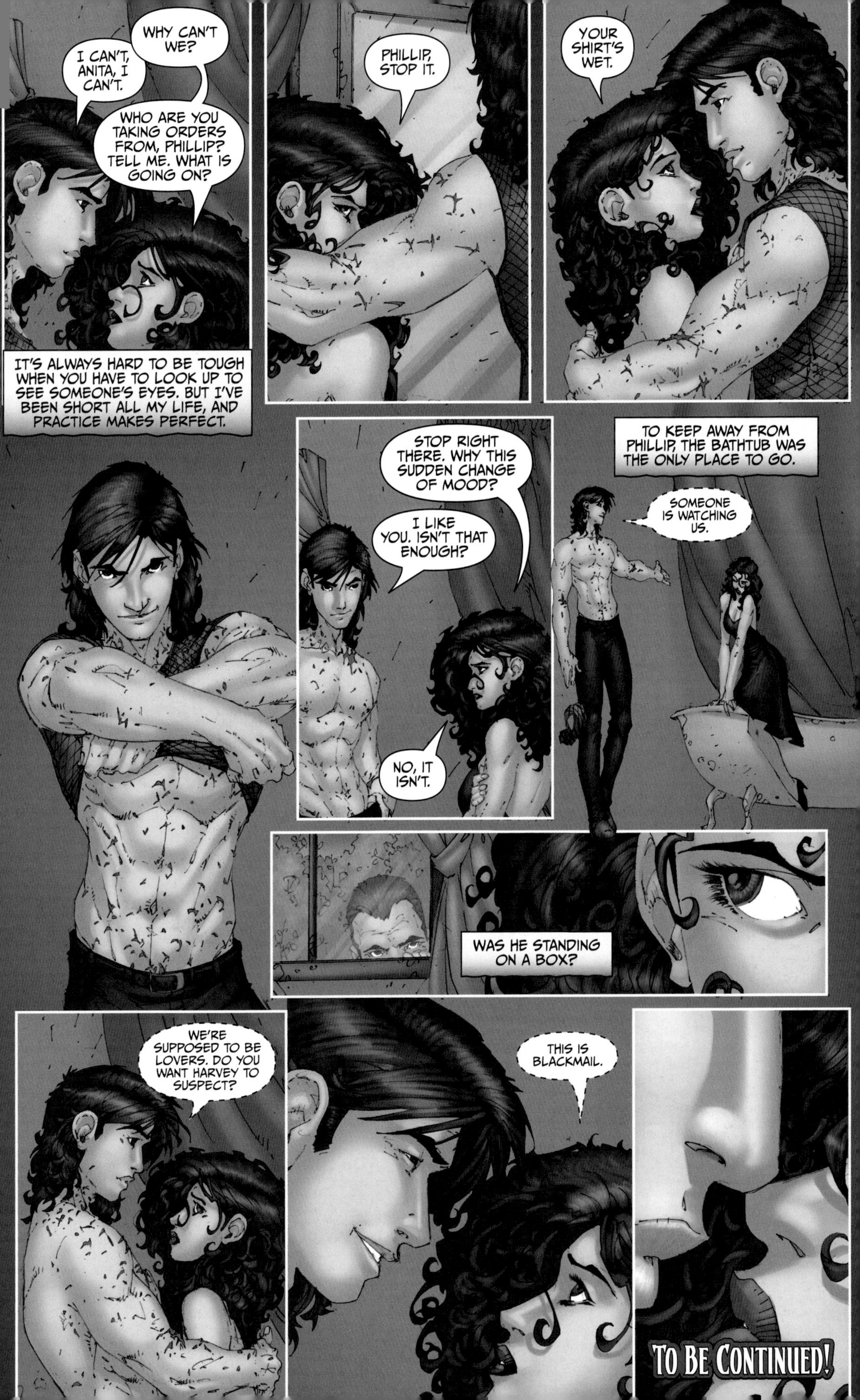

I CAN'T, ANITA, I CAN'T.
WHY CAN'T WE?
WHO ARE YOU TAKING ORDERS FROM, PHILLIP? TELL ME. WHAT IS GOING ON?
IT'S ALWAYS HARD TO BE TOUGH WHEN YOU HAVE TO LOOK UP TO SEE SOMEONE'S EYES. BUT I'VE BEEN SHORT ALL MY LIFE, AND PRACTICE MAKES PERFECT.
PHILLIP, STOP IT.
YOUR SHIRT'S WET.
STOP RIGHT THERE. WHY THIS SUDDEN CHANGE OF MOOD?
I LIKE YOU. ISN'T THAT ENOUGH?
NO, IT ISN'T.
TO KEEP AWAY FROM PHILLIP, THE BATHTUB WAS THE ONLY PLACE TO GO.
SOMEONE IS WATCHING US.
WAS HE STANDING ON A BOX?
WE'RE SUPPOSED TO BE LOVERS. DO YOU WANT HARVEY TO SUSPECT?
THIS IS BLACKMAIL.
TO BE CONTINUED!

VAMPIRE VICTIM

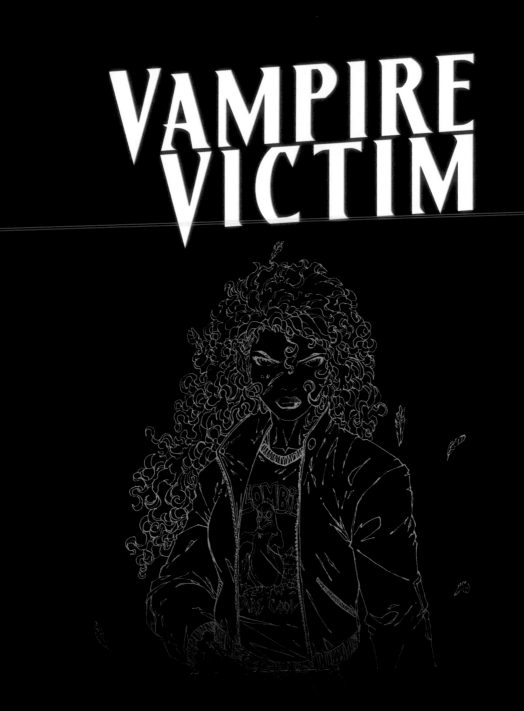

WRITER **LAURELL K. HAMILTON & JONATHON GREEN**

ARTWORK **BRETT BOOTH**

COLORS **LARRY MOLINAR** (SPECIAL THANKS TO JESS RUFFNER-BOOTH)

LETTERS **BILL TORTOLINI**

EDITOR **MIKE RAICHT**

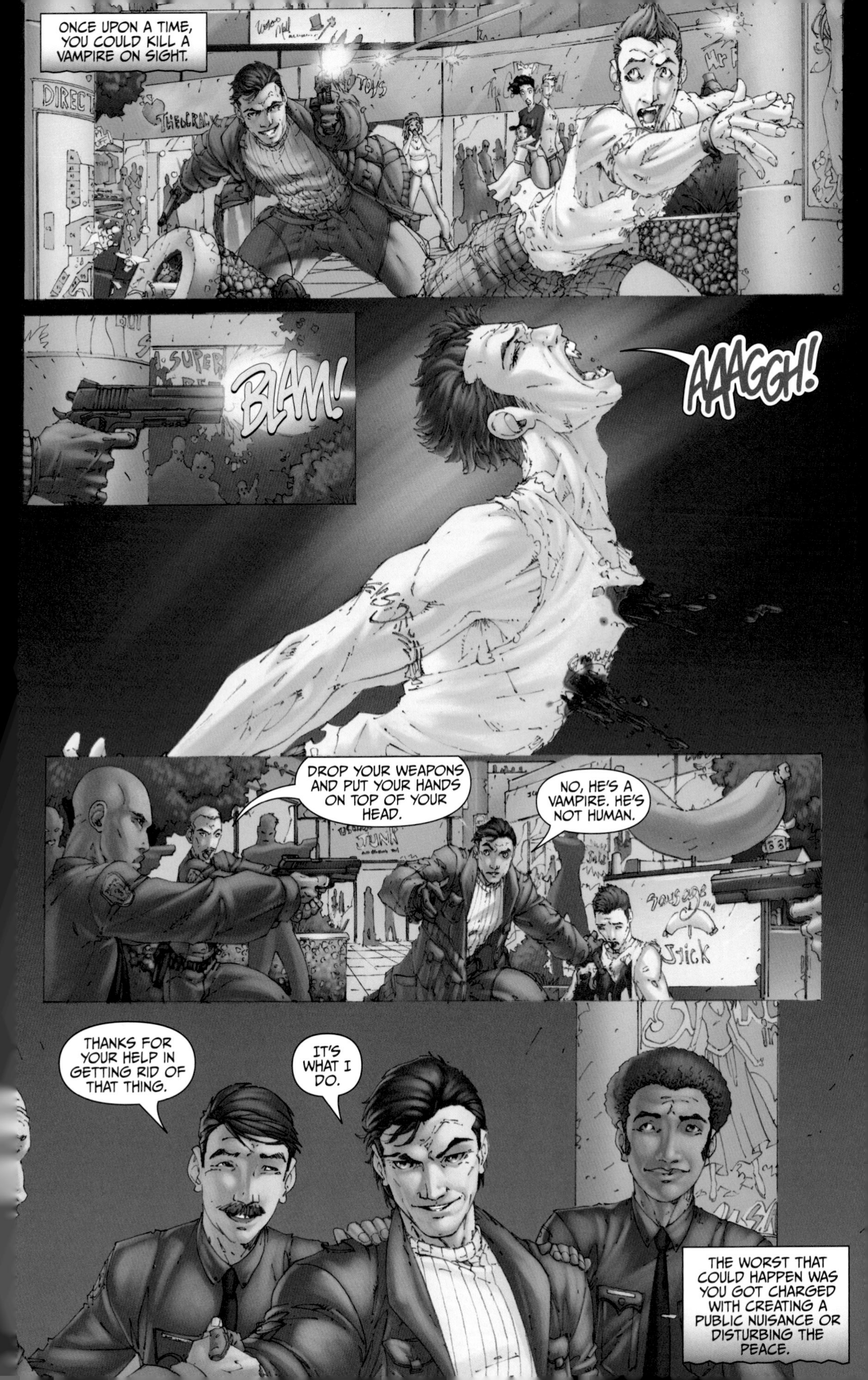
ONCE UPON A TIME, YOU COULD KILL A VAMPIRE ON SIGHT.
BLAM!
AAAGGH!
DROP YOUR WEAPONS AND PUT YOUR HANDS ON TOP OF YOUR HEAD.
NO, HE'S A VAMPIRE. HE'S NOT HUMAN.
THANKS FOR YOUR HELP IN GETTING RID OF THAT THING.
IT'S WHAT I DO.
THE WORST THAT COULD HAPPEN WAS YOU GOT CHARGED WITH CREATING A PUBLIC NUISANCE OR DISTURBING THE PEACE.

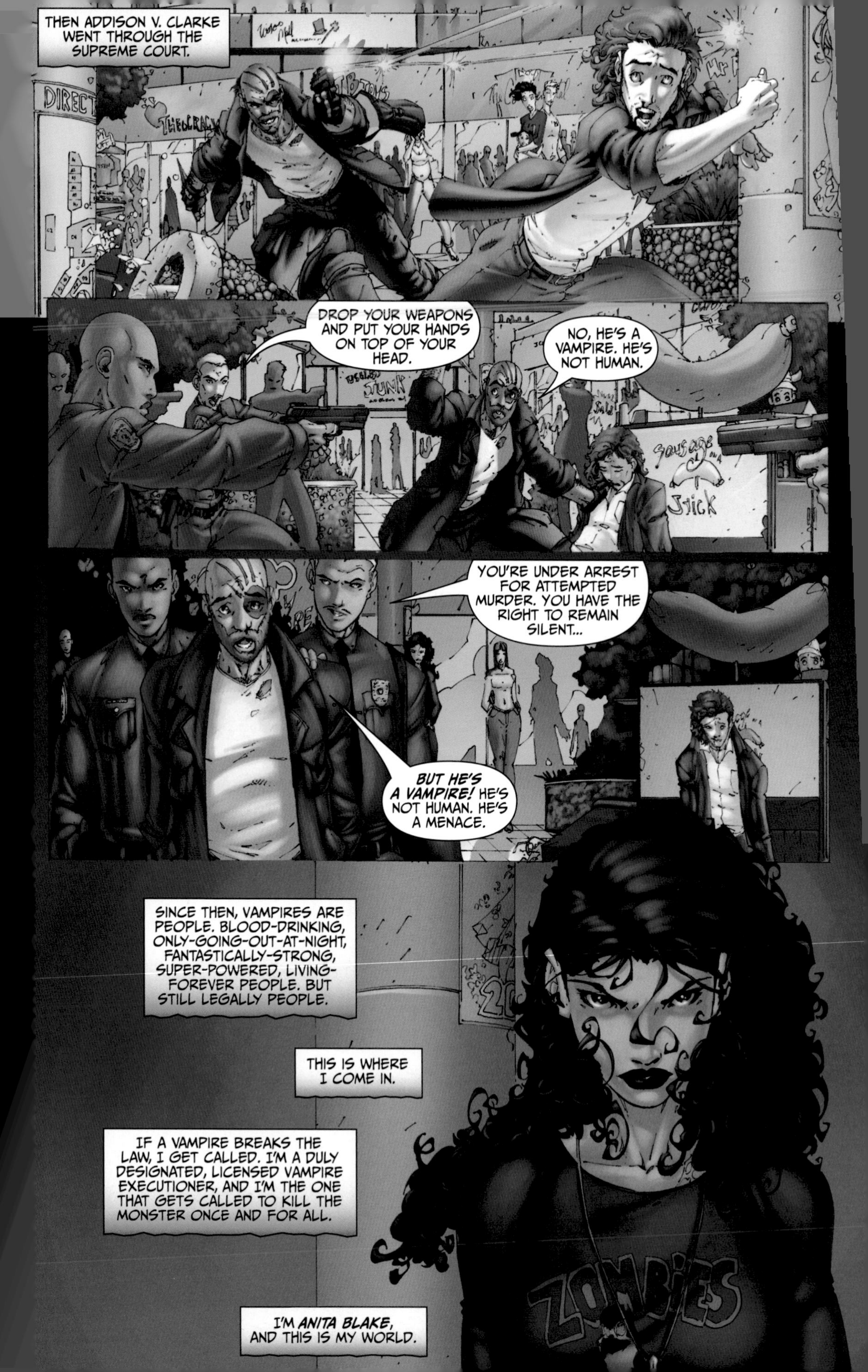

THEN ADDISON V. CLARKE WENT THROUGH THE SUPREME COURT.
DROP YOUR WEAPONS AND PUT YOUR HANDS ON TOP OF YOUR HEAD.
NO, HE'S A VAMPIRE. HE'S NOT HUMAN.
SAUSAGE ON A STICK
YOU'RE UNDER ARREST FOR ATTEMPTED MURDER. YOU HAVE THE RIGHT TO REMAIN SILENT...
BUT HE'S A VAMPIRE! HE'S NOT HUMAN. HE'S A MENACE.
SINCE THEN, VAMPIRES ARE PEOPLE. BLOOD-DRINKING, ONLY-GOING-OUT-AT-NIGHT, FANTASTICALLY-STRONG, SUPER-POWERED, LIVING-FOREVER PEOPLE. BUT STILL LEGALLY PEOPLE.
THIS IS WHERE I COME IN.
IF A VAMPIRE BREAKS THE LAW, I GET CALLED. I'M A DULY DESIGNATED, LICENSED VAMPIRE EXECUTIONER, AND I'M THE ONE THAT GETS CALLED TO KILL THE MONSTER ONCE AND FOR ALL.
ZOMBIES
I'M *ANITA BLAKE*, AND THIS IS MY WORLD.

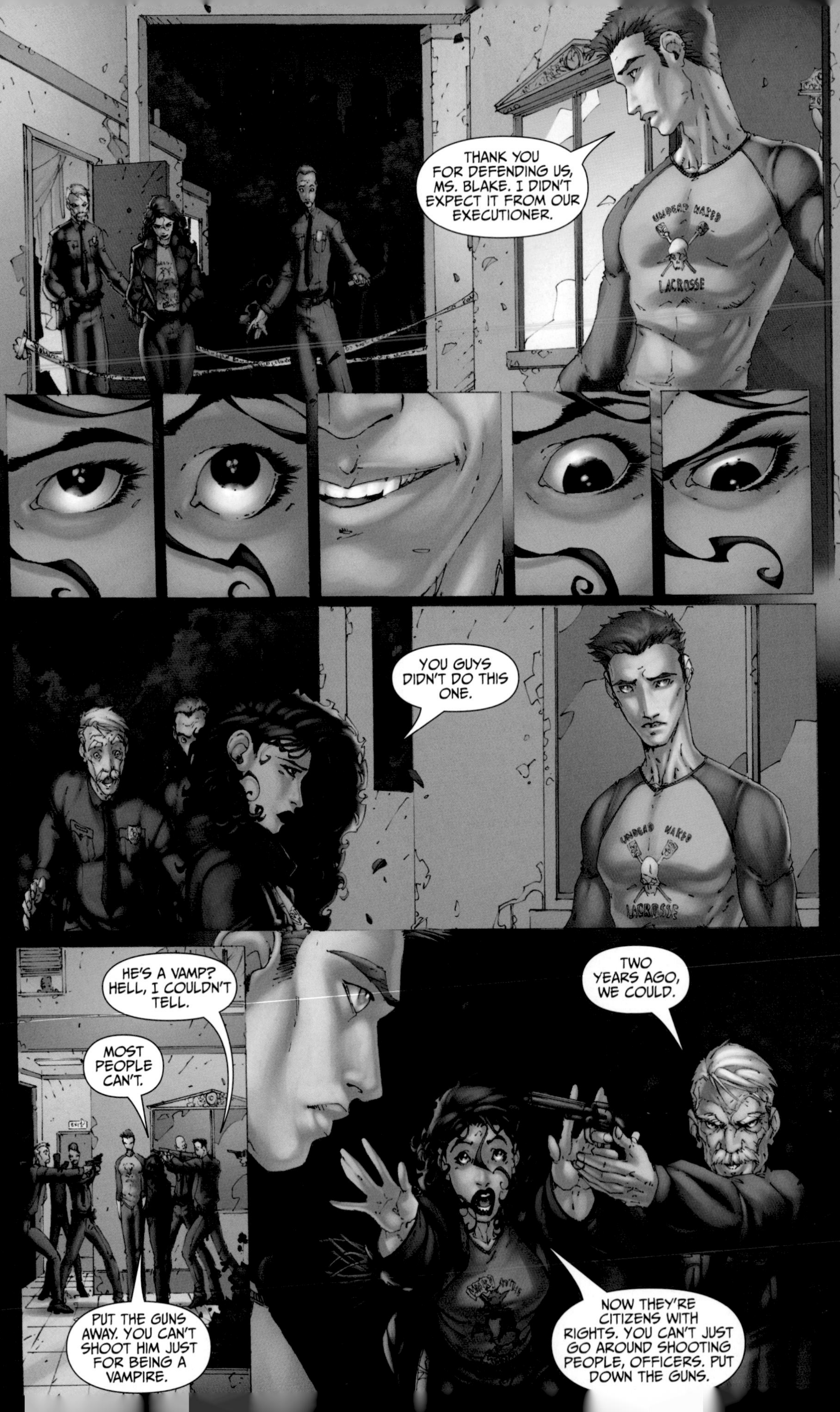
THANK YOU FOR DEFENDING US, MS. BLAKE. I DIDN'T EXPECT IT FROM OUR EXECUTIONER.
UNDEAD NAKED LACROSSE
YOU GUYS DIDN'T DO THIS ONE.
UNDEAD NAKED LACROSSE
HE'S A VAMP? HELL, I COULDN'T TELL.
MOST PEOPLE CAN'T.
PUT THE GUNS AWAY. YOU CAN'T SHOOT HIM JUST FOR BEING A VAMPIRE.
TWO YEARS AGO, WE COULD.
NOW THEY'RE CITIZENS WITH RIGHTS. YOU CAN'T JUST GO AROUND SHOOTING PEOPLE, OFFICERS. PUT DOWN THE GUNS.

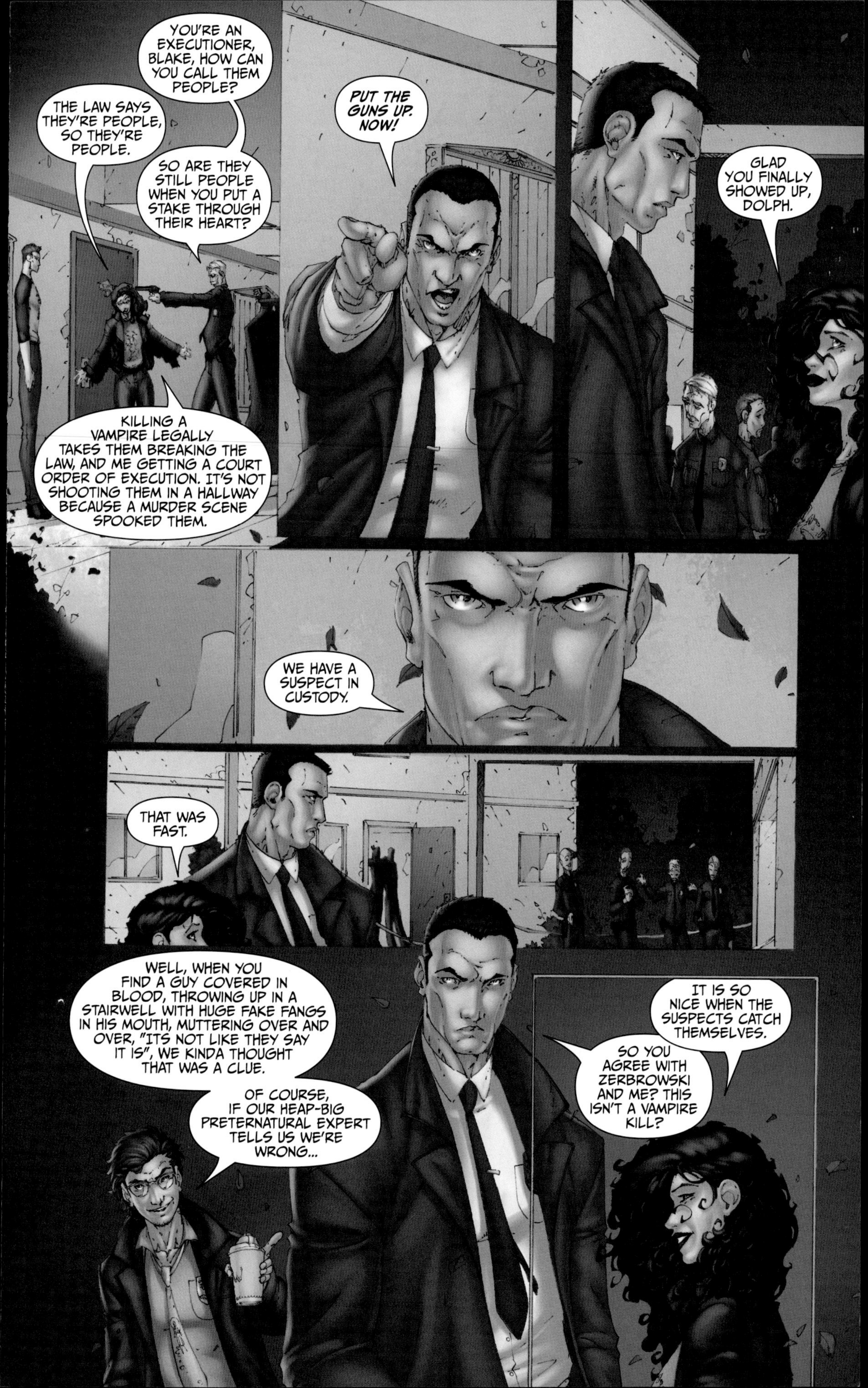
YOU'RE AN EXECUTIONER, BLAKE, HOW CAN YOU CALL THEM PEOPLE?
THE LAW SAYS THEY'RE PEOPLE, SO THEY'RE PEOPLE.
SO ARE THEY STILL PEOPLE WHEN YOU PUT A STAKE THROUGH THEIR HEART?
KILLING A VAMPIRE LEGALLY TAKES THEM BREAKING THE LAW, AND ME GETTING A COURT ORDER OF EXECUTION. IT'S NOT SHOOTING THEM IN A HALLWAY BECAUSE A MURDER SCENE SPOOKED THEM.
PUT THE GUNS UP. NOW!
GLAD YOU FINALLY SHOWED UP, DOLPH.
WE HAVE A SUSPECT IN CUSTODY.
THAT WAS FAST.
WELL, WHEN YOU FIND A GUY COVERED IN BLOOD, THROWING UP IN A STAIRWELL WITH HUGE FAKE FANGS IN HIS MOUTH, MUTTERING OVER AND OVER, "ITS NOT LIKE THEY SAY IT IS", WE KINDA THOUGHT THAT WAS A CLUE.
OF COURSE, IF OUR HEAP-BIG PRETERNATURAL EXPERT TELLS US WE'RE WRONG...
IT IS SO NICE WHEN THE SUSPECTS CATCH THEMSELVES.
SO YOU AGREE WITH ZERBROWSKI AND ME? THIS ISN'T A VAMPIRE KILL?

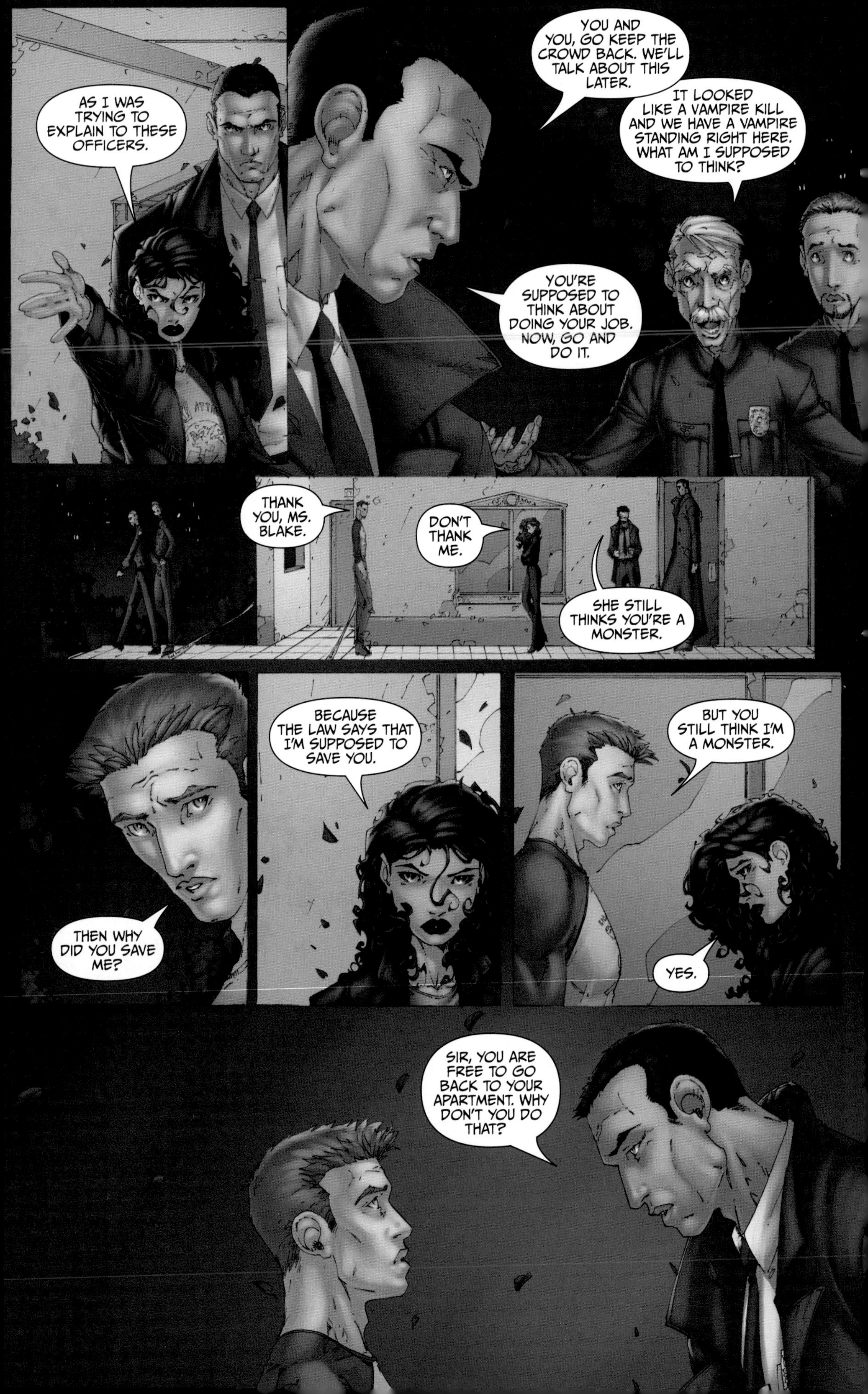
AS I WAS TRYING TO EXPLAIN TO THESE OFFICERS.
YOU AND YOU, GO KEEP THE CROWD BACK. WE'LL TALK ABOUT THIS LATER.
IT LOOKED LIKE A VAMPIRE KILL AND WE HAVE A VAMPIRE STANDING RIGHT HERE. WHAT AM I SUPPOSED TO THINK?
YOU'RE SUPPOSED TO THINK ABOUT DOING YOUR JOB. NOW, GO AND DO IT.
THANK YOU, MS. BLAKE.
DON'T THANK ME.
SHE STILL THINKS YOU'RE A MONSTER.
THEN WHY DID YOU SAVE ME?
BECAUSE THE LAW SAYS THAT I'M SUPPOSED TO SAVE YOU.
BUT YOU STILL THINK I'M A MONSTER.
YES.
SIR, YOU ARE FREE TO GO BACK TO YOUR APARTMENT. WHY DON'T YOU DO THAT?

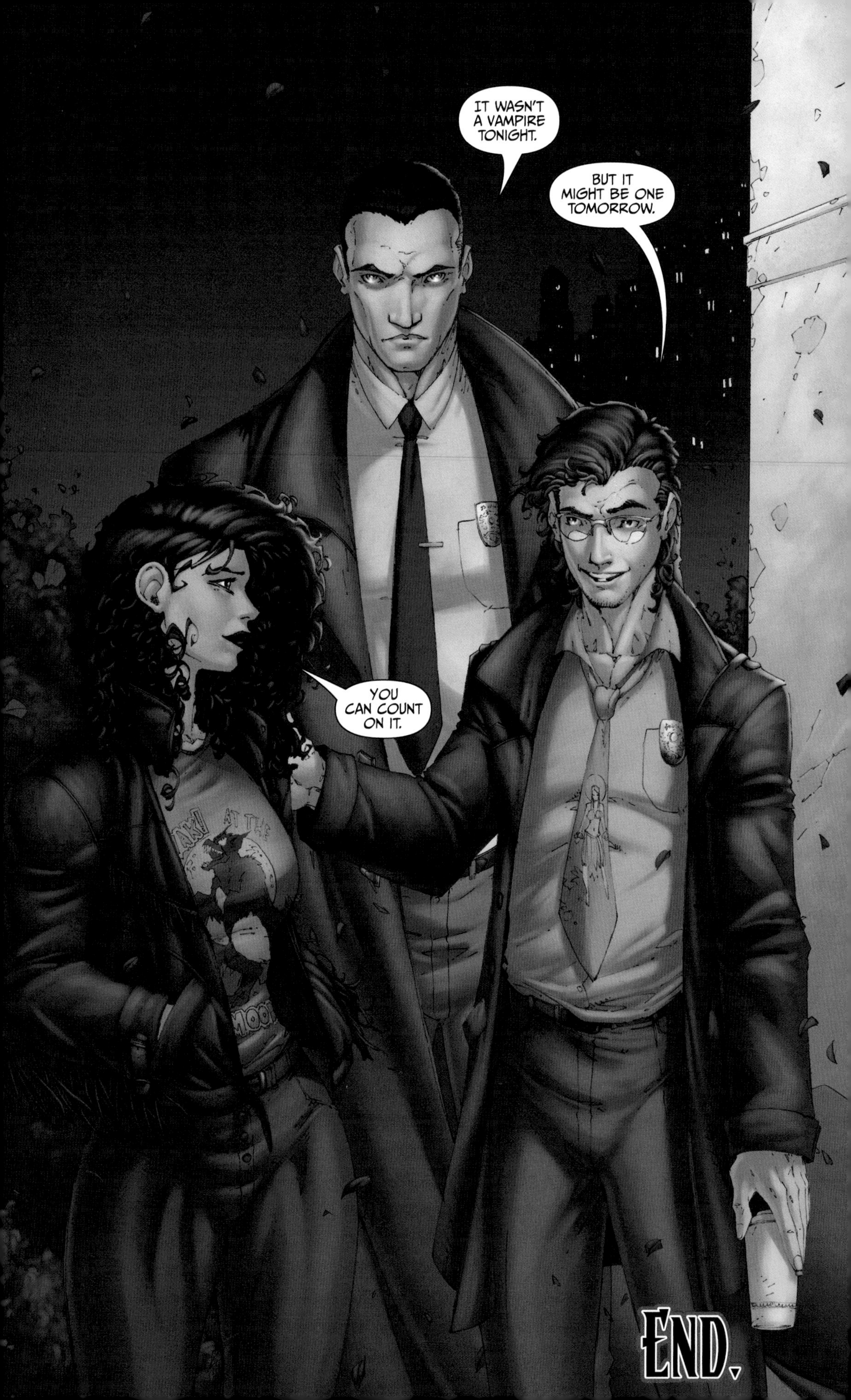
IT WASN'T A VAMPIRE TONIGHT.
BUT IT MIGHT BE ONE TOMORROW.
YOU CAN COUNT ON IT.
END.

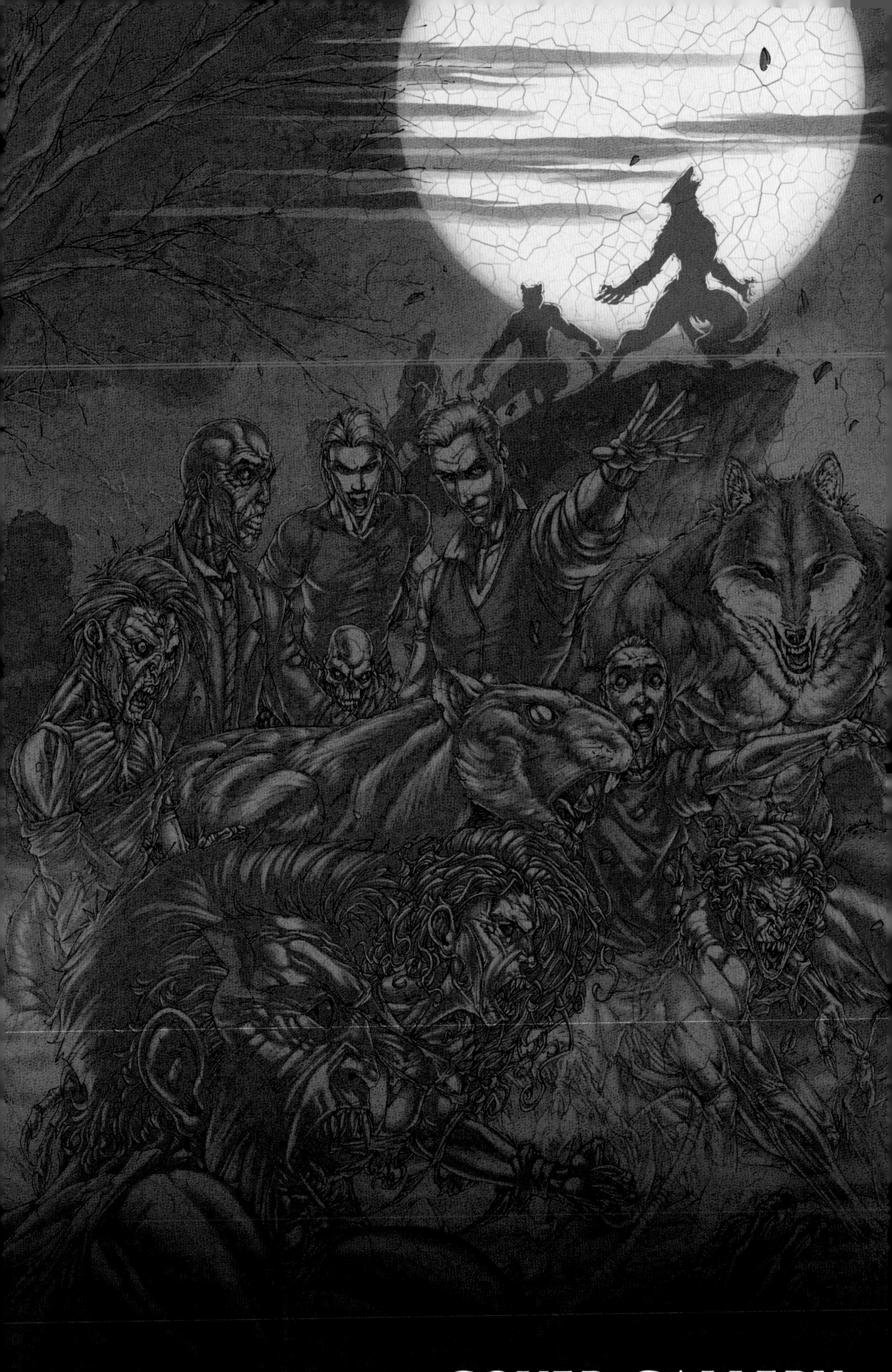

COVER GALLERY

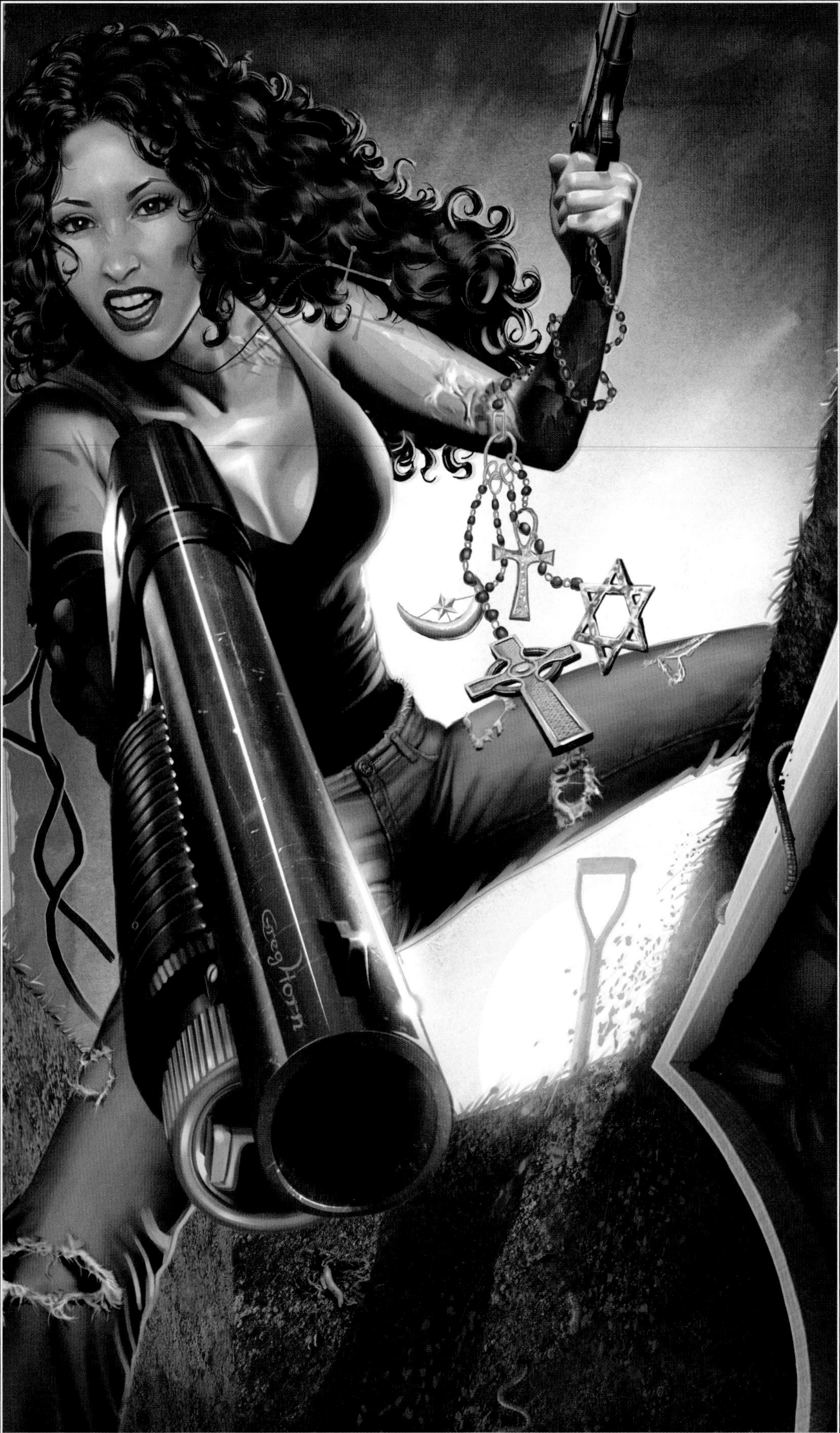
Greg Horn

ALTERNATE ISSUE #1 COVER BY: **GREG HORN**

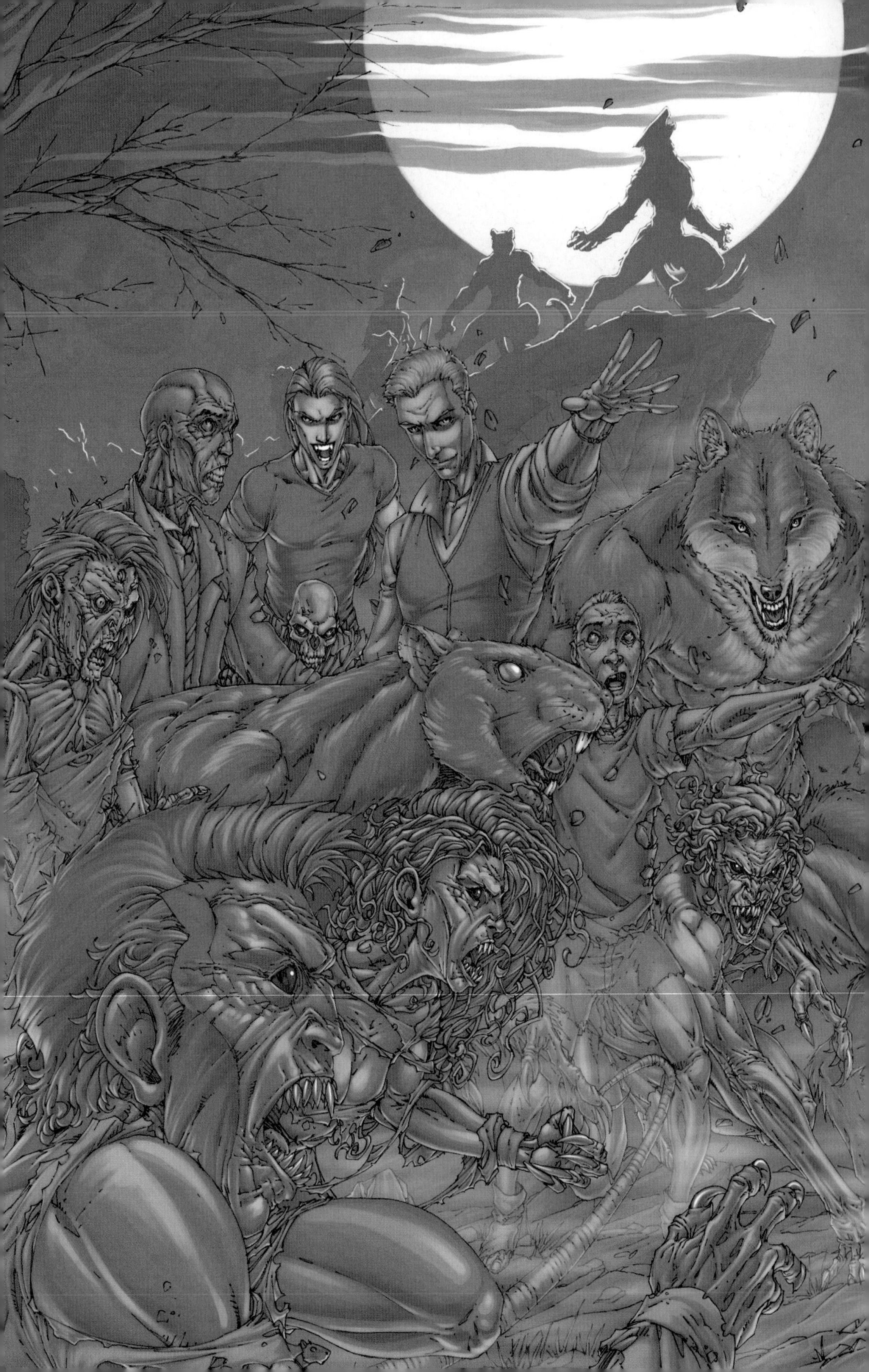

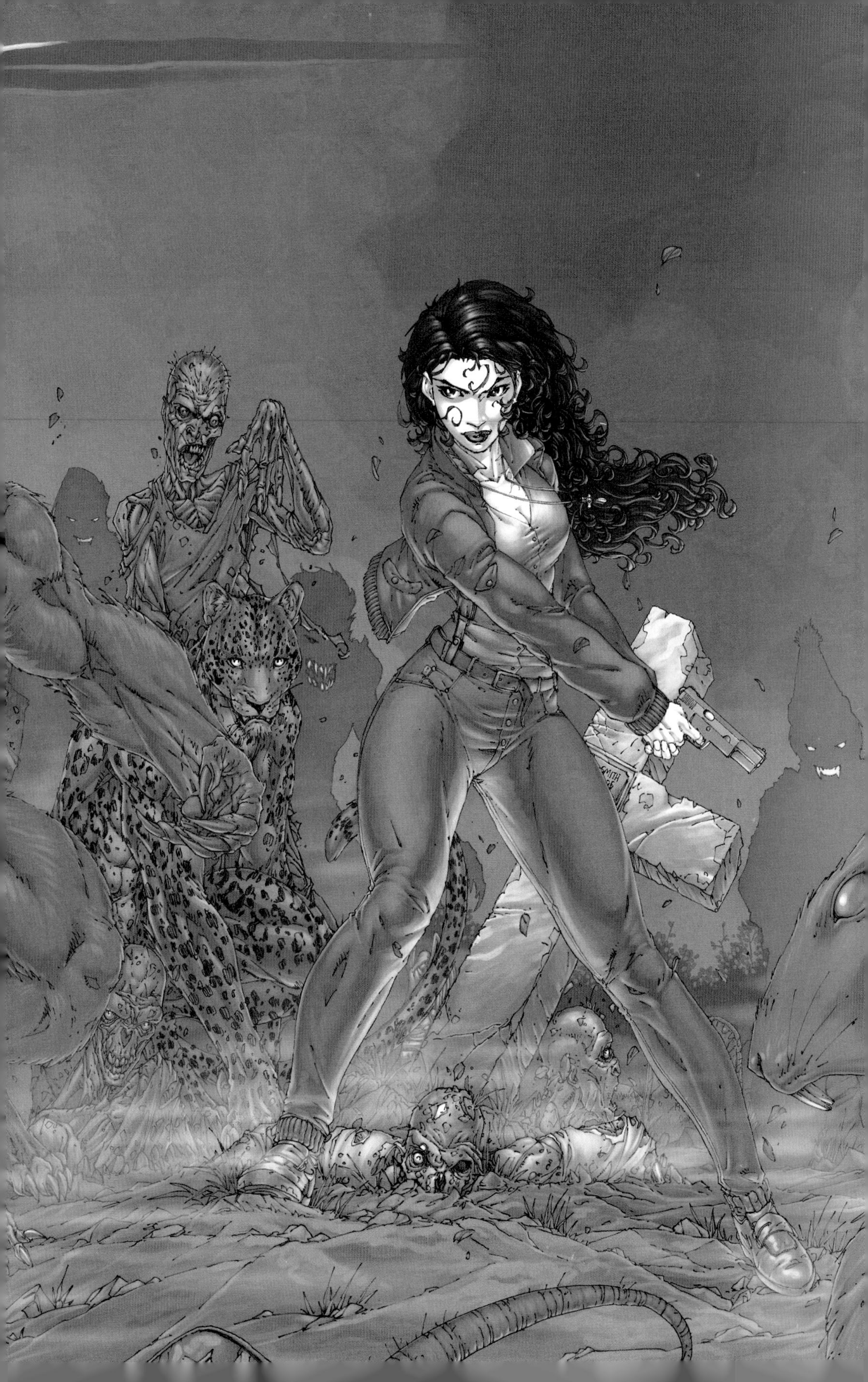

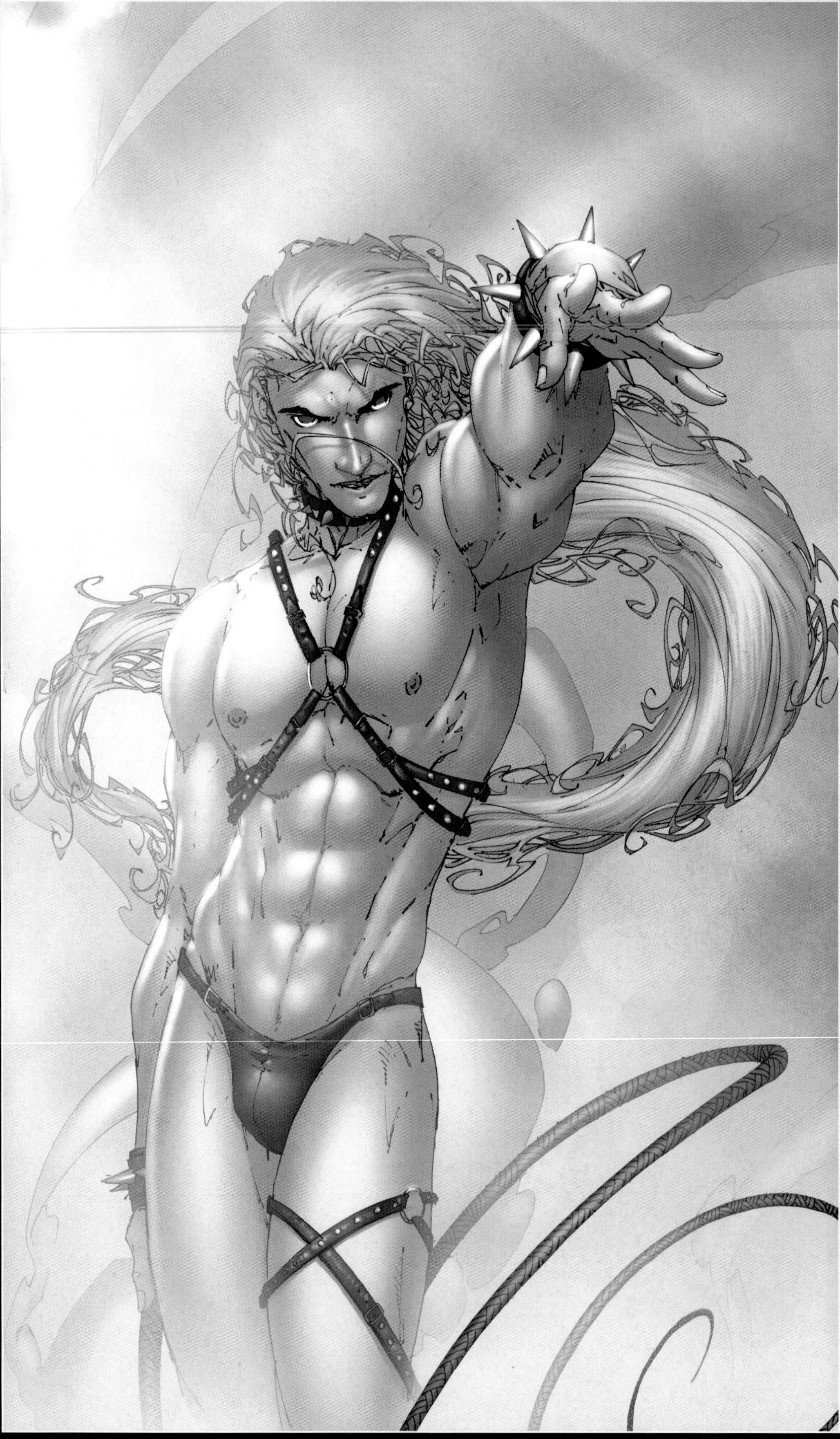

ISSUE #1 THIRD PRINTING COVER BY: **BRETT BOOTH & JESS RUFFNER-BOOTH**

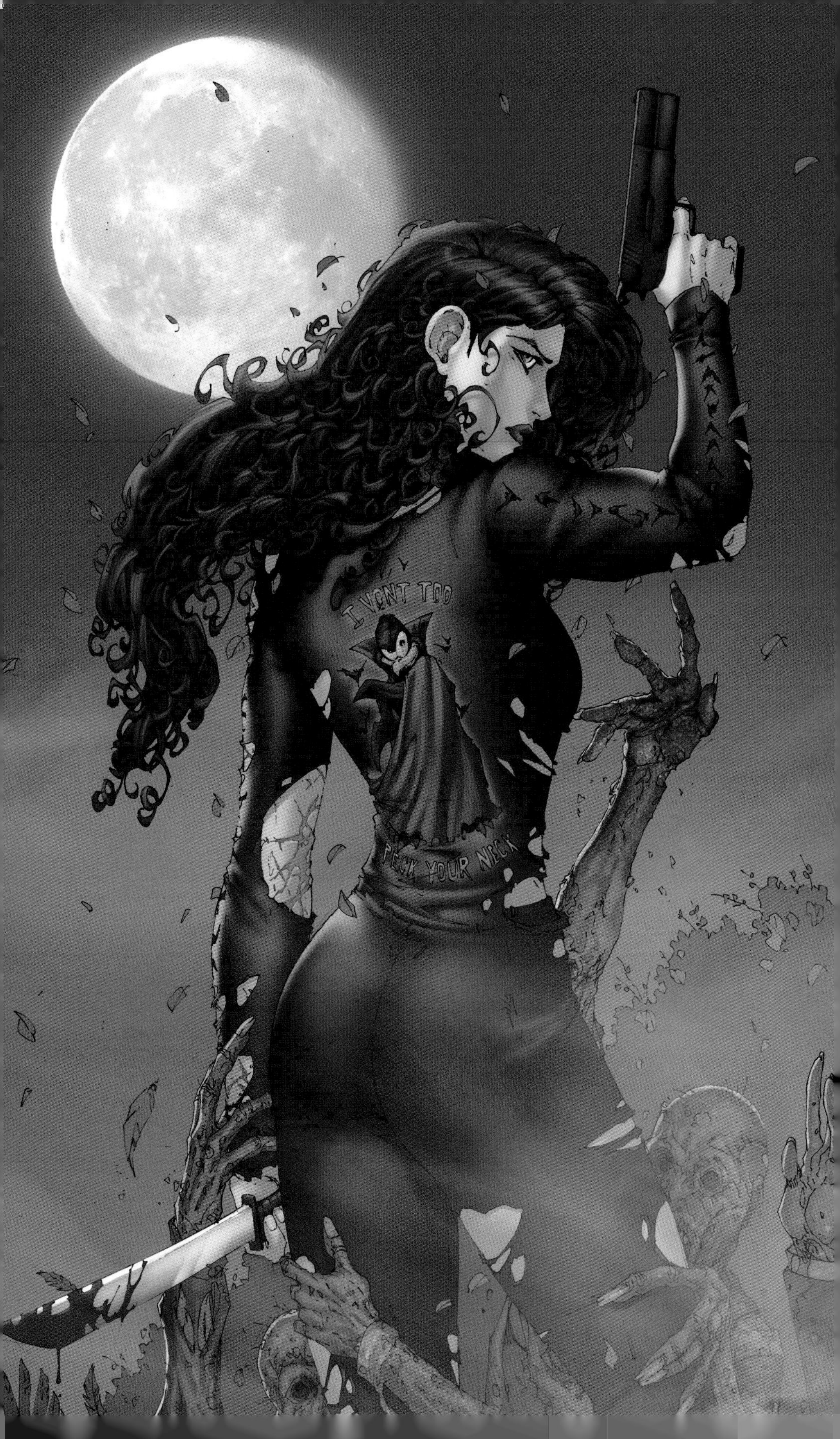

I VANT TOO
PECK YOUR NECK

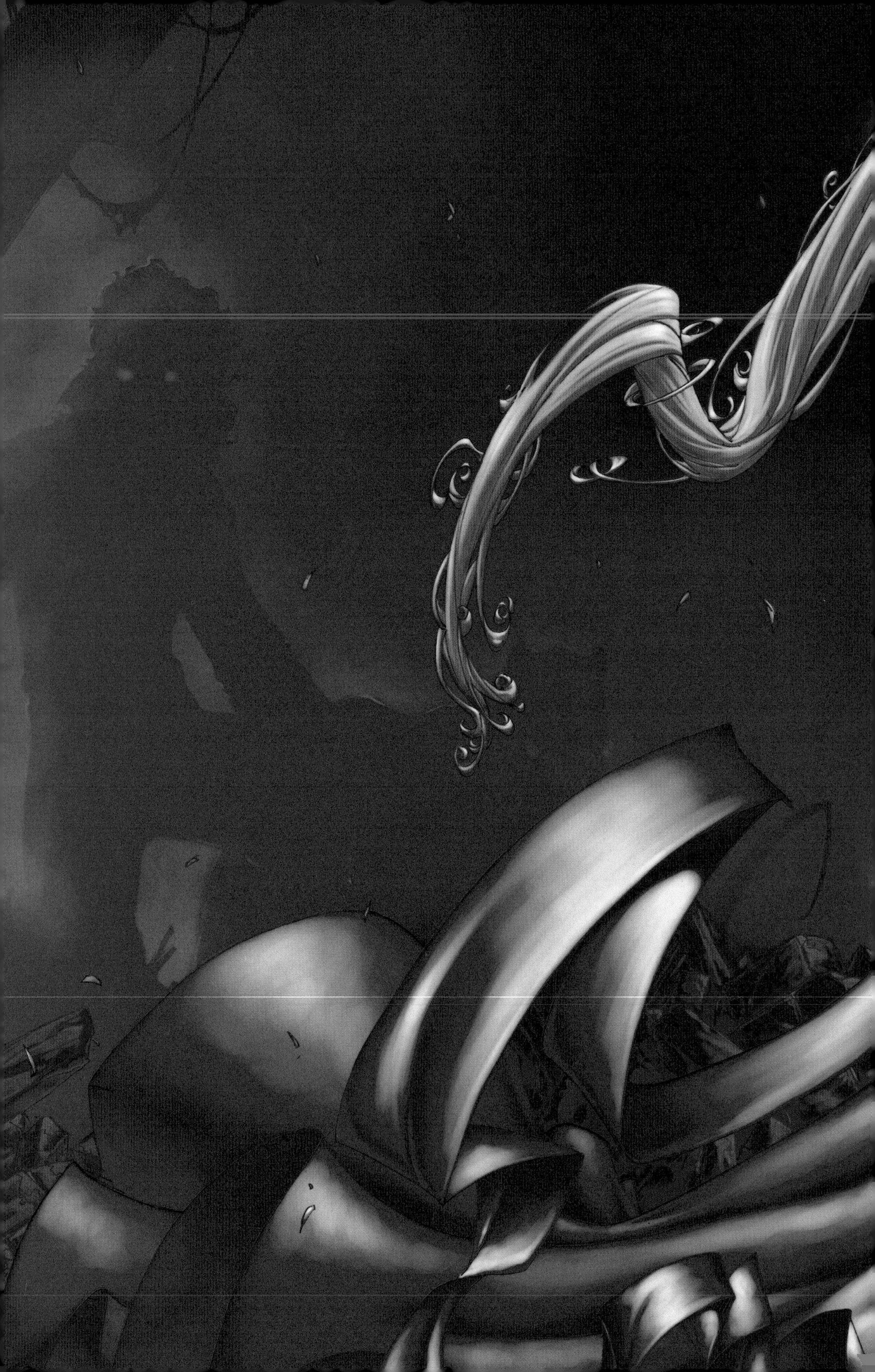

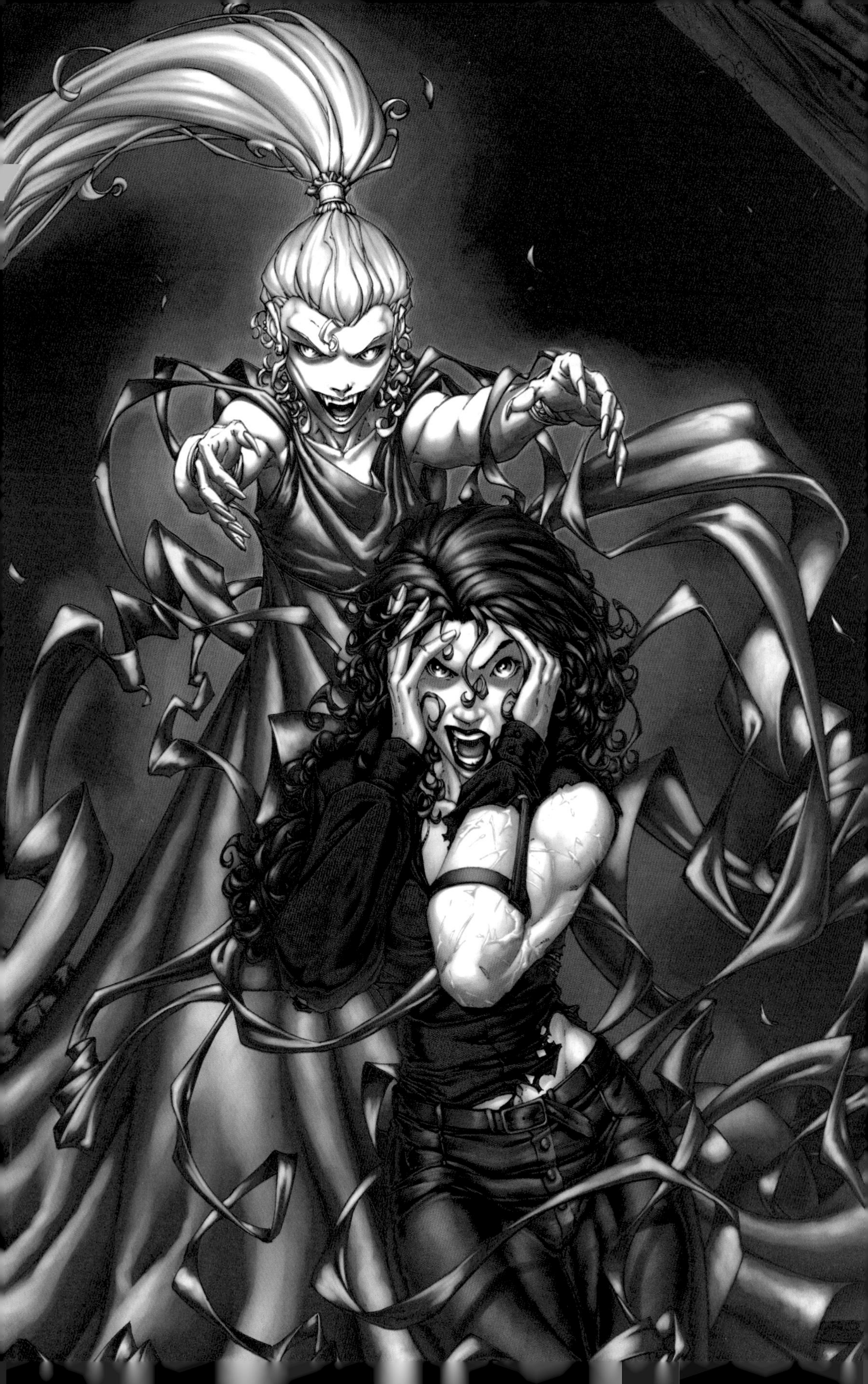

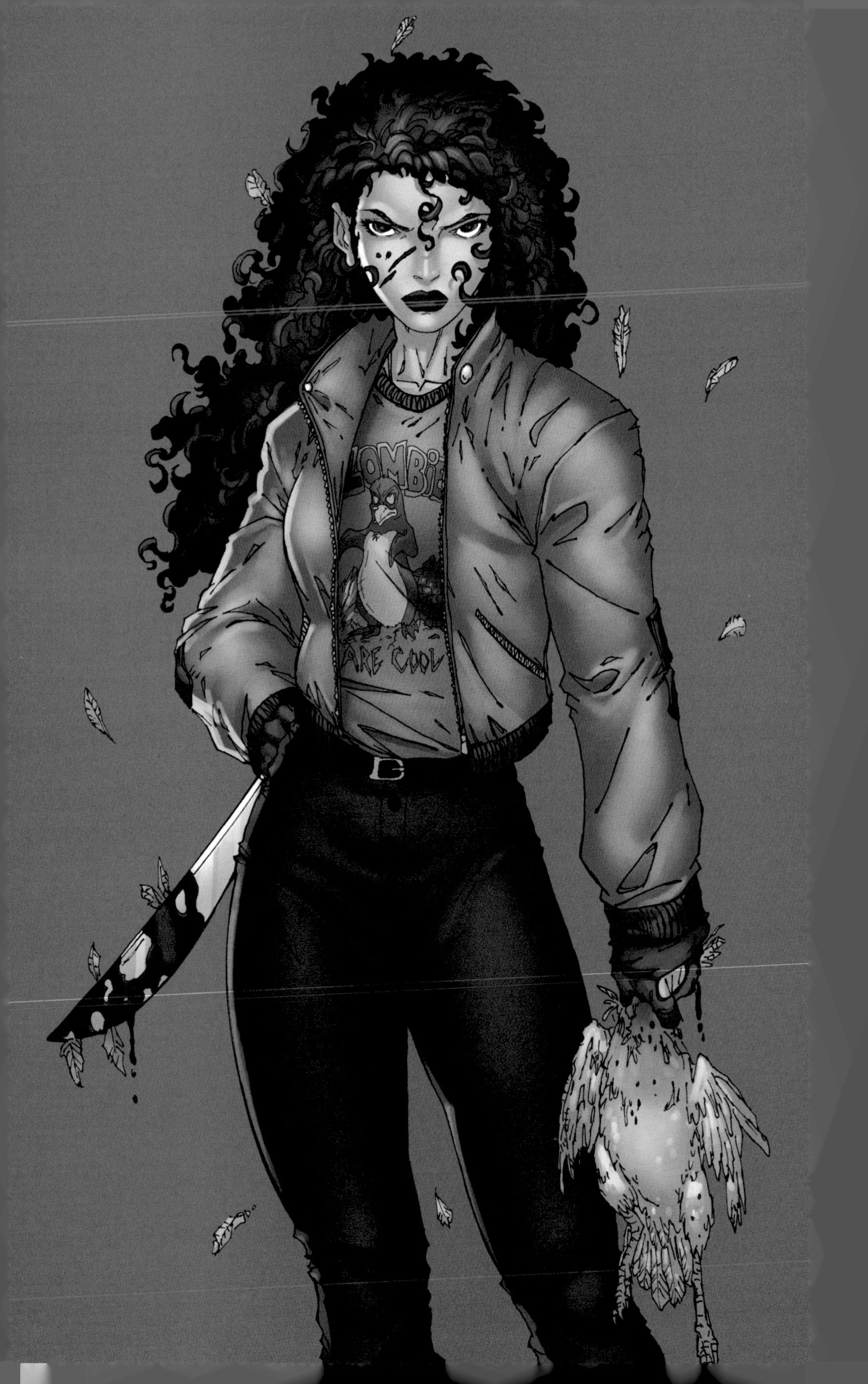
ZOMBIES
ARE COOL

LAURELL K.
HAMILTON
ZOMBIES
XIII
GEORGE R.R.
MARTIN
ORSON SCOTT
CARD
RAYMOND E.
FEIST
MONTE
COOK
ROBERT
SILVERBERG
R. A.
SALVATORE
The Highwayman
NEW TO
DB PRO!!
KINLEY
MACGREGOR
MacGregor
Sword of Darkness
NEW TO
DB PRO!!

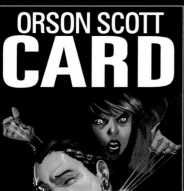

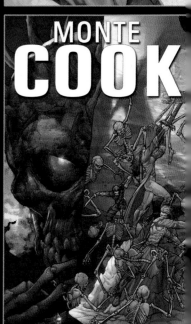

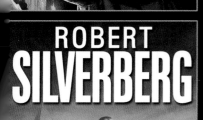

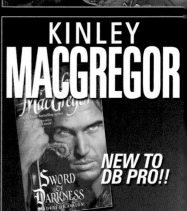

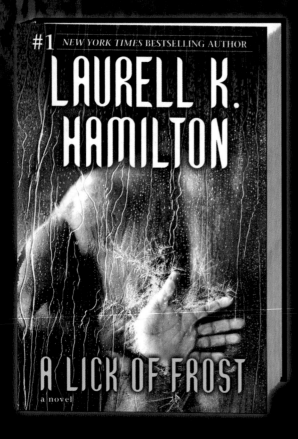

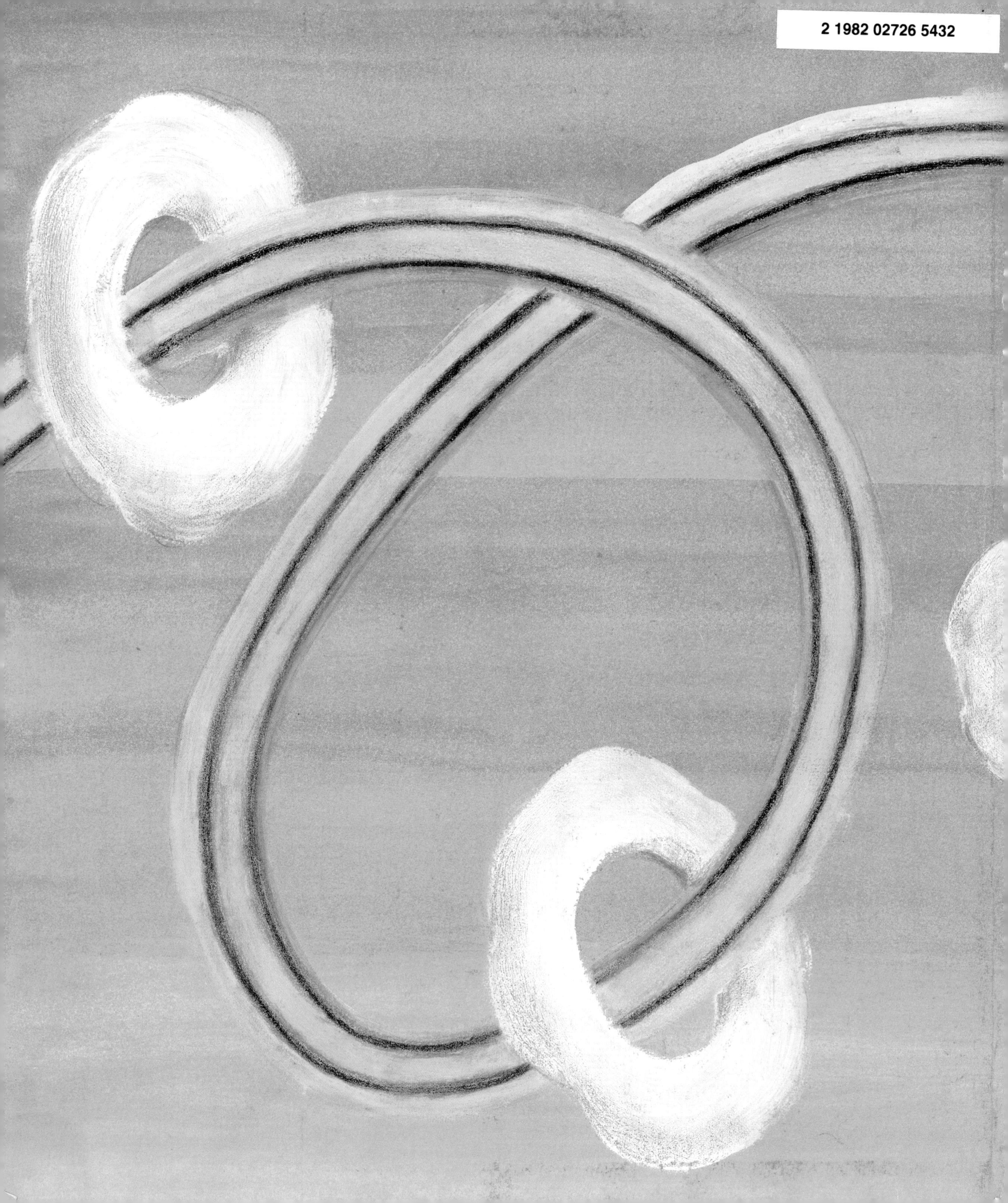

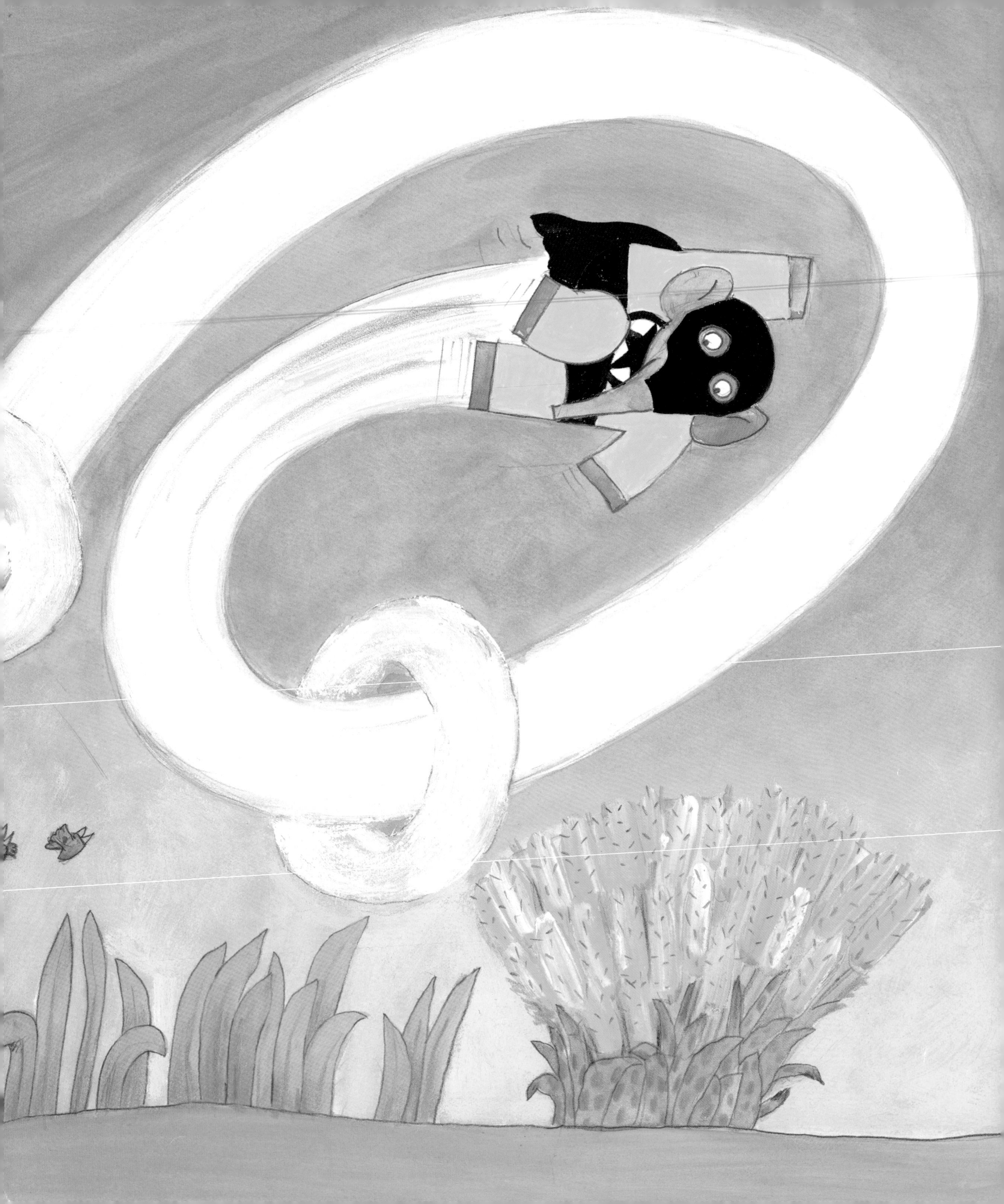

“Thank you! Now I feel super again,” said the little elephant. “I think you’re both wonderful. Maybe one day I can do something for you.”
With that, he shot off like a rocket into the sky.
He looped back just once to wave good-bye.
“If he’s going to rush about like that, he’ll rip his clothes again,” said Aunt Zelda.
“Probably,” said Elmer chuckling. “Probably.”

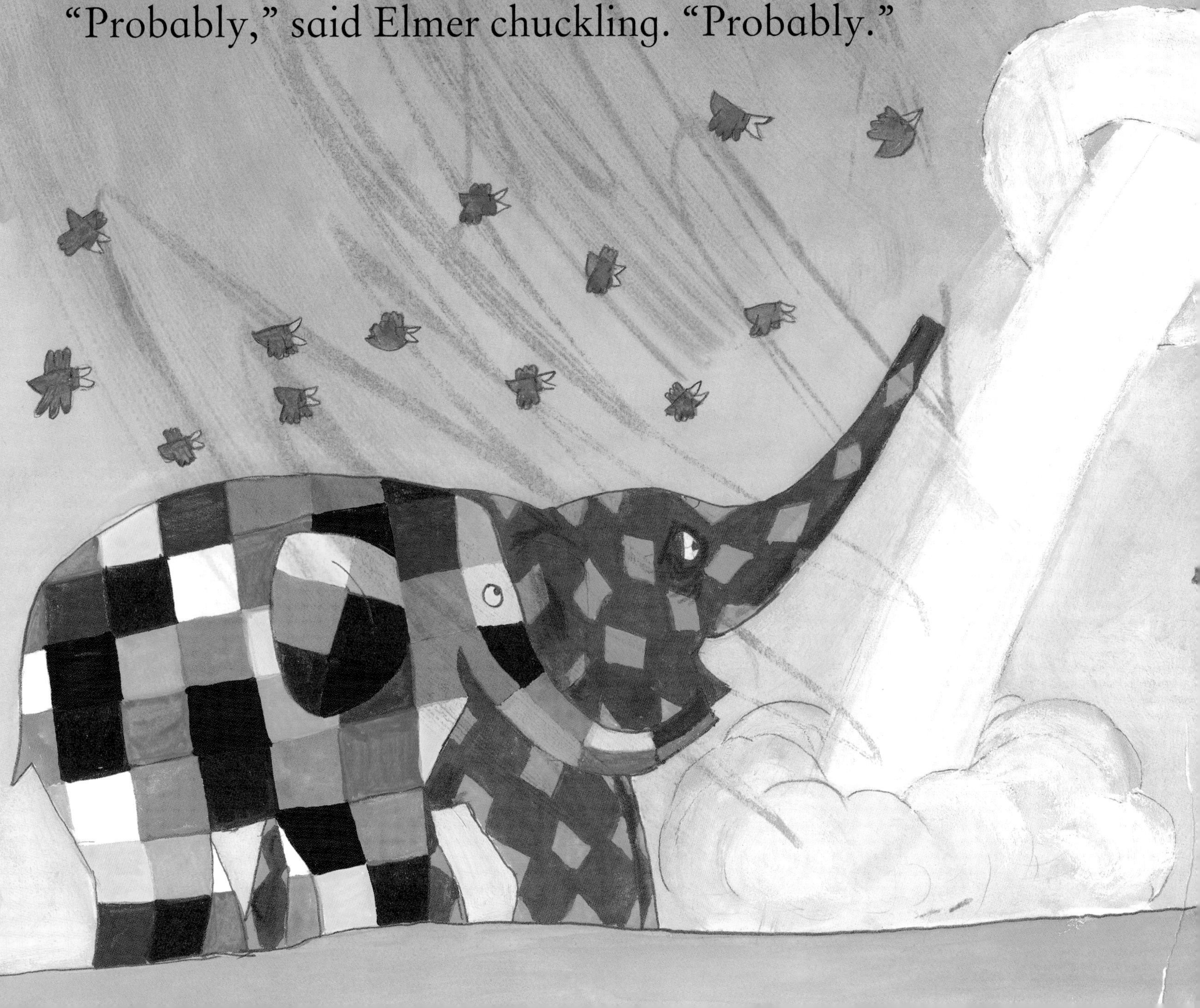

"Aunt Zelda," said Elmer, "you are a wonder."

"Thunder, dear? I didn't hear anything," said Aunt Zelda.

Super El smiled, and Aunt Zelda quickly finished the repairs.

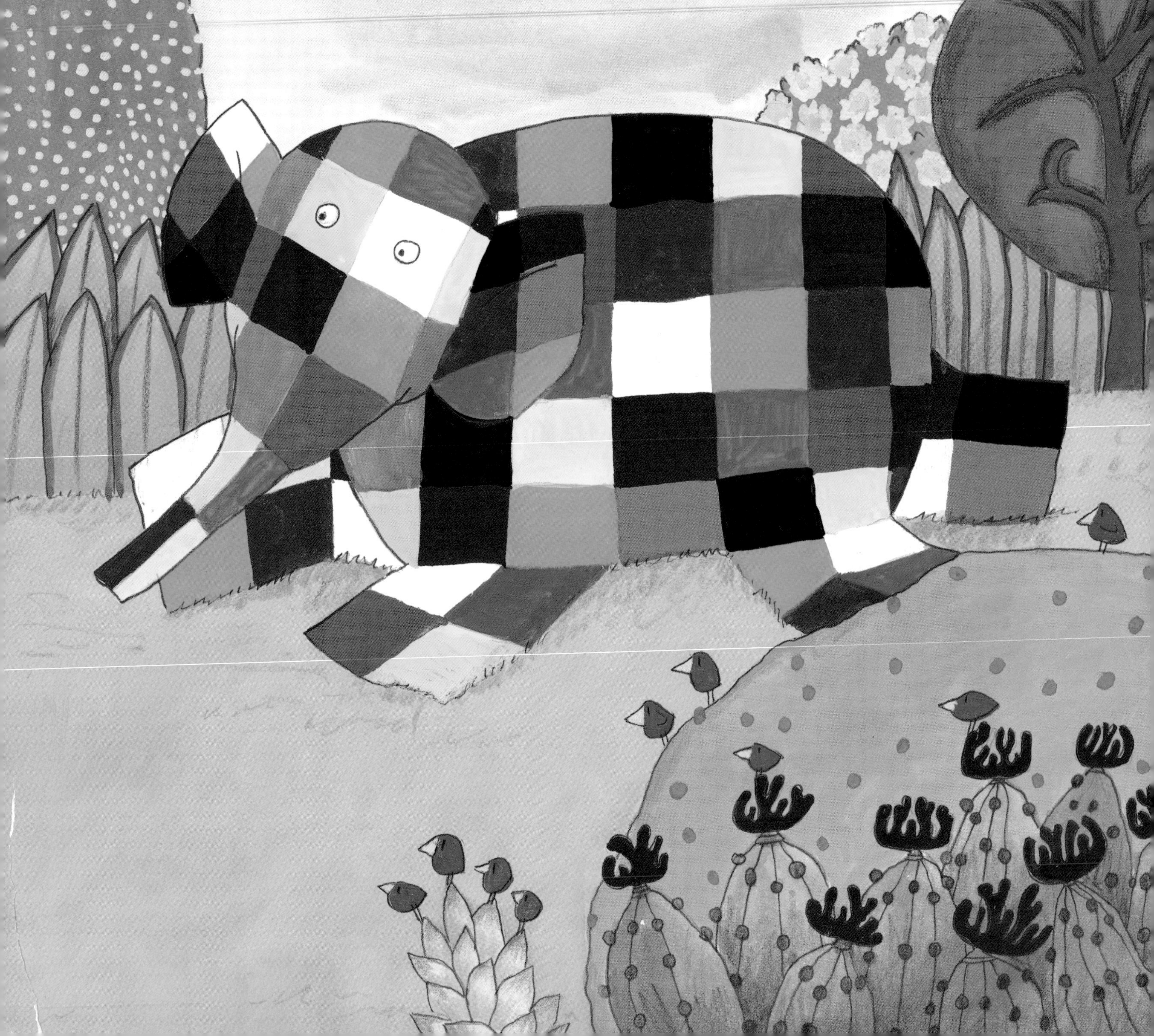

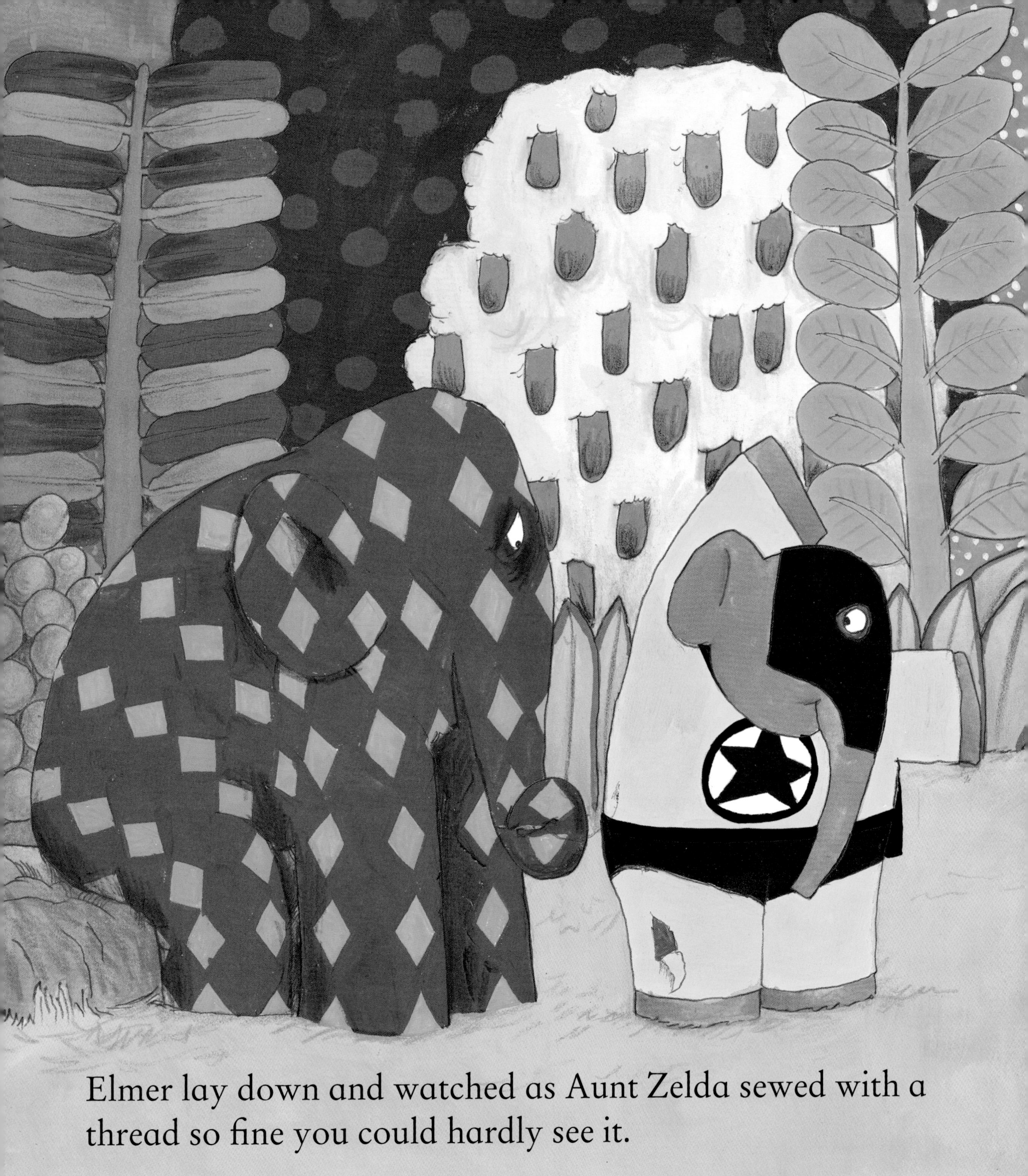

Elmer lay down and watched as Aunt Zelda sewed with a thread so fine you could hardly see it.

When the others had gone, Elmer said, “Hello, Aunt Zelda, this is my friend Super El.”

“Yes, I’m very well, thank you, Elmer dear,” said Aunt Zelda. “But your friend’s suit looks nearly worn out. Shall I mend it?”

“Oh yes, please!” said the little elephant.

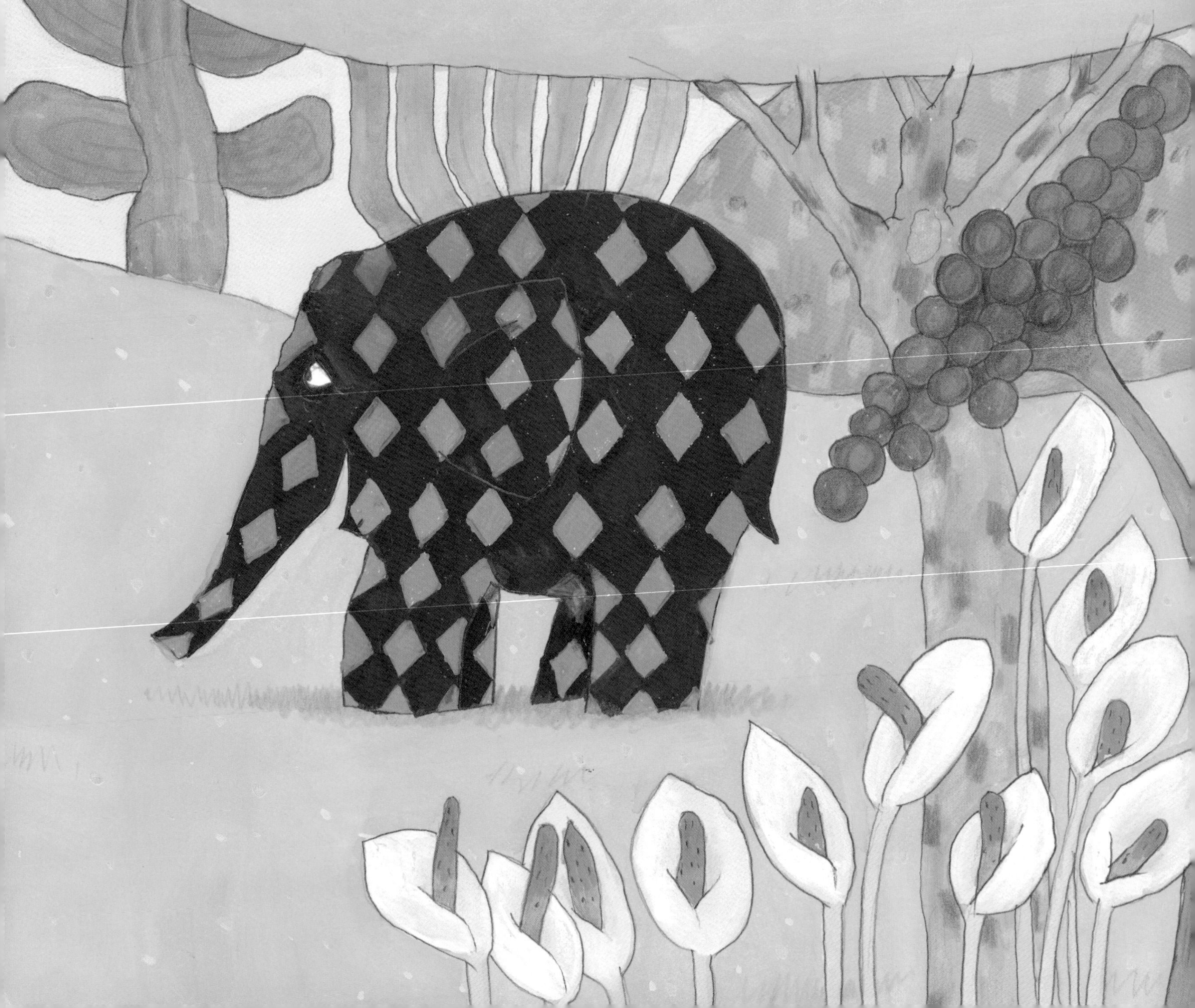

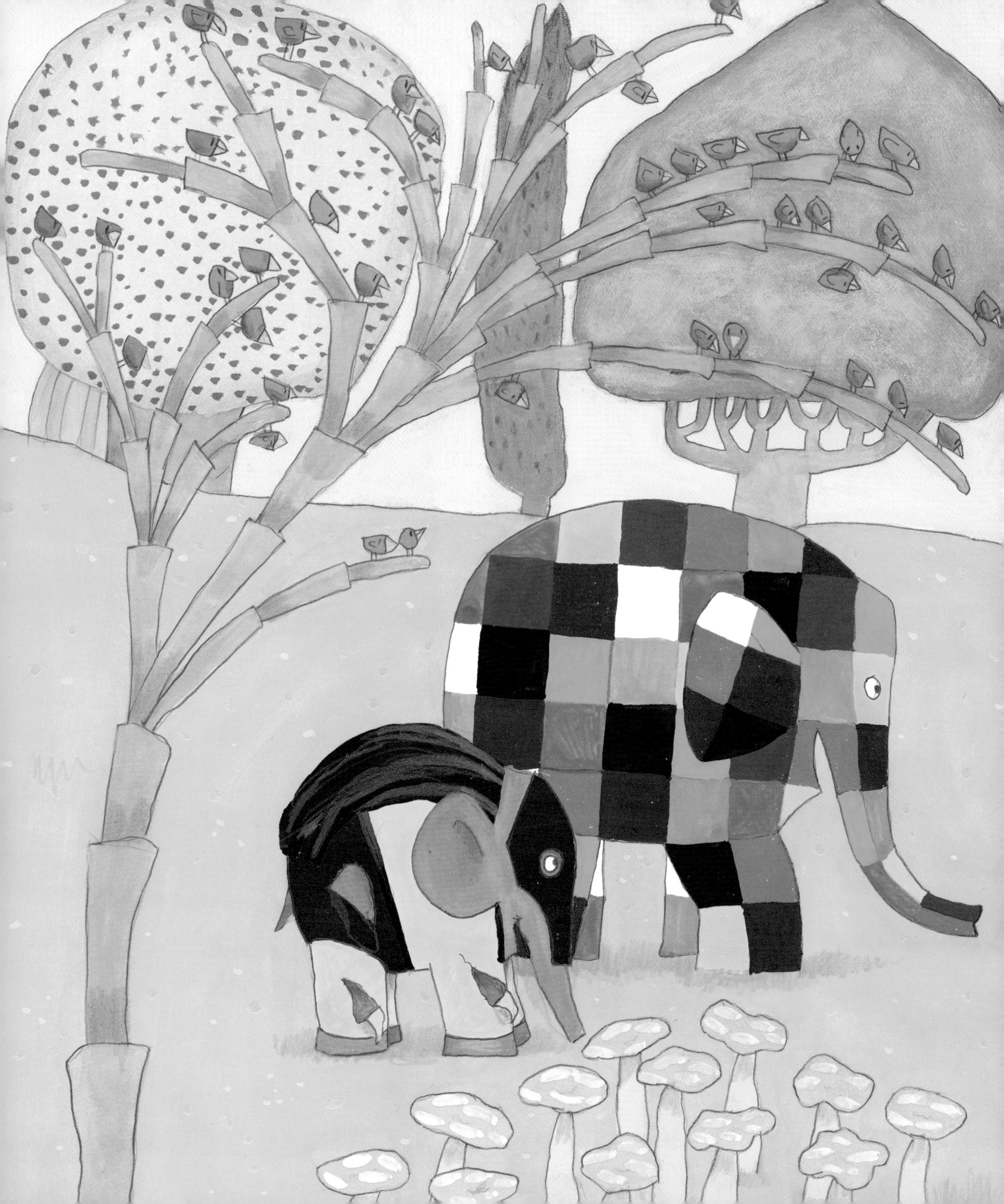

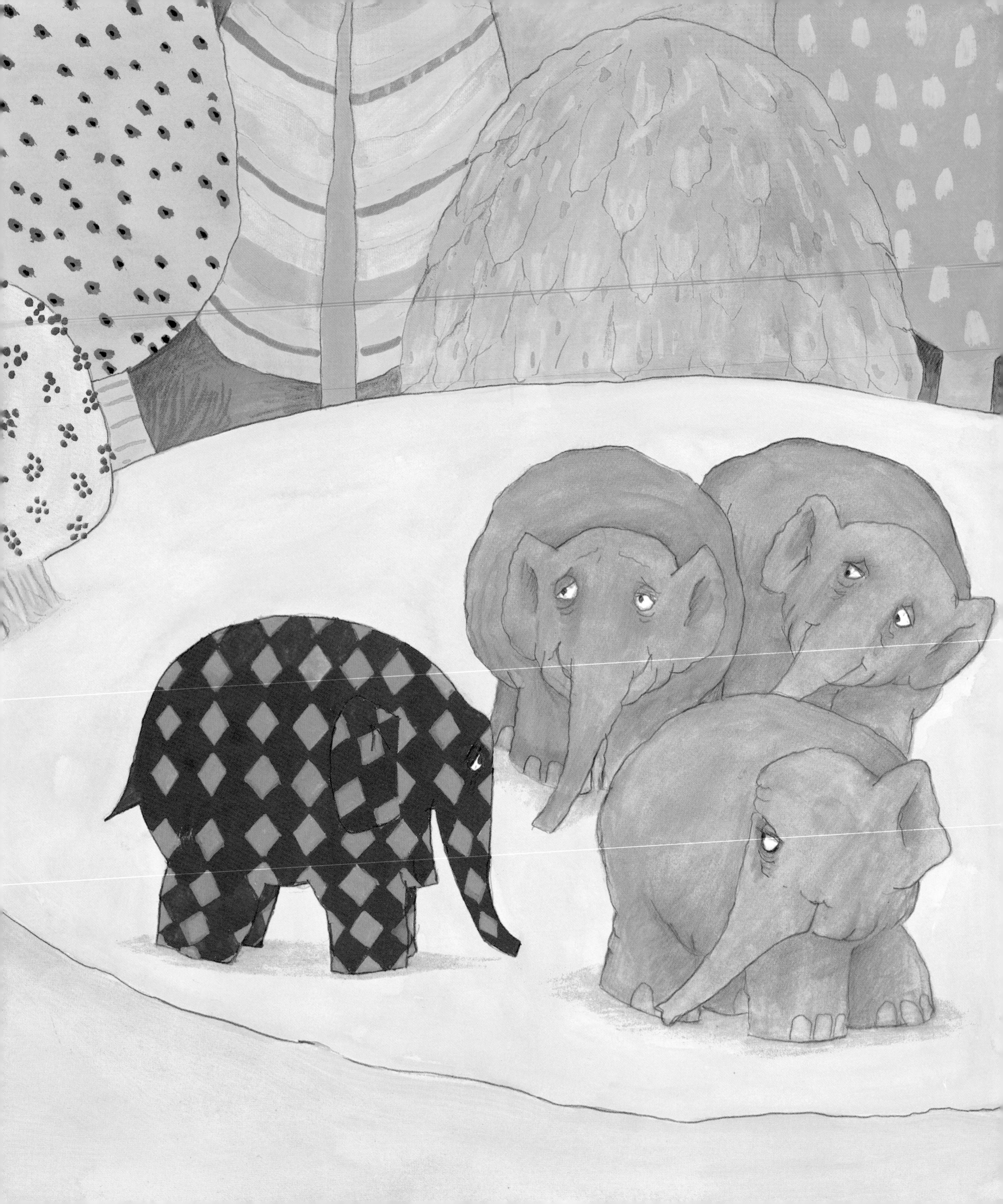

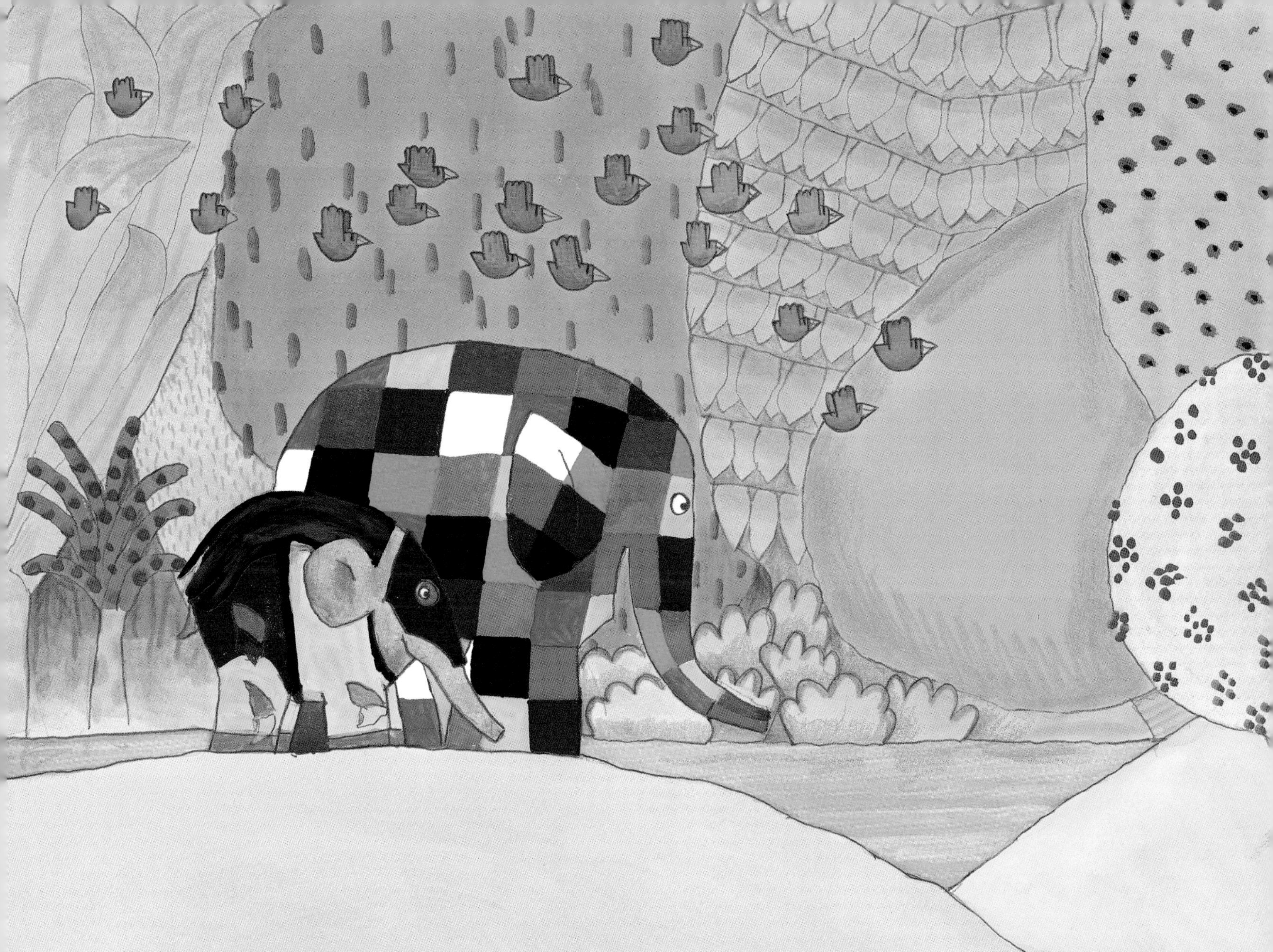

“Thanks, birds. You were fantastic!” said Elmer later. “Look, there’s Aunt Zelda saying good-bye to some friends. As soon as they’ve left, we’ll go to her. Remember, she doesn’t always hear too well.”

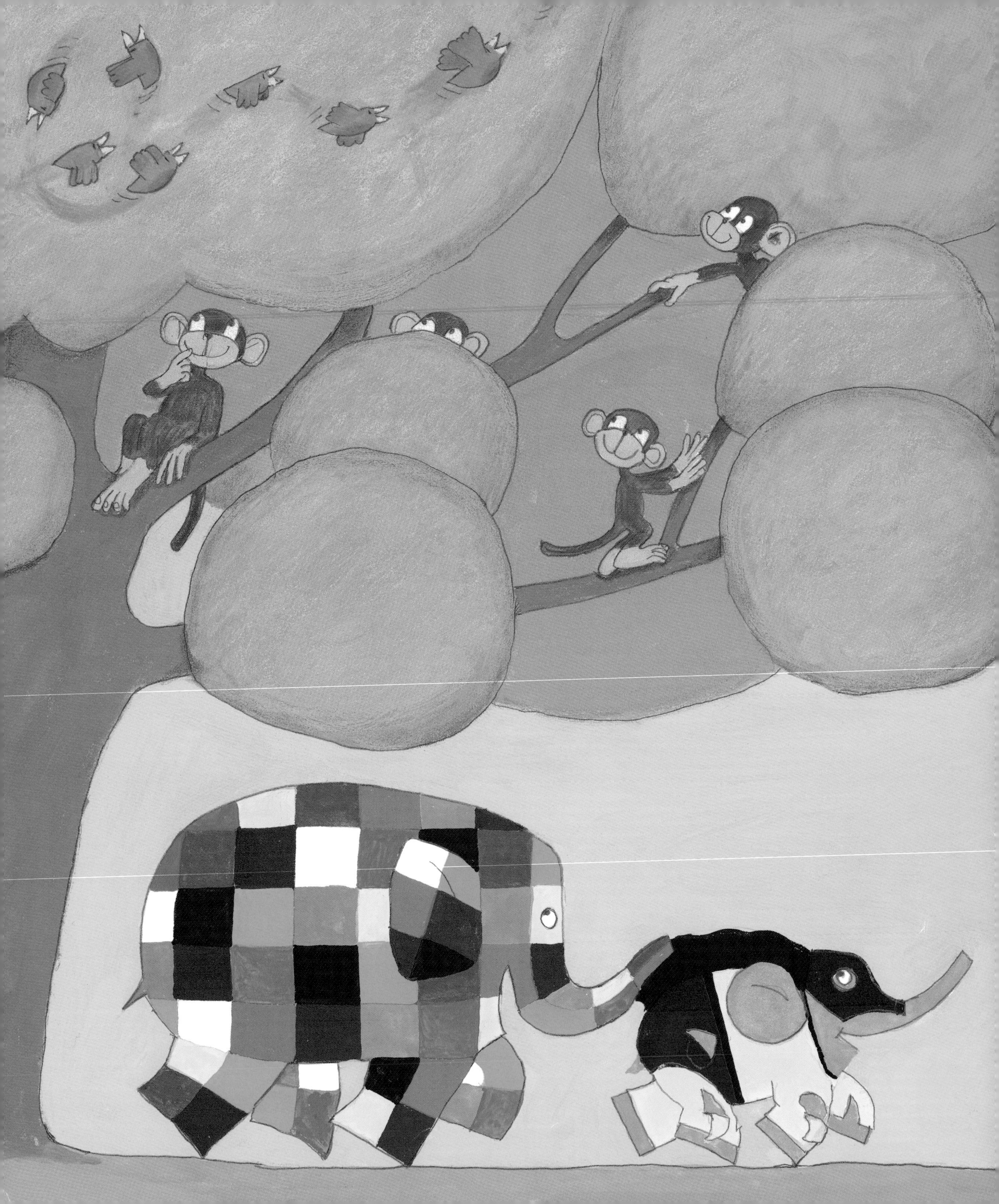

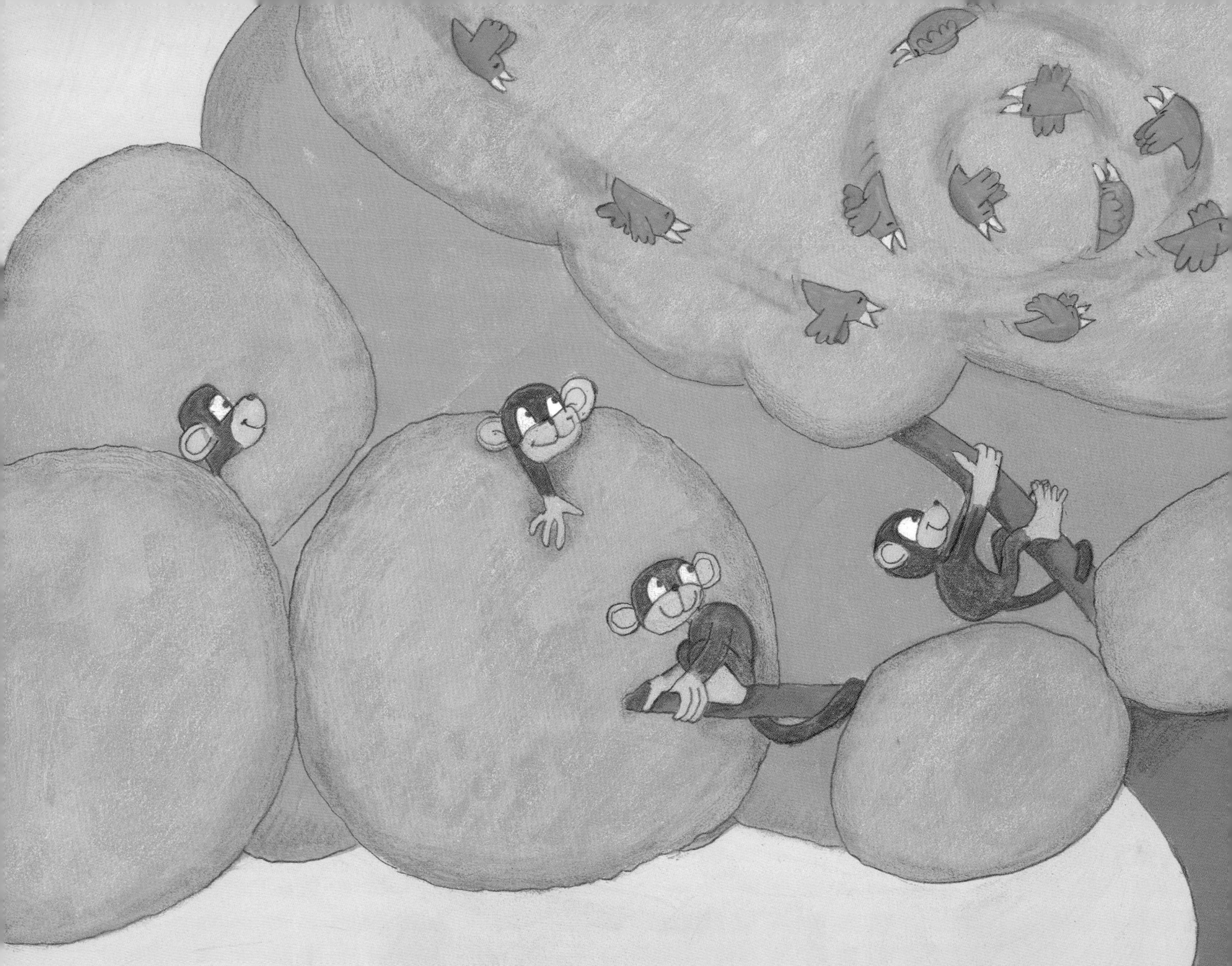

The birds were wonderful. They sang and flew in patterns above the monkeys' heads. The monkeys were too fascinated to notice the elephants. The little elephant nearly stopped to watch, but Elmer pushed him along.

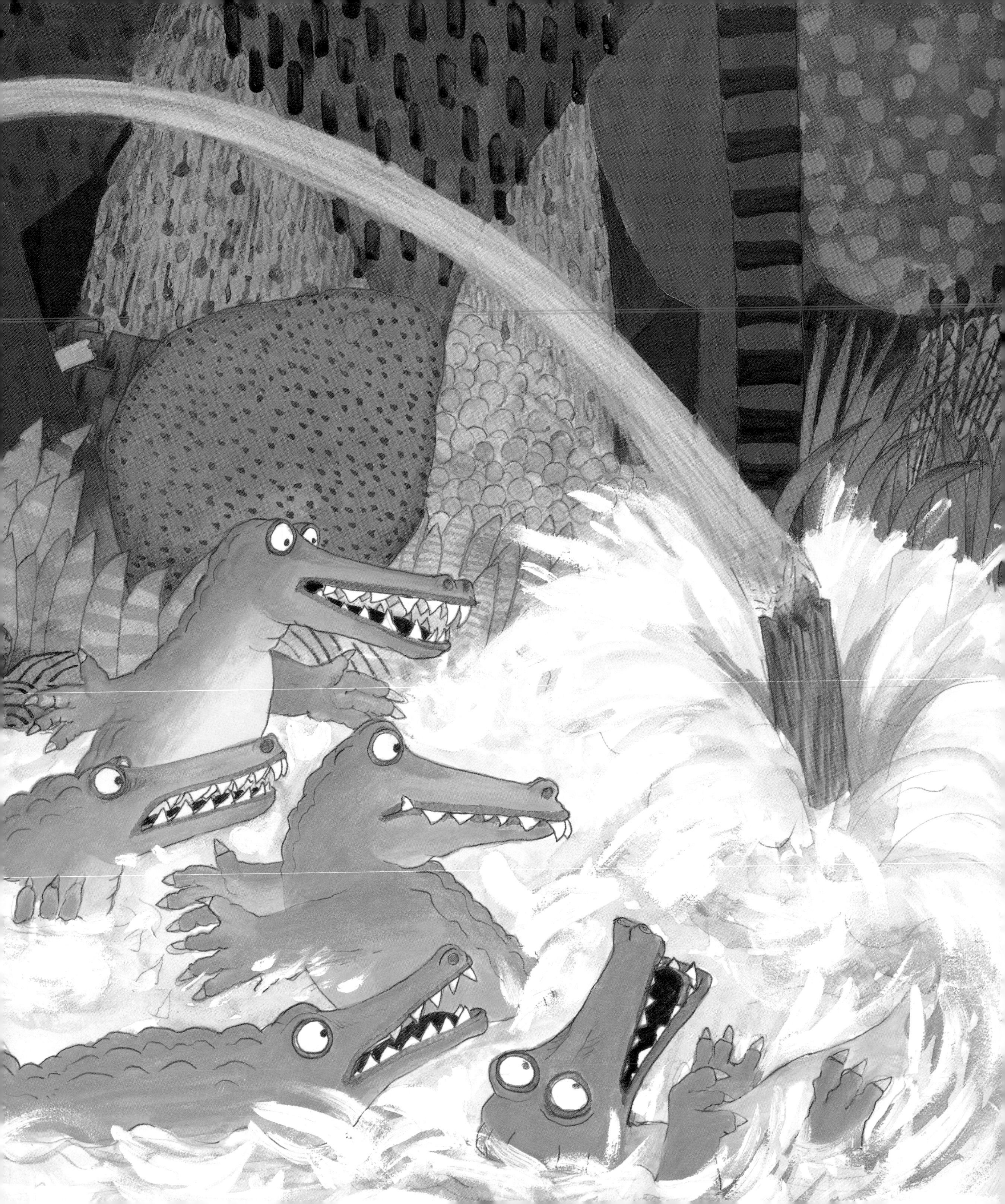

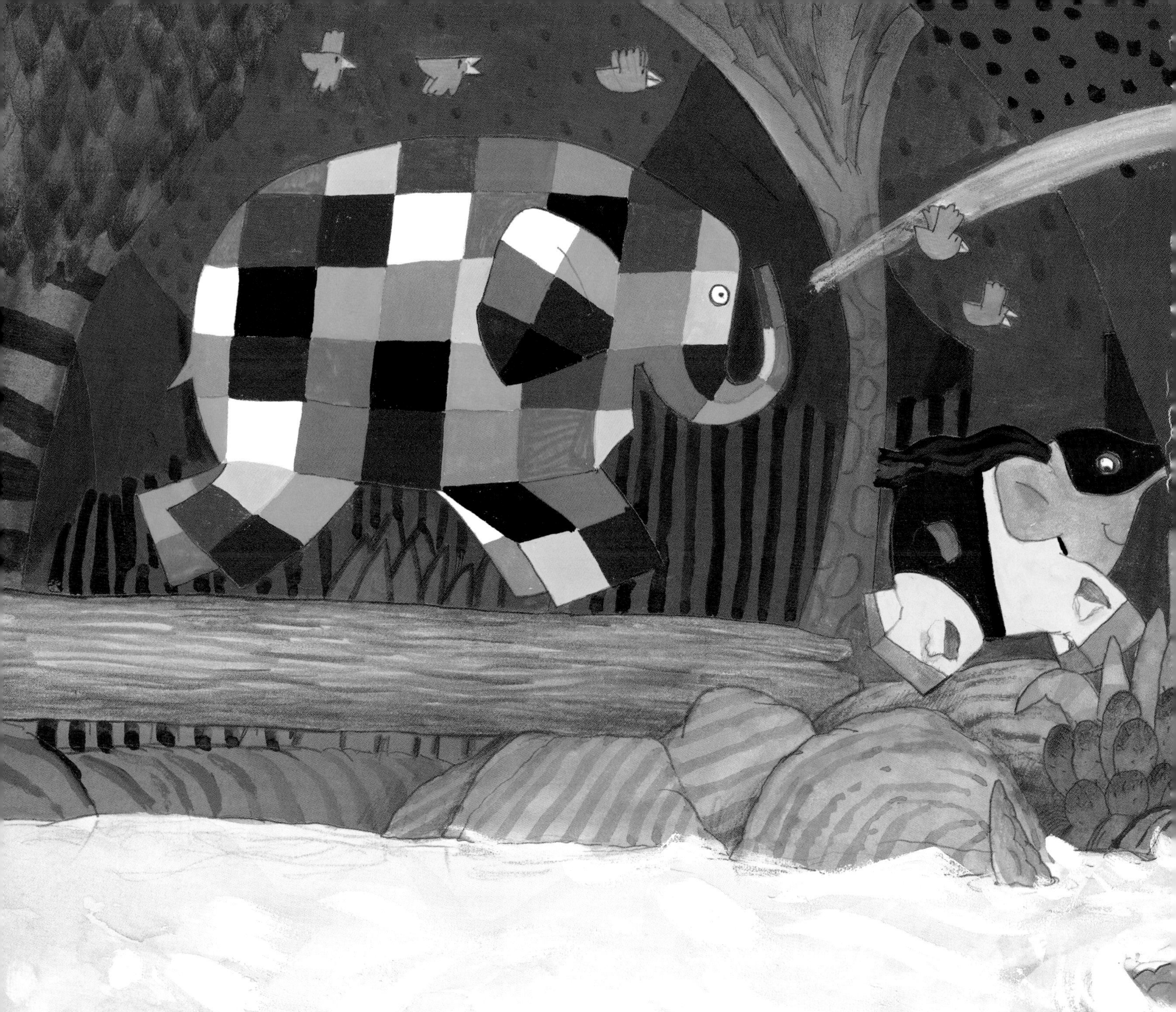

When they came to the crocodiles, Elmer threw a branch into the river to distract them. Then he and Super El crossed in the confusion that followed.

"It's not going to be easy to pass the monkeys," said Elmer. "Leave that to us," said the birds.

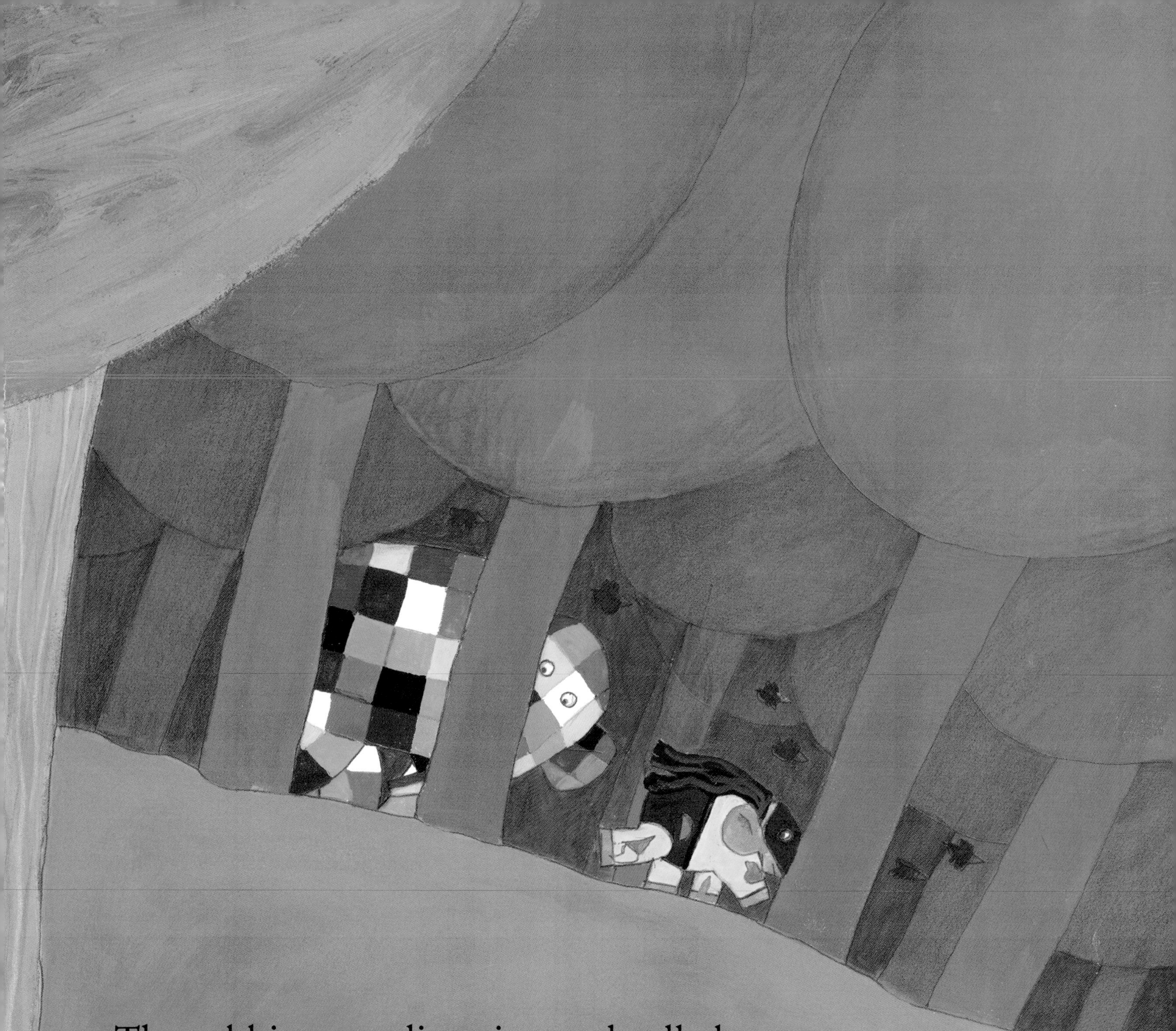

The rabbits were listening enthralled to Snake, as the two elephants slipped past them.

"What's going on?" whispered Super El.

"I asked Snake to tell the rabbits about the time he tricked me and the elephants," said Elmer. "He tells it beautifully. They haven't noticed us."

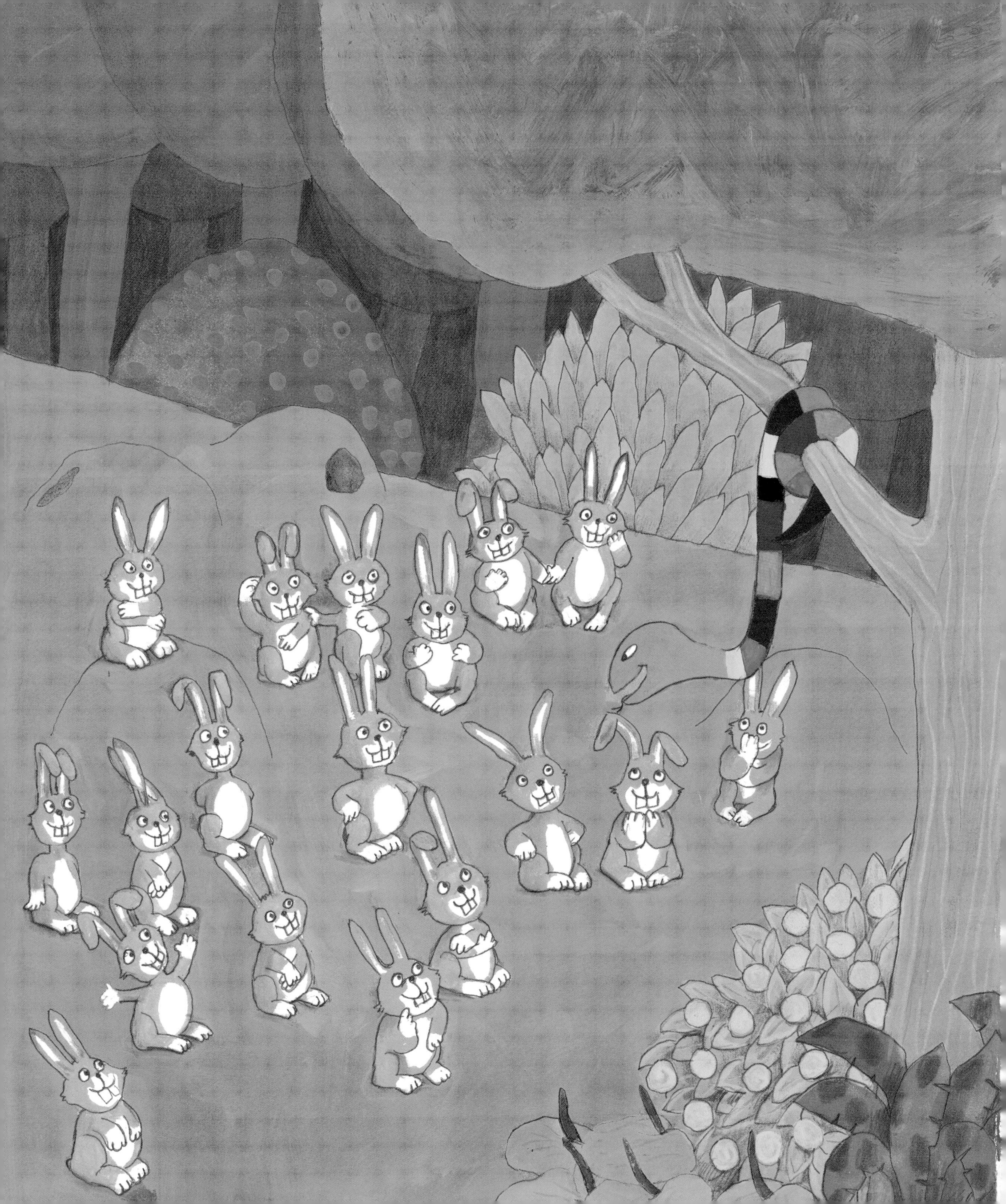

"We're near the hippos," said Elmer. He picked up a broken bush. "Hide behind this."

"Taking a bush for a walk, Elmer?" chuckled a hippo.

"There's an elephant behind it," Elmer replied.

"Always joking, Elmer," the hippos laughed.

Once Super El was safely past, Elmer said, "Wait here. I've an idea how we can get past both Snake and the rabbits."

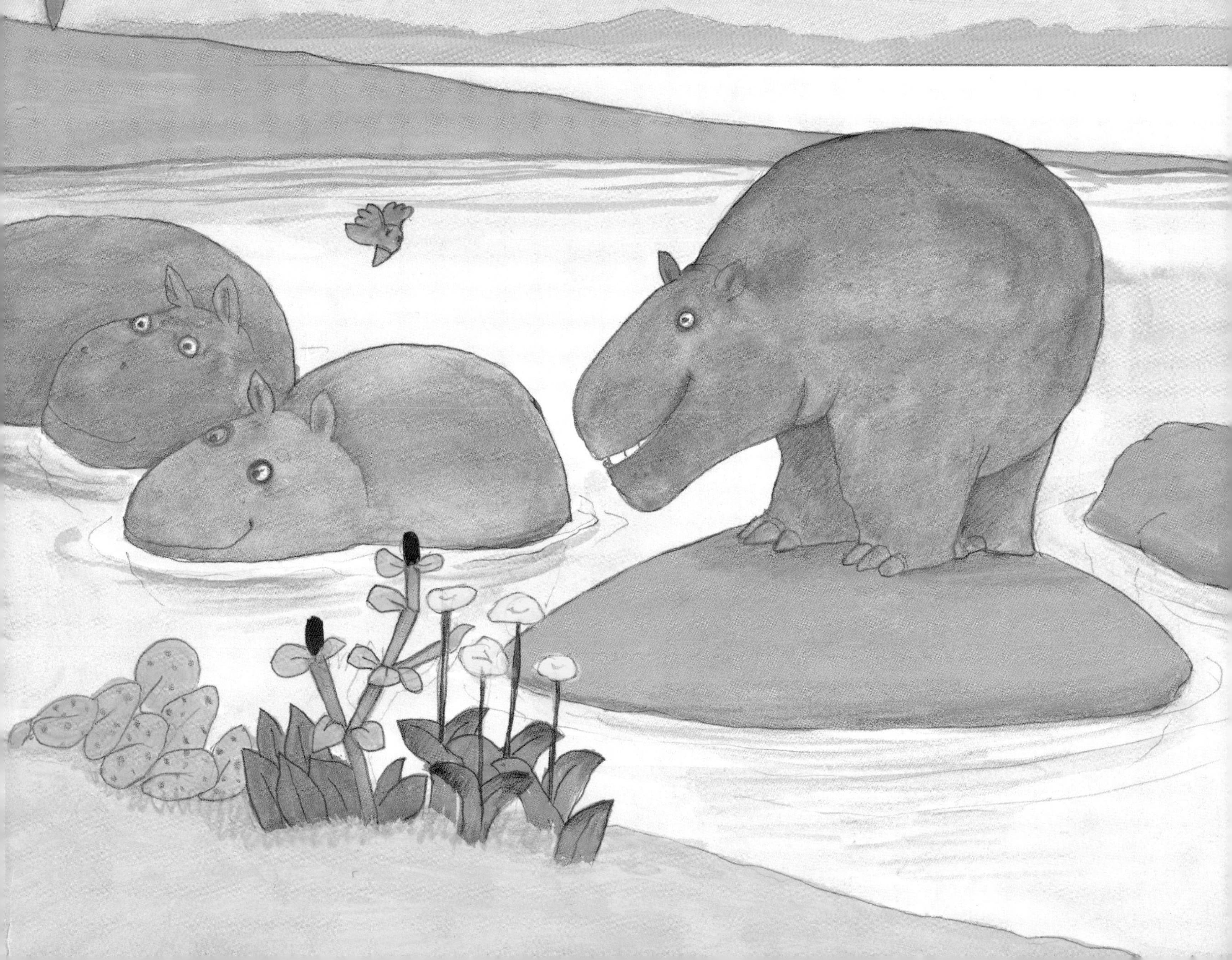

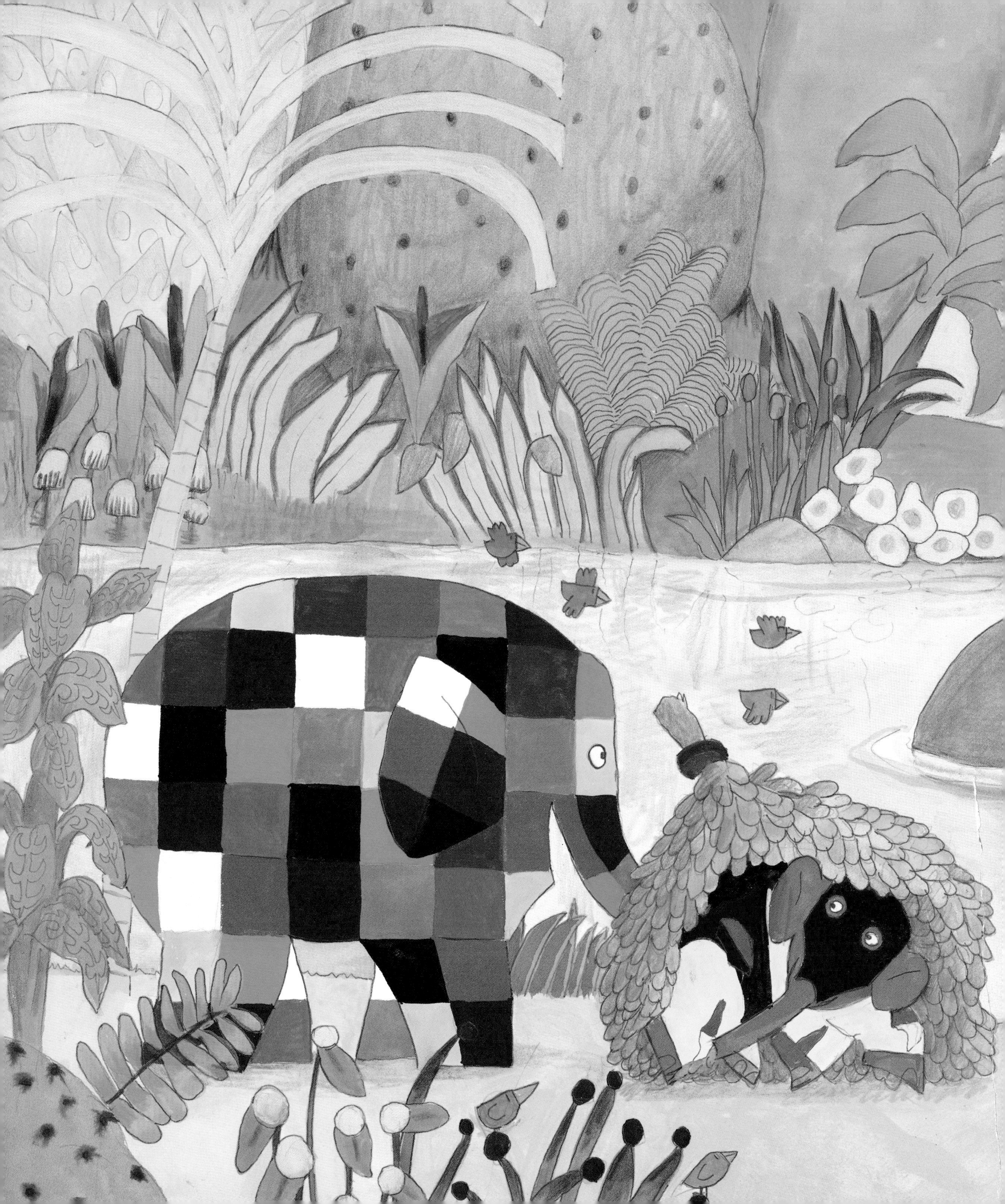

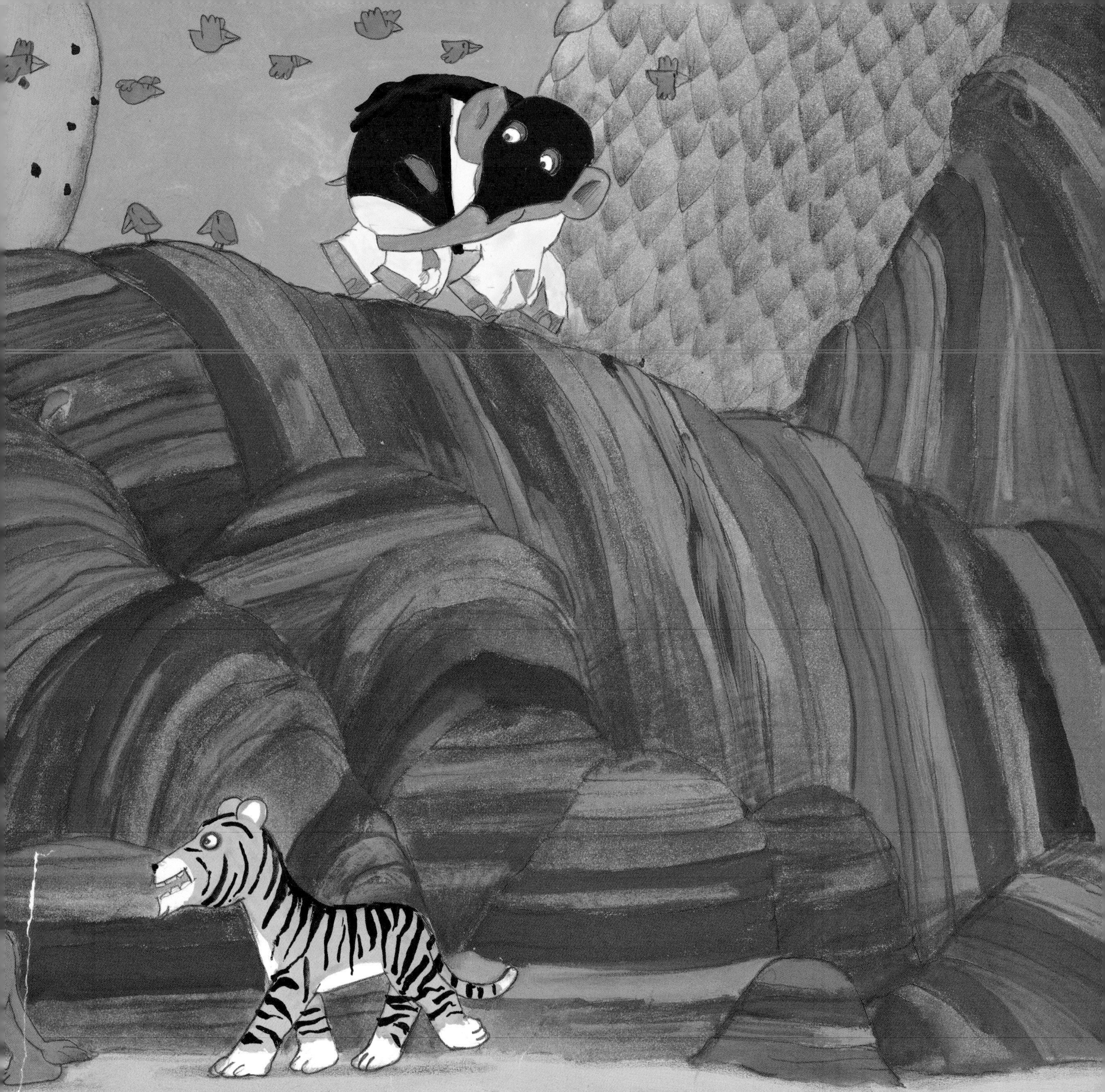

"Eh? Nice day for what?" asked Lion and Tiger together. They were confused enough not to notice the little elephant on the rocks above them.

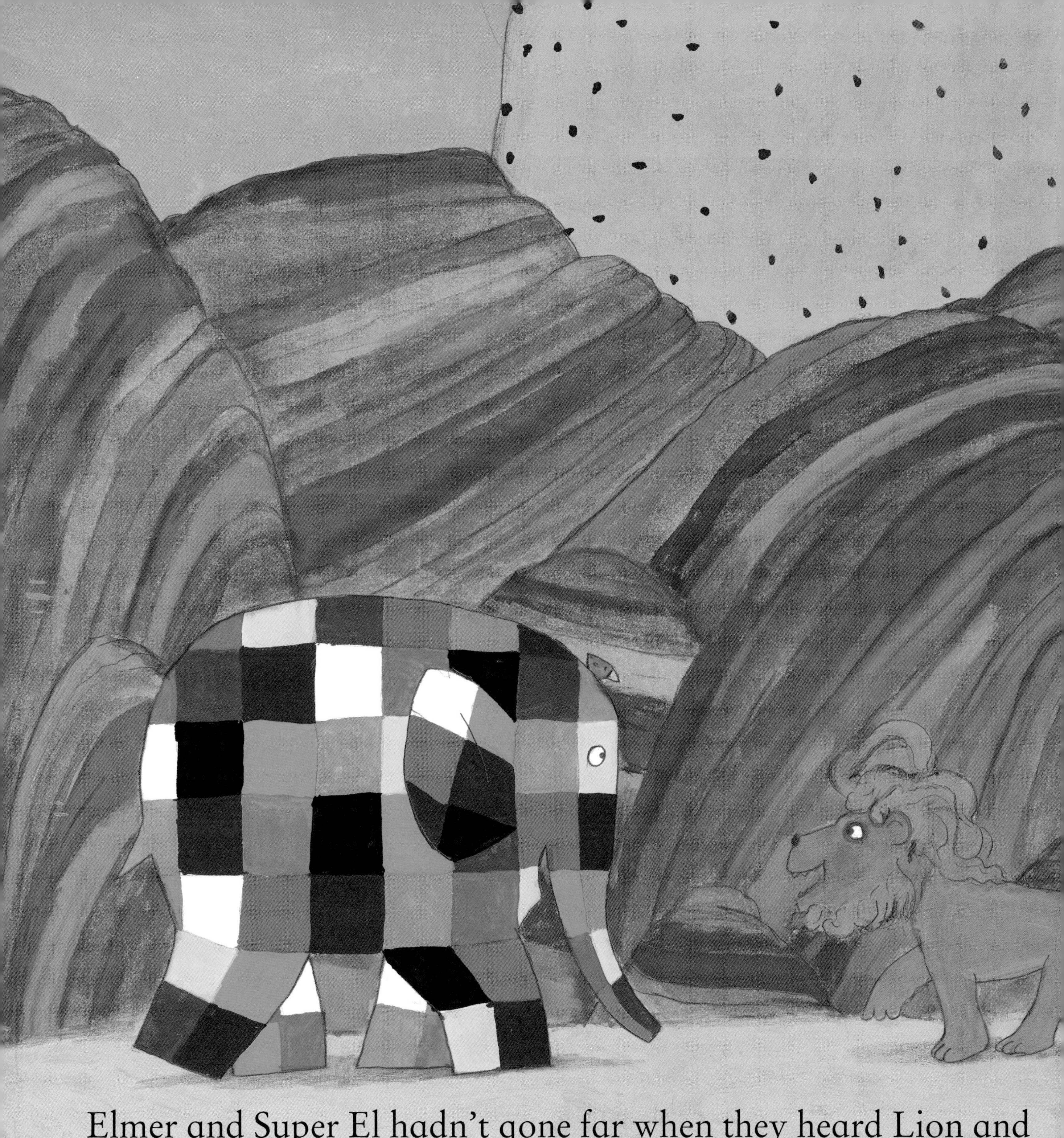

Elmer and Super El hadn't gone far when they heard Lion and Tiger approaching. "Hello," said Elmer. "Nice day for it."

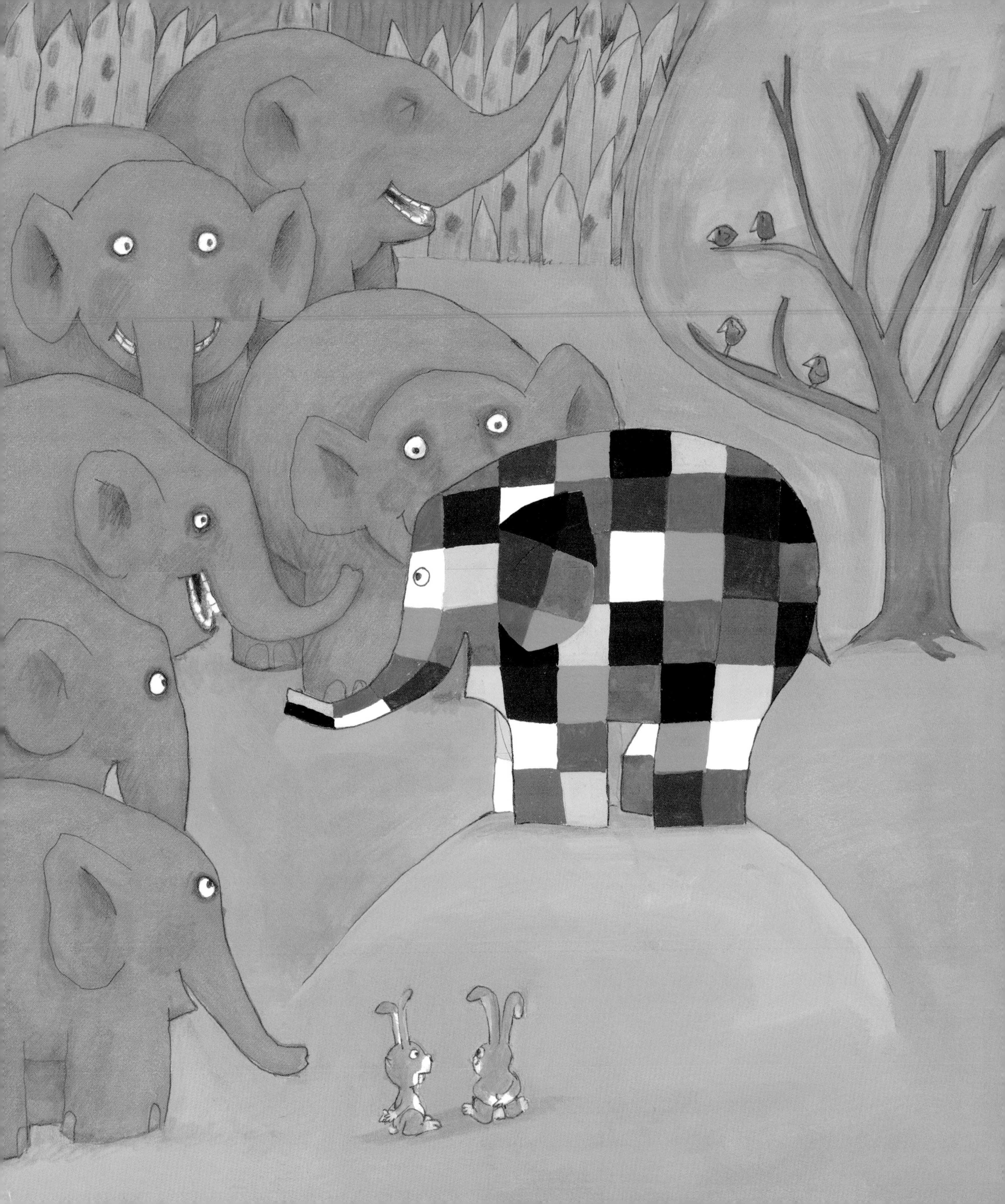

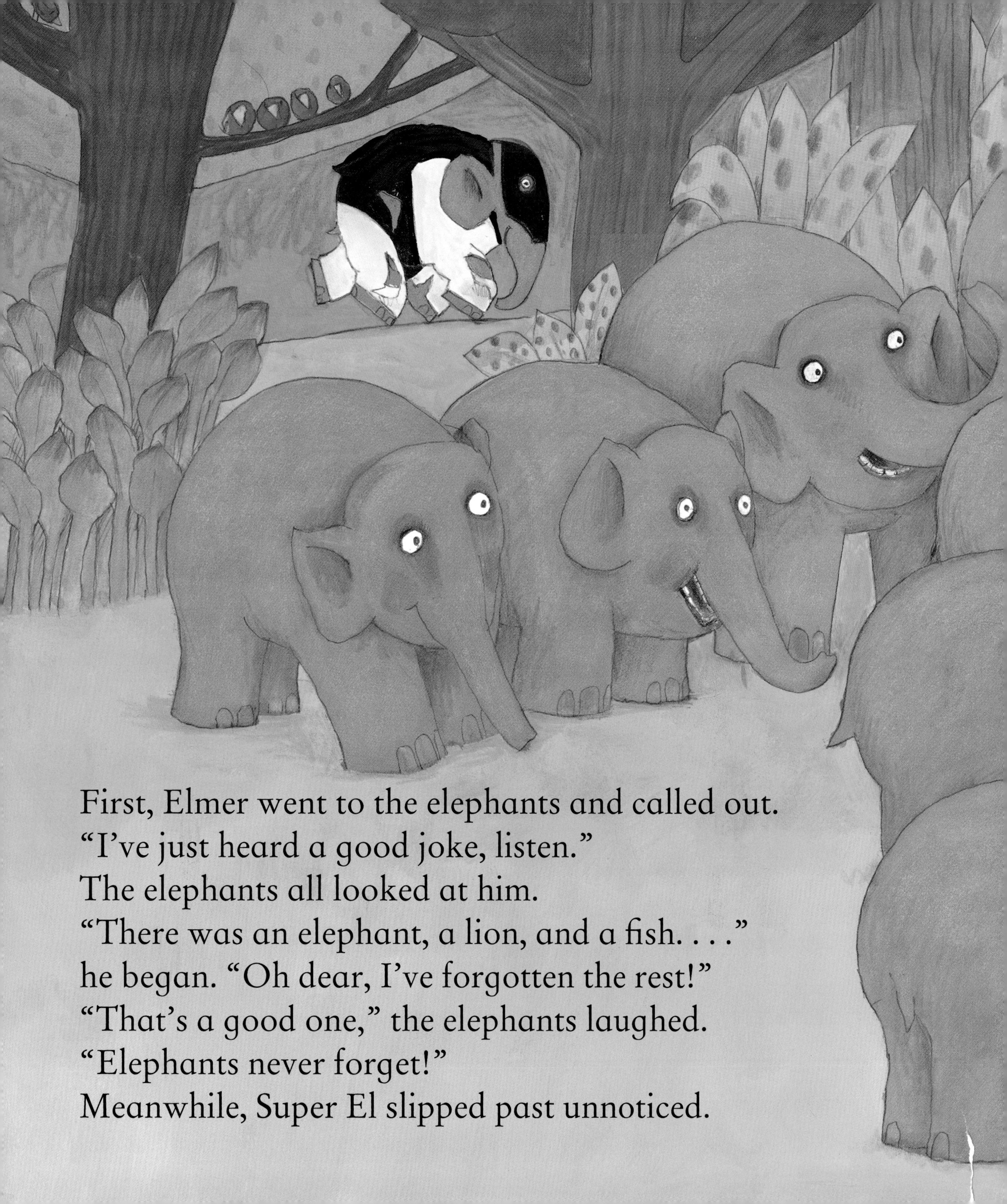

First, Elmer went to the elephants and called out.
"I've just heard a good joke, listen."
The elephants all looked at him.
"There was an elephant, a lion, and a fish. . . ."
he began. "Oh dear, I've forgotten the rest!"
"That's a good one," the elephants laughed.
"Elephants never forget!"
Meanwhile, Super El slipped past unnoticed.

"Look," said the small elephant, showing his torn outfit. "That thornbush attacked me! The other animals will laugh if they see me like this. That's not very super."

"Aunt Zelda can fix your outfit," said Elmer. "We'll just have to make sure no one sees you. I'll distract the other animals. Come on. It will be fun!"

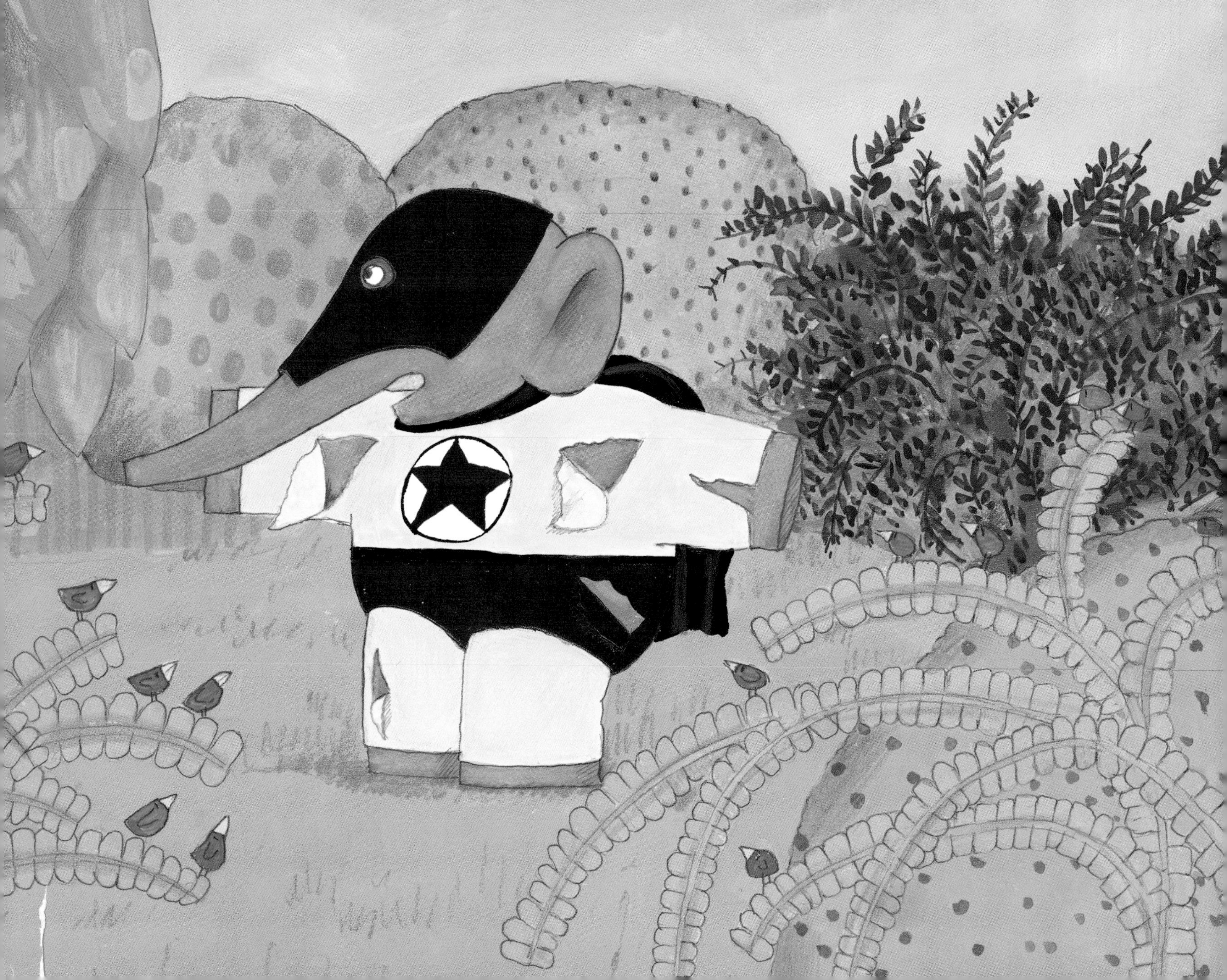

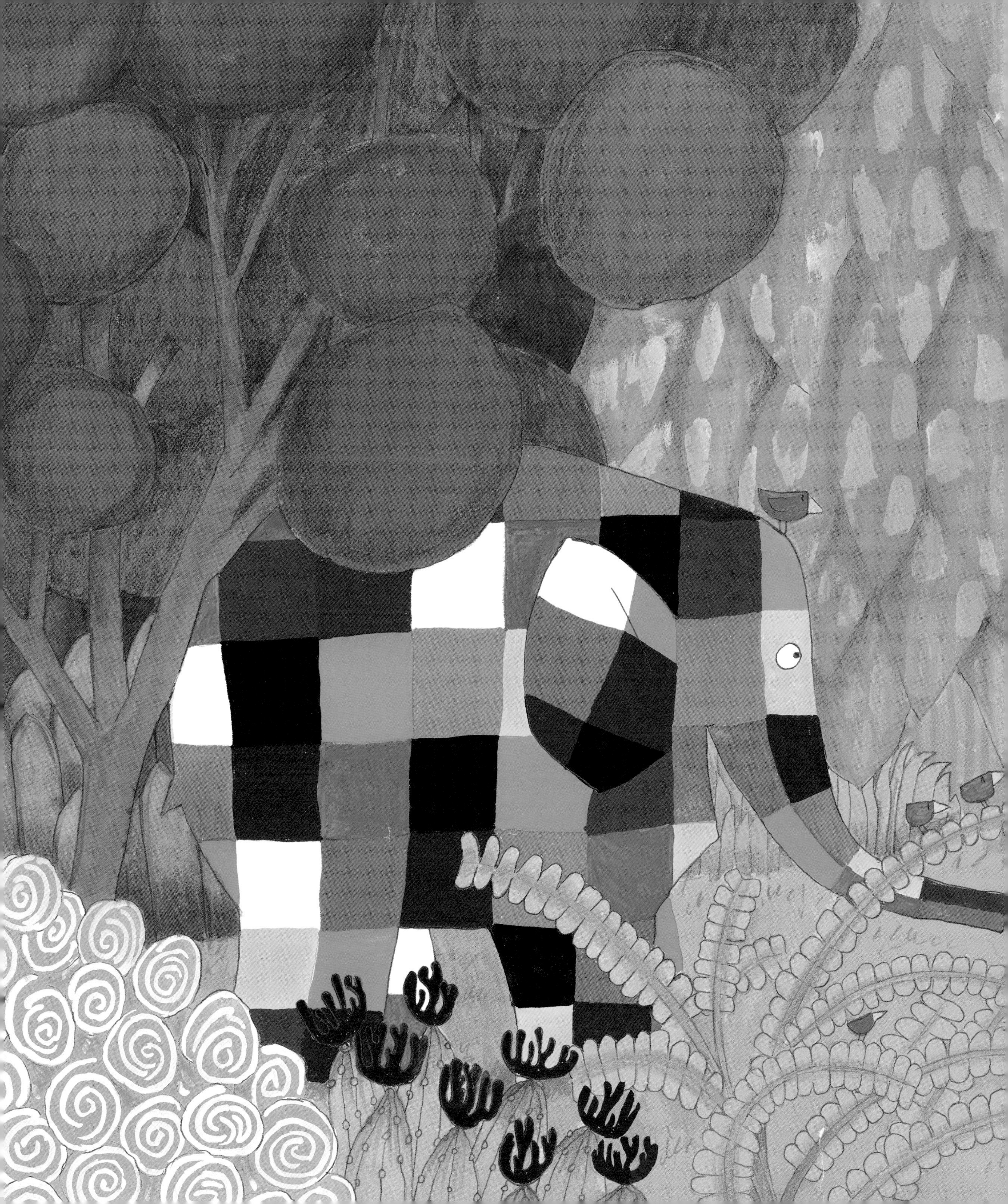

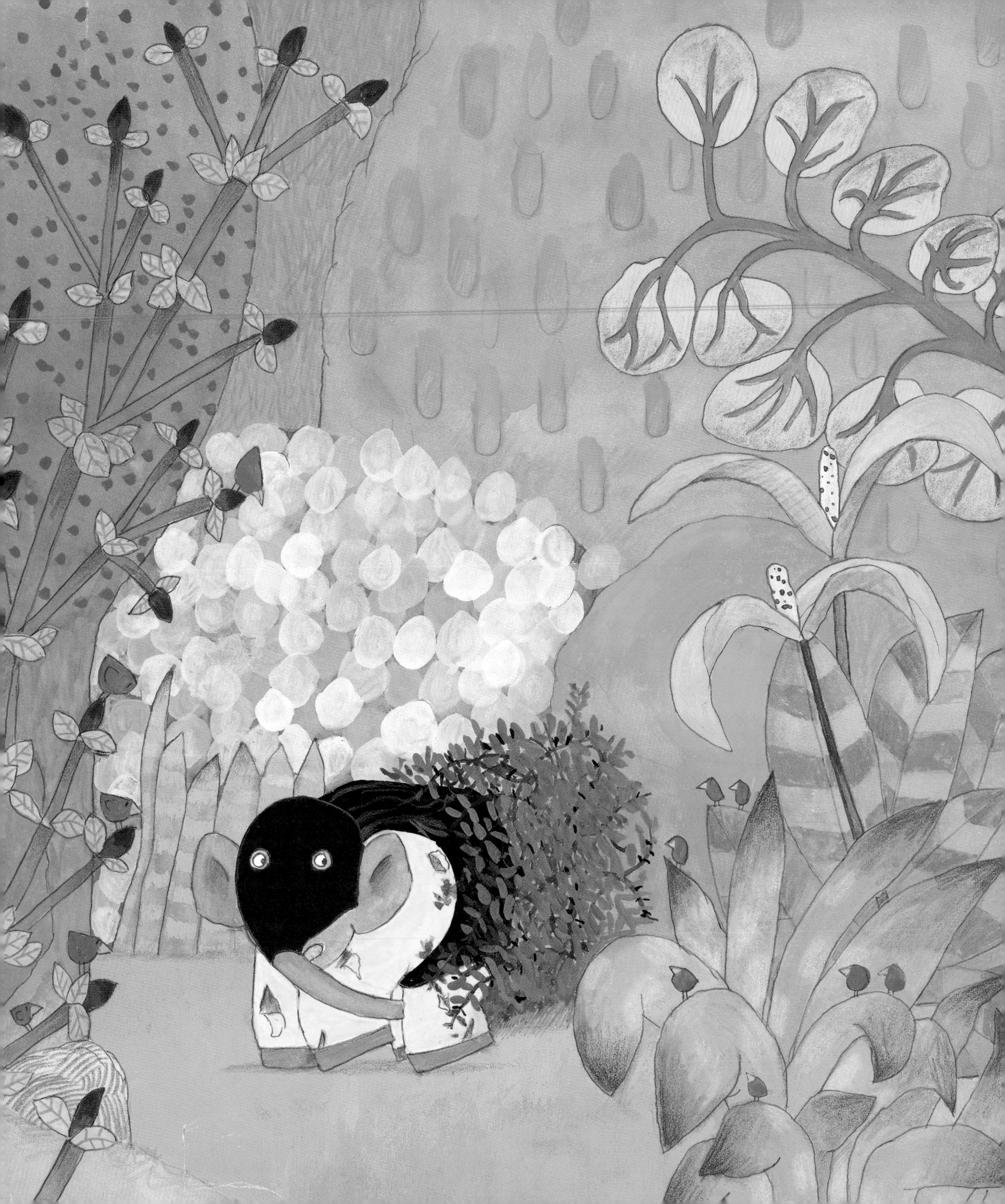

Elmer, the patchwork elephant, was taking his morning walk when he heard an “Oh no!” Looking around, he spotted a small elephant dressed in an outfit that he recognized.

“Hello, Super El,” Elmer said with a smile. “What’s the problem?”

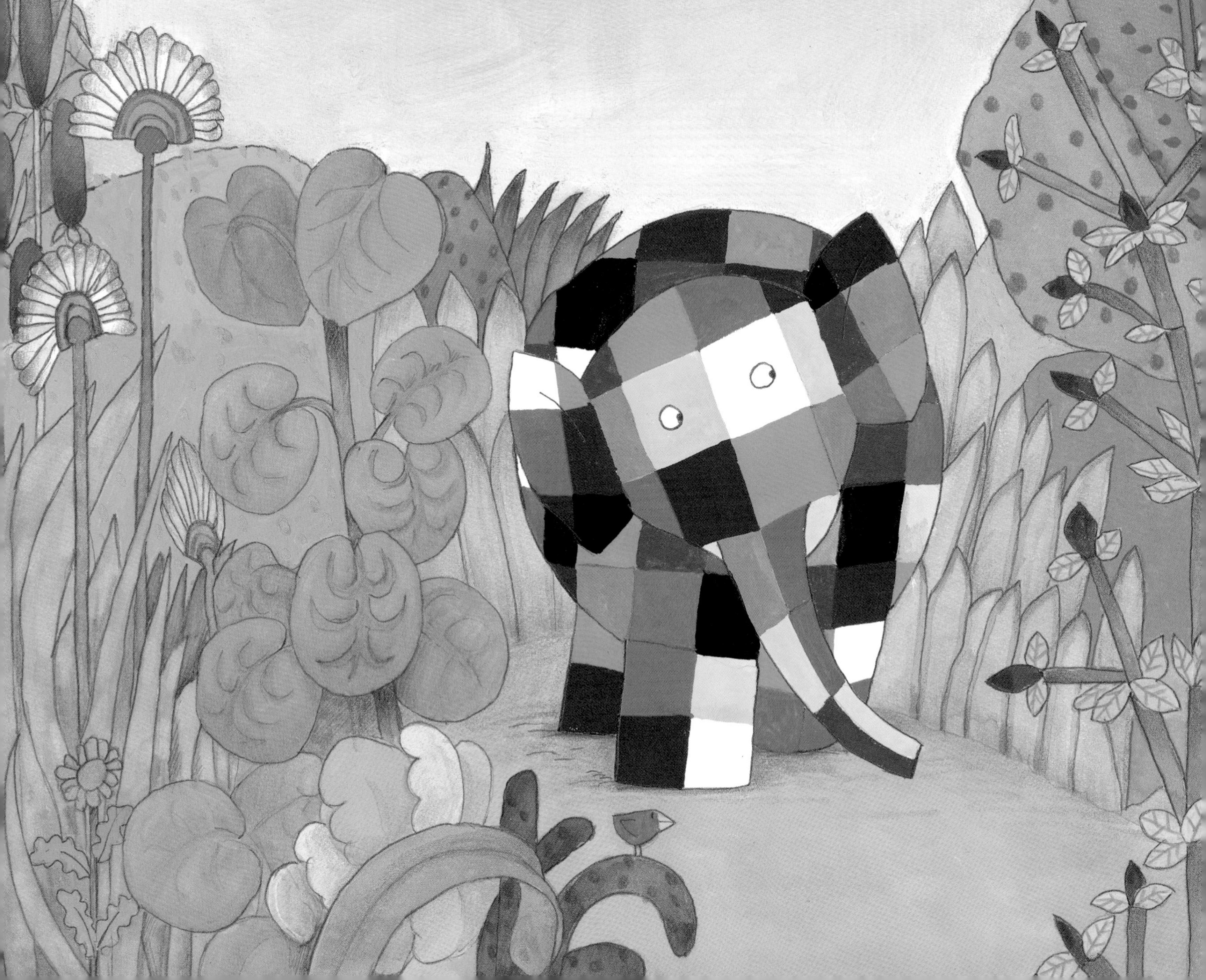

ELMER
and SUPER EL

David McKee

Andersen Press USA

For Super Amélie, Super Flynn, and Super Blake

Also by David McKee:
Elmer and Rose
Elmer and the Hippos
Elmer and the Rainbow
Elmer's Christmas
Elmer's Special Day

American edition published in 2012 by Andersen Press USA, an imprint of Andersen Press Ltd.
www.andersenpressusa.com

First published in Great Britain in 2011 by Andersen Press Ltd.,
20 Vauxhall Bridge Road, London SW1V 2SA.
Published in Australia by Random House Australia Pty.,
Level 3, 100 Pacific Highway, North Sydney, NSW 2060.

Distributed in the United States and Canada by
Lerner Publishing Group, Inc.
241 First Avenue North
Minneapolis, MN 55401 U.S.A.
www.lernerbooks.com

Color separated in Switzerland by Photolitho AG, Zürich.
Printed and bound in Singapore by Tien Wah Press.
David McKee works in gouache.

Library of Congress Cataloging-in-Publication Data Available.
ISBN: 978-0-7613-8989-7
1 – TWP – 12/31/11
This book has been printed on acid-free paper.

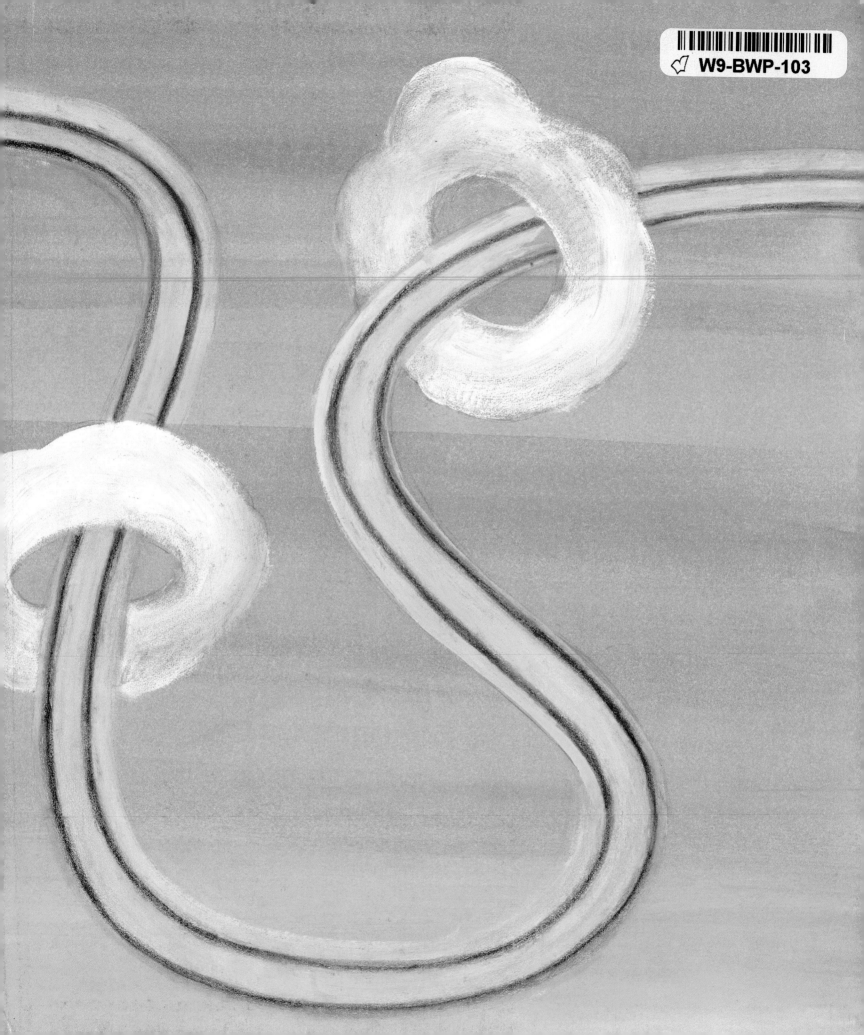